THE HISTORY OF THE ENGLISH NOVEL

Volumes Already Issued

THE HISTORY OF THE ENGLISH NOVEL

*

FROM THE BEGINNINGS TO THE RENAISSANCE

* *

THE ELIZABETHAN AGE AND AFTER

* * *

THE LATER ROMANCES AND THE ESTABLISHMENT OF REALISM

* * * *

INTELLECTUAL REALISM: FROM RICHARDSON TO STERNE

* * * * *

THE NOVEL OF SENTIMENT AND THE GOTHIC ROMANCE

* * * * * *

EDGEWORTH, AUSTEN, SCOTT

* * * * * * *

THE AGE OF DICKENS AND THACKERAY

* * * * * * * *

FROM THE BRONTËS TO MEREDITH: ROMANTICISM IN THE ENGLISH NOVEL

* * * * * * * * *

THE DAY BEFORE YESTERDAY

* * * * * * * * * *

YESTERDAY

Demy 8vo *16s. net each*

THE HISTORY OF THE ENGLISH NOVEL************

Yesterday. *By* Ernest A. Baker, D.Lit., M.A.

H. F. & G. WITHERBY LTD.
326 High Holborn, London, W.C.1

First published 1939

PRINTED FOR MESSRS H. F. & G. WITHERBY LTD.
BY THE RIVERSIDE PRESS, EDINBURGH

PRINTED IN GREAT BRITAIN

PREFACE

THIS is the end of an enormous task, and the tenth volume of a work that, as first projected, was to have finished in three. When, however, the first volume was ready for press, the publishers decided for technical reasons that it must be split into two. And, as the work went on, certain periods, and still more certain novelists, inexorably demanded more space than had been bargained for. The later volumes, in particular, far outgrew the original allowance. Even in this final one, Conrad, Katherine Mansfield, and D. H. Lawrence, in spite of every effort to compress, insisted on having proper elbow-room, with the result that this is the longest of all the ten.

At all events, it should be realized that this account of the English novel is the result of more than half a lifetime of reading, thought, and research, as well as enthusiasm for the subject. My first modest attempt at a survey of the field, entitled "A Handbook to Fiction," appeared in 1899, and was merely an annotated catalogue running to 150 pages. It fell into the hands of the late William Swan Sonnenschein, who induced me to undertake the more ambitious *Guide to the Best Fiction, English and American* (1903), which in its third edition (1932) had expanded into a quarto of 634 pages. The two small volumes *History in Fiction* (1908), also instigated by him, grew rapidly into a quarto of 566 pages, and one of my old students is now preparing a still larger edition of this chronological manual of historical novels and romances. It was Sonnenschein who long ago suggested that I should write a history of the English novel; but at that time I had neither the knowledge nor the temerity for such an undertaking. Work, many years ago, upon two series of reprints, "Half-forgotten Books" and "The Library of Early Novelists," which between them salvaged some thirty notable works that had long gone out of print, led me on instructive exploring trips into the past of the English novel, not to mention many reviews, chiefly for the more erudite periodicals. But the real beginning of this history of the English novel was the courses of lectures given for fifteen years at University College, London, with the concurrence of the late Professor W. P. Ker and his successor in the Chair of English, Dr W. B. Chambers. Long before these came to an end, I had published the first few volumes.

Among numerous acknowledgments, warm thanks are due first to Scotland Yard, for enabling me to trace the Sir Robert Anderson who I vaguely knew was Conrad's original for the Assistant Commissioner in *The Secret Agent* (see p. 51 below). For their kind permission to quote relevant passages from the novelists under scrutiny, I am indebted to the following: for any novels whatever published by them, to Messrs Chatto & Windus, Messrs William Heinemann, Ltd., and Messrs Methuen & Co., Ltd.; for Conrad, to Messrs William Blackwood & Sons, Ltd., Messrs J. M. Dent & Sons, Ltd., Messrs Ernest Benn, Ltd., Messrs Methuen & Co., Ltd., Messrs William Heinemann, Ltd., and Messrs J. B. Pinker & Son; for Mrs Oliphant, to Messrs William Blackwood & Sons, Ltd.; for "Ian Maclaren," to Messrs Hodder & Stoughton, Ltd.; for Kipling, to Mrs Kipling, Messrs Hodder & Stoughton, Ltd., Messrs Methuen & Co., Ltd., Messrs Macmillan & Co. Ltd., and Messrs A. P. Watt & Son; for Barrie, to Messrs Hodder & Stoughton, Ltd., Messrs Cassell & Co., Ltd.; and Lady Cynthia Asquith; for Mrs Craigie, to Messrs Ernest Benn, Ltd.; for Mary Webb, to Messrs Jonathan Cape, Ltd.; for Katherine Mansfield, to Mr J. Middleton Murry and Messrs Constable & Co., Ltd.; for Samuel Butler, to the Trustees of the Butler Estate and Messrs Jonathan Cape, Ltd.; for G. K. Chesterton, to Messrs Cassell & Co., Ltd., Messrs J. W. Arrowsmith, Ltd., Messrs Methuen & Co., Ltd., Messrs A. P. Watt & Son, and the Executrix of the late G. K. Chesterton; for Arnold Bennett, to the Trustees for the Estate of Arnold Bennett and to Messrs Hodder & Stoughton, Ltd.; for John Galsworthy, to Mrs Galsworthy; for D. H. Lawrence, to Messrs William Heinemann, Ltd., Mr

Frieda Lawrence, and Messrs Pearn Pollinger & Higham, Ltd.; and also for their kind services to Messrs J. B. Pinker & Son. If by an oversight my obligations to any others have not been gratefully acknowledged, I trust they will pardon the omission. I must also express my sincere gratitude to the printers of this long series of volumes for their unfailing watchfulness and their kindly forbearance. Dr Edith Batho, of University College, has again done me the invaluable service of revising the proofs, and I am deeply grateful.

E. A. B.

CONTENTS

CHAPTER		PAGE
I.	Conrad, the Teller of Tales	11
II.	Conrad the Novelist, with his next of kin	45
III.	Rudyard Kipling	105
IV.	The Scots Group and some Irish	157
V.	Some Women Novelists	199
VI.	Satirists and Utopians, Revolutionaries and Evolutionaries	244
VII.	Arnold Bennett and Galsworthy	288
VIII.	D. H. Lawrence	345
	Select Reading and Reference List	393
	Index	399

CHAPTER I

CONRAD, THE TELLER OF TALES

A Pole writing English

Joseph Conrad (1857–1924) does not fit easily and neatly into the history of the English novel after Hardy and Stevenson. Though a great realist, he was at the same time a great romantic; and it is tempting to view him as the natural sequel to the Stevensonians, and detect some analogy with the transition from romantic make-believe to a deeper and truer romanticism at the end of the eighteenth century. Conrad's was not indeed a solitary voice, though it sounded new and strange. His tales of distant parts and of adventure and heroism amid the wildest surroundings and the most outlandish types of humanity came at a time of widespread interest in travel and exploration and the study of alien races, when the accounts of their experiences by Stanley and Wallace, Tyndall and Whymper, George and Mary Kingsley, Layard, Doughty, and Sir Harry Johnston, were read with the same eagerness as the latest novel. Some of these wanderers and naturalists and observers of exotic peoples, W. H. Hudson, Marmaduke Pickthall, Cunninghame Graham, Sir Hugh Clifford, and Mr H. M. Tomlinson, put what they had to say, wholly or in part, into novels and stories. And there were gadabout novelists, conversely, who assumed the attitude of critical, amused, or ironical spectators, Edward Noble, master mariner, for instance, or C. E. Montague, or the omniscient Rudyard Kipling, whose *Plain Tales from the Hills* (1895) appeared eight years before Conrad his senior's first book, *Almayer's Folly*. The analogue of fiction pretending to be fact is fact recounted as fiction. There were also such phenomena as the young American Stephen Crane's vivid imaginative analysis of sensations on the battlefield and of men and women in other phases of violent activity and physical or moral hazard, subject of the longest of Conrad's *Last Essays*. All these writers, whether novelists or explorers, were realists, the technical accomplishment of those who wrote fiction coinciding with the veracity which was the principle all observed. And it might be said they were all romantics, inasmuch as the new discoveries and the exposures of old-established errors which they brought forward and the truer pictures which they drew appealed to deep instincts of curiosity, wonder, and sympathy, even for the wild and almost incredible.

But the mere circumstance that Conrad was not without rivals or coadjutors in his explorations of the outlying regions of human character is of minor relevance, beside the initial and obvious fact that he was not an Englishman. He is the solitary instance of a foreigner writing works of genius in English, and his foreignness is enough to explain all that seems strange or anomalous even in that large part of his fiction which is concerned with English characters. He had not long acquired the language, and was very far from well-versed in English literature, when he set out on his career in it, though he was amply to make up for this later on. His father was a Shakespearian scholar and had translated some of the plays into Polish. The boy read Captain Marryat and Fenimore Cooper, in translation; but apart from those two, who stimulated his imagination and zest for adventure to a degree he never forgot,[1] it was long before he became familiar with any important English novelist except Dickens. His chosen masters were French—Flaubert, "the last of the Romantics," [2] Maupassant, and in due time Anatole France, Daudet and Loti delighting him too. He knew French from childhood, and always spoke it fluently; but of English not a word till he was sixteen. He wrote his novels in English not French,[3]

[1] "Perhaps no two authors of fiction influenced so many lives and gave to so many the initial impulse towards a glorious or a useful career. Through the distances of space and time those two men of another race have shaped also the life of the writer of this appreciation" (*Notes on Life and Letters*, "Tales of the Sea").

[2] *A Personal Record*, opening sentence. He emphasized that "my Flaubert is the Flaubert of *St Antoine* and *Éducation Sentimentale*" (*Life and Letters*, ed. G. Jean-Aubry, ii. 206).

[3] "The legend set afloat by Hugh Clifford" about his hesitation between English

however, English prose cadences chiming with his emotional nature infinitely better, apart from the excellent reason that he was going to write largely about British seamen. Conrad was by birth a Russian citizen, but never knew Russian, and the only Russian novelist for whom he avowed admiration was Turgenev, whose works were introduced to him by Edward Garnett. Dostoevsky he jeered at, and would scornfully have repudiated any kinship or comparison, even on the strength of *A Secret Agent* or *Under Western Eyes*. Mencken's harping on his Slavonism infuriated him. He was a Pole; racially, he said, belonging to a group that derived their culture first from Italy and then from France.[1] His is a body of work as strange and solitary in English as Herman Melville's in American literature, though apart from the Dutch origin of his mother Melville was in no wise an alien. But, however the racial elements in Conrad's genius and temperament be assessed, the foreign heritage always outweighed the English characteristics that he acquired. To the end he remained a Pole.

Ancestry and early life

Jozef Teodor Konrad Nalęcz Korzeniowski (1857–1924), born in the Ukraine, then part of the empire of the Tsars, came of a Polish family of landowning gentry various members of which had fought in the long and intermittent struggle with Russia. The Nalęcz Korzeniowskis were noted for their martial spirit; the Bobrowskis, on his mother's side, tended to devote themselves more soberly to agriculture. But a grand-uncle, Nicholas Bobrowski, won fame under Napoleon, and is said to have been the original of the leading characters in "The Duel," "The Warrior's Soul," and *The Rover*. He figures in Conrad's *Personal Record* as "the unfortunate and miserable (but heroic) being who once upon a time had eaten a dog." Jozef's father, Apollo Nalęcz Korzeniowski, a man revered by his compatriots for his idealism and devotion and adored by his only son, was exiled to Vologda for his part in

and French as a writing language irritated Conrad, who said that when he wrote the first words of *Almayer's Folly* he "had been already for years and years *thinking* in English" (*Ibid.*, ii. 206). In the "Author's Note" to *A Personal Record* he stressed his Englishness—"it was I who was adopted by the genius of the language."

[1] See the long letter to G. T. Keating (*Ibid.*, ii. 289). Mégroz states categorically, "He was a Pole of the purest Slav type physically" (p. 224).

the rising of 1863, and died when the boy was not quite twelve; the mother, a woman of equally exalted character, had died in exile four years earlier. From them he inherited his passionate and chivalrous temperament and brooding compassion for the lot of man. The orphaned Conrad—to give him the anglicized name he afterwards adopted—remained in the charge of his kinsfolk. He had been sent to school at Cracow, and being the child of his father was a great reader, always dreaming of himself enacting what he read. The incident is well known—it has been recorded by himself and all his biographers—how the boy of nine or so was one day poring over the map of Africa, and putting his finger on a spot in the middle of the still dark continent said to himself, "When I grow up I shall go *there*." Like it or not, his relatives had to give in. It was in 1872 that he peremptorily declared his intention to be a sailor. Everyone disapproved and every obstacle was put in his way; two years later, however, at the age of seventeen, he made his way to Marseilles; and from now for twenty years Conrad followed the sea, first as a common sailor on French vessels and then in the English marine, and after 1880 as second or first mate and then as fully-qualified master. His first experiences were nondescript, one romantic episode being a spell of gun-running for the Carlists in Spain; but all fertile in impressions, especially of rough life and character, which he used later in his fiction. Much of this crowded epoch is chronicled in his *Mirror of the Sea*, which rivals the novels in brilliant pictures of the sea and ships and their inhabitants, in incidents brimming with dramatic interest, and the splendour of the prose.

Personal experi- ences the stuff of his fiction

Though so ample and varied, he must have wasted very few of his recollections, to judge by the wealth of incident, racy and diversified character, and the multifarious aspects of the mariner's existence, reproduced in his novels and tales. His biographers have indexed his ships and voyages, and shown methodically to which of them this and that personage or episode can be traced. His own adventures and those he witnessed gave him the stuff for his fiction, which consists essentially of anecdote and his recollections of characters that arrest the eye or provoke curiosity by something anomalous between their outer and their inner life. All was reshaped and set in a clearer light. But Conrad's imagination was not called upon to invent; he had the material ready, and all he had to do was to adapt and fit together and interpret. "Imagination, not invention, is the supreme master of art as of life," [1] was his ruling precept. Every patch of the earth's surface had its story attached, in Conrad's recollection. To put it summarily, his fiction is in method a sort of nautical yarning, developed into a fine art of sensuous impressionism and psychological elucidation. As a hard-bitten man of action, Conrad is perhaps unique among English novelists; he was everything romantic that Stevenson would like to have been. Not even Kipling, that other master of romantic realism or realistic romance,[2] knew more or was a more exact delineator of the miscellaneous shapes of life that he came in contact with. Like that other sailor Herman Melville's, his vision of life, his incidents in the general tragedy of the human adventure, his ordeals, perils, and deliverances, and his portrayals of salient personalities, are put in settings drawn from his own experiences of wild environments all over the world. Unwittingly in Conrad if not in Melville, a measure of symbolism creeps in: this and that wild scene is for the time being the universe, whether an ethical stage on which events of profound import are taking place or a neutral proscenium across which the absorbing spectacle proceeds. Like Melville again, he began as a very faithful chronicler of "life in the great world of waters." [3] But he was to be just as faithful, just as exact, when he turned to other themes and other kinds of experience. Though usually classed as a writer of the sea, Conrad said,

"I have always felt that I had no speciality in that or any other specific subject. . . . Sea life had been my life. It had been my own self-sufficient, self-satisfying possession. When the change came over the spirit of my dream (Calderon said

[1] *A Personal Record*, i., last paragraph.

[2] Mr H. G. Wells in a review of *An Outcast of the Islands* (*Saturday Review*, 16th May 1896) remarked, "Surely, this is real romance, the romance that is real!" (Aubry, i. 165).

[3] *Last Essays*, p. 211.

that 'Life is a Dream') my past had, by the very force of my work, become one of the sources of what I may call, for want of a better word, my inspiration—of the inner force which sets the pen in motion."

The sea tales are all authentic, "because they are the product of twenty years of life—my own life"; they are facts, and his business was to trace the clues for their full interpretation. But *Nostromo*, *The Secret Agent*, *Under Western Eyes*, and the dramas of mental and moral contention that followed, have a like authenticity, inasmuch or in so far as they are works of imagination rather than of invention.

Coloured by his peculiar mentality

Little escaped his observant eye; but the quality of his interest and the mode of his reactions were the result of his innate disposition and peculiar heritage. Though far from unsociable and loved by troops of friends, all having something akin to himself, Conrad was a lonely soul. There was something secret and inscrutable about that searching and inexorable thinker, standing apart from the rest of the world, absorbed in watching and unravelling by a process of imaginative self-identification the interplay and conflict of personalities and motives, and arriving at inflexible conclusions. He was an impressionist whose vision had a profundity, a penetration, that nothing could mislead. A conscience acutely, almost morbidly, sensitive enabled him to divine feelings and motives as far asunder as the antipodes. He was equally at home with individuals, like himself and his kindred, ready for the finest devotion and self-sacrifice; with those whose steadfastness broke down in the hour of trial and could never be re-established; and also with characters the very opposite, who were capable of the foulest deeds and mocked at scruples. Men and women so intensely individual as Conrad's are not to be classified; but they do sort themselves roughly into these three groups, typified by Captain Anthony, faithful old Singleton, or Captain Whalley; by Lord Jim or Razumov, who fail at the supreme moment but work out their own salvation; and by Willems, Kurtz, Heemskirk, and Donkin, a quaternion of the most thoroughpaced but well-differentiated miscreants ever drawn. The son of Apollo Korzeniowski regarded loyalty and self-devotion as the cardinal virtues, and his life at sea only deepened his primal convictions and supplied the wealth of circumstance to illustrate his favourite theme—these qualities brought to the test. Conrad had the reputation of an efficient and trustworthy officer; he was not lacking in the excellences he prized; but he was no mere slave to duty. There was a gallantry and an itch for adventure in Conrad which might have made his shipowners uneasy if they had not had his record of invariable success to rely upon. Tales were rife of risks he was prepared to run, like the skipper in "The Secret Sharer," who scares the mate and crew by shaving the rocks within a few inches, to give the man he has been sheltering a chance to swim ashore.[1] He made good his boyish prophecy by undertaking and bringing to a conclusion the Congo expedition of which the esoteric history is contained in "Heart of Darkness." Then one day, when in charge of a ship with a cargo for Mauritius, "*all of a sudden*, all the deep-lying historic sense *of the exploring adventures in the Pacific* surged up to the surface" and he wrote for permission to take his ship through Torres Strait. Instead of "the severe rap on the knuckles" that he expected, the owners allowed him to do so, and a voyage which called up vivid memories of the old navigators was successfully carried out. There is nothing of the merely sensational or sentimental romancer in Conrad. The actualities he relates, and the strong, live, determined men, are romantic enough, and he renders them with a vigour and gusto that shows how romantic they are. The doings and

[1] "Conrad would indulge in extremely dangerous manœuvres, going about within knife-blades of deadly shores whilst his officers and crew shivered—but over very small details of the stowing of spars and the like he would go out of his mind and swear the ship to pieces . . . in driving, he would shave stone posts like a madman, and then curse the stable-boy to pieces for letting him come out with the old instead of the new whip" (Ford, 107). It is odd to read in the monograph by R. L. Mégroz (81 *et seq.*): "Evidence is not wanting of his physically unadventurous temperament, and if he was not adventurous in the usual sense of the word, clearly his seamanship was the fruit of a fantastic impulse to live an ideal." The author of *Youth*, *Typhoon*, *The Nigger of the "Narcissus*," and scores of recitals of heroism and hairbreadth escapes, animated with a delight in strife and endurance and a glamorous spell rarely to be found at such a pitch in his boyhood's enchanters, Marryat and Fenimore Cooper, not adventurous! Scores of passages in *The Mirror of the Sea* and *Last Essays* contradict such a statement. His biographer rightly says that in his seafaring life he was "carried along by the ardour of his temperament and attracted by an almost unconscious longing for adventure" (Aubry, i. 142).

adventures are related with the coolness and aplomb of the man used to it all; heroism is part of the day's work. There is no swagger, no appeal for admiration, in the men who go through these feats and endurances, or in the narration. On the contrary, as Conrad gets his hand in, a slightly ironical air towards mere courage and address grows more shrewd, and more indicative of his attitude to a dense and supine world contemplating such queer heroics from the depths of their armchairs. It is typified by the nonchalant D'Hubert, in "The Duel," accepting the fire-eating Gascon's challenges as they come, and going through the silly business with calm efficiency; naturally annoyed at having to fight about a straw, but preserving his air of indifference and superiority to the deadliest risks. All this is not a pose, but the temperamental self-sufficiency of a proud man. Decoud, in *Nostromo*, is another. Or take the cynical collector of Chinese bronzes and porcelains, a man in the best society, who unmasks the double-dyed traitor, in "The Informer." "This monster was polished and even exquisite." In his "beautiful unruffled manner" he remarks casually, "There's no amendment to be got out of mankind except by terror and violence"; and with the savage irony of his "flaming red revolutionary pamphlets" and his active co-operation with the secret societies he is one of the most dangerous persons in Europe. The two scoundrels in *Victory*, the "gentleman" and the undisguised bandit, are of a still more sardonic brand. Conrad was in fact criticized for "a certain unemotional, grim acceptance of facts; of what the French would call *sécheresse de cœur*"; and defended himself with the plea that an element of autobiography was always latent in his work, and he was one of those "to whom an open display of sentiment is repugnant."[1] Writing fiction is a task "which mainly consists in laying one's soul more or less bare to the world"; but this can be done "with a regard for decency"; respect for one's own dignity is "inseparably united with the dignity of one's work."

Conrad relates how in the course of an eastern voyage he first saw Almayer, and heard about him afterwards from many

[1] *Personal Record*, preface.

How he became a novelist

different quarters. He was glad to go ashore and dine with the man; and from this contact with the original and a sympathetic reading of his past Conrad's first novel, *Almayer's Folly* (1895), gradually evolved. But for that incident, he said, "it is almost certain there would never have been a line of mine in print."[1] He was five years writing the book, carried the manuscript about with him on his voyages, having it with him for instance in the Congo adventure, several times all but lost it, and wrote the last chapters after he had left the sea, though he did not know then that it was for ever. He was nearly forty when it appeared. *Almayer's Folly* was the first of a whole series of stories which he set picturesquely in the tropical forests, rivers, and seas of Malaya, and furnished out with such figures of Europeans, natives, or half-castes as he had come into contact with during these voyages.[2] Conrad's interest in the case of Almayer is intelligible, though it was one to excite curiosity and make large demands upon his charity, rather than give much inspiration. The weak and broken Dutchman was the obverse of Conrad's heroic ideal, the negation that certified its rightness. The tragedy of failure and demoralization—the commonest of life's tragedies—was always to haunt him, and to alternate with his stories of achievement and steadfastness even in the jaws of disaster. This was his first and least successful attempt to convey it. It had merits, especially the vivid picturing of a remote world and unknown races, which commended it to Edward Garnett as a promising first novel and prompted him to ask for another. A second was soon written, with the same scenes and some of the identical people, though, instead of being a sequel, it harked back to the distant antecedents of Almayer's sad history. Conrad was often to make a regular method of such inverted chronology.

Twenty years before, when Captain Lingard was a power

[1] *Ibid.*, iv.

[2] Conrad had to admit to Sir Hugh Clifford, Governor of the Straits Settlements, who pointed out many inaccuracies, that his knowledge of the region and the natives was superficial. He was not an ethnologist, interested in the diversities of race. As elsewhere, he was intent on fathoming the man, and comprehending his moral ordeal to the last scruple.

"Almayer's Folly" and "The Outcast of the Islands"

in this region, Almayer was in charge of a station on the great river in one of the islands, carrying on a prosperous trade with the mysterious interior. But now Lingard is ruined and gone, a wily Arab has stolen the traffic, and Almayer is left in idleness at his tumbledown wharf. All he has to live for in these sad days is his daughter Nina, child of the Malay girl Lingard had over-persuaded him to marry. But he still nurses extravagant hopes. They will find the gold-mine in the far interior to which Dain, son of the neighbouring rajah, promises to guide them; and then they will go to Europe, their fortune made after all. But Dain and Nina are in love, and she flees with him. Almayer sinks under the blow. He is the first of many Europeans in Conrad's pages who succumb to the loneliness and the corrupting influences of the wild tropical environment, as much as to the paralysing emergencies they are called upon to face in their dealings with crafty and ferocious natives. *The Outcast of the Islands* (1896) goes back to the days when Sambir was a thriving station. Almayer though a weakling was an honest man. Willems, the agent of both Lingard and Almayer's ruin, is one of Conrad's earmarked reprobates who go utterly to the bad. Rescued from the consequences of a fraud, and provided by Lingard with a refuge at the trading-station, he is soon at daggers drawn with Almayer, goes mad after a native wench, and to make sure of her undertakes to pilot Abdulla, Lingard's Arab rival, up the dangerous mouth of the river. Lingard comes back, and sentences Willems to a fitting punishment. But the man has had enough of the savages and tries to escape; Aïssa gets hold of his own revolver and shoots him.

Conrad's characteristic method still undeveloped

In *Almayer*, Conrad tried in an elementary way to trace the unhappy Dutchman's mental and moral history, and succeeded only in leaving him shadowy and indistinct, except in the weird scene of anguish when the final blow has fallen and the man is beside himself. The method was too abstract; Almayer does not stand out clear, nothing like as clear, for instance, as the pair of intriguing Malay adventurers, Lakamba and one-eyed Babalatchi, "the Bohemians of their race," who are drawn with sharp irony and cut a lively figure in both these stories. The trite method of following the thread of thought and feeling in a man like Almayer failed in Conrad's hands [1]; a continuous process of analysis was not the method for him. But already there are glimpses of his inborn faculty for realizing with a vivid intensity sensations and emotional states at crucial moments. This, with his keenness of eye for the external traits of individuality, was soon to show itself fully matured. There is some forecast of it in those passages of spasmodic effort to maintain his dignity and his "unflinching firmness," when Almayer feels it is of the utmost importance that he should assure Nina "of his intention of never forgiving."

"I will never forgive you, Nina!" he shouted, leaping up madly in the sudden fear of his dream. This was the last time in his life that he was heard to raise his voice. Henceforth he spoke always in a monotonous whisper like an instrument of which all the strings but one are broken in a last ringing clamour under a heavy blow.

It appears again in the moral tussle in Willems' mind with the opportunity and the temptation, and in the duel of mad concupiscence and racial antagonism in Willems and Aïssa, when, as he would never have done when he had a stricter sense of artistic propriety, Conrad tries to lay bare the hearts of both, and symbolizes the eye of the universe in the primeval forest trees.

She stepped back, keeping her distance, her eyes on his face, watching on it the play of his doubts and of his hopes with a piercing gaze, that seemed to search out the innermost recesses of his thought; and it was if she had drawn slowly the darkness round her, wrapping herself in its undulating folds that made her indistinct and vague. He followed her step by step till at last they both stopped, facing each other under the big tree of the enclosure. The solitary exile of the forests, great, motionless and solemn in his abandonment, left alone

[1] Especially in a man like Almayer. "With Almayer one could never tell. He governed his conduct by considerations removed from the obvious, by incredible assumptions which rendered his logic impenetrable to any reasonable person. I learned all this later" (*A Personal Record*).

by the life of ages that had been pushed away from him by those pygmies that crept at his foot, towered high and straight above their heads. He seemed to look on, dispassionate and imposing, in his lonely greatness, spreading his branches wide in a gesture of lofty protection, as if to hide them in the sombre shelter of his innumerable leaves; as if moved by the disdainful compassion of the strong, by the scornful pity of an aged giant, to screen this struggle of two human hearts from the cold scrutiny of the glittering stars.

As he gained experience in his craft, Conrad learned how to co-ordinate these instants of passion and vision into the intelligible history of an individual—and to moderate his grandiloquence. What, as yet unknown to himself, was his goal appears in those two far finer variants of the same tragedy of frustration, *Lord Jim* and *Under Western Eyes*. When, in the latter, he has to reveal the soul of Razumov, tortured with anxieties and terrors, and at length justifying to himself the betrayal of Haldin, instead of endeavouring to straighten out the tangle of motives, which even Razumov could not have done, for he did not act with deliberate calculation and was less than half aware of why he acted, Conrad compels the reader to enter into and follow the sequences of apprehension and feverish revolt in a "mind hovering on the borders of delirium." States of mind are set out consecutively; but the issue is not a logical inference, it is that mental and emotional attitude which will infallibly supervene. *Lord Jim* was the first complete example of Conrad's psychological method. Here this impressionism of his takes a different course; the instants are not consecutive. The course of the narrative is so rambling and apparently fortuitous that there seems at first to be no method at all, only an accidental synthesis of the yarns told by this man and that man, the scarce reconcilable testimony of many different witnesses. This is what the board of inquiry are confronted with, when they have to reconstruct the history of the accident and the abandonment of the *Patna*: the reader has to perform the same operation. Marlow, who tells most of the story, states the whole theory of Conrad's impressionism in the remark:

"All this happened in much less time than it takes to tell, since I am trying to interpret for you into slow speech the instantaneous effect of visual impressions."

Later on Marlow says:

"I don't pretend I understood him. The views he let me have of himself were like those glimpses through the shifting rents in a thick fog—bits of vivid and vanishing detail, giving no connected idea of the general aspect of a country. They fed one's curiosity without satisfying it; they were no good for purposes of orientation. Upon the whole he was misleading. That's how I summed him up to myself after he left me late in the evening."

Impressionism like Sterne's

It is odd how in two respects Conrad is analogous to Sterne [1]; both were impressionists, and both were interested in the mutual incomprehensibility of individual minds. At least half the fun in *Tristram Shandy* arises from the total inability of such pairs as Mr Shandy and his wife, Mr Shandy and Uncle Toby, Toby and Corporal Trim, to understand what the other is talking about. And then, Sterne's mode of telling a tale is a standing puzzle. It has already been observed [2] how he plays ducks and drakes with time and method, solemnly referring the reader to Locke's theory of duration. In recounting an incident and what led up to it, he does not address himself to the intelligence, which has by now grown automatic, recognizing things for what they are and putting them in their proper place in the general world of facts. Instead of proceeding in the manner of Fielding, he pours out sensations and impressions as they occur to a spectator of curious sensibility, visual impressions especially, which we can put together and explain to ourselves, as we are doing at every moment of our existence. He goes back to the initial stages of experience, and gives what falls upon ear and eye, not the thing as the understanding grasps it. The ordinary

[1] He compares Crane and Sterne, in *Last Essays* (181): "the foremost impressionist of his time, as Sterne was the greatest impressionist, but in a different way, of his age."

[2] See Vol. IV. 252–255 and 263–266.

novelist observes an inherent logic, shows effects arising from causes: this is the realism of the intellect. The impressionist ignores any such logic. He gives our instantaneous reactions, the effect upon the senses, not a rational description of the things felt or seen or heard. But through the vivid impact of these impressions a sense is transmitted of our being in immediate contact with what is going on.[1] Conrad might well say that "all creative art is magic," for he was always evoking this illusion—it was the only way he could tell a story.[2] Such impressionism is far more compulsive than mere workaday realism, its effects being so much more like the raw sensations which are the original stuff of experience. For reality is not an intelligible story. The story is an orderly arrangement subsequently impressed, or a lucid connexion which has been deduced. And, when the understanding does presently seize and comprehend all that has been gathered in, it holds this with a vividness and firmness infinitely stronger than when things are recounted by the other method, which must needs be more abstract, however simultaneous the operation of our consciousness. Fiction thus comes close up to life. Swiftly or gradually, from the crowding impressions the full meaning emerges, order is perceived rising out of chaos. The illusion of multitudinous life has been conjured up, "the whole mirage of Nature," as Garnett puts it; and the reader is thus keenly alive to the unity, to the underlying significance, to all that which the imagination of poet and artist discerns in the complexity and apparent confusion.

Such impressionism in "Lord Jim"

Lord Jim is such impressionism from beginning to end. Take any incident at random; take, for instance, the accident to the *Patna* from which everything starts. The German engineer has been abusing the old ship "with her plates like brown paper—brown paper s'elp me!" though he protests "I don't know what fear is."

[1] It might be called intuition, a word that will be often used in this book as shorthand for the swift apprehension in which the "general bodily consciousness" is involved—"a tide of sensations of internal bodily origin comes into consciousness" (see *Principles of Literary Criticism*, by I. A. Richards, esp. chap. xiii., "Emotion and the Cœnesthesia").

[2] *A Personal Record* is put together with the same disregard for chronology as the novels.

"'Tain't safe, s'elp me, it ain't! Only I am one of them fearless fellows. . . ."

He let go the rail and made ample gestures as if demonstrating in the air the shape and extent of his valour; his thin voice darted in prolonged squeaks upon the sea, he tiptoed back and forth for the better emphasis of utterance, and suddenly pitched down head-first as though he had been clubbed from behind. He said " Damn!" as he tumbled; an instant of silence followed upon his screeching: Jim and the skipper staggered forward by common accord, and, catching themselves up, stood very stiff and still gazing, amazed, at the undisturbed level of the sea. Then they looked upwards at the stars.

What had happened? The wheezy thump of the engines went on. Had the earth been checked in her course? They could not understand; and suddenly the calm sea, the sky without a cloud, appeared formidably insecure in their immobility, as if poised on the brow of yawning destruction. The engineer rebounded vertically full length and collapsed again in a vague heap. This heap said "What's that?" in the muffled accents of profound grief. A faint noise as of thunder, of thunder infinitely remote, less than a sound, hardly more than a vibration, passed slowly, and the ship quivered in response, as if the thunder had growled deep down in the water. The eyes of the two Malays at the wheel glittered towards the white men, but their dark hands remained closed on the spokes. The sharp hull driving on its way seemed to rise a few inches in succession throughout its whole length, as though it had become pliable, and settled down again rigidly to its work of cleaving the smooth surface of the sea. Its quivering stopped, and the faint noise of thunder ceased all at once, as though the ship had steamed across a narrow belt of vibrating water and of humming air.

The story is a series of such incidents, causally connected; but it is not unfolded as a connected story, it has to be pieced together from a thousand such sense impressions. All the detached glimpses and private conjectures, all the disconnected reports and chance observations, gradually fall together, and it is as if the reader had been put through the episode himself. Conrad has achieved form, and the reader enters into Conrad's triumph, feels the intensity of each moment, from having shared in the elucidation of every single fact. Conrad was never anything else but an impressionist, whether in the evocation of scenery and the great phenomena of nature or in his way of conducting a story, though in the latter he did not always employ the complicated indirectness of *Lord Jim*. It was a mode of seeing and transcribing that came natural to him; it is very unlikely that he could ever have schooled himself to adopt any other. Superficially, there are parallels discernible between his method of indirection and Henry James's. Both tried to view the complex of motives and circumstance from several different angles. But, if there are approximations, there are no exact correspondences. Conrad read James admiringly for twenty years; but if he owed something in the way of warranty and confidence in his own art to his senior, he learned from him only to be more perfectly Conrad.[1] The visual and pictorial manner had become natural and spontaneous to many novelists, the most notable being the case of Hardy.[2] But no one ever relied so entirely as Conrad on sense impressions, almost to the exclusion of the intellect as collaborator.[3]

"The Nigger of the 'Narcissus'"

In his first two novels, in *Tales of Unrest* (1898), and *Lord Jim* (1900), Conrad told what he had seen or surmised; in *The Nigger of the "Narcissus"* (1897), in "Youth," "Heart of Darkness," "Typhoon," and a number of other stories, he recounted what he had gone through himself. He said that

[1] Conrad wrote an appreciation of James (1905), collected in *Notes on Life and Letters*, which is singularly unilluminating, except on the coincidence of the ethical and the æsthetic points of view. In an article, "The New Novel," dealing with the fiction before the public in 1914 (*Notes on Novelists*, 249–287), James has nothing more illuminating to say on Conrad than that the author of *Chance* stands "absolutely alone as a votary of the way to do a thing that shall make it undergo most doing," which is a poor and an erroneous compliment. It is as if both were, quite sincerely, trying to be as polite as possible to each other, but had no important insight into each other's genius. See also Vol. IX, pp. 261 and 286.

[2] See the excursus on Hardy's pictorial method in Vol. IX., 37.

[3] "Il règne par toute l'œuvre de Conrad un grand silence de la raison, un mépris audacieux et grave de la persuasion logique ou oratoire." "L'art de Conrad est donc le contraire de l'art descriptif, notamment de celui de Balzac; il ne calque pas la réalité devant l'homme mais l'homme devant la réalité; il évoke des expériences subjectivement intégrales parce que l'impression équivaut a la totalité de la perception, et parce que l'homme la subit tout entier et de toutes ses forces. Sa grande originalité est d'avoir appliqué cet impressionnisme à la connaissance des êtres humains" (Ramon Fernandez, *Messages*, 110 and 112).

in his sea-books, these and *The Mirror of the Sea* (1906), which is not a novel but could never have been written by one who was not a novelist, he had "tried with an almost filial regard to render the vibration of life in the great world of waters, in the hearts of the simple men who have for ages traversed its solitudes, and also that something sentient which seems to dwell in ships—the creatures of their hands and the objects of their care."[1] These are not novels, if a novel must be a work of some length and scope, with a plot, central idea, drift, sentiment, calling for a definite conclusion, a proper coherence and completeness. Each is rounded and compact; it has its own unity. Yet they might be described as episodes in an epical recital of heroic endeavour and endurance; yarns setting forth the life of the seaman in all its grimness, grandeur, squalor, and grotesquerie. *The Nigger*, "a tale of the forecastle," was the first of his books to bring Conrad fame. It was a brilliant presentation of a subject by no means new, the old-fashioned voyage home round the Cape. The novelty was in the impressionist picturing of the brute facts of life on shipboard, exalted and ennobled by the moments of superhuman conflict with external forces, but turned into an almost gruesome tragi-comedy by the presence of the negro, who takes such an unconscionable time in dying and exerts such an uncanny influence on officers and men.

He overshadowed the ship. Invulnerable in his promise of speedy corruption he trampled on our self-respect, he demonstrated to us daily our want of moral courage; he tainted our lives. Had we been a miserable gang of wretched immortals, unhallowed alike by hope and fear, he could not have lorded it over us with a more pitiless assertion of his sublime privilege.

There is plenty of broad humour and horse-play, in which general disgust at the effrontery and baseness of the slum-bird Donkin is a big item, setting off and throwing into curious relief the subtler comedy of the Nigger and the spell he throws on the crew. Donkin is a figure in Smollett's vein.

[1] *A Personal Record*: a familiar preface.

A taciturn, long-armed shell-back, with hooked fingers, who had been lying on his back smoking, turned in his bed to examine him dispassionately, then, over his head, sent a long jet of clear saliva towards the door. They all knew him! He was the man that cannot steer, that cannot splice, that dodges the work on dark nights; that, aloft, holds on frantically with both arms and legs, and swears at the wind, the sleet, the darkness; the man who curses the sea while others work. The man who is the last out and the first in when all hands are called. The man who can't do most things and won't do the rest.[1]

Conrad might have been trying to beat Loti's description of a storm in *Mon frère Yves*,[2] which he had no doubt read; and certainly his cyclone, in the same Indian Ocean, is a bigger and more decisive episode, focusing the dramatic idea of man's perpetual struggle with overwhelming forces without and within. For with Conrad Nature is as much a personage in the drama as with Hardy; life is the same struggle with cosmic forces. But Conrad sees the struggle as the test of manhood. Life is always trying us; any chance affair may be a platform and a fulcrum for the assertion of personality. Donkin and the Nigger are one sort of visitation; the gale is another.

Most seamen remember in their life one or two such nights of a culminating gale. Nothing seems left of the whole universe but darkness, clamour, fury—and the ship. And like the last vestige of a shattered creation she drifts, bearing an anguished remnant of sinful mankind, through the distress, tumult, and pain of an avenging terror.

But it is only in his later books that Conrad yields to the Manichean temptation to perceive malice in the unseen, and talks of "the unexpected that seemed to hover about one,

[1] It is tempting to think that Conrad had taken a character, Jackson, from his literary kinsman Herman Melville's *Redburn*, and evolved out of that rich personality and his similar plight on board the *Highlander* both the Nigger and Donkin. Jackson "was a horrid desperado . . . he seemed to run amuck at heaven and earth. . . . He was a Cain afloat . . . going about corrupting and searing every heart that beat near him." But "every day this Jackson seemed to grow worse and worse, both in body and mind. He seldom spoke, but to contradict, deride, or curse; and all the time, though his face grew thinner and thinner, his eyes seemed to kindle more and more, as if he were going to die out at last, and leave them burning like tapers before a corpse" (*Redburn*, xxii).

[2] Chapters xxvii.–xxviii.

ready to stretch out its stealthy hand in a touch sudden, familiar, and appalling."[1]

Youth, a narrative, and two other stories (1902), and *Typhoon*, "*Youth*" *and other stories* (1903), the two books following *Lord Jim*, and "*Ty-phoon*" are autobiography in basis. "Youth," Conrad said, "is a feat of memory," whilst in "Heart of Darkness" experience is "pushed a little (and only very little) beyond the actual facts of the case," to bring it home to the minds and bosoms of the readers. "Youth" was a treasured recollection of early days, when hope and spirit were unconquerable and survived the most shattering tests. With "Heart of Darkness" and "The End of the Tether" "it typified," he said, "the three ages of man."[2] It was his second contribution to "Maga"; but is more memorable as the first piece in which Marlow figures, that "most discreet, understanding man," a second self deputed to bear witness, to explain, and sometimes to put a very definite construction upon, the things related. Marlow was twenty then, and joined the ship as second mate, "a really responsible officer." She was the *Judea*—Conrad hardly troubled even to change the name of her original, the *Palestine*.[3] Her motto "Do or Die" was painted on her stern. A coffin ship, if ever there was one. She encountered a gale, and was sixteen days getting from London to the Tyne. Then a steamer collided with her, and provided six weeks of repairs. All went well down Channel; but three hundred miles or so west of the Lizard the gale began. "The *Judea*, hove to, wallowed on the Atlantic like an old candle-box. It blew, day after day: it blew with spite, without interval, without mercy, without rest. The world was nothing but an immensity of great foaming waves rushing at us, under a sky low enough to touch with the hand and dirty like a smoked ceiling." They are driven back, and put in at Falmouth. The *Judea*, "the barque that's going to Bankok—has been here six months—put back three times," becomes a byword. "Where you bound to?—Bankok?" they jeered. At length,

[1] *The Rescue*, iii.
[2] Letter to F. N. Doubleday (Aubry, ii. 338).
[3] In the case of the *Narcissus* he did not change it at all.

she gets away again. But, long before they are anywhere near Bankok, the cargo is on fire. The coal had got wet, spontaneous combustion sets in. And now ensues a long and desperate fight with a smoking volcano, which blows up from time to time. She goes down at last, trying viciously to scorch the boat's crew who are the last to quit her. And they get to the East—derelict; still, they are there! "But for me all the East is contained in that vision of my youth. . . . I came upon it from a tussle with the sea, and I was a young man—and I saw it looking at me. And this is all that is left of it! Only a moment; a moment of strength, of romance, of glamour—of youth!" So Marlow. But the ground-bass to that seducing theme is still the same—man's irrepressible though maybe inconsequent and useless endurance, his innate and treasured stoicism. This is the burden also of "Typhoon," another reminiscence of a tremendous storm. Conrad's prosaic, unimaginative, imperturbable Captain MacWhirr, who brings the *Nan-Shan* through without turning a hair, has become a synonym for sober efficiency.

> Captain MacWhirr was trying to do up the top button of his oilskin coat with unwonted haste. The hurricane, with its power to madden the seas, to sink ships, to uproot trees, to overturn strong walls and dash the very birds of the air to the ground, had found this taciturn man in its path, and, doing its utmost, had managed to wring out a few words. Before the renewed wrath of winds swooped on his ship, Captain MacWhirr was moved to declare, in a tone of vexation, as it were: "I wouldn't like to lose her."
>
> He was spared that annoyance.

"Heart of Darkness" and other stories

"Heart of Darkness," one of the two stories accompanying "Youth," is another episode looming out of the past, Marlow's past, which is here frankly identified with Conrad's. In fundamentals, Conrad said, it is "quite as authentic" as "Youth"; but the facts are avowedly enhanced, for an effect that he infallibly secures. Conrad desired to give a sombre theme "a sinister resonance, a tonality of its own," and contrived to make it all the more uncanny by leaving the climax enigmatic. An indefinable moral shock is experienced, an unnerving "pure abstract terror, unconnected with any distinct shape of physical danger," which stuns and subdues the ardent young fellow, when with his crowd of greedy, backbiting, intriguing Belgians he makes his way at length up the never-ending river to the unholy spot in the tropical forest where Mr Kurtz has his lair and where he exerts some monstrous, reciprocal influence over the natives. The heart of darkness is not the heart of Central Africa but the darkness into which Kurtz has descended. "His was an impenetrable darkness." What the secret was is never revealed. But as he lies dying, the prey of unimaginable terrors, his would-be friend is fascinated. "It was as though a veil had been rent. I saw on that ivory face the expression of sombre pride, of ruthless power, of craven terror—of an intense and hopeless despair. Did he live his life again in every detail of desire, temptation, and surrender during that moment of complete knowledge? He cried in a whisper at some image, at some vision—he cried out twice, a cry that was no more than a breath—'The horror! The horror!' "[1]

Already, in *The Outcast of the Islands*, for instance, Conrad had dilated on "the tremendous fact of our isolation, of the loneliness impenetrable and transparent, elusive and everlasting; of the indestructible loneliness that surrounds, envelops, clothes every human soul from the cradle to the grave, and, perhaps, beyond." Marlow too has his say here on this haunting question: "No," he says, "it is impossible, it is impossible to convey the life-sensation of any given epoch of one's existence—that which makes its truth, its meaning—its subtle and penetrating essence. It is impossible. We live, as we dream—alone." And so even the savage, Captain Whalley's serang, in "The End of the Tether": "His placid mind had remained as incapable of penetrating the simplest motives of those he served as they themselves were incapable of detecting through the crust of the earth the secret nature of its heart, which may be fire or may be stone." In "Heart

[1] There is some parallel between *Heart of Darkness* and *Le Roman d'un Spahi* (1890) of Pierre Loti, in the enervating and demoralizing effect of the African *milieu* on a European.

of Darkness," Marlow peeped over the edge. "Life is a greater riddle than some of us think it to be."

"The End of the Tether"

"The End of the Tether" is too much encumbered with Conrad's word-painting of Malay seas and shores, fine as that admittedly is. It can boast, however, a little galaxy of striking characters, prompting the question, how much Conrad owed to Dickens. Dickens, at any rate, could never have drawn that beautiful old man Captain Whalley, and he would have made laughing-stocks or incredible scoundrels of the rest, and given them too pointedly their deserts. For it was his way to administer poetic justice even in the characterization. Conrad, with his avenging irony, let them show themselves as they are beneath their plausible surface; though he criticized Maupassant for being almost too austere and impassive,[1] he also as a rule was too true an artist to paint the lily or vent his detestation on the weeds. So they present themselves unprejudiced by any indictment, for the reader to scrutinize—the "clever scoundrel" Massy, the lottery maniac, first engineer on the ship he has bought in order to be "best" with the superior officers who have trampled on him; the misanthropic second engineer, with his sullen fits of drunkenness and "the wild and incoherent tale of his infatuation for the wife of a sergeant in an Irish marching regiment"; and Sterne the mate, deferential and treacherous, cunning yet stupid, who spies on Captain Whalley and hopes to get his job. He does find out the captain's blindness, but misses his hard-earned reward. But the comedy arises, characteristically, from their mutual inscrutability, the gulf between their separate selves—"something profound and subtle and incalculable, like an unexpressed understanding, a secret mistrust, or some sort of fear." Conrad is in his own element when he follows the ship on her hazardous passage between the rocky islets and the submerged reefs: the captain of the *Sofala* "had had to take her through at night more than once"; he could

[1] In an essay a trifle *décousu* in its reasoning (*Notes on Life and Letters*)—it was published two years after "The End of the Tether"—Conrad admits "His determinism, barren of praise, blame, and consolation, has all the merit of his conscientious art. The worth of every conviction consists precisely in the steadfastness with which it is held."

almost have done it with his eyes shut. But the villainous Massy has hung his coat with the pockets full of rusty iron bolts close to the binnacle, and he succeeds in wrecking her, in broad daylight, for the insurance money. All which is but the last heroic scene of Captain Whalley's death. He has kept going in spite of the blindness that has crept on him, which he thinks no one has found out; all to preserve intact the little fund saved up for his daughter. The ship is sinking. They shout to him to leap; but he will not leap. "God had not answered his prayers. The light had finished ebbing out of the world; not a glimmer. It was a dark waste; but it was unseemly that a Whalley who had gone so far to carry a point should continue to live. He must pay the price." [1]

More stories—"Tales of Unrest," etc.

Other stories came before, and some were written or at any rate collected after Conrad began to weave his memories and imaginative transmutations into longer narratives, having the fuller compass and greater intricacy of a novel. *Lord Jim* (1900) represents the culmination of his art in this earlier period; it has the length, a good deal of the elaboration, and the symmetrical winding-up of the typical novel. Yet, if it be carefully compared with *Nostromo* (1904), with which the new phase opens, it is seen to be only the story of an act and its ulterior results. If Conrad still abjured invention, and relied on the imaginative rendering of what he had experienced or been told, at all events in these ampler constructions he had to plan, contrive, and manipulate to an extent he had hitherto avoided. Of the five in *Tales of Unrest* (1898), one, "The Lagoon," is interesting as the first he ever wrote, and for intrinsic beauties. The Malay who let his brother fall whilst he carried off the woman he loved is one of those who fail in loyalty and are ever after racked by remorse. The tale is told in a poetic, elegiac way, the surroundings of tropical, forest-girt lagoon blending like a musical accompaniment. "Karain" is more laboured, the story of a savage, "loyal to a vision, betrayed by his dream, spurned by his illusion, and

[1] Aubry states that Conrad himself at this time "was very uneasy about his eyesight" (i. 200). Was it in brooding over this that he conceived Captain Whalley's terrible ordeal, and then devised a story giving it dramatic significance?

coming to us unbelievers for help—against a thought." But the Conradian touch is felt most in the ironic contrast between the primitive, intense manhood of the indigene and the intrinsic meanness of civilization to-day.[1] The contact of two scions of our highly organized social existence with "pure unmitigate savagery" is the theme, again, of "An Outpost of Progress," "the lightest part of the loot I carried off from Central Africa."[2] This pair of stupid incompetents left in charge of a trading-station, a tiny spot in a great void, are a remarkable antithesis to the ideals of efficiency that Kipling was now preaching. The monotony, the maddening boredom, are conveyed with Conrad's usual vividness. The end of the pair, one shooting the other in a fit of fever and terror and then hanging himself when the siren announces the arrival of the relief-boat, is almost farcical in its tragic completeness. By far the best tale in *A Set of Six* (1908) is "The Duel," already mentioned. It is told with a workmanlike economy and a style like the brilliant sword-play with which it has so much to do, that were new in Conrad's stories. In lieu of the elaborate painting of tropical environments, he gives just such glimpses of surroundings as are felt to be of dynamic significance for the actors, of dramatic significance for the spectators:

In the deepening purple twilight of the fields spread with vine leaves, backed by a low band of sombre crimson in the west, the voice of the old ex-officer in the army of the Princes sounded collected, punctiliously civil.

"Do I dream? Is this a pleasantry? Or am I to understand that you have been hatching an affair of honour for sixteen years?"

"It has clung to me for that length of time. That is my precise meaning. The quarrel itself is not to be explained

[1] Most critics have alluded to the story that Sir Hugh Clifford, governor of Malaya, told Conrad that he knew nothing about Malays, and that Conrad accepted the impeachment. Sir Frank Swettenham coincided. Conrad's Malays, and no doubt others of his characters, were the result of lightning impressions on a swift and receptive imagination. As Fernandez puts it, a *coup d'œil* was enough for Conrad, instancing Marlow's portrait of the financial magnate in the third chapter of *Chance*. Marlow had seen him only that once, but it sufficed (Fernandez, 113).

[2] *Last Essays*, "The Congo Diary," 236. See also above, p. 19, n. 2.

easily. We met on the ground several times during that time, of course."

"What manners! What horrible perversion of manliness! Nothing can account for such inhumanity but the sanguinary madness of the Revolution which has tainted a whole generation," mused the returned *émigré* in a low tone.

"The Duel" is indeed, incidentally, a trenchant conspectus of the Napoleonic wars and the retreat from Moscow, as powerful in its brevity as Hardy's panorama in *The Dynasts*, completed that same year. "The Informer" is another good story the pith of which has been given already, and one that certainly called for some inventiveness from Conrad in plotting the climax. How his impressionism works at moments of suspense may be judged from the paragraph following the alarm that the police are raiding the cellar. The informer takes it all coolly, until the moment when he sees the girl who has captivated him enter.

With the appearance of the girl he became obviously alarmed. It was plain. I could see it grow. The change of his expression was swift and startling. And I did not know why. The reason never occurred to me. I was merely astonished at the extreme alteration of the man's face. Of course he had not been aware of her presence in the other cellar. But that did not explain the shock her advent had given him. For a moment he seemed to have been reduced to imbecility. He opened his mouth as if to shout, or perhaps only to gasp. At any rate, it was somebody else who shouted. This somebody else was the heroic comrade whom I had detected swallowing a piece of paper. With laudable presence of mind he let out a warning yell:

"It's the police! Back! Back! Run back, and bolt the door behind you."

"The Brute" is a ship, a huge, unwieldy vessel that squashed a shipwright as she went off the ways, and goes on killing someone or smashing something on every voyage. She seems to be endowed with a clumsy malevolence; and, before she flings herself on a reef, she catches a charming, petted girl in the fluke of her anchor and hurls her to the bottom. In "An Anarchist," Conrad lets out at modern advertising and other aversions of his; but in the main this is an account of how in his opinion red revolutionaries and terrorists are made—in those days all alike were labelled "Anarchists." It is a Conradian pendant to "Crainquebille," that little masterpiece which he singles out in an admiring essay on Anatole France.[1] The poor devil gets involved in a street row, and is charged by the police with assault and seditious propaganda, of which he is as innocent as a babe. "But whatever chance he had was done away with by a young Socialist lawyer who volunteered to undertake his defence. In vain he assured him that he was no Anarchist; that he was a quiet, respectable mechanic, only too anxious to work ten hours per day at his trade. He was represented at the trial as the victim of society and his drunken shoutings as the expression of infinite suffering. The young lawyer had his way to make, and this case was just what he wanted for a start. The speech for the defence was pronounced magnificent." The victim gets the maximum penalty, and is ever after at the mercy of the comrades, a relentless set of criminals. Conrad hated what he called "Anarchists." Nothing annoyed him more than to have the patriotic enmity of his countrymen to Russia styled revolutionary.

"Gaspar Ruiz" is a sensational story of the Chilean war of independence, and as far below his South American novel, *Nostromo*, as it is below Hudson's inimitable tale of the Pampas, "El Ombú" (1902), with which it inevitably provokes comparison. But that exquisite trifle, mingling irony and pathos —and astonishment—with a curious ingenuity, "Il Conde," with its delicate portrait of the fine old Neapolitan aristocrat, would make amends for far worse than this.

"'Twixt Land and Sea" and later stories

The longest of the three stories in *'Twixt Land and Sea* (1912) is a tragedy on pure classical lines, and at the same time a characteristic expression of Conrad's romanticism. "Freya of the Seven Isles" is the tale of a dashing young sailor-lover, who owns a beautiful brig, another *Tremolino*, and loves

[1] "Anatole France," 1904 (*Notes on Life and Letters*).

her like a sentient being, as Captain Lingard in that later elaborate novel, *The Rescue*, loves his. To both, the brig is all their fortune; if they lose her, there is nothing to live for or to live by.

The brig's business was on uncivilized coasts, with obscure rajahs dwelling in nearly unknown bays; with native settlements up mysterious rivers opening their sombre, forest-lined estuaries among a welter of pale green reefs and dazzling sandbanks, in lonely straits of calm blue water all aglitter with sunshine. Alone, far from the beaten tracks, she glided, all white, round dark, frowning headlands, stole out, silent like a ghost, from behind points of land stretching out all black in the moonlight; or lay hove-to, like a sleeping sea-bird, under the shadow of some nameless mountain waiting for a signal. She would be glimpsed suddenly on misty, squally days dashing disdainfully aside the short aggressive waves of the Java Sea; or be seen far, far away, a tiny dazzling white speck flying across the brooding purple masses of thunderclouds piled up on the horizon.

Jasper Allen means to carry off the exquisite Freya, as soon as she is twenty-one, when her grumpy father will have no further right to say him nay. But he has a rival in Heemskirk, captain of the Dutch gun-boat on patrol duty in the Archipelago. Conrad had as much though a different sort of dislike for the Dutch as for Belgians, and he spares no pains in making Heemskirk a diabolical scoundrel. He has never caught Jasper in any illegal traffic; but, maddened at seeing Freya embrace him, Heemskirk plots his ruin. Jasper's overweening self-confidence is one shape of that romanticism which Conrad knows is hated and hunted down by the ignoble but unvanquishable forces of evil in the world. He suffers the revenge of fate, at the hands of Heemskirk. Robbed of his ship, which was to have been his wife's home, robbed of Freya, who falls into a decline, he sinks into apathy, destitution, madness. Freya is the usual scapegoat of destiny, which awards capital punishment to the weak rather than the erring, to the Ophelias and Desdemonas in the higher tragedy. Jasper becomes one of the disreputable crowd of sea-loafers;

his lot is the extinction of all human dignity. In "A Smile of Fortune," which is patently a reminiscence,[1] Conrad's impressionism creates an atmosphere, and leaves off on a note of interrogation. The young captain's first sight of "The Pearl of the Ocean," a blue, pinnacled apparition, "almost transparent against the light of the sky," is a masterly opening, a good introduction to the Arabian Nights' mysteriousness of sleek, stealthy, inscrutable Jacobus, the curtained house, and the sulky young beauty who repulses him, but in saying good-bye just misses his lips with "a hasty, awkward, haphazard kiss." "The Secret Sharer," again, is invested with the peculiar Conradian glamour, by the insistent feeling of inscrutability and a queer sense that the man concealed and saved by the captain who tells the story is his double. Of the four stories, *Within the Tides* (1915), the only one perhaps that counts is "The Partner," which Conrad left, so to speak, "in the raw." Its reality is vindicated by the admirably incoherent but unquestionable witness of the chief actors. And it contains another of Conrad's admirable scoundrels in Cloete.

"Tales of Hearsay"

Finally, *Tales of Hearsay* (1925) was a collection made after his death, though Cunninghame Graham in the preface states that the last of the four items, "The Black Mate," was written somewhere about 1884, that is, before *Almayer's Folly*. This is a trifle distinguished by a brilliant comic denouement. "Prince Roman," written in 1911, is the only tale of his in which Conrad lays the scene in Poland, the Poland of 1831, year of the great rising. It is an eloquent vindication of his patriotism, and the portrait of an heroic, self-devoted soul is obviously meant as his epicedium on the Nałęcz Korzeniowskis. He returned to the retreat from Moscow in "The Warrior's Soul," which is an anecdote heard from a grey old officer who was one of the stragglers. The terrible actuality is equalled by the dramatic force. It is, as it were, the last scene in a tale that is not told, a final scene hinting at things unknown which are still more dreadful. Conrad's impressionism had lost none of its power of grim suggestion. Nor in this respect is there any falling off in "The Tale," a sailor's yarn of the Great War.

[1] See Aubry, i. 113.

Here, too, the abrupt exordium imparts the air of a chapter in a story still going on. The terrible fog on the ironbound coast, infested with enemy submarines and suspicious neutrals, is a counterpart to the darkness of doubt and hesitation through which the young officer cuts his way by the light of intuition, and sends the equivocal stranger to death on the reef. In war-time there is no giving the benefit of the doubt. In war-stories one need not be particular about a moral!

> "Yes, I gave that course to him. It seemed to me a supreme test. I believe—no, I don't believe. I don't know. At the time I was certain. They all went down; and I don't know whether I have done stern retribution—or murder; whether I have added to the corpses that litter the bed of the unreadable sea the bodies of men completely innocent or basely guilty. I don't know. I shall never know."

Lord Jim (1900) is Conrad's *Hamlet*, the tragedy of the man of imagination who is so morbidly aware of the possible consequences of doing anything at a moment of terrible emergency, that his capacity for decisive action is paralysed, he cannot act at all. The story centres in one event, Conrad's account of which has already been cited as an outstanding example of his impressionist method. A young seaman, Jim is second officer on a ship carrying eight hundred pilgrims, when she strikes by night on some half-sunken wreckage and appears to be sinking. The panic-stricken captain and engineers leave the ship; and Jim, his brain reeling with indecision, and called upon to jump, finds himself in the boat. The *Patna* is discovered by another vessel, still afloat. The deserting captain is caught in his own lie, and Jim stands trial and forfeits his master's certificate. He carries his stricken self about with him, brooding over his failure; but he gets his chance again, in Malaya.[1] Here, as counsellor to a native potentate, he regains his dignity as a man of honour and a trusted leader, only to meet his death as the result of a

"*Lord Jim*"

[1] As Edward Garnett pointed out to Conrad, who had to admit it and feel proper compunction, this entailed a cleavage of the book into two parts. This was the "plague-spot" that made him feel "as if he were left with a lump of clay into which he had failed to breathe the right sort of life" (Aubry, 298–299).

chivalrous error, a deed of mistaken generosity. Such is the gist of the story, showing the linkage of cause and effect. But, as already seen, Conrad delivers it as a succession of instantaneous pictures, impressions on the senses, that have to be connected together and made intelligible. Here is Marlow putting his own construction on what he has learned:

"His confounded imagination had evoked for him all the horrors of panic, the trampling rush, the pitiful screams, boats swamped—all the appalling incidents of a disaster at sea he had ever heard of. He might have been resigned to die, but I suspect he wanted to die without added terrors, quietly, in a sort of peaceful trance. A certain readiness to perish is not so very rare, but it is seldom that you meet men whose souls, steeled in the impenetrable armour of resolution, are ready to fight a losing battle to the last, the desire of peace waxes stronger as hope declines, till at last it conquers the very desire of life."

On the next page he is interpreting Jim's state of mind, when he pictures in imagination "the sudden swing upwards of the dark sky-line, the sudden tilt up of the vast plain of the sea, the swift still rise, the brutal fling, the grasp of the abyss, the struggle without hope, the starlight closing over his head for ever like the vault of a tomb—the revolt of his young life—the black end." But Marlow comes closer to the facts and puts the reader in immediate contact with them in his report of his talk with Jim, and Jim's savage indignation at the dastards who betrayed him, and at himself for being betrayed.

"They called out to me from aft," said Jim, "as though we had been chums together. I heard them. They were begging me to be sensible and drop that 'blooming piece of wood.' Why *would* I carry on so? They hadn't done me any harm—had they? There had been no harm. . . . No harm!"

His face crimsoned as though he could not get rid of the air in his lungs.

"No harm!" he burst out. "I leave it to you. You can understand. Can't you? You see it—don't you? No harm!

Good God! What more could they have done? Oh yes, I know very well—I jumped. Certainly. I jumped! I told you I jumped; but I tell you they were too much for any man. It was their doing as plainly as if they had reached up with a boat-hook and pulled me over. Can't you see it? You must see it. Come. Speak—straight out."

Alleged didacticism

Some critics are so alarmed at the idea of seeming to countenance any sort of edification that they are always scenting a moral; even *Lord Jim* has been taken for a didactic story—dereliction, remorse, atonement—with the appropriate lesson to mankind.[1] This is the risk that has to be run by the novelist who deals in ideas, especially moral ideas. If *Hamlet* and *Othello* appeared to-day, they would be viewed with the same apprehension by the pedantic æsthete. But in *Lord Jim* the question is not of guilt and remorse; it is simply the question of a man's honour, the respect of his fellows, his own sense of probity. All the trouble hinges on the fact that the *Patna* did not sink. If she had gone down, as there was every reason to expect, the ship's officers, including Jim, would certainly not have added lustre to their records, but they would not have been cashiered: Jim's career would not have been wrecked. It was not Conrad's wont to preach. The task he set himself was to represent the conflict that life is, as he envisaged it, a conflict with circumstances which seem to be arrayed against us. That conflict, however the apparent hostility be interpreted, is one to try character, it is the test of manhood, it is eminently a moral predicament. The moral dilemma is implied, at any rate inferentially, in every genuine work of art, for the simple reason that the ethical is the most momentous and most insistent aspect of the human situation to man as a self-conscious being. But to be moralistic, to draw a formal conclusion and demonstrate a thesis, to turn the work of art into the utilitarian illustration of a dogma, would

[1] It is since his death that these insinuations have been made. Conrad said, in his preface to *Chance*, "I do not mean to hint that anybody had ever done me the injury (I don't mean insult, I mean injury) of charging a single one of my pages with didactic purpose. But every subject in the region of intellect and emotion must have a morality of its own if it is treated at all sincerely; and even the most artful of writers will give himself (and his morality) away in about every third sentence."

not merely have offended against Conrad's feeling for artistic decorum, it would have run counter to his reliance on sense impressions. True, he had Marlow to act as commentator if he thought fit. But though Marlow does from time to time let fall a personal observation—it was part of his character to do so—his definite function, even in such spontaneous remarks, was to clarify the story. He stands somewhere between the reader and Conrad himself, seeing things as Conrad sees them. In *The Nigger of the "Narcissus,"* in "Youth" and "Typhoon," man is shown at strife with nature, the sea, and ultimately with fate—and triumphing against fearful odds. In *Lord Jim*, *Nostromo*, and most of the novels and stories right down to *The Rover*, the conflict with inimical circumstance is uppermost; whilst in "Heart of Darkness," *Chance*, *Victory*, and divers others, it is the devil in man himself that is the foe. In nearly every single instance, man comes to grief; but to Conrad this does not mean that man is defeated. On the contrary, he writes a novel, *Victory*, which closes in death for a pair of his most exalted lovers, for it is at the moment of death that all the barriers are overthrown, and they have achieved themselves and the bliss of full spiritual communion. For the poetic justice beloved of the sentimental romancer Conrad had nothing but scorn; it was usurping the prerogative of divine omnipotence.[1]

Tragedy in Conrad

And to him, as to all the great ones, tragedy is not a sad thing, but exhilarating, vitalizing, dynamic; in short, it is a triumph. A triumph of pity? By no means. Pity implies some contempt. It is the triumph of human personality. The finest tragedy does not fill the onlooker with infinite regret, but with a sense of wonder and joy at a splendid achievement. We glory in the strength of the human spirit conquering all the ills and disasters of mortality and meeting the end serenely. Fate seems to have had the best of it, but that is a false seeming: the soul is nobler and sublimer than fate. Lear and Cordelia have reached a spiritual plane above

[1] "Why the reading public which, as a body, has never laid upon a story-teller the command to be an artist, should demand from him this sham of Divine Omnipotence, is utterly incomprehensible" (*Notes on Life and Letters*, "Henry James").

all the evil in the world. The outcome in prosperity or failure is nothing; it is the ripeness of human personality which is the enduring consummation:

Nothing is here for tears.

Conrad does not appear to have been a reader of George Eliot or Hardy. He would have spurned at the didacticism of the former; but his rendering of the tragedy of the human lot approximates to that of both when they were at their finest. The upshot in the great majority of his stories is parallel to the austere conclusion of *The Woodlanders*, and to the catastrophe that immortalizes Tom and Maggie in *The Mill on the Floss*, when they have attained mutual understanding and forgiveness. Like George Eliot too, he sometimes invoked the aid of melodrama at such crises. He might discuss the virtue of patience and resignation in the abstract. "Not that I think resignation the last word of wisdom. I am too much the creature of my time for that."[1] He was, indeed. Rebellion and unremitting warfare were much more to his mind. He was so grievously aware of the predominance of evil that he asked himself whether any ethical view of the universe was not utterly fallacious. "I have come to suspect that the aim of creation cannot be ethical at all. I would firmly believe that its object is purely spectacular: a spectacle for awe, love, adoration, or hatred, if you like, but in this view—and in this view alone—never for despair. . . . The unwearied self-forgetful attention to every phase of the living universe may be our appointed task on this earth."[2] He was himself brought up in the Roman Catholic religion; but he abjured and denounced all the creeds of supernaturalism. His religion was based on the spirituality of man. Man is apparently the one atom of self-consciousness in the whole cosmos. His realization of man's uniqueness and loneliness in an indifferent and inscrutable universe, the acute sense of man's dignity and man's self-responsibility, and a sense, equally acute, equally profound, not merely of abstract justice, but of the superlative value to man of courage, endurance, and

[1] *A Personal Record*, preface. [2] *Ibid.*, v.

loyalty to his fellow-men—it was all this that constituted his religion for Conrad. And it was eminently the religion for a man of letters, a great artist; for is not art itself thus identified with religion, with worship of the highest, of the truly spiritual? Through art alone is discerned and realized that perfection which the soul craves and can find nowhere outside itself. Such is the reasoning to which his convictions lead, and which the heroic and aspiring issue of his imagination corroborate.

CHAPTER II

CONRAD THE NOVELIST, WITH HIS NEXT OF KIN

"*Nostromo*"

Nostromo, a tale of the seaboard (1904), opens a new chapter for Conrad. So far he had been content to tell stories, stories of the sea; even *Lord Jim*, though in mere length a novel, is rightly called "a Tale"; and his characters, however far they stood out from the average and commonplace, were simple at bottom as the sailors and sea-captains who were their originals. They might find themselves in staggering predicaments; but there was never a touch of complexity or subtlety in their own compositions. But after finishing *Typhoon, and other stories*, Conrad was feeling exhausted. "Things are bad with me," he writes to a correspondent, and to another, Arnold Bennett, he talks of "the terrible worry of having to rewrite a story" and "the impossibility of concocting a reasonable sentence confronting me at every turn. It was like a nightmare."[1] He felt that his vein was exhausted, as for the time being it was. About now he was collaborating with Ford Madox Ford in a novel of adventure candidly entitled *Romance* (1903), and this experience may have influenced him in what was a new departure. For, as he told his agent Pinker, *Nostromo* "is more of a Novel pure and simple than anything I've done since *Almayer's Folly*."[2] So now, instead of his lonely souls engaged in a duel with hostile forces, he evolves a more complex drama, in which the intricacies of human relations are the chief factor, and the beings reacting together are a prey to modern perplexities and disillusionments. Yet, as before, he relied on his own acquaintance with a distant land, though it had been little more than a glimpse, and drew

[1] Aubry, i. 306. [2] *Ibid.*, 316.

again from the originals who from time to time and in remote places had set his imagination brooding. It had not been the practice of the impressionist story-teller to prepare events beforehand, in order that the outcome, however surprising, would appear inevitable. His was the opposite way, to copy life, and let the explanation gradually emerge. Conrad knew the value of suspense; he gave that very title to the last of his novels; but he declined to make deliberate use of it in a mechanical plot. In this, his greatest creative effort, he could not help availing himself of some of the machinery of professional fiction. His task, this time, was to weave a good many strands, some of which would have made dramatic stories by themselves, into a complicated tissue; he had to show what existence was like in strange and strangely-diversified places and circumstances, and at the same time present a large and tempestuous piece of history. Hence his brilliant opening, setting the grandiose stage, and the glimpses of a tragic past premonitory of what will follow; hence the more or less regular development, the terrible episodes cunningly linked in, and the theatrical conclusion according to accepted usage. The spaciousness and opulence of *Nostromo* are beyond dispute, whatever its shortcomings. It is real romance, according to Stevenson's formula: "The right kind of thing . . . in the right kind of place," made actual, with real men of action, real passions, real deeds; and even when there is a spice of melodrama, the events are made to come about in a markedly natural way.

Origin and growth of "Nostromo"

Conrad himself recalls how in a voyage to the West Indies, when he was only an apprentice, he heard the story of a man said "to have stolen single-handed a whole lighterful of silver somewhere on the Tierra Firme seaboard during the troubles of a revolution."[1] This, with what he saw of the coast of South America in sailing along it and surmised of what peoples and passions lay behind, was the germ, so long dormant, which a fertilizing imagination now had to develop. Nostromo himself was one of the avatars of a character that had impressed himself on Conrad at that same period, the Dominic Cervoni,

[1] Aubry, i. 380. He enlarges upon it in his "Author's Note."

padrone of the *Tremolino*, who is the memorable figure of those chapters in *The Mirror of the Sea* headed by the name of that dare-devil craft. This audacious, "astute and ruthless" type of a Mediterranean seaman, with his foibles of personal vanity and "perfectly remorseless irony," admittedly was also the stem from which sprang that fine sailor Captain Lingard, Peyrol of *The Rover*, and Attilio, in *Suspense*.[1] But, it is noteworthy, they are by no means duplicates. Conrad never repeated himself; the corollary to his belief in the loneliness of the individual is the intense individuality of each. He had to devise the "revolutionary troubles," and find a role for Nostromo in which his escape with the lighterful of ingots would come in as a plausible dramatic incident. The vast spectacle of life in all its aspects of peace and turmoil in the Republic of Costaguana, where revolution was an annual event; the scheme for establishing a separate state of Sulaco on the other side of the Cordilleras, where the San Tomé mine was situated; the risings and massacres and raids of the revolutionary factions; and such breathless episodes as Nostromo's ride on the locomotive to give the alarm, the terror at the approach of Sotillo, that "soul of gloomy hatred, irresolution, avarice, and fury," with his greedy and murderous hordes; and Nostromo and Decoud's hairbreadth escape with the cargo of silver from the mine, compose a tremendous drama, within the infernal clashing of which the more intimate drama of Carlos Gould and his adorable wife, of Decoud and Antonia, Nostromo, old Viola and his daughters, and the rest of the aristocrats and their partisans, pursues its course. Conrad's impressionism is by no means laid aside; but the narration is mostly direct, or put in the mouths of the people implicated, who stamp themselves with peculiar vividness by the traits of mien and voice which reveal. It is Conrad's visual drama at its strongest. He falls back at times, however, on a substitute for Marlow, in the French boulevardier Decoud, whose flippant mockery changes now and again to the more searching irony of his creator. Of his country he used to say to his French associates:

[1] *Ibid.*, 37, n.

"Imagine an atmosphere of opera-bouffe in which all the comic business of stage statesmen, brigands, etc., etc., all their farcical stealing, intriguing, and stabbing is done in real earnest. It is screamingly funny; the blood flows all the time, and the actors believe themselves to be influencing the fate of the universe."

But when the opera-bouffe has turned to deadly earnest he sums up the situation more tellingly and shows himself no laggard in action:

"I have read somewhere that Drake, who was the greatest of these men, used to dine alone in his cabin on board ship to the sound of trumpets. In those days this town was full of wealth. Those men came to take it. Now the whole land is like a treasure-house, and all these people are breaking into it, whilst we are cutting each other's throats. The only thing that keeps them out is mutual jealousy. But they'll come to an agreement some day—and by the time we've settled our quarrels and become decent and honourable, there'll be nothing left for us. It has always been the same. We are a wonderful people, but it has always been our fate to be"—he did not say "robbed," but added, after a pause—"exploited!"

Decoud is "a dilettante in life"; yet he is the most clear-sighted in the whole vast crowd, unless Mrs Gould's serene, disillusioned vision is not even more penetrating. It is Decoud who conceives the idea of separation and a new State of Sulaco; no one knows better than he that the fate of the rebellion turns on possession of the mine: it would be a prize for the piratical generals and for the savage mob, it can be a weapon for the loyalists. Don Carlos Gould is a sentimentalist disguised as a man of iron, as Decoud clearly perceives. He has avenged his father by rehabilitating the world's confidence in the mine, which he will blow up rather than let it fall into the hands of a predatory government. His faith in the mine is a religion: "After all this misery I simply could not have touched it for money alone." He hates to hear his millionaire partner in San Francisco discuss it as a mere business proposition. "A man must work to some end." But "he holds to it," says the sceptical Decoud, "as some men hold to the idea of love—or revenge. . . . A passion has crept into his cold and idealistic life"—the mine is an emblem, a fetish—an emblem of what? To Charles Gould, of right and justice, a purpose for which to live and work; to the ruck of the politicians, armed brigands, and the half-starved proletariat, it is the symbol of plutocracy and slavery of the people. He and the wonderful Mrs Gould are lovers and stanch husband and wife; yet their personal worlds are as far apart as Sirius and Aldebaran. "Poor boy! She had a clear vision of the grey hairs on his temples. He was perfect—perfect. What more could she have expected? It was a colossal and lasting success; and love was only a short moment of forgetfulness, a short intoxication, whose delight one remembered with a sense of sadness, as if it had been a deep grief lived through." She detects the root of all the trouble—the greed, unrest, and so-called democratic fury of the ignorant crowd; the idealism of Don Carlos and the pseudo-religion of Holroyd, the corruption of Nostromo's primitive integrity, based on self-esteem, or, if you like, vanity. Ultimately, the contest is between material interests and everything spiritual, including love. "These material interests of the foreigners," fulminates the Cardinal Archbishop, that patient, undaunted, unscrupulous worker for his Church and the restoration of its confiscated property. "There is no peace and no rest in the development of material interests," Dr Monygham tells her, he who calls Charles Gould "incorrigible." She sees the San Tomé mine—

possessing, consuming, burning up the life of the last of the Costaguan Goulds; mastering the energetic spirit of the son as it had mastered the lamentable weakness of the father. A terrible success for the last of the Goulds. The last! . . . An immense desolation, the dread of her own continued life, descended upon the first lady of Sulaco. With prophetic vision she saw herself surviving alone the degradation of her young ideal of life, of love, of work—all alone in the Treasure House of the World.

And where does Nostromo come in? The Captain of the Sulaco Cargadores, though he gives the book its title, is after

Nostromo and other figures

all a minor character; but his is the part that hits the moral on the head. He, the disinterested, the incorruptible, partly out of injured pride, seeing himself made a tool for the benefit of his superiors, but still more through being himself corrupted at last by the same material interests; now taught to see things clearly by Decoud's irony and stung by the sharper plain-speaking of Dr Monygham, looks out for himself, and, when Decoud takes four ingots of the treasure, he hoodwinks his conscience with the argument that what the supercilious gentry do must be right for him. So he yields to the magic of all that wealth, and becomes its slave and ultimately its victim. "The rich lived on wealth stolen from the people, but he had taken from the rich nothing—nothing that was not lost to them already by their folly and their betrayal. For he had been betrayed—he said—deceived, tempted." Material interest has him at last, as it has had the others all along. Decoud takes the four ingots when, left alone on the Great Isabel by Nostromo, he commits suicide, "a victim of the disillusioned weariness which is the retribution meted out to intellectual audacity." He puts them in his pockets; and when he shoots himself on the gunwale of the boat they carry him down. It would be unfair to ask who chronicled the last moments of Decoud; Conrad reverts for the most part here to narrative that enforces itself by its own vividness. It is the richest of all his books in varied human shapes, from the best to the vilest. Those of the stamp of Don Pépé, General Barrios, Sotillo, the inquisitioner Father Beron, the two Monteros, and their myrmidons, are contemptuously allowed to brand themselves as covetous rogues glozing over their lusts and atrocities. The beautiful Antonia, he confessed in his "Author's Note," was modelled on Conrad's own first love. But the parallel between himself and Decoud is not otherwise very close.[1] Another figure it is impossible to forget is Dr Monygham. He is loyalty and integrity incarnate, but his soul has been maimed by the "confession" wrung from him by torture long ago by the repulsive Beron, tool of one of Costaguana's patriotic "liberators." Monygham is as clear-

[1] Morf lays much stress on this "parallel"; see below (p. 78) and Morf (p. 128).

sighted as Decoud, and is not afraid to tell Mrs Gould some home truths or to correct Charles Gould's wild idealism. He fills the post of Marlow when required; and at the last it is Dr Monygham, after the old Garibaldian Viola has killed Nostromo in mistake for Ramirez, that recognizes who is the hero of the whole piece. Linda will never forget Nostromo, "Never! Gian Battista!"

It was another of Nostromo's triumphs, the greatest, the most enviable, the most sinister of all. In that true cry of undying passion that seemed to ring aloud from Punta Mala to Azuera and away to the bright line of the horizon, overhung by a big white cloud shining like a mass of solid silver, the genius of the magnificent Capataz de Cargadores dominated the black gulf containing his conquests of treasure and love.[1]

"The Secret Agent"

The Secret Agent (1907) also had its foundation in facts known to Conrad simply by hearsay.[2] It is his inner history of the attempt in 1894 to blow up Greenwich observatory. His version, apparently based on a suggestion of Ford Madox Ford's, is that the attempt was the outcome of a hint from the Russian embassy to a certain spy in its pay that concrete facts were wanted, to rouse public opinion against the Anarchists and goad the police into activity. Verloc accordingly acts as "agent provocateur," and stirs up his soft-headed and soft-hearted brother-in-law Stevie to strike this blow for the cause of humanity. But the bomb goes off in Stevie's hands, and the lad is blown to pieces. As a theory it sounds over-subtle; but Conrad was delighted to find afterwards that some of his guesses came remarkably close to facts of which he had been unaware.[3] *The Secret Agent* is a new kind of detective story, as different from Conan Doyle's as Henry James is from Cutcliffe Hyne. Conrad endows the Assistant Commissioner of Police, said to have been drawn from Sir Robert Anderson (1841–1918), with his own clairvoyance.[4] The scene where

[1] Cunninghame Graham spoke of *Nostromo* as "a sort of South American epic, written by someone who had seen right to its heart" (*Nouvelle Revue française*, December 1924).

[2] He was abroad at the time, and knew nothing but the bare facts. He "never read what was printed in the newspapers at the time" (Aubry, ii. 322).

[3] *Ibid.*

[4] See Anderson's autobiography, *The Lighter Side of my Official Life* (1910).

this astute official reads the mind of Chief Inspector Heat, and detects just what that estimable functionary, not merely left unsaid, but tried with all his craftiness to keep unsuspected, is a telling bit of psychological drama. Little is said, but mystification and officialdom are stripped naked. The Assistant Commissioner has found a clue which he keeps to himself, and, being like Conrad a man of imagination, reconstructs the whole case, even to the part played by the nefarious embassy. Later on, when all the information has been put together, he is in a position to dumbfound the high and mighty Vladimir at the embassy, in a little chat which gratified Conrad's Russophobia.

"We've got hold of a man called Verloc," he announced, casually.

Mr Vladimir did not stumble, did not stagger back, did not change his stride. But he could not prevent himself from exclaiming: "What!" The Assistant Commissioner did not repeat his statement. "You know him," he went on in the same tone.

"What makes you say that?"

"I don't. It's Verloc who says that."

"A lying dog of some sort," said Mr Vladimir in somewhat Oriental phraseology. But in his heart he was almost awed by the miraculous cleverness of the English police. The change of his opinion on the subject was so violent that it made him feel slightly sick. He threw away his cigar, and moved on.

An ironical story

The straight contest between the intuitive and the deductive, the imaginative and artistic and the orthodox police methods of investigation, is indirectly a manifesto of Conrad's artistic principles. There are missing links in the case. For instance, it is not made too clear how Verloc persuaded the half-idiot Stevie to undertake the fatal job. The reader is left to supply certain details, if he feels there is no inherent unlikelihood. Conrad called it "a simple story"; but even up to this point it is an ugly one, threading the mazes of a hideous underworld of criminals, terrorists, and plotters. The only characters for whom one can feel a vestige of human sympathy, apart from an intellectual admiration for the Assistant Commissioner, are the hoodwinked Mrs Verloc and the witless boy. How was such a story to be told? There was no room here for a Marlow. Yet Conrad must present the facts from a definite angle. Fortunately, he wrote a preface for the revised edition in which he fully discusses the problem, and reveals how he was brought by purely artistic considerations to "the earnest belief that ironic treatment alone would enable me to say all I felt I would have to say in scorn as well as in pity." Observe that he does not aim, here at any rate, at preserving the impassive attitude of a Maupassant. The ironic point of view is maintained with almost unfailing consistency, though scorn and pity break through at times, especially in the harrowing sequel, when after stabbing the husband who sent her brother to be blown to bits Winnie Verloc flies with the unspeakable Ossipon, and being tricked and left in the lurch by that scoundrel drowns herself in the Channel. Conrad himself was compelled by his imaginative realization of Winnie Verloc's "maternal passion" for Stevie to regard it all as her story: so he leaves it to be understood in his preface. But, if this was a theme that emerged and asserted itself, the original object, to explain the outrage, and show up the concealed forces of terrorist crime that Conrad loathed, afforded enough outlet for scorn and satirical irony. It begins at once, with Mr Verloc's walk through the park and along the Row, when he contemplates with mixed feelings the loitering procession of the well-to-do, whilst "a peculiarly London sun—against which nothing could be said except that it looked bloodshot—glorified all this by its stare. It hung at a moderate elevation above Hyde Park Corner with an air of punctual and benign vigilance." "All these people had to be protected. Protection is the first necessity of opulence and luxury." "Mr Verloc was not devoid of intelligence—and at the notion of a menaced social order he would perhaps have winked to himself if there had not been an effort to make in that sign of scepticism." Dread, intensified by the irony, is the ground-note of the chapters that follow Verloc's trip to the embassy, when the secret region of the underworld of London is opened up, infested by the terrorist plotters and their more sordid hangers-on, and by spies of the Verloc stamp. The atmosphere is charged with a ghastliness as sinister as that of "Heart of Darkness," which deepens into soul-numbing horror with the ironic, cold-blooded narrative of the sombre menaces fulfilling themselves in acts. Conrad shows the repulsive or grotesque outsides of the beings in his Chamber of Horrors, and somehow lets light into their very brains and nerve-centres. Complex or simple, shifty or rabidly idealist, stupid or acute, they are laid bare like transparent anatomies. Michaelis, "the ticket-of-leave apostle," is done in the Daumier style; Ossipon, foul, bloodthirsty, ready to sell the cause and any shred of soul he may have to get hold of Verloc's savings, would do credit to Rops at his most sardonic; the gentle, hard-headed, wrong-headed, fanatical "Professor," sane in his insanity, labouring to find the perfect detonator, is a walking terror hardly to be matched outside Conrad. Correlative with all this is his intuitive comprehension of the half-imbecile Stevie.

Supremely wise in knowing his own powerlessness, Stevie was not wise enough to restrain his passions. The tenderness of his universal charity had two phases as indissolubly joined and connected as the reverse and obverse sides of a medal. The anguish of immoderate compassion was succeeded by the pain of an innocent but pitiless rage.

Conrad senses the soul in the poor boy, a soul in the brainless. With a like understanding, he looks into the depths of the agonized Mrs Verloc, and sees her in the grip of the terrible hallucination which quietly impels her to take hold of the carving-knife and bury it in the breast of her remorseless husband.

"I wish to goodness," he growled, huskily, "I had never seen Greenwich Park or anything belonging to it."

The veiled sound filled the small room with its moderate volume, well adapted to the modest nature of the wish. The waves of air of the proper length, propagated in accordance with correct mathematical formulas, lapped against Mrs Verloc's head as if it had been a head of stone. And incredible as it may appear, the eyes of Mrs Verloc seemed to grow still larger. The audible wish of Mr Verloc's overflowing heart flowed into an empty place in his wife's memory. Greenwich Park. A park! That's where the boy was killed. A park—smashed branches, torn leaves, gravel, bits of brotherly flesh and bone, all spouting up together in the manner of a firework. She remembered now what she had heard, and she remembered it pictorially. They had to gather him up with the shovel. Trembling all over with irrepressible shudders, she saw before her the very implement with its ghastly load scraped up from the ground. Mrs Verloc closed her eyes desperately, throwing upon that vision the night of her eyelids, where after a rainlike fall of mangled limbs the decapitated head of Stevie lingered suspended alone, and fading out slowly like the last star of a pyrotechnic display. Mrs Verloc opened her eyes.

"Under Western Eyes"

The sky is still overcast in *Under Western Eyes*, the prevailing atmosphere of which is as ominous of obscure terrors as in a novel of Dostoevsky, that "grimacing, haunted creature, who is under a curse."[1] It is a study in the pathology of fear, distrust, villainy, remorse, which has been compared with *Crime and Punishment*; it is at the same time another exposure, this time of the misguided scheming of the Russian revolutionaries. In writing what his mouthpiece in the book calls "a Russian story for Western ears, which . . . are not attuned to certain tones of cynicism and cruelty," he underwent two years of "terrible moral stress"; he found it "a confounded difficult novel."[2] For in spite of his hatred of Nihilism and his aristocratic prejudices, and in spite of the Russophobia due to the wrongs of Poland, Conrad strove not to be hard on the Russians.[3] He depicts their misery and absolute servitude under the Tsarist autocracy as a simple inferno. But two or any number of wrongs do not make a right; and, for all his

[1] Letter to Garnett (Aubry, ii. 192).

[2] Letter to Rothenstein (*Ibid.*, 104). He makes his elderly English teacher remark, "I suppose one must be a Russian to understand Russian simplicity, a terrible corroding simplicity in which mystic phrases clothe a naïve and hopeless cynicism. I think sometimes that the psychological secret of the profound difference of that people consists in this, that they detest life, the irremediable life of the earth as it is, whereas we westerners cherish it with perhaps an equal exaggeration of its sentimental value" (*Under Western Eyes*, medallion ed., 104).

[3] See Aubry, i. 54–55, on Conrad's bitter resentment towards Tsarist Russia. But this is not a condemnation of Russia or a merely hostile exposure of Nihilism; it is a sincere effort to understand and portray the Russians as human beings (see Mégroz, 125–126).

efforts to grasp and sympathize, he depicts the general crowd of revolutionaries as senseless dreamers or conceited mountebanks, bloodthirsty cut-throats or simple traitors, selling their services and their accomplices to the secret police. Haldin stands out as a pure idealist, confronting death for the cause, though the deed he performs does not advance it a single step.

The mental conflict in Razumov

But the central point of the huge canvas is the soul of Razumov, who betrays Haldin and becomes a paid spy. Razumov is another man of fine potentialities who yields to temptation or fear at the critical moment, like Lord Jim, Willems, Nostromo, and so many others of Conrad's people. But he is of different mettle from these. He is a Russian; an abstracted, self-analysing, questioning Slav; who asks himself satirically what is the real worth of a lofty purpose, what in truth is there in faith, loyalty, in any sort of enthusiasm. He has that Russian "cynicism" ingrained in him which Conrad diagnoses:

> Ziemianitch's passionate surrender to sorrow and consolation had baffled him. That was the people. A true Russian man! Razumov was glad he had beaten that brute—the "bright soul" of the other. Here they were: the people and the enthusiast. Between the two he was done for. Between the drunkenness of the peasant incapable of action and the idealist incapable of perceiving the reason of things, and the true character of men. It was a sort of terrible childishness. But children had their masters. "Ah! the stick, the stick, the stern hand," thought Razumov, longing for power to hurt and destroy.

Razumov is the product of a racial disposition and a political state of things that Conrad strains every nerve to see clearly, making all possible allowances for what is foreign to himself. The strain is apparent here and there, mainly because Conrad handicapped himself in this book with such a clumsy substitute for Marlow as his teacher of languages, who protests his artlessness, yet has to piece together Razumov's self-revealing record with the account of what went on under his own eyes, filling in the gaps with what Miss Haldin tells him of her conversation with the *dame de compagnie* to Peter Ivanovitch, and the history of the journeyman lithographer who was tortured into giving information. Nevertheless, no one has ever come nearer to Dostoevski than Conrad in the crucial points of the story—Razumov's act of perfidy, and his revulsion when, maddened by the gratitude and worship of the sister of the man he had betrayed, though the inevitable result will be to lose the woman he loves and there is now no risk of his being unmasked, he confesses all. Razumov, before he betrays Haldin, is like a being only half conscious of himself and what he is doing, in a dim, mysterious universe; trying spasmodically to co-ordinate his perceptions and the significance of his acts, but not sure of what he sees or what he does. Yet he sees certain things only too acutely; he knows only too well the peril to himself and his ambitions into which Haldin's desperate appeal for aid has thrown him, a motive combining only too easily with the conservatism that means playing for safety. It is in a state of mind bordering upon hallucination that the conflicting motives fight it out within him.

> Razumov stood on the point of conversion. He was fascinated by its approach, by its overpowering logic. For a train of thought is never false. The falsehood lies deep in the necessities of existence, in secret fears and half-formed ambitions, in the secret confidence combined with a secret mistrust of ourselves, in the love of hope and the dread of uncertain days.

Presently he throws down the book that he has not been reading, and takes a sheet of paper "with a vague notion of going on with the writing of his essay—but his pen remained poised over the sheet." Then he begins to write, the last of the five lines growing unsteady, almost childish.

> "History not Theory.
> Patriotism not Internationalism.
> Evolution not Revolution.
> Direction not Destruction.
> Unity not Disruption."

He stabs the paper to the wall, and then he lies down, and dreams of walking through the snows of Russia, "as completely alone as any betrayed autocrat could be." How he chooses between the alternatives, and comes to give Haldin up to the authorities, is not explained, not stated; but the sequences of thought and mood are thus shadowed forth in a "mind hovering on the borders of delirium." And it is as the final stage of a like process of self-accusation and self-torment that he arrives at the consciousness that he can no longer be "a living, acting, speaking lie," and makes his confession. In the "Author's Note," added later, Conrad enumerated his objects in writing *Under Western Eyes*, and does only justice to the figures typifying the Russian bureaucracy and those selected from the "purely Utopian revolutionism" which it had brought into being. He did not mean anything monstrous in Razumov.

> Nobody is exhibited as a monster here—neither the simple-minded Tekla nor the wrong-headed Sophia Antonovna. Peter Ivanovitch and Madame de S. are fair game. They are the apes of a sinister jungle and are treated as their grimaces deserve. As to Nikita—nicknamed Necator—he is the perfect flower of the terroristic wilderness. What troubled me most in dealing with him was not his monstrosity but his banality.
>
> Both sets were good artistic pendants to the shapes of evil in *The Secret Agent.*

"*Chance*" In his preface to *Chance* (1913) in the collected edition of his works, Conrad said, "My intention was to interest people in my vision of things, which is indissolubly allied to the style in which it is expressed." His vision, his theory of life, his scale of values, are crystallized in a small group of recurring ideas. One that he was always harping upon was the loneliness of each of us, the impossibility of complete intimacy. As Arnold had put it long ago,

> Yes, in the sea of life enisled,
> . . . .
> We mortal millions live alone.

It was a theme implicit in his sea-stories, which taken together might almost be called an epic of individualism,[1] so

[1] The word "epic" is used here in a general, perhaps metaphorical, sense. Mr Herbert Read contends, "Conrad cannot be claimed as an epic novelist. He does not idealize the heroic, or make it more than the expression of an individual temperament" (*Reason and Romanticism*, 208)—a statement not wholly beyond dispute.

solitary and inscrutable are even the simplest of his characters, even when they are not outcasts. Sterne had made some such idea the occasion of infinite jest. To Conrad it is sometimes a romantic, but always a tragic theme. In *Chance*, the anguish of two kindred beings unable to confide in each other across the impassable gulf is the dominant theme. But the other, indicated in the title, is hardly less significant. Everything important in the story occurs through the haphazards of cause and effect, from such a secondary incident as Fyne's marriage, a pure accident, to the revelation that comes at last and unites the lovers. But mark the irony. The chances are wofully small in this ill-arranged world of any such happy consummation; and yet in this instance mere hazard has brought it to pass. Chance, yes; but such a strange complication and convergence of chances! Possibly, too, at the back of his mind there was another and a more personal thought. The narrative seems to proceed in the happy-go-lucky way of a picaresque romance. But the apparent haphazards have been devised with unwonted forethought: nothing has been left to chance. And it is the most complicated of all Conrad's novels in the number of points of view, one reporter reported by another, and so on, with further comment and elucidation, all for the sake of pure objectivity. Intricacy of design and infinity of pains to secure the ends desired make the title more ironic.

The story

They are two of Conrad's rarest and most generous creations—Miss Smith or Flora de Barral, daughter of the fraudulent financier, the great De Barral, another Whitaker Wright or Jabez Balfour; and the chivalrous seaman, Captain Anthony, son of the poet. Briefly, if incredibly, the story is this. De Barral goes to gaol, leaving Flora unprotected. Insulted by the servants and her governess, she finds a temporary refuge with the stupid, upright Fyne and his conventional literary wife—Fyne, by another stroke of Conrad's irony, is one of the chroniclers of her story. Then she is carried off by a not disinterested relative, in whose house she endures unspeakable outrage, till she runs away again to the Fynes. Here Marlow comes in. By chance, he saves her from suicide. Without a soul to trust or a hope to live for, she has calmly determined to go out of the world. By chance again, Captain Anthony, Mrs Fyne's brother, discovers her state of desperation, and more by luck than intention preserves her again from putting an end to herself. The next thing Marlow hears is that Flora and Anthony have eloped, much to the indignation of the Fynes. What had happened is this. The captain, in love with the shrinking girl, has humbly offered to rescue her for good by taking her away, to sea, as his wife. There is something else behind. De Barral will soon be out of prison, Flora's father, tenderly loved, and the only thing she has of her own in a friendless world. What will become of him, more than friendless, firmly believed by her to be the victim of a monstrous conspiracy, all the world against one man? Anthony's magnanimity is sublime enough not only to lend the girl the shelter of his name, conscious that she has only gratitude, not love, and cannot be his wife in anything but form, but also to give asylum on board his ship to the man whom he believes to be an abject scoundrel. And now the story is chiefly in the hands of Powell, the youthful second officer on Anthony's ship, though it is retailed at second-hand by Marlow, with his inimitable flashes of irony mingled of cynical distaste for average humanity and reticent appreciation of what is sterling. De Barral still believes in himself; he wants only the opportunity to make another colossal fortune on better foundations. He regards the ship as a prison and the captain as his gaoler. Flora, long after, puts her position between them thus:

"I really believed I was selling myself, Mr Marlow. And I was proud of it. What I suffered afterwards I couldn't tell you; because I only discovered my love for poor Roderick through agonies of rage and humiliation. I came to suspect him of despising me; but I could not put it to the test because of my father. . . . Oh! I have been miserable! That night when my poor father died suddenly I am certain they had some sort of discussion, about me. But I did not want to hold out any longer against my own heart! I could not."

So year after year the strange trio sail about in the *Ferndale*,

Roderick and Flora passionately in love but kept ever asunder, the one by his sublime delicacy, the other convinced that Roderick's act is simply one of immense generosity and disinterestedness. The villainous old convict is on the watch, awaiting his chance, till the dramatic moment when, by another stroke of incalculable hazard, revelation comes to the lovers.

Anthony had entered with extreme precipitation the enchanted gardens of Armida saying to himself, "At last!" As to Armida herself, he was not going to offer her any violence. But now he had discovered that all the enchantment was in Armida herself, in Armida's smiles. This Armida did not smile. She existed, unapproachable, behind the blank wall of his renunciation. His force, fit for action, experienced the impatience, the indignation, almost the despair of his vitality arrested, bound, stifled, progressively worn down, frittered away by Time; by that force blind and insensible, which seems inert and yet uses one's life up by its imperceptible action, dropping minute by minute on one's living heart like drops of water wearing down a stone.

It would occur to Anthony at the end of such meditations that death was not an unfriendly visitor after all. No wonder then that even young Powell, his faculties having been put on the alert, began to think that there was something unusual about the man who had given him his chance in life. Yes, decidedly, his captain was "strange." There was something wrong somewhere, he said to himself, never guessing that his young and candid eyes were in presence of a passion profound, tyrannical, and mortal, discovering its own existence, astounded at feeling itself helpless and dismayed at finding itself incurable.

Irony suffuses the story from beginning to end, for Marlow is the chief narrator, though he is usually telling what he has learned from the reluctant and only half understanding lips of Powell. It is heard also in the stolid propriety of the intellectual, Fyne.

"Good little Fyne! You have no idea what infernal mischief he had worked during his call at the hotel. But then who could have suspected Anthony of being a heroic creature?

There are several kinds of heroism, and one of them at least is idiotic. It is the one which wears the aspect of sublime delicacy. It is apparently the one of which the son of the delicate poet was capable.

"I call a woman sincere when she volunteers a statement resembling remotely in form what she would really like to say, what she really thinks ought to be said if it were not for the necessity to spare the stupid sensitiveness of men. The women's rougher, simpler, more upright judgment embraces the whole truth, which their tact, their distrust of masculine idealism, ever prevents them from speaking in its entirety. And their tact is unerring. We could not stand women speaking the truth. We could not bear it. It would cause infinite misery and bring about most awful disturbances in this rather mediocre, but still idealistic fool's paradise in which each of us lives his own little life—the unit in the great sum of existence. And they know it. They are merciful."

"*Victory*"

To give the story thus in its broad outlines has been imperative. Character is not subordinate to action nor action to character in a novel by Conrad; they are complementary to each other. Life being a conflict, personality is developed through action.[1] The story would be nothing without his rare and exquisite or plain but heroic characters; the characters would be half-fledged, would be still-born, without the acts which expound them and make them solid and real. So it is again in *Victory* (1915), another novel skirting the region of pure idealism, and even penetrating some way beyond the borders. Conrad put into it some of his final or at least his most definite and "immovable" conclusions.[2] Here the

[1] See his recognition of the same in *Notes on Life and Art*, "Henry James" (15–16). "Warfare, sacrifice, renunciation are the secret, and the token of success is a fine conscience" (*Ibid.*, 17).

[2] He perhaps implied or hinted at meanings only vaguely formulated, to judge from a letter from an inquirer as to what he was driving at: "Coming now to the subject of your inquiry, I wish at first to put before you a general proposition: that a work of art is very seldom limited to one exclusive meaning and not necessarily tending to a definite conclusion. And this for the reason that the nearer it approaches art, the more it acquires a symbolic character. This statement may surprise you, who may imagine that I am alluding to the Symbolist School of poets or prose writers. Theirs, however, is only a literary proceeding against which I have nothing to say. I am concerned here with something much larger. . . . So I will call your attention to the fact that the symbolic conception of a work of art has this advantage, that it makes a triple appeal covering the whole field of life. All the great creations

technique is different; Conrad has taken the easier path, and the narrative goes on ordinary lines with less regard for strict objectivity. Conrad hears a good deal about Heyst and his doings and peculiar character from Davidson; but this is only a pretence of attestation by a near acquaintance, and is quickly abandoned for straightforward story-telling. The gist of it is a sort of transposition of that of *Chance*—another persecuted girl saved from infamy by a chivalrous hero, and their inability to achieve full mutual understanding till they are about to be sundered by death. Heyst is as rare a character as Captain Anthony. He is a Swede, son of a man of letters who preached quietism, avoidance of action, for the world is evil: therefore keep aloof, live your own life, "as the best way of cheating the time which is allotted to us whether we want it or not." He has drifted to this lonely outpost of Samburan, in the Archipelago, disenchanted with life through having been beguiled into action, gnawed by the pain of useless apostasy and by remorse for having, as he believes, been the cause of a man's death. By a mere chance Heyst rescues Lena from a disreputable band of musicians and from the libidinous advances of the hotel-keeper Schomberg, and they retire to his remote station on an isle inhabited by harmless Malay natives. They are in love, but each is baffled by the mysterious background of the other's mind. Then their solitude is suddenly broken in upon by three desperadoes, lured there by Schomberg's malicious gossip about the supposed riches of Heyst. From this point the story becomes more and more sensational, and the question arises whether figures of that order and risks so repulsive do not seriously impair a tragedy involving finer issues. True, there is sensationalism as lurid in some of Shakespeare's tragedies; but it has none of these nauseous implications. The agonizing scenes in which Heyst finds himself unarmed and helpless to defend the girl from these ruffians mar the beauty and dignity of the close—perfect understanding attained only in the hour of death.

Conrad had known Heyst: "we became very friendly for a

of literature have been symbolic, and in that way have gained in complexity, in power, in depth, and in beauty" (Letter to B. H. Clark, Aubry, ii. 204–205).

Incongruous elements

time." He had had a glimpse of the gentlemanly Mr Jones, though "the characteristic insolence belongs to another man." [1] His bloodthirsty secretary Ricardo he had come across in his early voyage to the West Indies; and he had set eyes on their bestial servant, the quondam alligator-hunter Pedro, and the shock was enough to put him to flight. He had been charmed by the "dreamy innocence" of Lena's original. In short, Conrad, as usual, assembled a number of characters that had appealed to his imagination, and put them here into dramatic contact, without enough regard for artistic fitness. It was one thing that at the advent of the appalling three, who far outdo Stevenson's horrific villains, Pew, Long John Silver, and Black Dog, Heyst, the man of universal detachment, should lose "his mental self-possession, that fine attitude before the universally irremediable which wears the name of stoicism." The evil of the world has broken into his retreat with a vengeance. But it is quite another thing to mix this up with the tragic idyll: the misanthropic comedy of crime free and easy does not blend harmoniously with that. In the dreadful finale of suspense and terror, Conrad reverts to his old impressionism. The things that happen just happen, and the meaning of it all gradually becomes plain, with the force of immediate contact with the events. The sardonic comedy of the three ruffians terrorizing Schomberg and thoroughly enjoying themselves at such a congenial game is a good preparation for the subsequent frightfulness.

"He's a gentleman," testified Martin Ricardo, with a sudden snap of the lips, after which his moustaches stirred by themselves in an odd, feline manner.

"Oh, I wasn't thinking of that," said plain Mr Jones, while Schomberg, dumb and planted heavily in his chair, looked from one to the other, leaning forward a little. "Of course I am that; but Ricardo attaches too much importance to a social advantage. What I mean, for instance, is that he, quiet and inoffensive as you see him sitting here, would think nothing of setting fire to this house of entertainment of yours. It would blaze like a box of matches. Think of that! It

[1] Preface, in collective ed.

wouldn't advance your affairs much, would it?—whatever happened to us."

"Come, come, gentlemen," remonstrated Schomberg in a murmur. "This is very wild talk!"

"And you have been used to deal with tame people, haven't you? But we aren't tame. We once kept a whole angry town at bay for two days, and then we got away with our plunder. It was in Venezuela. Ask Martin here—he can tell you."

Mr Jones is a more ghastly incarnation of pure evil even than the ugly malefactors in *The Secret Agent* and *Under Western Eyes*.

"You can't tell how a gentleman takes that sort of thing. They don't lose their temper. It's bad form. You'll never see him lose his temper—not for anybody to see, anyhow. Ferocity ain't good form, either—that much I've learned by this time, and more, too. I've had that schooling that you couldn't tell by my face if I meant to rip you up the next minute—as of course I could do in less than a jiffy. I have a knife up the leg of my trousers."

"Do you want me to understand, sir, that you mind there being one life more or less on this earth?" I asked him, a few hours after we got away.

"Certainly not," says he.

"Well, then, why did you stop me?"

"'There's a proper way of doing things. You'll have to learn to be more correct. There's also unnecessary exertion. That must be avoided, too—if only for the look of the thing.' A gentleman's way of putting things to you—and no mistake."

Life only a spectacle

It was inevitable, said his biographer of Conrad, "that his ardour and intellect should suffer profoundly in contact with the mediocrity of the world."[1] Out-and-out villainy interested him more: he brands vulgarity and baseness, but the dull average person hardly puts in an appearance in his books. Heyst and his father voice his philosophic musings, since Conrad himself harboured the thought that "this world, for the wise, is nothing but an amusing spectacle." "Truth,

[1] Aubry, i. 148.

work, ambition, love itself, may be only counters in the lamentable and despicable game." "Man on this earth is an unforeseen accident which does not stand close investigation." In the characters and attitudes of beings like Heyst and Lena, Anthony and Flora, Charles and Doña Emilia Gould, in their exalted passions and aspiring motives, Conrad hints at an ideal world dimly perceived beyond the imperfection of reality. The order of nature is a mirage: there all is accident and confusion. Man is the sole repository of order and goodness in a derelict universe. Only in the mind of man is there any glimpse of perfection. There is the heaven which the finer arts strive to possess—music, painting, architecture, the poetic imagination. This, whether distinctly formulated or not, was the basis of Conrad's idealism; virtually, it was his religion, as to many who think that art is the ritual and worship directed to the highest they are able to conceive. The artists do, indeed, as Garnett said, bring "new worlds" along with them [1]: they order this confused, baffling, immitigable world with that illumination, being themselves in contact with another, their own universe of order and perfection. Heyst sought to make his life "a masterpiece of aloofness." But man cannot live alone; the outer world broke in upon his quietude, and his last words to Davidson spoke his agony: "Ah! Davidson, woe to the man whose heart has not learned while young to hope, to love—and to put its trust in life!"

"The Shadow-Line"

A pair of novels, or rather stories, may be bracketed together, as romanticized versions of autobiographical episodes. *The Nigger of the "Narcissus"* was intended to be a short story; *The Shadow-Line* is not much more. The title has symbolical allusion to the young sailor's passage "from youth, care-free and fervent, to the more self-conscious and more poignant" experiences of maturity.[2] Conrad had already served up some of the same incidents in "Falk," about the man who like his uncle had dined on inhuman food, only this time the fare was not dog but the flesh of a fellow-creature. "A Confession" he calls *The Shadow Line*, and puts it in the mouth of the hero

[1] *Friday Nights*, "Mr Joseph Conrad," 86.
[2] Preface to collective ed.

of the exploit. Chance makes him skipper of a vessel, the late master of which has died leaving her in a far eastern port; he, as a young man, has to bring her home. But all "the immense forces of the world" seem to be against him. The ship is becalmed, the crew are down with fever, and the stock of quinine has mysteriously vanished. The chief mate declares that the old devil of a captain, who had left behind him a fiddle-case full of unreceipted bills and other compromising papers, and was buried at sea in lat. 8° 20′, will never let them pass. It is a near thing. When at the last gasp they get into port, there is not a man but the skipper left with strength to let go a sheet or hold the wheel. It is another story of heroic endurance, not weakened in the slightest by the fact that the chief actor relates it, for his admiration goes out to the fever-stricken sailors, who work like men inspired when their bones are turned to water. It is also a story of something occult. Was the evil soul of the dead captain fighting against them? There is no answer; but in his later preface Conrad explains that Mr Burns had received a severe shock in his relations with his late captain, and his diseased mind turned it into "a superstitious fancy compounded of fear and animosity." Conrad unfolds the moving panorama of what goes on, without trying to clear up what is strange or inexplicable, at any rate till much later on. Thus there is the incident of the letter kept back by the steward, at the officers' home. It is left a sheer enigma, till, when the affair is all but forgotten, the motive, the steward's hope that one of his friends would get the job rather than Captain Anon, clears that up. And, if one puzzling circumstance can be explained, others will be accepted that are never explained. So the question whether the captain's ghost did waylay the ship remains a puzzle to be solved or not, according to taste. Or take the bottles of quinine which are discovered to have been emptied and filled up with salt. This surprise, with all its paralysing consequences—the plight of the fever-stricken ship, without the one remedy that would have kept the crew fit for duty—falls like a thunderbolt. Everyone is nonplussed, too much disturbed to ask questions. But even that mystery is unobtrusively explained by the remark that quinine is expensive, and may fetch a handsome price in the eastern tropics, where it is almost unprocurable. It comes so casually that the other alternative, that the diabolical skipper may have played a diabolical trick, slips into oblivion.

"*The Arrow of Gold*"

The Arrow of Gold (1919) is subtitled "a story between two notes," and is a romantic expansion of the doings of the *Tremolino* and of Doña Rita, the facts of which fill the liveliest chapters in *The Mirror of the Sea.* It is the tale of two lovers in a "world eaten up with charlatanism of all sorts so that even we, the simple, don't know any longer how to trust each other." Their particular world is the Carlist society of the mid seventies, when the Pretender is somewhere in Spain, and his supporters in France and elsewhere are plotting, intriguing, and gun-running to keep him afoot. Mr George becomes a gun-runner, or at least sticks to the job, out of devotion to Doña Rita, the lovely, unfathomable being who was originally a peasant, was adopted and left a millionaire heiress by a great painter, and then seems to have been the mistress of Don Carlos, and is further credited by general report with the frailties of a Ninon de l'Enclos. But youth answers to youth in Monsieur George and Rita. Honesty, sincerity, even purity of soul, are incarnated in this exquisite creature, who cannot surrender herself to the man she passionately loves because she is who she is. Mr George, who is Conrad himself, kept notes or a diary, meant for one woman's eyes, and this is as satisfactory for maintaining illusion as ever Marlow would have been. But the story is told in the regular Conradian way, of one trying to probe a mystery, piecing together vague intimations, passing on hints to the reader, who may or may not make more of them. Hence, when the true nature of the characters is seized, the reader grasps them with a firmness as of at length understanding someone in real life who has puzzled or misled him—a slow but certain method of apprehension. Rita grows clearer as George's mind grows more definite about her; but there remains a veil, a penumbra, like the inscrutable smile of Mona Lisa. Scathing is the irony, the revulsion of feeling, with which the world of sordid cabals, treacherous foes, and slippery friends is drawn; it is an inferno of shapeless fears that chill like a contagion.

The Rescue (1920) is one of Conrad's most ambitious novels, and a great deal too long, owing to iteration of the same sentiments and the same or all but the same situation. His shrewd divination of the mind and soul of the savage is used here again to bring out the clash between the tame world and the wild one. The bumptious futility of our over-civilization brought up against elemental human forces is charmingly typified in Mr Travers, the multi-millionaire, standing on his empty dignity, unable to take in the position of things; with the result that he falls into the hands of the natives, and his life for weeks is not worth a moment's purchase. But it is also a love-story, and one in which Conrad lays himself open to the charge of sentimentalism, if that consists in dwelling on the beauty and pathos of the situation for its own sake. Captain Lingard and Mrs Travers have too many final interviews. For Conrad's ancient hero Tom Lingard here makes his last appearance, and his simple young manhood is tainted with modern sophistication. Unlike the Whalleys and MacWhirrs of yore, he falls in love, and betrays his native integrity. He has made immense preparations to restore his two friends, the Rajah Hassim and his sister Immada, to their kingdom. Munitions have been stored in a concealed hulk, hostile or lukewarm chiefs and piratical intriguers have been pacified: all is in readiness for the blow. Then, at the critical moment, the millionaire's yacht gets stranded at the very place of the grand rendezvous, and all is jeopardized. Lingard might have left the strangers to their own devices; but, unfortunately, he conceives a lofty and chivalrous passion for Mrs Travers. She understands the complexity of all that is at stake, and at no small personal risk goes alone to the native compound to give Lingard a ring betokening that his two friends are in deadly peril. She never hands over the ring; but that would not have mended matters, for Lingard has broken his trust from the moment he let his mind be divided between Mrs Travers and his pledge to the young Rajah. The Spaniard D'Alcacer, "a true Latin," who "was not afraid of a little

"*The Rescue*"

introspection," and plays part of Marlow's customary role, has more than a glimpse of what is in the wind, and stuns Lingard with his shrewd paraphrase of Lingard's own code of loyalty.

"It is a very binding agreement with which sincerity and good faith and honour have nothing to do. Very binding. Woe to him or her who breaks it. Directly they leave the pageant they get lost. . . . They get lost in a maze. . . . They wander in it lamenting over themselves. I would shudder at that fate for anything I loved. Do you know, Captain Lingard, how people lost in a maze end?" he went on, holding Lingard by a steadfast stare. "No? . . . I will tell you then. They end by hating their very selves, and they die in disillusion and despair."

The end comes with a completeness that ruins Captain Lingard's emprise, and leaves him nothing to live for. The Traverses sail away. His love is a dream. He remains, defeated and disillusioned, without even the credit of Lord Jim's last self-sacrifice.[1]

The last two

Conrad said *The Rover* (1923) was a story that grew of itself into a novel; it was one of the more rambling and inconsequent tales that came together spontaneously out of casual reminiscences, this time of the *Tremolino* business again. Such unity as it has pertains to the heroic Peyrol, another embodiment of Dominic Cervoni, and his contacts with the revolutionary movements in and round Toulon, when Nelson was blockading the coast before Trafalgar. It revolves rather ambiguously round a mission entrusted to Peyrol to sail with faked letters and dispatches, which were to be intercepted by the English and persuade Nelson that the fleet fitting out at Toulon was destined for Egypt and the East. Peyrol is a man, if ever there was one; the French mariner at his best, though of doubtful antecedents, privateer, adventurer, maybe even

[1] Lingard was, of course, a real person, to whom there are numerous references in Aubry. At the moment of writing, a brief article, "Almayer and Lord Jim," appears in *The Times* (22nd August 1938), epitomizing F. Harold Gray's account, in a magazine printed at Sarawak, of existent memories of Lingard and Almayer, on the river Pantai, on the east coast of Borneo. On the chart, the words "Oversteek Lingard," or Lingard's Passage, still recall *An Outcast of the Islands*. Almayer's house is still called "La Folie."

pirate. But this "calmly terrible" man has his sense of duty, duty to his own manhood and dignity, above all; and he dies a patriot's death in the mission which he takes on his own shoulders by outwitting the jealous Lieutenant Réal. Réal, "who on emerging from boyhood had laid for himself a rigidly straight line of conduct amongst the unbridled passions and the clamouring falsehoods of revolution," and who at heart cherishes scorn and loathing for the Revolution, makes the "awful discovery" that he loves and is loved by a poor creature with a mind darkened by an atrocious experience—beautiful, but "body without mind!" as he repeats with "angry derision directed at himself." Arlette is a penetrating and compassionate study of unselfish love in a mind diseased; but Conrad destines her after all for happiness. Peyrol, like Heyst, had gone through trials with faithless friends and his own passions, which had put into him "a drop of universal scorn, a wonderful sedative"; but, as in so many other cases, Conrad leaves the out-of-the-way corners of his soul obscure. On the other hand, he is perfectly clear about Citizen Scevola, the *sans-culotte*, the blood-drinker, his idea of a revolutionary. He regarded him, frankly, as "a pathological case."[1] Peyrol is excellent on the English, and the duty and pleasure of tricking them; but—

"What—that Nelson? Ah! but he is a cunning one."

As to the novel *Suspense* (1925), which Conrad left unfinished, it belongs to the genre of *Nostromo*; in method it is description and straightforward narrative, not indirect reporting of impressions. In plan and atmosphere it is romantic, the beginnings of some large complication that defies conjecture and whets the appetite. The time is that of Napoleon's incarceration on Elba; and the chief scene is Genoa, where hopes and fears focused upon the captive emperor are at high tension. A rich young English squire has arrived, and finds himself in mysterious contact with spies, secret agents, and police. He comes across a beautiful friend of his boyhood's days, and appearances indicate an elopement from her husband —one of Conrad's most sinister figures—or at the least a

[1] Aubry, ii. 326.

love-affair. Keen suspense has been stirred up, the actors have been brought forward and made vividly known, the first heavy links of the chain of events have rattled forward; then comes the standstill, and what was toward can only be guessed.

Two modes of story-telling

Conrad assented to the claim put forward by Henry James that fiction is a form of history. "Fiction is history, human history, or it is nothing. But it is also more than that; it stands on firmer ground, being based on the reality of forms and the observation of social phenomena, whereas history is based on documents . . . on second-hand impression."[1] Thus the novelist is a very serious and responsible person, especially when he deals with the motives and acts of those around him by such a close scrutiny as Conrad's, implying immediate contact with men and women and their doings. M. Fernandez has pointed out that Conrad had two distinct manners, distinct though aiming alike at the evocation of reality. The one is illustrated in *The Nigger of the "Narcissus,"* "Youth," "Typhoon," and "Heart of Darkness; the other in *Lord Jim* and *Chance*. It might be added that the first is typical of his most dramatic stories, the other of the ampler and more leisurely novel. In the one, he conjures up "the collective adventure of a vessel through a series of perceptions composing an actual dramatic state of things, a compelling, hallucinating present." In the other, the tension relaxed, he transmutes the past slowly and minutely into the present,[2] dealing leisurely with the consequences and the problems hingeing on the event, which itself may have been presented with the same intense actuality. *Nostromo*, *The Secret Agent*, *Under Western Eyes*, and his other novels that are definitely novels, are obviously the result of this leisurely, reflective process. But in these too the moments of critical action impinge with the same fierce actuality; reflection is suspended for the time being, and the illusion is evoked of sheer contact with the things

[1] *Notes on Life and Letters*, "Henry James" (p. 17).

[2] "La plupart de ses histoires proprement maritimes évoquent directement l'aventure collective d'un navire par une suite de perceptions qui composent un état dramatique actuel, un *présent* hallucinant et oppressif." "La deuxième manière . . . correspond aux périodes de congé et de détente. Là tout est repos, méditation, nonchalance" (*Messages*, "L'Art de Conrad," 115).

going on. Conrad, however, did not invariably apply his system of eye-witnesses and reporters or other devices for creating the illusion of direct contact with realities. And he had his moments of inadvertence. Lapses from the single point of view have been detected in *The Nigger of the "Narcissus,"* [1] where the man who tells the story sometimes dilates on things he manifestly could not have known; and he does at times, if rarely, forget himself elsewhere. In *Victory*, the device is employed perfunctorily, and degenerates into a mere pretence of authentic hearsay. In *Chance*, Marlow is often not much more than a literary elegance, an oracle, a mouthpiece for wit and irony, though he is still invaluable in certain passages for showing the complex of circumstance and motive at different angles. As elsewhere, this accounts for the to-and-fro movement of the narrative. Observe the circumstantial preamble, Powell signing on and telling Marlow all about it. Then Marlow takes up the tale; and, recalling Powell's experiences as a puzzled observer, in a rambling, gossipy way he pieces the story together and makes everything intelligible. Marlow is represented as a man of vision, with a faculty for seeing in a flash vital points that escape ordinary attention. Through his piercing and experienced eye, the latent conflict becomes a visible drama, easy to comprehend in all its intricacies and implications.

His characters

Impressionism does not see its characters as syntheses of qualities and intelligences sharply aware of their predicaments. Conrad is not one of the thoroughgoing analysts. Though often so like James in method, he is essentially different. He rarely anatomizes; it is only in the novels of his decline, at least after the two Almayer novels, that he formally states what is going on in the mind of his significant personages. He sees his creations as wholes, acting on impulse or habit, or from a complex of emotions they themselves could not define. They are to be known by intuition, for they are animated with "feelings of universal import." [2] The reader is put in contact with them; the blankness of the conventional hero is abolished, both by James and Conrad. Even the laboratory cases, such

[1] See, *e.g.* Crankshaw, 148–150.

[2] *Last Essays*, 213.

as the idiot boy and the fanatics in *The Secret Agent* or the tormented consciousness of Razumov, are not vivisected. Whether simple or complex, each is recognizable as a being of marked individuality reacting to the shocks of circumstance. But his characters do not yield their secrets easily, if they ever yield them quite. No small part of their unity and uniqueness is owing to the fact that there is an essence in each that cannot be segregated and defined. Marlow says of Lord Jim, "I don't pretend I understood him. The views he let me have of himself were like those glimpses through the shifting rents in a thick fog—bits of vivid and vanishing detail, giving no connected idea of the general aspect of a country." There is something that remains inexplicable, "a darkness he cannot pierce,"[1] another point of likeness to real life.[2] "Queer enough they were," Marlow remarks of the Fynes. "Is there a human being that isn't that—more or less secretly?" "When it comes to dealing with human beings, anything, anything may be expected." It is the exact contrary to the rule that the artist, the novelist especially, must simplify, must clarify, make intelligible. Life is not to be simplified and made completely intelligible; Conrad sees it as infinitely complex, and at the last an insoluble mystery.[3] And to him, unlike Sterne, this inscrutability of the individual was a tragic theme. Possibly there is such a thing as a psychology of the crowd, for the vast majority suppress and live down any insubordinate traits they may be aware of, making it a point of honour to be the same as their neighbours. With them, personality is undeveloped; what traces exist are feeble and unobtrusive in both quality and quantity. There are some, however, who obstinately run counter to the general, repudiating the ancient

[1] Freeman, 259.

[2] Aldous Huxley's criticism that Conrad is unable to fathom his own creations is one that cuts both ways. Perhaps it is the finest eulogy. As M. Fernandez puts it, "Il demeure tangent à la réalité; d'où vient que l'opacité de l'individu, de la scène, n'est jamais complètement dissipée—en droit du moins—puisque l'analyse appuie tant qu'elle peut sans dissoudre cette épaisseur de mystère, refuge de la vie. La pointe d'incertitude la fait dévier sans cesse, l'évènement est à la fois compris et impénétrable" (*Messages*, "L'Art de Conrad," 117).

[3] "Une maîtrise pensive de l'impensable, telle est l'impression que nous laissent ses meilleurs livres" (*Ibid.*, 111). "Ce grand silence autour des personnages de Conrad n'est rien de moins que le complément de leur verité" (*Ibid.*, 114).

collective impulse born of fear. Most novels give the herd instinct—types, averages, everyman. Conrad prefers the more interesting opposite. His reader stands at gaze whilst these daring, self-sufficient beings perform their feats, think their thoughts, experience their strange emotions, and overwhelm with the force of inherent greatness. Think of Weller, Mr Pecksniff, Mrs Gamp, Becky Sharp, Major Pendennis, Mrs Proudie—obvious emanations of the herd instinct or its excesses and eccentricities, rather than strong and original personalities. Then think of those lonely souls, Lord Jim, Dr Monygham, Mrs Gould, Captain Anthony, Heyst, and even Conrad's black sheep, who are by no means all tarred with the collective brush. Their distant relatives are the exquisite beings exquisitely displayed in all the variousness of their contacts with life by Henry James. Such people may or may not be rich and rare, in having uncommon gifts of soul or intellect; but, at any rate, they are individuals, not stamped with the gregariousness and imitativeness of the crowd, or their success in courting the admiration of their similars. Conrad was not interested in snobbishness, that vulgar aberration of the herd instinct. Those who portrayed the very souls of Jane Eyre, Lucy Snowe, and Paul Emanuel, and of Heathcliff and Catherine Earnshaw, were the nearest akin of his predecessors; for the Brontë sisters and Conrad alike participated in a romanticism that neighbours poetry, the other shape of it.[1] Bear in mind that Conrad expressed his artistic allegiance to imagination, not invention.[2] Like Dickens in his rich diversity, he is unlike in that his interests are internal, psychological, psychical, moral, anything but the mere enjoyment of humours. The comedy and satire are sardonic, not warm and genial. Dickens was content as often as not to hit off external peculiarities, and to individualize with a few odd traits. Every one of Conrad's figures is an integer, a definite person; even the most minor character is never a mere cipher. He sees his characters as wholes; whether heroes or scoundrels, they stand there with their history written on them. It is as if each

[1] See what was said on the Brontëan romanticism in Vol. VII., chapters i.–ii.

[2] See above, p. 15.

were the potential centre of a story, even if that particular story is not told.

A new scale of values—irony

Conrad works to a scale of values entirely his own, based on his view of life as a state of incessant conflict. He remains taciturn, impassive, apparently neutral; but can any alert reader fail for a moment to recognize those values, though they are not definitely formulated? What he thought of poetic justice has been seen already.[1] Irony was his alternative mode of indicating his own values. It may show in the doings and utterances of the characters, or in the shape of the conjunctures in which they are placed, or in the ultimate turn of events; irony is always there, an irony that is no mere literary pungency but goes to the root of the matter, is as fundamental as his general vision of the world. It is at its deadliest, perhaps, in *The Secret Agent* and *Under Western Eyes*; but, as there is now no need to prove, it is never quite in abeyance. The general configuration of his stories, including those expanding into novels, is of two divergent kinds; and he has two corresponding sets of characters: the irony comes out in both, largely through the implicit contrasts. In *The Nigger of the "Narcissus,"* in "Youth," "Typhoon," "The End of the Tether," and less simply and unambiguously in other novels and stories, loyalty and endurance are seen heroically contending with the forces of mischief, and emerging unbroken. In *Lord Jim*, *Nostromo*, *Under Western Eyes*, "Freya of the Seven Isles," and *The Rescue*, man comes to grief through some inner weakness or some dereliction, which perchance he may strive to amend and rehabilitate his selfhood. Parallel to this there is a sharper dichotomy of those who reach or only just fail to reach the heroic standard, and, on the other hand, the sheer incarnations of evil or the simple moral wreckage who are the negative to his positive ideal. It is as if the laches and the downright villainies were essential to his full theme. Comrade Ossipon and Mr Vladimir, Mr Jones and Ricardo, Scevola the *sans-culotte*, and their like, give, as it were, the counterpoint. Hardy with his myths and tyrannical hierarchy, in which he did not believe, and his Immanent Will in which he did believe,

[1] See above, p. 42.

had a target for his irony, a target standing for the universe itself. Conrad does not accuse the universe, nor like Hardy anathematize Fate. As to ultimate causes, he admitted that he knew nothing. Perhaps all we see is but a spectacle [1]; nevertheless, man is an ethical being, and when the heavens seem most hostile it may be only the supreme test. The worst evils we have to contend with on this earth are human—men's falsehood, baseness, malevolence, or the good intentions which are paralysed by weakness of will. There is no Providence to be relied on to help man in his tribulations. But, if he takes himself seriously, he has scope to make at least a good fight. Conrad has faith in the ability of the human soul to assert and save itself. The heavens may be black; but, instead of railing at the heavens, he directs his irony at the cowardice or the lack of intelligence, or the purposes that come to nothing through the weakness or the falsehood that betrays. As to the selfishness and malevolence that make earth blacker than the heavens, these are too gross for irony, and are simply laid bare in all their ugliness. His bitterest irony was for the belief of friends and relatives in a scoundrel's loyalty and devotion: that was indeed mistaking evil for good. The irony in "Heart of Darkness" rises to a fiercer tension when Marlow recounts his interview with the girl at Brussels, to whom he hands over the slim packet of letters Kurtz had left for "his Intended."

"'Forgive me. I—I—have mourned so long in silence—in silence. . . . You were with him—to the last? I think of his loneliness. Nobody near to understand him as I would have understood. Perhaps no one to hear . . .'

"'To the very end,' I said, shakily. 'I heard his very last words . . .' I stopped in a fright.

"'Repeat them,' she murmured in a heart-broken tone. 'I want—I want—something—something—to live with.'

"I was on the point of crying at her, 'Don't you hear them?' The dusk was repeating them in a persistent whisper all around us, in a whisper that seemed to swell menacingly like the first whisper of a rising wind. 'The horror! the horror!'

[1] See above, p. 43.

"'His last word—to live with,' she insisted. 'Don't you understand I loved him—I loved him—I loved him!'

"I pulled myself together and spoke slowly.

"'The last word he pronounced was—your name.'

"I heard a light sigh and then my heart stood still, stopped dead short by an exulting and terrible cry, by the cry of inconceivable triumph and of unspeakable pain. 'I knew it —I was sure!' . . . She knew. She was sure. I heard her weeping; she had hidden her face in her hands. It seemed to me that the house would collapse before I could escape, that the heavens would fall upon my head. But nothing happened. The heavens do not fall for such a trifle."

An alleged "guilt-complex"

There has been an able and formidable attempt by a Freudian critic to narrow down Conrad's tragic outlook on the world, and to attribute his obsession with cases of moral dereliction to some intimate personal motive, in short, to demonstrate that it was all the result of a "complex."[1] This is supposed to have been his suppressed and only half conscious remorse for having deserted Poland in her "hour of trial." The critic points to the number of stories turning upon some act of disloyalty or desertion. Even Almayer is said to be a symbolization of this suppressed side of his author's life; whilst Willems, his detested colleague, who pilots the rival trader Abdulla up Lingard's river, is guilty of the same act of treachery as so many later delinquents. It is urged that Conrad repeatedly showed himself sorely exercised in spirit over questions of breach of faith. In touching on the why and wherefore he had left a land bedewed with the blood of patriots, he said, "there are men of unstained rectitude who are ready to murmur scornfully the word desertion."[2] He deprecates the random use of such terms as "faithlessness" and "betrayal," and wanders off into what seems a rather pointless reminiscence of the man who told him, a boy of fifteen, that he was "an incorrigible, hopeless Don Quixote."[3] The cap fitted, it is contended, for the Don was another who to escape intolerable realities "sallied forth from his native place" and put his own ideals before the obligations of patriotism. "The

[1] *The Polish Heritage of Joseph Conrad*, by Gustav Morf (1930).
[2] *A Personal Record*, ii.
[3] Morf, 221 and 199.

conscious Conrad was realistic, the unconscious Conrad, ever dissatisfied and unhappy, was incurably romantic." So an obsession, for which there were ample grounds, with acts of failure determined the cardinal motives of *Lord Jim*, *Under Western Eyes*, *The Secret Agent*, and many other novels and stories. "*Lord Jim* is more than a novel, it is a confession." In the language of psycho-analysis, Jim is "the projection of Conrad's unconscious wishes for compensation. Mentally and morally, he is, on the other hand, the projection of Conrad's suppressed fears." Everything he does or that happens to him is ingeniously identified with facts in Conrad's life and the haunting "fear that the desertion of his native country might ultimately prove a fault by which he had forfeited his honour." [1] Razumov commits a heinous breach of trust, and actually revolves the question whether there is any such thing as remorse. *Victory* restates the "father-son problem" as it confronted Conrad: "Shall I be faithful to my father's ideas?" In *Nostromo*, the sturdy old Garibaldian Viola stands for Apollo Korzeniowski, and Decoud is Conrad at the period of light-hearted insubordination at Marseilles. The same prick of conscience actuates the personal drama—an identification reinforced by Conrad's acknowledgment that Antonia was modelled on his first love. He knew little of Venezuela; but it was easy to transfer characters from Poland, and imagine the country in a state of unrest and perennial revolution such as was only too familiar to Conrad. More startling is the invitation to accept "The Secret Sharer" as a case of self-identification with a murderer, which would imply that when Conrad retold the story once heard he was unwittingly biased by a "wish-complex" like that with which certain critics explain the paralysis of will in *Hamlet*.[2] When Conrad in 1920 was planning *The Rover*, "Polish patriots were shedding their blood, fighting against the Russian invader." Hence it is not surprising that at such a moment he should recall the tale of a man's self-immolation for his country. But the psycho-analyst goes further, and makes this an unintentional allegory of Conrad's relations with Poland, an allegory of

[1] *Ibid.*, 164. [2] *Ibid.*, 157–158.

desertion and expiation, and fortifies his theory with numerous coincidences, both men losing their mothers at the same age, both revisiting their native countries at the same period of life, and so on.

The real versus the imputed debt to Poland

Admittedly, an esoteric significance does seem to hover over many of Conrad's stories. He always insisted that "explicitness is fatal to glamour," and one is lured on and on without craving anything so recondite as the revelation of a buried complex. Up to a certain point, some of these arguments sound plausible enough; but they are pushed to extremes such as characterize the school. The coincidences and identifications are suspiciously neat and to the point, the regular symptoms of a fixed idea. And one suddenly notices that they are proving far too much, far more than is relevant to the issue, and that the best part of Conrad's work is being resolved into a vast cryptogram. And yet he is assumed to have been entirely unaware of what he was doing. Surely, one exclaims, it was perfectly natural, it was inevitable, if Conrad's most cherished virtue, the one in which he perceived man's one and only means of moral salvation, was truth to himself and fidelity to his fellow-beings, that his tragedies should be concerned with breaches of loyalty, failure to honour and observe the most precious canons of human behaviour. What need to suppose he was unburdening his conscience in half the things he wrote? Conrad is a great deal more intelligible and consistent seen from the ground level than from this artificial platform.[1] The net result of the

[1] It is satisfactory to find that the latest first-class study of Conrad, that of M. Las Vergnas, does not accord Dr Morf anything more than an attentive hearing. It is pointed out that Conrad always scoffed at psycho-analysis. He would have been stupefied and enraged at what H. L. Mencken calls this "Freudian autopsy upon a genius" (p. 180). That may be neither here nor there; Conrad may have been prejudiced and narrow-minded. But at all events it rules out any supposition that he knew he was hinting at more than he was saying, or suspected his unconscious self of being engaged in such illicit transactions. It also renders it extremely improbable that he could himself harbour the same sort of wish-complexes and suppressed fears as he derided. Conrad would have enjoyed the passage describing the alliterative clues with which Dr Morf amplifies a perfectly reasonable suggestion that Conrad often had at the back of his mind regrets and compunctions that he could do nothing to help Poland into a huge fabric of unconscious symbolism. "Dire que Pologne se masque inconsciemment sous la sonorité des noms de Patna, de Patusan, voire de Peyrol, voire surtout de Porquerolles (!) outrepasse l'habituelle liberté de lire

new and more minute investigation is to throw further light on the immense value to the novelist of his Polish heritage, not only of the personal memories that went to the making of his finest originals, but also of the lofty standards of integrity and devotion assimilated from his near and distant ancestors. All is grist that comes to the novelist's mill, especially to one who relied so much on the creative interpretation of historical fact, in other words, on a rich and poetic memory.[1] It is clear whence he derived his adventurous spirit, as well as his ardent sense of chivalry, rectitude, and fidelity. "The life-history of the earth must in the last instance be a history of a really relentless warfare," he writes, even in a comment on Henry James.[2] Faith, tenacity, and, if required, self-abnegation, are the weapons. "All adventure, all love, every success, is resumed in the supreme energy of an act of renunciation." The prize is a good conscience. "Mr Henry James is the historian of fine consciences." "That a sacrifice must be made, that something has to be given up, is the truth engraved in the innermost recesses of the fair temple built for our edification by the masters of fiction." He himself was also an historian of fine consciences. His Polish heritage was the profound conviction of the pre-eminence of these human qualities; it inspired his vital and vivifying embodiment of them; it also impelled him to show the conflict which is the test, and bring forward as the logical complement his grim congeries of the base, the treacherous, and the malevolent, his Donkins, Verlocs, Ricardos, Nikitas, Vladimirs, the negative to his affirmations. He showed both sides of the world, miserable humanity as it actually is.[3]

entre les lignes. L'imagination se donne des fêtes, mais ce système de dépistage allitératif paraît bien étrange" (Las Vergnas, 178).

[1] "Fiction is history," etc. (see above, p. 72. "Fiction is nearer truth," etc. (*Notes on Life and Letters*, "Henry James," 17).

[2] "The interest of a reader in a work of imagination is either ethical or that of simple curiosity. Both are perfectly legitimate, since there is both a moral and an excitement to be found in a faithful rendering of life" (*Ibid.*, "Guy de Maupassant," 26). Maupassant satisfied both kinds of interest, it is contended, and he is praised for the impassiveness and austerity with which he avoids the pitfalls of sentiment, humour, pathos, etc.

[3] At Conrad's death the *Nouvelle Revue française* (December 1924) had a sheaf of "Souvenirs" by Galsworthy, André Gide, Paul Valéry, H. R. Lenormand, Cunninghame Graham, etc., and short essays on "L'Œuvre" by Edmond Estaunié,

Conrad's style

Conrad's style is too large a constituent of his art to be left unnoticed, and this by no means chiefly on account of his astonishing mastery of a foreign language.[1] It is really a matter of styles; for his style not merely developed, but underwent radical changes, with his progress in craftsmanship, and more particularly a growing proclivity to scepticism and irony, in unveiling the conflict between human illusions and reality. Whilst his early impressionism aimed at making the reader feel and see as he himself felt and saw, the later went deeper, to inner realities. That his earlier style was rhetorical and over-elaborate is evident in the very fact that it attracts so much attention; the reader is often fascinated by the verbal magic rather than the vision evoked. It is too copious in adjectives, too obviously bent on being impressive, like much of Stevenson's prose. His account of the nigger James Wait's overpowering effect on the ship's company, in *The Nigger of the "Narcissus,"* is undeniably a brilliant success, but at a terrific outlay of vehement language. Conrad was always feeling for the right word, and did not invariably get it at the first try. "Give me the right word and the right accent and I will move the world. . . . Because written words have their accents too. Yes! Let me only find the right word! Surely it must be lying somewhere."[2] But it is not merely the right word for what he wants to say that he seeks so strenuously, for he lets it out further on that he has "never sought in the written word anything else but a form of the beautiful,"[3] which is equivalent to Oscar Wilde's avowed aim, to be impressive rather than expressive. Conrad writes for effect, and he gets it; he seeks beauty, and he attains it, but at some cost, the conquest of a grace or splendour too obviously courted and importuned. In some of the passages already quoted, he can be observed striving laboriously for his effects: the strain is as evident as the parade of art. There is no denying the power

André Chevrillon, André Maurois, E. Kessel, Ramon Fernandez, etc. M. Lenormand is good on Conrad's attitude to psycho-analysis.

[1] Grammatical martinets have busied themselves in detecting traces of Conrad's native idioms and even elementary mistakes of syntax, a schoolboy task that in such an illustrious case of accomplishment in another language than his own seems peculiarly uncalled-for.

[2] *A Personal Record*, "a faithful preface."

[3] *Ibid.*

and magnificence of those great storm-pieces, *The Nigger of the "Narcissus"* and "Typhoon," the vivid picturing of tropical forests and eastern seas in "Heart of Darkness," "Karain," "The End of the Tether," and of every aspect of the mariner's existence in *The Mirror of the Sea*; there is often a veritable orchestration of chords and cadences in the sound and colour of the language. But so far as there is a temptation to single out gorgeous passages, it is really a criticism of a writer's taste and discretion.

Later, more restraint

On the other hand, the reader is spell-bound by the purple draping of Conrad's theatre of events in *Nostromo*, and yet it is here that his prose is least trammelled by the cult of pomp and circumstance, or by his studied romanesque cadences. Scenery has always been a golden opportunity for the display of style. Conrad has shown, however, that there is by no means less scope for the finer graces in the portrayal of men and women, their outer and their inner physiognomy, in the manner of the narration, and in that vital part of any dramatic story, the dialogue. He was too intelligent an artist, as well as too conscientious, not to aim at a comprehensive and homogeneous fabric and contexture; and he was now experienced enough to attain this with the ease of self-disciplined genius. Formerly, he used to rise to the occasion; he knew now that the occasion was always present. In "Youth" he had proved that a whole philosophy of life could be expressed in the very poise of the words, the sound of the verbs and adjectives. Henceforth, his prose, stripped of the old rhetoric, shows itself supple and sinewy, wielded with the freedom and spontaneity of a master hand, seizing its metaphors in what lies nearest, dealing easily and felicitously with every contingency that arises. There is no attenuation of the sensuous force of his impressionism, or in the almost symbolic glimpses of external nature. That dynamic power was at its height in the early sea-stories; but is he less dynamic in this momentary glance at Captain Anthony, in *Chance*, watched by Powell, whose curiosity all but discovers the captain's secret pangs?—

"The captain walked up and down looking straight before him, the helmsman steered, looking upwards at the sails, the old gent on the skylight looked down on his daughter—and Mr Powell confessed to me[1] that he didn't know where to look, feeling as though he had blundered in where he had no business—which was absurd. At last he fastened his eyes on the compass card, took refuge, in spirit, inside the binnacle. He felt chilled more than he should have been by the chilly dusk falling on the muddy green sea of the soundings from a smoothly clouded sky. A fitful wind swept the cheerless waste, and the ship, hauled up so close as to check her way, seemed to progress by languid fits and starts against the short seas which swept along her sides with a snarling sound. Young Powell thought that this was the dreariest evening aspect of the sea he had ever seen. He was glad when the other occupants of the poop left it at the sound of the bell. The captain first, with a sudden swerve in his walk towards the companion, and not even looking towards his wife and his wife's father. Those two got up and moved towards the companion, the old gent very erect, his thin locks stirring gently about the nape of his neck, and carrying the rugs over his arm. The girl who was Mrs Anthony went down first. The murky twilight had settled in deep shadow on her face. She looked at Mr Powell in passing. He thought that she was very pale. Cold perhaps."[2]

No emphasis even; but the atmosphere so quietly evoked makes the pulses beat in unison with the perplexed and aching hearts of Captain Anthony and Flora. Or take this casual but downright expression of a whole attitude of mind, through one of nature's most familiar aspects:

"It was one of those dewy, clear, starry nights, oppressing our spirit, crushing our pride, by the brilliant evidence of the awful loneliness, of the hopeless obscure insignificance of our globe lost in the splendid revelation of a glittering, soulless universe. I hate such skies. Daylight is friendly to man toiling under a sun that warms his heart; and cloudy soft nights are more kindly to our littleness."

And so far from a set piece is this snatch of ulterior vision, that the next sentence takes up good little Fyne, "fussing in

[1] Marlow. [2] Part II., chap. ii.

a knickerbocker suit before the hosts of heaven"; and Marlow's story goes serenely on. There is irony here; irony, indeed, has now become second-nature to Conrad; it is a constant attitude of his mature art, the essence of his outlook, no form of mere literary vivacity, but the reflex of a whole philosophy. And there is style in his lightest raillery, as in the ferocious persiflage already quoted from *Victory*. There had been signs of all this as long ago as *Lord Jim*, where it was remarked that Jim's father "possessed such certain knowledge of the Unknowable as made for the righteousness of people in cottages without disturbing the ease of mind of those whom an unerring Providence enables to live in mansions." Later on, Marlow saturates with his irony the account which he has extracted from Jim of what went on in the *Patna*'s boat after the supposed catastrophe.

"Trust a boat on the high seas to bring out the Irrational that lurks at the bottom of every thought, sentiment, sensation, emotion. It was part of the burlesque meanness pervading that particular disaster at sea that they did not come to blows. It was all threats, all a terribly effective feint, a sham from beginning to end, planned by the tremendous disdain of the Dark Powers whose real terrors, always on the verge of triumph, are perpetually foiled by the steadfastness of men. I asked, after waiting for a while, 'Well, what happened?' A futile question. I knew too much already to hope for the grace of a single uplifting touch, for the favour of hinted madness, of shadowed horror. 'Nothing,' he said. 'I meant business, but they meant noise only. Nothing happened.'"

So much then for Conrad's style, a matter of yet further importance. For it is his style as much as any feature of his art that puts him at the head of a line of novelists and portrait-painters of exotic peoples and of men called of a sudden to live dangerously, every one of whom, from W. H. Hudson to C. E. Montague, was distinguished by parallel gifts, used perhaps very differently and yet to much the same purpose. It was the same with that most pungent of local colourists, Rudyard Kipling, who had come into the field several years earlier. Not that any of them were mere disciples of Conrad;

rather were they his literary kith and kin, who might have written as they did had he never been heard of.

Hudson and others

In reading the early Conrad, the teller of tales, or W. H. Hudson and Kipling, or such contentious men of letters as Cunninghame Graham or Montague, one cannot escape the thought that art is life, that literature itself is action. It is a reflection not more relevant to them, indeed, than to some who did not strain after such a close facsimile of life in its more strenuous phases. Who can question it in reading those who came a short while before, Carlyle, Ruskin, Tolstoy, not to speak of Milton and Shakespeare, or of Dante, Sophocles, Homer? How mistaken to regard the artist as a man cloistered from the world, be he writer or painter, musician or architect! The great writer—poet, dramatist, or novelist—is not an abstracted, academic virtuoso, or connoisseur of things that have little to do with general human activities. Great literature is life at the highest pitch, the utmost significance, the most completely human, put on record, cast into forms more stable than bronze, to nourish and expand the soul of the race. Conrad put himself and his own most fateful experiences into his works, and so did Hudson. William Henry Hudson (1841–1922) was not a novelist, in any sense that would affiliate him to the typical exemplars. He wrote two nondescript romances and some excellent stories, of his own adventures or of occurrences he had heard of in South America, when these had ripened in memory and perhaps been considerably transfigured by a ruminating imagination. But all his work, despite elementary faults of craftsmanship, has that note of authenticity which comes from his having lived his books before writing them. He had not a trace of Conrad's creative genius: none of the group had that, though they were Conrad's best-qualified admirers, and Hudson and Cunninghame Graham paid him comrades' tribute with eloquence.[1] But

[1] Hudson calls part at least of Conrad's chapter on the winds, in *The Mirror of the Sea*, "one of the sublimest passages in recent literature" (*Far Away and Long Ago*, 73). Cunninghame Graham wrote the preface to Conrad's *Tales of Hearsay*—an "exordium" that was also an epicedium. Here he remarks that both Conrad and Hudson talked more and more like foreigners as they grew old Their admiration for his work did not go unreciprocated.

they started with a fund of experience on a par with his, which they utilized to the full, each with a style that approximated in various fashions and degrees to his at its most vivid and most athletic. Hudson's first book appeared ten years before Conrad's, and he never attained, or even cultivated, the subtleties of art and style of which Conrad was to show such mastery. He adhered to the primitive, entirely simple mode of telling a tale; but instinctively, and as it were artlessly, he charged every incident, every lineament, accent, emotion, with all its human import. Hudson is like a child of nature who, without art or learning, speaks the tongue of the simple and innocent, which is not so far from the tongue of the angels.

"Far Away and Long Ago"

The best introduction to his fiction is *Far Away and Long Ago* (1918), which, almost confessedly, was prompted by Aksakov's *History of my Childhood*.[1] It is the chronicle of his boyhood in the Argentine, his life on the pampas, the growth of his passionate love of birds and animals and everything alive, and recollections of terrible events which later on gave sombre colour to the tragic element in his fiction. He read Dickens: but it is the alert eye of Borrow for grotesque and astonishing character that might have caught the outward features of such a procession as the lad's schoolmaster Mr Trigg and his successor Father O'Keefe, Zango the old horse and the dog Cæsar, Barboza the fighter and Jack the killer, Don Evaristo and his six wives, and the dictator Rosas, "the Tiger of Palermo," his fool Eusebio and the traitor Urquiza. But more characteristic of Hudson than the humanity so tellingly pictured is the wealth of observation of natural phenomena, observation that goes to the soul of things, human or infra-human; this it was that makes him unique among story-tellers, for he saw man confronted by the mighty spectacle of creation, and but one item in the great universe of life. Hudson gives a lucid account of this faculty of his,[2] in his chapter on "A

[1] *Far Away and Long Ago*, 226.

[2] Edward Garnett, who knew Hudson intimately, speaks of him as a pantheist, with a mystic insight into nature's secrets and infinite fecundity. He owed nothing to science, for the scientist is crippled by his specialization, and scientific method is only an auxiliary to instinctive perception, ignoring the actual spirit of life. That is the very thing that Hudson seizes and comprehends in his synthesis, which Garnett likens to the key employed by Shakespeare and the other great interpreters of human

Boy's Animism." From his earliest days, he used to wander out, perhaps by moonlight, among the trees; "and at such times the sense of mystery would grow until a sensation of delight would change to fear, and the fear increase until it was no longer to be borne, and I would hastily escape to recover the sense of reality and safety indoors, where there was light and company." [1] "This faculty or instinct of the dawning mind seemed to me essentially religious in character; undoubtedly it is the root of all nature-worship, from fetishism to the highest pantheistic development." But it exists in many persons; he instances George Herbert and Cowper. In the Romantic "feeling for nature" "it has become intertwined with the æsthetic feeling." Traherne's poetry was "distinctly animistic, with Christianity grafted on it. Wordsworth's pantheism is a subtilized animism; but there are moments when his feeling is like that of the child or savage when he is convinced that the flower enjoys the air it breathes." [2] This penetrating insight is to be explained, no doubt, as the imaginative and emotional comprehension developed from Hudson's close communion with nature from boyhood onwards. It is exquisitely personified in the witching shape of Rima, in *Green Mansions*:

> And to Rima has been given this quickness of mind and power to divine distant things; it is hers, just as swiftness and grace and changeful, brilliant colour are the humming-bird's; therefore she need not that anyone dwelling in the blue should instruct her.

Hudson's works of fiction should be put on the same shelf as his *Naturalist in La Plata*, *Idle Days in Patagonia*, *Nature in Downland*, *Adventures among Birds*, *A Shepherd's Life*, and *Hampshire Days*. They are different; they are an excursion from his main path; but their intrinsic values are of the same order.

Actually, he wrote three romances; but the second, *A*

nature. It is a species of poetic divination; but Hudson goes even further than the poets, for instance, in his *Hampshire Days* and *Nature in Downland*. "The real force of his spiritual vision arises from his *refusal to divide man's life off from nature's life*," like Tolstoy in *Resurrection* (*Friday Nights*, "Hudson's nature books," 15–35).

[1] *Far Away and Long Ago*, xvii., "A Boy's Animism," 231. [2] *Ibid.*, 235

Crystal Age (1887), a "Utopia" in which he pushed his bright idealism beyond all the limits of credibility and imagined a society as blameless and perfect as that of the bees, has ceased to count. The case is not much better with his first, *The Purple Land* (1885), the gist of which is in the sub-title, "the narrative of one Richard Lamb's adventures in the Banda Orientál, in South America, as told by himself." This, however, is no pastoral; the spirit of it is stern acceptance, so far as Richard's misfortunes are concerned, though the renegade from the Whites in Montevideo and from his adored wife Paquíta is such a scapegrace, and so fond of invoking the shades of Gil Blas, that the book is often classed as picaresque. At all events, it contains the first rough sketch for Rima, in the child Margarita, and some anticipations of Hudson's mature philosophy. "We had only to conquer Nature," Bacon taught; but that is seeking happiness in the wrong way. "It was with us once and ours, but we despised it." For Hudson always held that happiness is here and now, if we would only recognize what is good for us; and, certainly, he proved it for himself, in spite of incessant ill-health and more disasters than fall to most men. *His romances*

Green Mansions (1904) is free from this uncertainty of aim and this incoherence, being a more spontaneous work; it is a prose poem to be compared with such classics as *Paul et Virginie*, Chateaubriand's *Atala*, and Pierre Loti's *Rarahu*. Some of it is clumsy: Rima is better as a sprite than as a woman to be domesticated; she loses her glamour in her conventional love-making with Abel; and Hudson should have followed Kipling's example in the parallel case of Mowgli, instead of making her twitter like a bird. But, whereas there is something factitious in the older attempts to body forth the unsullied beauty and innocence of nature, the writers' imagination being clogged with their own sentimentalism, this is the direct and authentic issue of Hudson's mystical philosophy; Rima is the perfection that he glimpses behind nature's failures and shortcomings, her own child speaking for the universal mother. She is one of Hudson's dreams that he tries to make true. *"Green Mansions"*

"Living alone in the wood she had only God's creatures to play and make friends with; and wild animals, I have heard it said, know those who are friendly towards them."

Rima's alleged grandfather, old Nuflo, is speaking, a character into whom Hudson tried unwisely to infuse a little humour. Rima shuns him, for he is an eater of flesh; but he dare not hunt in the wood. "For in that wood there is one law, the law that Rima imposes, and outside it a different law." The beasts, even the venomous serpents, are all her kindred. Through Rima, the fugitive Venezuelan Abel apprehends the vital forces animating the cosmos; the universe is spiritual and divine in essence—her beauty is the sign of it—an idea by no means at variance with the belief that she is a chance survivor of a vanished race, who went down in the strife and inhuman havoc of pillaging whites and debased Indian tribes in years gone by. But this lovely being, like a flower dropped from on high, falls a victim to the savages who hate her; and Abel, who could endure much and be patient, is driven to blasphemy and murder by the fiendish destruction of so much beauty. In him Hudson depicts a sense of the malignancy of fate, of cruelty "beyond all cruelty," more lacerating even than Hardy's.

Not nature the instrument, not the keen sword that cuts into the bleeding tissues, but the hand that wields it—the unseen unknown something, or person, that manifests itself in the horrible workings of nature.

Abel looks up at the stars and curses the Author of his being, and calls on Him to "take back the abhorred gift of life." But he comes at length to see that his philosophy was a false one, "it was not the whole truth." Hudson's is a sterner, saner, more clear-eyed philosophy. Abel subdues himself to accept the consequences he has deserved. His cries touch not the Supreme Being, though they bruise his own soul "with wounds that will not heal." Revolt is vain. But he is not without hope. Rima is in his mind, inhabiting it. "Heaven itself, she said, could not undo that which I had done; and she also said that if I forgave myself Heaven would say no word, nor would she." Man is alone, and is alone responsible for himself. "Prayers, austerities, good works—they avail nothing, and there is no intercession, and outside of the soul there is no forgiveness in heaven or earth for sin." Nevertheless, there is a way. "In that way I have walked; and, self-forgiven and self-absolved, I know that if she were to return once more and appear to me—even here where her ashes are—I know that her divine eyes would no longer refuse to look into mine, since the sorrow which seemed eternal and would have slain me to see would not now be in them."

"El Ombú"

This stoicism is like Conrad's; both he and Hudson decline to palter with the facts of existence. In his other stories also there is implicit a definite argument against Manicheism. The four in *El Ombú* (1902) are like four movements in a tragic symphony: theme, the cruelty and remorselessness of man in his unregenerate state, no matter if white or black, civilized or savage. The scene of all is the South American pampas; the characters are Spanish soldiers of different ranks, opulent ranchers, poor whites, half-breeds, and pure Indians. Even the reader is called upon for a certain stoicism—to refrain from execrations on the wanton barbarity of such hideous deeds. The truth of it all is driven in by the simple, objective style, tingling with suppressed passion, suppressed by an heroic effort. Hudson is like a compassionate physician, who must needs preserve his calm whilst witnessing fearful agonies. That is the difference from Conrad's imperturbable sang-froid. "Strange and terrible scenes have I witnessed," says old Nicandro, in relating the history of El Ombú, "but never a sadder one than this! Tell me, señor, are these things told in books—does the world know them?" This is not a rounded and integral account of an action or a dramatic complication of events, but an extract from Hudson's recollections of terrible incidents connected with an old house on the pampas. It is "mostly a true story," though the details have been re-arranged.[1] Some of the same reminiscences appear in *Far Away and Long Ago*, where Barboza figures at great length, Barboza, the redoubtable fighter and Government general,

[1] Appendix to *El Ombú*, at end.

who fell when Valparaiso was captured by the insurgents in 1891. Santos Ugarte and poor Valerio de la Cueva are two contrasted characters of a time of revolution and moral chaos. Valerio was one of those who, as Nicandro puts it, make you say, "Here is one who is like no other man in the world."

"Perhaps on rising and going out, on some clear morning in summer, he looked at the sun when it rose, and perceived an angel sitting in it, and as he gazed, something from that being fell upon him and passed into and remained with him. Such a man was Valerio. I have known no other like him."

Santos has a devil in his heart. It is related with Defoe-like terseness how he dealt with his favourite Meliton, who had saved enough to purchase his freedom, and prayed to be allowed henceforth to serve his master without payment.

Santos took the money into his hand, and spoke, "It was for this then that you saved, even the money I gave you to spend and to run with, and the money you made by selling the animals I gave you—you saved it for this! Ingrate, with a heart blacker than your skin! Take back the money, and go from my presence, and never cross my path again if you wish for a long life." And with that he hurled the handful of silver and gold into the young man's face, that he was cut and bruised with the coins and wellnigh stunned. He went back staggering to his horse, and mounting, rode away, sobbing like a child, the blood running from his face.

Two years later, he comes back, and the old man greets him jovially; he thinks he is forgiven when he is asked to shake hands.

The other, glad to think he was forgiven, alighted, and advancing, put out his hand. Santos took it in his, only to crush it with so powerful a grip that the young man cried out aloud, and blinded with tears of pain, he did not see that his master had the big brass pistol in his left hand, and did not know that his last moment had come. He fell with a bullet in his heart.

Nicandro remarks of Valerio's time of humble prosperity, "The peace did not last long; for when misfortune has singled out a man for its prey, it will follow him to the end, and he shall not escape from it though he mount up to the clouds like a falcon, or thrust himself deep down into the earth like the armadillos."

"Marta Riquelme," etc.

The "Story of a Piebald Horse," "Niño Diablo," and the terrible "Marta Riquelme" have the same tragic burden. The first is of two foster-brothers, in love with their foster-sister; it is a story alive with feeling, and shapely in its picturesque denouement. But "Niño Diablo" alone is lightened with a happy escape. It has touches of Hudson's animism. Niño grew up a captive with the Indians, and learned all their craft and subtlety; so he is able to go among them in disguise and rescue a woman who has been carried off from her husband. But "Marta Riquelme" is so merciless and relentless in its crescendo of anguish, closing on the question of Marta's ultimate fate, after she has been driven insane by outrage, cruelty, and abandonment, that the old priest who tells the fearful tale is driven to believe that the old Quicha gods, Pachacamac, Tupa, and Viracocho, are indeed mighty spiritual entities, having power even "to suspend the order of nature" in their strife with the true God. "The old gods and demons retired into this secluded country," and have their fastnesses now among the peaks and chasms of the Cordilleras.

> Although the lost spirits cannot harm they are always near me, watching all my movements, ever striving to frustrate my designs. Nor am I unmindful of their presence. Even here, sitting in my study and looking out on the mountains, rising like stupendous stairs towards heaven and losing their summits in the gathering clouds, I seem to see the awful shadowy form of Pachacamac, supreme among the old gods. Though his temples are in ruins, where the Pharaohs of the Andes and their millions of slaves worshipped him for a thousand years, he is awful still in his majesty and wrath that plays like lightning on his furrowed brows, kindling his stern countenance and the beard which rolls downward like an immense white cloud to his knees. Around him gather other tremendous forms in their cloudy vestments—the Strong-comer, the Lord of the Dead, the Avenger, the Ruler of Men, and many others whose names were once mighty throughout the continent.

They have met to take counsel together; I hear their voices in the thunder hoarsely rolling from the hills, and in the wind stirring the forest before the coming tempest. Their faces are towards me, they are pointing to me with their cloudy hands, they are speaking of me—even of me, an old, feeble, worn-out man! But I do not quail before them; my soul is firm though my flesh is weak; though my knees tremble while I gaze, I dare look forward even to win another victory over them before I depart.

Cunninghame Graham

Hudson's friend, Robert Bontine Cunninghame Graham (1852–1936), never pretended to be a novelist, and the contents of his numerous volumes of what purports to be fiction, even when he gives them such titles as "Thirteen Stories," turn out to be, not stories at all, but the miscellaneous output of a brilliant reporter, who has travelled far, seen everything, and is determined to show the average man what a dull and ignorant creature he is, and how much better it would be to fail in glorious fashion than to stay at home and comfortably vegetate. By birth and inheritance a Scots laird, of ancient and romantic lineage, with a not quite unfounded claim to the Scottish crown, partly Spanish through his grandmother and a childhood spent in Cadiz, he went at the age of sixteen to South America, was a rancher in the Argentine, served in the Uruguayan army, explored Paraguay, farmed in Mexico, and amassed much the same sort of wild experiences as Hudson put into his tales and his own biography. But he was a more travelled man than Hudson. He knew enough of the western world and its past, for example, to write an authoritative life of Hernando de Soto. And the knowledge subsequently gained of the other hemisphere was just as intimate and extensive. He went to Morocco, and, disguised as a Turkish physician, tried to penetrate beyond the Atlas, the account of his attempt and his arrest and captivity, *Mogreb-el-Acksa* (1898), being by general consent the best of his books. He went farther east, on the pilgrimage to Mecca, for instance; and he seems to have been as familiar with Mohammedan ways of life and thought as with the Gauchos or the Apaches.

Commencing with *The Ipané* (1899) and ending, the year

Assortments of stories

of his death, with *Mirages* (1936), Cunninghame Graham put forth, every twelve months or so, little assortments of travellers' yarns and reminiscences, the kind of rough material that a novelist would have licked into shape as furniture for a story—sketches of racial types or odd characters and physiognomies from as far afield as South America and Mexico and all parts of the Eastern world, and as near home as the Scottish lowlands—vignettes and caustic etchings, or, it might be said, instantaneous photographs, bits of dialogue and chance scenes of elemental drama—all of it anything but impersonal or impartial in the rendering, for if the observation was eagle-eyed the phrases in which it was bitten in cut and rankled with the venom in them. An inveterate Ishmaelite, he was one to prefer the fierce sincerities of the savage or the shameless effrontery of the thief and exploiter, who like the animals simply fulfils his nature, to the shams, the meanness, and ineradicable vulgarity of our machine-made civilization. If he loved a rough-rider, he also loved the beast he bestrode; and one of his many links with Hudson is his tenderness for animals, movingly displayed in such tales as "Calvary,"[1] of the brutal commerce in horses, and "Sor Candida and the Dying Bird,"[2] or an interjection like "The overladen ass, girth-galled and patient, treading its weary Calvary which leads to no heaven, except the rest from toil that death affords." "All that we write," he said in the preface to *Faith* (1909), "is but a bringing forth again of something we have seen or heard about. What makes it art is but the handling of it, and the imagination that is brought to bear upon the theme out of the writer's brain." It was also the basis of Conrad's far superior art. If a moral is drawn, it is only a sarcastic touch to soothe the sentimentalist and make fun of him at the same time. "Virtue" in none of these stories "is in the least atom better rewarded than it is actually rewarded in the world."[3] He almost tried conclusions with Conrad in "S.S. *Atlas*," the story of a tramp crossing the Atlantic.[4]

[1] *Thirteen Stories.*
[2] *Faith.* The quotation is from "A Saint," in the same book.
[3] Preface to *Faith.*
[4] *The Ipané.*

"Victory" is a caustic picture of American rejoicing at the heroic end of Admiral Cervera—Cunninghame Graham hated Yankees.[1] "Hegira," the tale of a raid by Apaches and the long pursuit, is memorable for the admiration it wrings out for the poor, tough, irreconcilable last of the band, and pity for his little dog howling and scratching the turned-up earth on his grave. The point of "Success" is in the sentence, "How few successful men are interesting!" "Progress" (1905) is a cold-blooded account of the wiping-out of a Mexican community by the forces of law and order. *His People* (1906) chiefly consists of the failures, the desolate and oppressed, and every other tale has a dig at our boasted civilization. *Faith* (1909) is very representative. Then there is "A Silhouette," a ghastly picture of war, painted with a cold horror, a sort of cruel gusto. "A Saint" presents a poor, foolish, but guileless and devoted Anarchist; and in "An Idealist," Cunninghame Graham gives the portrait of one of his own Socialist comrades.

His irony His only idea of comedy was haughty and disdainful irony, one of his few approaches to humour being the incident "At the River," where the Sultan who with his army has struggled across the great stream calls for the grand piano, which has been brought in sections on mules and camels: "Bring me the Biano, I want to play on it," and there in the desert with the troops looking on he picks out with one finger and making several wrong notes the Spanish Royal March. Cunninghame Graham is full of detestations—of missionaries, of the "curse of progress," of Government iniquities perpetrated on Maori natives. "God seems to sit, presiding blindly, over a world which either mocks Him, or is mocked at by Him." The same strain continues in *Hope* (1910), *Charity* (1912), *A Hatchment* (1913), and the *Thirty Tales and Sketches* (1929) collected by Edward Garnett. But the man was at least as interesting as his works, this "Scottish hidalgo" as he was dubbed in the obituary notices, "Don Roberto" as his biographer calls him,[2] with the airs of a conquistador, with

[1] *Thirteen Stories.*

[2] *Don Roberto, life and works of R. B. Cunninghame-Graham*, by A. F. Tschiffely (1937).

knowledge enough for an ethnographer yet a wholesale contempt for the average man everywhere, hard-headed, and, as he liked to make out, hard-hearted, but actually nothing of the sort. Unfortunately, Cunninghame Graham always had his lofty and scornful personality to maintain, in his books and elsewhere, which must have cost him as much unremitting effort as his picturesque appearance as cavalier or cowboy, Mohammedan physician or militant Socialist. He himself was his finest work of fiction, and it will not stand re-reading: in his life and his work he was too much of the journalist, a man of the impressive moment. But fiction cannot be made out of nothing; and there was a certain foundation of greatness in Cunninghame Graham, as both friends and enemies attest.

Pickthall's "Saïd the Fisherman"

The same year as Cunninghame Graham, died one who had a singular career and wrote a novel and certain tales that are unique in English. Marmaduke William Pickthall (1875–1936) became a Mohammedan, and late in life was Imam at the Woking mosque. He had lived among the Druses of Lebanon and in Egypt, and afterwards went to India, where he was for a long while editor of the *Bombay Chronicle* and then the *Hyderabad Quarterly*. He was a great Orientalist on both the literary and the political and social side. One of his big works was a translation of the *Koran*; but the book by which he achieved lasting fame was *Saïd the Fisherman* (1903), whilst he also wrote some novels of English life, two or three others of Egypt and Arabia, and a set of tales, *Oriental Encounters, Palestine and Syria* (1918), almost as good as *Lavengro* in its racy pictures of character and manners. *Saïd the Fisherman* easily stands comparison as a lifelike representation of Eastern life with Thomas Hope's *Anastasius* or J. J. Morier's *Hajji Baba of Ispahan*, and falls little short in comedy of the picaresque order; it is in every way superior to the *Pandurang Hari* of W. B. Hockley.[1] It is the unvarnished biography of an Arab adventurer during the years 1860 to 1882, that is, from just before the time of the massacre at Damascus, when the cowardly rascal manages to steal the hoard of a murdered

[1] For *Anastasius*, *Hajji Baba*, and *Pandurang Hari*, see Vol. VII. 65–76.

Druse and make off with his daughter, to the bombardment of Alexandria after Arabi's rebellion. Saïd is a lying, spiteful, vainglorious scamp, who deserts his wife and lives on his friends, both wife and friends, however, sticking to him through thick and thin, testifying to some queer personal charm. But the reader feels no compunction whatever when the tables are turned on the sanctimonious old wretch, and he dies a raving maniac amid the bursting of the shells. It is all written in a style as objective as Defoe's, and with self-effacing neutrality. Shrewd, if far from charitable, maxims drop from the lips of Saïd or his familiars, unless they are his own unuttered thoughts, as when he reflects upon his deserted wife, left behind when he just escapes with his skin:

> He had not done much to revive Hasneh, it was true; but then, he had supposed her dead, and none but a fool would wantonly waste his time in trying to bring a dead woman back to life. He had now little doubt that she lived, thanks to the old woman's scornful suggestions. In his heart he cursed the crone for breaking in upon him just when he had brought his mind to a peaceful contemplation of his wife's dead body.

The old beggar who first leads him astray is another of the same kidney. "There is no trade like ours," he assures him.

> "All the day long we cringe, we flatter, we weep, and none can resist us. And afterwards, when the evening is come, we laugh and are merry, with eating and drinking, with music and women. Behold I love thee, for thy likeness to my son, Mansûr, who forsook me."

And the bilious-looking person who has been looking on at a case managed with inadequate attention to the demands of bribery, tells the plaintiff:

> "Twenty piastres will buy thee a plausible fellow who will swear to aught that pleases thee. The Cadi will count the witnesses on either side, and will give judgment for the greater number—if he have not sold his verdict beforehand, which

is most likely. Bakshish is lord of all. A wise man does not fall out with the rich. It is the same all the world over. They tell of countries where justice is for rich and poor alike; but that is all a lie!"

It is this satirical, imperturbably picaresque spirit that renders *Saïd the Fisherman* much superior to the more romantic *Hermann Agha, an Eastern narrative* (1872), of another Orientalist, William Gifford Palgrave (1826–1888), who had been a Jesuit missionary in the East and was later employed there as a British diplomatist. He is best known probably for his *Year's Journey through Central and Eastern Arabia* (1865). It is an historical novel, of adventures in war and love, the titular hero being a German who went East, was for a time ruler of Egypt, and bore a leading part in the revolt against the Porte in 1768. Palgrave affirms that "it is not fiction, but reality; not invention, but narration," and invokes the authority of manuscript records in Cairo. Its fault, if it be a fault, is that it is constructed and written on the established lines of historical romance; it is an eminently respectable and at times a brilliant performance, but the disreputable Saïd is far more entertaining—and far more human.

C. E. Montague

If style could have sufficed, Charles Edward Montague (1867–1928), another man both of action and of letters, would have made a brilliant novelist. He was one of the brightest stars of the *Manchester Guardian*; and, before the Great War, in *A Hind let Loose* (1910), gave an inside view of newspaper life in a provincial town, and of the ceaseless campaigning between the Tory and the Radical organs, *The Warden* and *The Stalwart*. It is a hollow conflict. Fay the leader-writer, without imperilling his honour, is sometimes called upon to exercise his pen on both sides. The sensitive and over-conscientious Dick, with his fastidiousness for style—and even a passion for mountaineering—is patently Montague himself. When Pinn the Radical editor, his office being burnt out, has to petition the rival editor Brumby to machine his next issue, the suppressed humour of the scene almost atones for the weakness of the character-drawing, for Montague wanted to make every man jack an original, with the result that he often left out what would have made him lifelike.[1] But Montague, though well over age, chivalrously went to the front, and saw the war from start to finish, saw it from two opposite points of view. Being a trained publicist as well as a man of piercing intelligence, he came through bitterly disillusioned, his very soul wounded and bleeding, with what he had been confronted by or ferreted out of the shams, corruption, and jobbery, the self-complacency and blunders of those in high positions, which were responsible, not only in large part for the holocausts, but also for the social and economic evils of our post-war world, the meanness and futility of which he compared with historic periods of decadence.

"*Right off the Map*"

He vented his discontents in an urbane but devastating anatomy of the age, *Disenchantment* (1922), and in several volumes of fiction. *Right off the Map* (1927), a novel based on a play, is satire. Montague had three engrossing interests, the war, journalism, mountaineering, and here he exploits them all. It is the history of a war between South American republics, a war mainly due to the intrigues of great industrial corporations, but also in no small part to influential journalists who ought to have detected and exposed their machinations but were too witless or too corrupt. So Roya has its army annihilated and becomes a province of its arrogant neighbour. The war is fought in a region of lofty mountains that might have been suggested by *Nostromo*, though the rout of the defending army is more like the butchery when the Argentines and Brazilians defeated Rosas, as described by Hudson. It is a cold-blooded, blood-curdling picture of modern scientific warfare under remorseless, dictatorial leadership. Even the forlorn hope, led by a veteran cragsman along a dangerous traverse, up the cliffs and across the snow-fields, to a concealed valley opening on the enemy's rear, comes to nothing. But the proceedings on the home front, which spin the narrative out to the dimensions of a novel—the love-affairs, the problem of the fluent editor and his

[1] Arnold Bennett, in a mood of irritation, denounced *A Hind let Loose* as "not a book for the intelligent masses." "It is for the secretly arrogant few," *i.e.* the intellectual Pharisees (*Books and Persons*, 201).

high-strung wife, who cannot live with a husband who is not a hero and a statesman, and the other psychological perplexities that Montague revelled in—blunt the satire, in spite of the side-hits at swindling contractors supplying papier-mâché boots and armament firms selling munitions to both sides, or the fire-eating bishop intoning,

> How nobly natures form
> Under the war's red rain,

and then denouncing the wickedness of everybody when the news is bad.

"Fiery Particles"

Fiery Particles (1923) consists of nine stories, mostly of the war-time, and shows Montague's mordant, epigrammatic, quick-step style at its finest. It is the style of an accomplished journalist whose wits have been braced, as he put it of someone else, by coming "under the stinging shower-bath of sparkling spray from Meredith's astringent wit." Dixon Scott called it a "pizzicato" style: "did you ever hear such a dancing of dactyls, and tripping of trochees, and ruthless absence of iambs and ease?"[1] Which remark is corroborated by Fay, in *A Hind let Loose*, when he exclaims of Dick's prose, "Why, it scans!" Another mannerism that was ofttimes an elegance is that Montague's language is tessellated with familiar tags. "In Brumby's elocution any quotations he made were fenced round with audible inverted commas." Montague was not so crude. Much neater to observe of the big guns "idyllically emplaced" behind the woodlands and flowery alps, "There did they see no enemy but autumn and rough weather," or of the "brass hat's" motor-car that it was "like Tennyson's full tide that moving seems asleep." This from "Honours Easy," tale of the competition between two aristocratic war-shirkers who never got far from the seaboard, "washed by such tides as a man may take at the flood and be led on to fortune." By sticking to the base and a discreet opportunism, without ever exposing their skins, they proved the rightness of the maxim "that on the average the number of ribbons a British officer gets in this war varies in direct proportion to

[1] *Men of Letters*, "C. E. Montague," 222.

the square of his distance from the front." Montague can even mix his metaphors with impunity: "How're we to win if they're always taking the heart out of the backbone of the army?" He knew his Shakespeare, and could use him deftly for his Shakespearian Publicity Trust, in "My Friend the Swan"; and he could handle the brogue, as in "A propos de bottes," story of the Madame Tussaud's that melted and was then run as "The End of the World." Finer still are the hyperboles in praise of old Farrell's whisky, in "Another Temple Gone," panegyric of an illicit still:

"What sort of hivven's delight is this you've invented for all souls in glory?"

"Half-way am I now, as you can see for yourselves, to transformin' the body of anny slushy old drink you'd get in a town into the soul of all kindness an' joy that our blessed Lord put into the water the good people had at the wedding. Nothin' at all to do but walk straight on, the way I was going, to work the stuff up to the pitch that you'd not feel it wettin' your throat, but only the love of God and of man an' the true wisdom of life, and comperhension of this and of that, flowin' softly into your mind."

But the humour turns macabre in such tales as "The First Blood Sweep," in which a trenchful of Tommies under drum-fire make up a sweepstake on the first to be killed. In "Two or Three Witnesses," Montague reverts to journalism. A young reporter who has to attend a distinguished funeral spends the evening with three seasoned confreres, who talk to him grandiloquently of the dignity of their profession:

"Mind, he who writes for the *Day* writes history. He who writes history makes it."

The three did not hear that the archbishop had fallen ill and the funeral was postponed. Their reports duly appear, with the archbishop's discourse. The young fellow waits and attends the actual ceremony, sends in the facts, and is reprimanded for being so glaringly at variance with the accounts in three leading papers.

In all his fiction, Montague can be seen fascinated by such psychological problems as of the boy who unwittingly wins

Psychological problems

the sweep, and is heart-struck by the suspicion that his sergeant exposed himself to the fatal bullet just to save him, or the conundrum in "Judith"—will the German spy, who has recognized in the English spy in Cologne the officer who fell in love and rescued her in Amiens, give him up? Montague's arbitrary solutions are not always beyond dispute; but that is not the case with "Action," the title-piece in his last collection (1928). An elderly disillusioned man, ripe for suicide but disliking the nastiness of such an end, thinks it honestly out. He is a climber. Why not realize that haunting dream of scaling a wall of rock or ice, and see how far, with nothing to lose, he can pare away the margin of safety? So he goes to Zinal, when the season is all over, and starts on the terrible ice-wall between the Weisshorn and Schallihorn. At the supreme moment, when with body spent he says to himself, "I'm done!" he hears a cry, and sees a woman helpless at the end of a rope above him; and in the next half-hour he is able to rescue a climber and his wife from a hopeless position. The call to action has healed him. What a pity that the stark improbability of his finding a pair of mountaineers at that altitude, after sunset and when everybody has gone home, spoils a thrilling bit of practical psycho-analysis! Of the satirical pieces in the same volume "A Cock and Bull Story" is the grimmest. The touchiness of a French colonel who will not take orders from an English officer of inferior rank working in concert, results in frightful carnage for the troops of both. "Sleep, gentle Sleep," is about one of those opportunities never seized because never perceived which might have ended the war at a blow. Montague's characters, unfortunately, never quite come to life: they are psychological problems, very absorbing, but only abstractions. He talks intelligently about them, and they talk about themselves; but it is as if the decisions and the acts were arrived at on insufficient evidence —the fabric is too unsubstantial to bear the dramatic weight imposed upon it.[1] This and the more obvious shallowness of

[1] He confirmed this view himself—"it is really only abstract ideas togged out to look like human" (from letter to his future biographer, Elton, 67). He said he cared most for the characters in another novel, which brings in the Great War, *Rough Justice* (1926). This partiality is confessed in a letter to H. W. Norman (Elton, 288).

Cunninghame Graham throws into greater relief the depth and solidity of Conrad's people, whose very souls are known to us, even as we perceive them behind the solid paint in a Velasquez. Conrad's influence is not quite spent. One of his followers, one not unaffected also by Kipling, Mr Edward Noble, has written a small library of novels of the sea and the mercantile marine, beginning with *The Edge of Circumstance* (1904), which is not sparing in sarcasm at the expense of ship-owners and the tyranny of wealth, whilst *Waves of Fate* is a curious variation of the story told in *Lord Jim*.

CHAPTER III

RUDYARD KIPLING

From journalism to literature

The nearest to Conrad and that group in the matter and method of his art, though himself not to be bracketed with anyone else whatever, is Rudyard Kipling (1865–1936). Conrad's junior by nearly a decade, he had leapt into fame a decade before the other began to make any great impression. Kipling, in fact, achieved at a blow both popularity and literary prestige; the public were simply told by the reviewers why and how rightly they had been thrilled. He was at once a classic and a "best-seller"—something unexampled in an age when there is a gulf of no small dimensions between the well-regulated standards of the critic and impulsive appreciation by the crowd. It seemed as if he must have been born mature, so infallible were eye, judgment, and pen, the reason being that he had learned assurance and swiftness in the school of practical journalism. Son of the versatile John Lockwood Kipling, who was to illustrate some of his books, and of the sister to three notable women, he was born at Bombay, whence the family soon removed to Lahore on the father's appointment to the curatorship of the Government museum—see the opening scene of *Kim*.[1] At six, the boy was sent to be educated in England, and in a year or two entered the United Services College at Westward Ho! What that school did for Kipling may be discerned even through the horse-play and ribaldry of *Stalky & Co.* Still in his teens, he went back to work as a reporter and then sub-editor on the *Civil and Military Gazette* of Lahore, also writing for the *Pioneer* of Allahabad and other papers. His earliest stories and poems, apart from

[1] John Lockwood Kipling was the author of that notable book, *Man and Beast in India* (1891).

a private collection of *Schoolboy Lyrics* (1881), came out to begin with in these journals, the first book given to the world being a small volume, *Departmental Ditties* (1886), roughly produced in the office and published by himself; he was just twenty-one. It was rapidly followed by *Plain Tales from the Hills* (1888), mostly written before he was twenty and collected from the *Gazette*, in which he introduced his three musketeers, Mulvaney, Ortheris, and Learoyd, showed something of the under side of idle life at Simla, and sent an exploring eye into mysterious native purlieus; and this by half-a-dozen pamphlet-like volumes, *Soldiers Three*, *The Story of the Gadsbys*, *In Black and White*, *Under the Deodars*, *The Phantom 'Rickshaw*, and *Wee Willie Winkie* (1888–1889), telling more of the peerless trio and a host of others, many aspects of Indian and Anglo-Indian life being mirrored with the same pungent realism, realism matched by the brilliance of the story-telling.

Letters of travel, poems, more stories

Sent to England by the *Gazette* and the *Pioneer*, Kipling travelled by way of China, Japan, and the United States, the articles written for the two papers on his journey across India and on the other countries visited ultimately securing permanence in the two volumes *From Sea to Sea* (1900). These "Letters of Travel" are as candid, racy, and sparkling as his fiction. He arrived in England to find himself already a celebrity. He stayed here for the time being, and meeting a young American, Wolcott Balestier, he collaborated with him on a novel, *The Naulahka* (1892), and married his sister. This amusing contrast of Western commercialism and Oriental manners was preceded in publication by a longish story which is almost a novel, *The Light that Failed* (1891), and by *Life's Handicap* (1891), first of three sets of more mature stories of the same India, white and black, the two others being *Many Inventions* (1893) and *The Day's Work* (1898). *Barrack-room Ballads* (1892), in the same strain as *Departmental Ditties*, was followed by *The Seven Seas* (1896), the miscellaneous themes of which show an outlook on a broader world; and after the South African war he tempered patriotism with grave admonition in another set of occasional poems, *The Five Nations* (1903). But, like some others, Kipling was more of a poet in some of his prose works, and that not only in the snatches of verse, often his very best, forming chapter-headings. Among the fruits of a stay with the Balestiers in Vermont was *Captains Courageous* (1897), a story of the New England cod-fishers. It was here also that he began *The Jungle Book* (1894), which with *The Second Jungle Book* (1895) reveals a depth and catholicity of vision rivalling *Kim* (1901), his amplest portrayal of the life of modern India, native and European. He had given his own version of his schoolboy years in *Stalky & Co.* (1899); and now, having lost the elder of his two daughters, he offered as it were a libation to the dead in his *Just-so Stories for Little Children* (1902), playful and engaging tales to be followed after a while by *Puck of Pook's Hill* (1906) and its sequel, *Rewards and Fairies* (1910).

His last phase

Kipling was now living in a beautiful old house under the Sussex downs, in a countryside haunted by old legends; and his imagination, softened and mellowed by the loss of his child, found comfort in weaving such tales of old England and of fairyland, or such a piece of serious fancy as "They," the scene of which is the same old house adjoining the other world. The last of his miscellaneous stories, however, *Debits and Credits* (1926) and *Limits and Renewals* (1932), though as deft as ever in mere technique, added nothing to his record. He watched with an apprehensive eye all that was going on at home and abroad, and from time to time gave the nation the benefit of his judgments and misgivings. Now a poem or song, and now an article, speech, or interview, proclaimed his views with uncompromising trenchancy; he was always stirring and often provocative. He revisited South Africa in 1898 and again during the Boer war. He was in Canada in 1907. These were occasions for solemn admonitions in the Press. He had long prophesied war with Germany—and, for that matter, with Russia. When the Great War of 1914 broke out, he threw himself into the campaign for national service with all his energy, and he celebrated the deeds of the submarines and destroyers with the old force and vividness. His only son was one of the missing at Ypres. To the end he retained his distinction as poet and novelist of the Empire; he was certainly not one of those prophets whom their own country fails to recognize. And among his many honours it is not irrelevant that he followed Scott, Meredith, and Hardy, in being a recipient of the gold medal of the Royal Society of Literature. He had been awarded the Nobel Prize for Literature in 1907.

Kipling's first stories

When Kipling arrived in this country in the wake of his earliest stories, people were growing tired of the affectations of the æsthetes and the perversions of cherished formulas and venerated platitudes by those who boasted their decadence. His glorification of strength and manhood was welcomed as a just reprisal; it was indeed a more effective counterblast than all the parodies and caricatures.[1] Here was the natural man in his element, uncouth and unregenerate maybe, but refreshingly free from the morbid self-consciousness and self-questioning of the artist in attitudes. Terence Mulvancy, Stanley Ortheris, and John Learoyd might be rough diamonds, at any rate they had all the marks of being genuine. And their deeds and adventures, their tragic predicaments, or the rowdy pranks in which they disported themselves, were not mere episodes in a literary farrago: these were unmistakably pages torn from the daily register of life as it goes on, if such a record is kept on earth or elsewhere. Kipling wasted no time on methodical portraits or psychological analysis; that was not his way. The immortal three are rough-hewn in a few curt phrases, almost as tersely as in a playbill. They are given just enough definite traits to carry on, and what they say and do, and the way they say and do it, fills out the likeness and gives it palpable reality. In short, he lets them present themselves. Kipling had taught himself the art in his work for the Press: his business had been first to know and then to impart all he knew in terms that would make his readers see and hear and feel with the same lively sense of actuality. He had fastened instinctively on the truly revealing aspects of life in India for the contributions to his journal; when these

[1] Richard le Gallienne waited and then hit back, in a review of *Many Inventions* (June, 1893, see *Retrospective Reviews*, i. 275–281), which is by no means unfair, but smiles at the introductory prayer "to the true Romance," at Kipling's gesture of "drawing back from his clay statuettes, with all the solemnity of the Creator resting on the seventh day," and the continual affectation of bloodthirstiness.

were collected for the public at home, they were to show the realities, the wealth of picturesque and incongruous character, and the underlying romance of the Indian scene. Kipling with his insatiable curiosity and uncanny insight into all sorts and conditions had absorbed the Orient, the life and mind of the native, as well as the diverse characters, feelings, and mental perspectives of those engaged in governing the vast dependency.

Essentially a story-teller

As critics have thought it fair to point out, he was not one who made a cult of realism for the sake of realism.[1] His purpose was to display the salient types, and present those phases of the human drama which had struck himself with the same force and vividness; and he had, moreover, his own anxious but resolute interpretation of life in general to assert for the benefit of the world. His imagination saw all this in the form of stories that must be told, vital bits of the human drama ready shaped; corresponding to his intuitions lay waiting the artistic forms into which to cast them. There has been no finer story-teller in English. Some said he was an imitator of Bret Harte, whose pithy yarns were also about rough and outlandish breeds of the human stock.[2] There is, in fact, a near resemblance; both drew sensational and comic effects from the lawless and uncouth; both made brilliant use of a slangy vernacular; and, be it added, both unearthed romance in the grimiest corners of a sordid world, and did not shrink, at a pinch, from melodramatic devices in bringing out the latent contradictions. To Bret Harte was largely due the vogue of the short, racy, dramatic story. He was a concise and, specifically, an American Dickens. There was not much left of Dickens in Kipling's art, except when he let

[1] See, *e.g.*, Jackson (233) on his difference from the French realists who "looked upon mere frankness as an end in itself."

[2] Andrew Lang (*Essays in Little*, 199–200) mentions this view, but concedes only that if Kipling had a literary progenitor it is Bret Harte. M. Firmin Roz (*Le Roman anglais contemporain*, 194) simply recognizes that the short story of this stamp was a peculiarly American product, and that in this sense Kipling may be grouped with Poe, Bret Harte, and Mark Twain. Lang very aptly compares the author of *The Gadsbys* and some other tales of flirting matrons and of men and women playing fast and loose with moral prohibitions with that sprightly novelist Gyp. He might be "an Anglo-Indian disciple, trammelled by certain English conventions."

sentimentalism now and then play ducks and drakes with honest realism.

"Plain Tales from the Hills"

The *Plain Tales* are nearly all very brief; many are simple anecdotes, with invention at a discount. They appealed by their freshness and self-evident veracity, as much as by an art that was surely capable of still finer exploits. And, swiftly and surely, this elemental fiction of his was to develop into compact histories of some episode in a life, of complications in which character and everything of any earthly value were at stake, or into the broad humours of some colossal hoax. The book is a prelusive epitome, a sort of table of contents, to all of Kipling's fiction that was to follow: nothing is missed. The British army in India, especially the British private, the frivolities at Simla, the prosaic lot of the civil servants, fraught however with all kinds of golden opportunities did they but know it, the many sides of native life, including the darker and more mysterious, the tireless self-immolation to duty of such as his Strickland, the romantic here and the sordid there, are all transcribed with the Argus-eyed scrutiny of a keen journalist, but also given a wider import by a poet's imagination. He seemed to have the run of two distinct worlds.

Something I owe to the soil that grew—
More to the life that fed—
But most to Allah that gave me two
Separate sides to my head.

I would go without shirts or shoes,
Friends, tobacco or bread,
Sooner than for an instant lose
Either side of my head.

A twofold vision

This snatch of song preceding one of the chapters in *Kim* has been quoted more than once to indicate the existence in Kipling of a twofold outlook, almost of two cultures, two racial souls, implanted one by his English schooling and the other by his intimacy with the Oriental mind.[1] The visionary

[1] This is well observed by Chevrillon (20-21). M. Firmin Roz (194) interprets the "two separate sides to my head" as two contradictory elements in the English mind—"la coexistence dans l'esprit anglais de deux caractères, le sens du réel et la faculté de rêve intense." This is hardly M. Chevrillon's meaning.

East with its craving for the absolute and the infinite held him spell-bound, and he could throw himself into all its ardours. Yet he came back invariably and inevitably to the realistic point of view of the English, the conviction that effects are the result of causes, that the occult is merely the unexplained, and that in the practical and in the moral sphere order and obedience will ensure efficiency and happiness, and it is folly to rely too placidly on such doubtful powers as fate and chance. Despite the flippancy of tone in a good many of *Plain Tales from the Hills*, this is the practical philosophy implied in the main trend; to some of the stories that followed it gives a positively didactic bearing. But in these first Kipling maintained a pose of imperturbable nonchalance, whilst pointing to the most startling, confounding, and almost unmentionable facts. The air of levity and indifference was put on, of course, in irony. But it was not much more than the arrogant and condescending manner of a clever young journalist, brutal enough to enjoy shocking the sensitive and exasperating others with his airs of superiority. It was all superficial; Kipling was thoroughly serious at bottom, though he did not alter his tone yet awhile. And it was realism, and no mistake. Some said it was photographic, and the glare which lighted up the dirtiest corners made the squeamish talk about the callous indifference of a searchlight. If it can be said that the characters depict themselves by their behaviour, it may be added that the stories seem to tell themselves, so little is the art of it allowed to show. Psychology is telescoped, or taken for granted; so little of what goes on inside us is ever mentioned that critics have deplored the emptiness of his figures. But his vision is by no means only skin-deep, though it may seem not much more than the perspicacity of any shrewd person of experience intently watching. Yet even that not so exceptional person may divine more than he sees with the naked eye, and have a pretty accurate idea of what is going on under the surface. Such is the attitude assumed by Kipling; and, when with his usual vigour he has stated all he perceives, there is certainly no need for confessions or vivisections. And further, with his friendly air of confiding in the reader, he imparts the sense of a sort of clairvoyance in which both share. The one is now in the secret as much as the other.

Range of his earlier story-books

It was not Kipling's practice to dismiss a picturesque or entertaining character at the end of the first performance. The three privates keep on reappearing in all sorts of roles and situations, tragic as well as comic, from *Plain Tales* to *Life's Handicap* and *Many Inventions*, and they figure repeatedly in his books of verse. Gross and raffish externally, each has his own inner life, to be divined from tale after tale; and it is the same with such select types as Mrs Hauksbee, Strickland, and even Mowgli, who gave a strange charm to the story "In the Rukh" before he became the hero of the two *Jungle Books*. This continual reappearance of prominent characters, and indeed the family traits and racial and professional links and loyalties that tie practically all the rest into well-marked groups, imparts something like the unity and centralized import of a novel to the whole huge miscellany of tales. Love is a master-theme that cannot be evaded in such a wholesale survey, however Kipling may fight shy of it; it has its place even in the turbulent existence of the stalwart three. But in these early stories Kipling handled the subject with a markedly slighting regard for common sentimental foibles. Love, or what passed for it, was material for satire in the sketches of society at Simla, where it is a main occupation for the idle and a serious business for the predatory. There the unmarried, the mismarried, and the breakers of marriages, lie in wait for the unwary, though unions worthy of a better place are sometimes made there. Kipling goes out of his usual way to usher in formally one of the predacious, Mrs Reiver, and one of her opposites, the more uncommon and more intricate Mrs Hauksbee, who snatches the enamoured Pluffles out of her very claws.

There was nothing good about Mrs Reiver, unless it was her dress. She was bad from her hair—which started life on a Brittany girl's head—to her boot-heels, which were two and three-eighth inches high. She was not honestly mischievous like Mrs Hauksbee; she was wicked in a business-like way. There was never any scandal—she had not enough generous impulses for that. She was an exception that proved the rule that Anglo-Indian ladies are in every way as nice as their sisters at Home. She spent her life proving that rule.

Journalism almost refined into literature, like the companion portrait—

Mrs Hauksbee was honest—honest as her own front-teeth —and, but for her love of mischief, would have been a woman's woman. . . . At a moderate estimate there were about three-and-twenty sides to that lady's character. Some men say more.

Mrs Hauksbee appears again and again, and sometimes has to pocket a rebuff, as in "Three and—an Extra," where however she avenges herself in the aphorism, "Take my word for it, the silliest woman can manage a clever man; but it needs a very clever woman to manage a fool." Kipling concedes rather more to honest sentiment in "False Dawn," the tale of the youth who proposed to the wrong sister in a dust-storm; and there is real tenderness in "A Bank Fraud." But that is about a poor young fellow's love for his mother. He dies of consumption, sending her his last month's salary, unaware that he had been sacked by the directors. The fraud was Reggie Burke's, who nurses him to the end, and to keep him from breaking down has paid the cheque month after month out of his own purse. But for the other kind of love Kipling is almost cynical, on the man especially, as, for instance, the self-centred Phil in "Yoked with an Unbeliever," who plays fast and loose with an English girl and marries a hill-woman, for he knew they make excellent housekeepers.

Now the particular sin and shame of the whole business is that Phil, who really is not worth thinking of twice, was and is loved by Dunmaya, and more than loved by Agnes, the whole of whose life he seems to have spoilt. Worst of all, Dunmaya is making a decent man of him; and he will ultimately be saved from perdition through her training.

"Georgie Porgie," etc.

It is nearly always the man who is the culprit in these tragedies. Georgie Porgie, in the tale in *Life's Handicap*, enters into temporary wedlock with a Burmese, who works her fingers to the bone for his lordship; but he thinks to himself "how much more comfortable would he be with a sweet English maiden who would not smoke cheroots, and would play upon a piano instead of a banjo." So he slips off home, and does indeed come back with an English wife. But not to the same station. Georgina finds him after walking half across India, and half dead with fatigue and privations looks in at the drawing-room window to gaze on the happy pair. After dinner they come out on the veranda, and the bride asks what is the noise they can hear in the distance.

"Oh," said Georgie Porgie, "I suppose some brute of a hill-man has been beating his wife."

"Beating — his — wife! how ghastly!" said the Bride. "Fancy *your* beating *me*!" She slipped an arm round her husband's waist, and, leaning her hand against his shoulder, looked out across the cloud-filled valley in deep content and security.

But it was Georgina crying, all by herself, down the hillside, among the stones of the watercourse where the washermen wash the clothes.

Sardonic, truly; but impatience of sentimentalism is far from arguing defect of feeling. The eight pieces of dialogue recounting *The Story of the Gadsbys* (1888) had given the ups and downs, the small annoyances and frictions, the mistrusts and semi-disloyalties, reproaches and forgivenesses, of married life in the officers' quarters. One, "The Tents of Kedar," had with inimitable force unveiled the tempests of passion and anguish concealed under a smooth surface of social decorum.

Mrs H. "If you denied everything you've said this evening and declared it was all in fun (*a long pause*), I'd trust you. Not otherwise. All I ask is, don't tell me her name. *Please* don't. A man might forget: a woman never would. (*Looks up table and sees hostess beginning to collect eyes.*) So it's all ended, through no fault of mine. Haven't I behaved beautifully? I've accepted your dismissal, and you managed it as cruelly as you could, and I have made you respect my sex, haven't I? (*Arranging gloves and fan.*) I only pray that she'll know you some day as I know you now. I wouldn't be you then, for I think even your conceit will be hurt. I hope she'll pay you back the humiliation you've brought on me. I hope—— No, I don't. I *can't* give you up! I must have something to look forward to or I shall go crazy. When it's all over, come back to me, and you'll find that you're my Pip still!" [1]

"Beyond the Pale"

But, again, for the tragedy that shocks and lacerates turn to that other tale of a liaison with a native, "Beyond the Pale," in which the jealous husband misses his stab in the dark at Trejago, who has, however, a terrible greeting from Bisesa when he taps at the familiar casement. "From the black dark Bisesa held out her arms into the moonlight. Both hands had been cut off at the wrists, and the stumps were nearly healed." And without even that much melodrama, for cholera is the avenger, the end of Holden's girl-wife and child, in "Without Benefit of Clergy," outdoes even this in elemental pathos. It is in *Life's Handicap*, which came out the same year as *The Light that Failed* (1891), Kipling's first near approach to a novel, and so almost inevitably a story of love. But love here, though Maisie takes up nearly as much of the canvas as Dick, is essentially a minor factor in the total disillusionment of the young painter, going blind before his work is half done, and seeing all that he has lived for sliding into the abyss. Of an opposite trend, and in truth a model story of the kind that "hold quite as much romance as is good for us," is "Miss Youghal's Sais," one of the early stories in *Plain Tales*. Strickland is the hero, and Miss Youghal is worthy even of him. But her parents do not consider him good enough; so the expert at native disguises clothes himself in a blanket and for two months shadows her as her *sais*. He finds the experience pretty trying, though he gets out of it much of his vast insight into native ways. But when an old and distinguished general tries to flirt with the young lady there is a scene. Happily, the general has a keen sense of humour. When the disguise comes off and he realizes the situation, he

[1] M. André Chevrillon has achieved a moving translation of a large part of this, as well as of "Love-o'-Women," and other profoundly tragic pieces, into French dialogue that comes up to the terrible original (*Rudyard Kipling*, 33–35, cp. 58–61).

not only bursts into fits of laughter and makes due apology to Strickland, but also prevails upon the reluctant parents to give their consent. In *Plain Tales from the Hills* there are illustrations of simple proverbs, such as "The Arrest of Lieutenant Golightly," the dandified officer who is out in a rainstorm and cannot prove that he is not a runaway private; one of the earliest and most charming of Kipling's sketches of children, "Tod's Amendment"; several of his magnificent farces, "The Taking of Lungtungpen," "A Germ-Destroyer," and "His Wedded Wife"; and a number of tales of natives, particularly "In the House of Suddhoo" and "The Bisara of Pooree," both concerned with talismans and black magic, and "The Gate of the Hundred Sorrows," in which the poor devil who has found perfect peace in the opium-den tells such a matter-of-fact yet heart-rending story of his dreams of life and death. *Plain Tales of the Hills* misses hardly a single one of Kipling's particular themes, though we must look elsewhere for the fuller development of some.

The three privates

His three privates, the Irishman, the Cockney, and the Yorkshireman, each talking his own dialect, enriched with barrack-room slang, and each individualized in no small degree by his racial or tribal moulding, are the protagonists of *Soldiers Three*; but they are always lurking in the background ready to come on the scene, and their finest epiphany is in stories as late as *Life's Handicap* and *Many Inventions*. No one will forget the peppery little Cockney's fit of the blues in the first series, "The Madness of Private Ortheris," when he talks seriously of deserting.

"I'm a Tommy—a bloomin' eight-anna, dog-stealin' Tommy, with a number instead of a decent name. Wot's the good o' me? If I 'ad a stayed ot 'Ome, I might a married a gal and a kep a little shorp in the 'Ammersmith 'Igh.—'S. Orth'ris, Prac-ti-cal Taxi-der-mist.' With a stuff' fox, like they 'as in the Haylesbury Dairies, in the winder, an' a little case of blue and yaller glass-heyes, an' a little wife to call 'shorp!' 'shorp!' when the door-bell rung. As it *his*, I'm on'y a Tommy—a Bloomin' Gawd-forsaken Tommy. 'Rest on your harms—'*versed*. Stan' at—*hease*; '*Shun*.

'Verse—*harms*. Right an' lef'—*tarrn*. Slow—*march*. 'Alt—*front*. With blank-cartridge—*load*.' An' that's the end o' me."

"No," he says later, "I ain't mammysick, because my uncle brung me up, but I'm sick for London again; sick for the sounds of 'er; orange-peel and hasphalte an' gas comin' in over Vaux'all Bridge," and all the rest of the familiar sensations of long before he put on khaki for "the Widder." It is Mulvaney who corrects him, Mulvaney who also has "vultures tearing his liver," as another notable story of the old days was to tell. Those in *Soldiers Three* are of a more trivial cast, bragging tales of practical jokes and the like. They are droll enough in the telling, though Kipling's humour was not at its best unless he was letting drive at something. It tended rather to be scathing and sardonic, or to the jest worked up into sheer extravaganza. "Private Learoyd's Story" of the sergeant's dog, purloined, and its skin dyed by Ortheris to pass it off as the animal coveted by the unscrupulous old lady, is perhaps the best here.

"Don't say steal," says Mrs DeSussa; "he shall have the happiest home. Dogs often get lost, you know, and then they stray, an' he likes me and I like him as I niver liked a dog yet, an' I *must* hev him."

But, after all, there were some as good if not a great deal better in *Plain Tales*, including that rumbustious farce, "The Taking of Lungtungpen," and the milder jocularities, "A Germ-Destroyer," and "His Wedded Wife." "Lungtungpen" is a masterpiece of its particular kind. The second is the anecdote of Mellish, the bagman with the fumigatory to sell, who is let loose on the Viceroy himself through being taken for the important Mellishe of Madras. The third is one of Kipling's cherished hoaxes; the good-looking young subaltern with a gift for amateur theatricals passing himself off for a wager as the beloved wife of his senior officer.

Life at Simla

As to *The Story of the Gadsbys*, this is a great technical success, a novelette entirely in dialogue, and so lifelike that the mere instantaneous photography rivets attention. But the people are a commonplace lot, though they are of the stagnant, mediocre class that Kipling always approved as if they were the backbone of a secure society.[1] He did the same kind of thing still better in *Under the Deodars*, half-a-dozen tales of "men and women playing at tennis with the seventh commandment." There Mrs Hauksbee is to the fore again; this is, indeed, a candid study of the fast set at Simla, the dangerous women. They may be dangerous, but the men deserve them; and, on the whole, their hearts are shown to be in the right place. Thus Otis Yeare, in the first tale, having mistaken Mrs Hauksbee's good-natured efforts to smarten him up for a desperate flirtation and fallen seriously in love, is skilfully and drastically restored to a state of comparative sanity. Jane Austen, if she had only been up to date enough in the technical terms, might have written the little chat over his case between Mrs Hauksbee and Mrs Mallowe. In "A Second-rate Woman" these two appear again, to applaud the dowdy who turns out to be a heroine.

The supernatural and the marvellous

The title-story in *The Phantom 'Rickshaw* is also about Simla and the sad doings that have given the place a bad name; though its interest is that it is one of Kipling's earliest and one of his most cogent ghost-stories.[2] Within the same pair of covers, follows immediately, as if for a challenge, one in the older, orthodox style, "My own True Ghost Story," the one in which the cause of all the affright proves to be a rat behind the wainscoting. But Kipling's dealings with the supernatural are a topic so mixed up with illicit appeals to credulity or else so pregnant with ulterior implications that

[1] "Par là Kipling diffère des purs réalistes. Si comme eux, il accepte ou recherche le laid ou le grossier, toujours il écarte le médiocre" (Chevrillon, *Kipling*, 50). This is true in the sense that the whole "slice of life" is never mediocre. As M. Chevrillon goes on to say, Kipling accentuates the lines and shows how life is exalted by exceptional circumstances. "Des faits qui composent le monde de l'âme, il ne garde que ceux qui sont des *maxima*." These people have few ideas, only commonplace sentiments; but temperament breaks the crust at intervals, and does raise life to higher levels. See, *e.g.*, above, 131.

[2] M. Firmin Roz is reminded by it of *Le Horla* of Maupassant, whilst he points out that it is a good illustration of M. André Chevrillon's remark on "la coexistence dans l'esprit anglais de deux caractères, en apparence antagonistiques, le sens du réel et la faculté de rêve intense" (194–195). But M. Chevrillon insists rather on the two ethnic spirits coexisting in Kipling, one native, the other absorbed from the East (see above, p. 110, n. 1).

they had better stand over till certain other apposite examples come into view. Both are definitely realistic narratives; and the two that follow are equally stories of the marvellous, though they keep within unquestionable limits without losing a jot of their sensational effects. "The Strange Ride of Morrowbie Jukes" originated in a gruesome experience the young reporter had heard about: "There is no invention about this tale." It is the story of the man out for a ride whose horse runs away with him, man and beast tumbling down a slope of sand into a crater-like hollow shut in by the Sutlej. He has fallen into one of those places where Hindus who have come round after a fit of catalepsy are relegated, instead of to the burning-ghaut; and sixty-five human beings appear from the badger-holes at the bottom when Morrowbie opens his eyes. In one of them he recognizes Gunga Dass, the native he had once known as a minor official and an expert at bad puns in English. Gunga Dass initiates him into the ghastly life of the place, and shows him how to snare crow, the only provender. There is a boat moored in the river, and a rifle-shot warns him of the futility of trying to escape. The worst of the situation is, not merely its hopelessness, but the fact that positions are reversed, and the Englishman finds himself at the beck and call of the unclean native. Gunga Dass means to murder him, and will probably have his way. Morrowbie Jukes is in a state bordering upon insanity, when at length his faithful dog-boy, who has tracked the hoof-prints through the jungle, prevails on his reluctant fellow-servants to come with a long rope and rescue their master from the village of the dead. "The Man who would be King" is the wildest romanticism substantiated by the realism of hard fact. Who will forget the grotesque farewell of Dravot and his pal, the couple who are down and out, starting up the Khyber on camels laden with Martinis and a cargo of gauds and trinkets, to find their realm at the back of beyond and make themselves kings? And they succeed. Carnehan turns up again, a summer and winter later, and tells the story. It was partly the rifles, with which they arm the natives and take a decisive part in a tribal war; but what clinches the matter and proves them superhuman beings is that they have the Freemason's grip. The priests know the Craft.

"It's Gord's truth. I've known these long years that the Afghans knew up to the Fellow Craft Degree, but this is a miracle. A God and a Grand-Master of the Craft am I. . . . It's a master-stroke of policy," says Dravot. "It means running the country as easy as a four-wheeled bogie on a down grade."

Dravot's views are Napoleonic.

"They're the Lost Tribes, or something like it, and they've grown to be English. . . . Two million people—two hundred and fifty thousand fighting men—and all English! They only want the rifles and a little drilling. Two hundred and fifty thousand men, ready to cut in on Russia's right flank when she tries for India! Peachey, man," he says, chewing his beard in great hunks, "we shall be Emperors—Emperors of the Earth! Rajah Brooke will be a suckling to us."

But, alas! the bubble is pricked, when in spite of his friend's remonstrances Dravot insists on taking a consort and the hysterical girl runs in and bites him, drawing blood. They are human, after all. Peachey by a miracle gets through the mountains. He has been tortured, he has been crucified; he has seen Dravot hurled into a ravine in Kafiristan, and has brought back his leader's dried and withered head. He shambles into the office, and they extract the story, only a day or two before he expires in the missionaries' asylum. Even this brief epitome makes comment superfluous. And then those tales of children, *Wee Willie Winkie* and "Baa baa, black Sheep," how sympathetically they show the working of a small boy's mind! Kipling, later on, was to come forward as a veritable pundit in the lore and mentality of children; and already he is severe on the time-honoured methods of bringing them up, "when the fear of the Lord was so often the beginning of falsehood." That was how Punch fell, who straightway becomes Black Sheep.

Auntie Rosa had credited him in the past with petty cunning and stratagem that had never entered into his head. By the light of the sordid knowledge that she had revealed to him he paid her back full tale.

The last item in this batch is "The Drums of the Fore and Aft," which shows up the errors of the way men are trained to face fire, and tells how a regiment made amends for an earlier panic. The fighting with Ghazis and Afghans is in Kipling's best style; the heroes are the two drummer-boys, Jakin and Lew. And the tales supposed to be translated from native originals, *In Black and White*, give completeness and symmetry, and are a useful measuring-rod for some in the future when he had to rely on that incomparable memory of his.

Kipling in England—Poems

Kipling had surveyed the whole length and breadth of the Anglo-Indian world, not omitting the darker recesses, and had produced as close a copy as lies within the compass of a verbal rendering. No one has ever pushed the art of representing actual life in words nearer to its extreme limits. On his arrival in this country, he was acclaimed as the novelist of both the English in India and the varicoloured myriads of natives. The eye of the world was now upon him, he was no longer a mere adventurer anxious to make his mark; and in the works that follow a certain sense of responsibility and a more conscious regard for the demands of art may both be discerned; the stories are mostly on an ampler scale, and invention is no longer pretermitted, if only for the sake of point and symmetry. *Departmental Ditties* was now followed by *Barrack-room Ballads* (1892). Both are the impromptus of a fluent rhymester, with almost as many rhythms and metres as Swinburne's at easy command. As realistic and matter-of-fact as his prose stories, they strike the ear, for the most part, as mechanical and metallic, skits and parodies and comic catches that went round the office, or marching songs for Tommy Atkins, fierce with the bellicose imperialism which was to be the dominant note in *The Seven Seas* (1896) and *The Five Nations* (1903). But now and again a purer music makes itself heard, in such moments of vision as lift some of the tales into a halcyon air, or change the rhymed prose to a lyric. And Kipling drops his barrack-room slang and outlandish vernaculars for cadences from the Bible and the Psalms, when, in his graver moods, he intones his creed of law, order, obedience, duty, efficiency, which was now the lesson of half his stories. But it is the poet of "Tam o' Shanter" and "Holy Willie's Prayer" that we seem to be listening to in "Tomlinson," the man that is "neither spirit nor spirk," that is "neither book nor brute."

Over the coal they chased the Soul, and racked it all abroad,
As children rifle a caddis-case or the raven's foolish hoard.
And back they came with the tattered Thing, as children after play,
And they said: "The soul that he got from God he has bartered clean
 away.
We have threshed a stook of print and book and winnowed a chatter-
 ing wind,
And many a soul wherefrom he stole, but his we cannot find:
We have handled him, we have dandled him, we have seared him to
 the bone,
And sure if tooth and nail show truth he has no soul of his own.

"The Light that Failed"

The Naulahka (1892), in which he collaborated with Balestier, is a pleasantry in which Kipling's knowledge of the East was the most valuable asset. But Kipling is a novelist who never wrote a novel himself. *The Light that Failed* (1891), which he wrote out of his feelings about art and the violent dislikes vented in "Tomlinson," has the simplicity of a story and not very much more than the length of one. *Captains Courageous* (1897) is hardly more than a string of pictorial sketches of a wild and strenuous variety of life and action. *Kim* is a panorama of the Indian world, a procession of the different aspects of that multitudinous life passing one after the other before the eyes of Kim and the wise old Lama. *The Light that Failed* is not autobiography, but Kipling frankly unbosoms himself here of the scorns and hatreds he felt for much that he saw around him in the home country. In Dick Helder, the man whose illusions are savagely laid waste, are personified the whole tribe of journalists, war-correspondents, and the rest of Kipling's brothers-in-arms. Dick is a young painter of genius, the same sort of genius as Kipling's, and it is Kipling's own realism that he expounds:

"You see the sort of things I paint. D'you like it?"

Maisie looked at the wild whirling rush of a field-battery

going into action under fire. Two artillerymen stood behind her in the crowd.

"They've chucked the off lead-'orse," said one to the other. "'E's tore up awful, but they're makin' good time with the others. That lead-driver drives better nor you, Tom. See 'ow cunnin' 'e's nursin' 'is 'orse."

"Number Three'll be off the limber, next jolt," was the answer.

"No, 'e won't. See 'ow 'is foot's braced against the iron? 'E's all right."

Dick, that "aggressive, cocksure, you-be-damned fellow," has the right gospel, too.

"Don't you understand, darling? Good work has nothing to do with—doesn't belong to—the person who does it. It's put into him or her from outside."

"But how does that affect——"

"Wait a minute. All we can do is to learn how to do our work, to be masters of our materials instead of servants, and never to be afraid of anything."

The unresponsiveness of the girl whom he has idealized and idolized tortures Dick. For a moment it looks as if his magnanimity will awaken hers; but—

Not for nothing is a man permitted to ally himself to the wrong woman. The first pang—the first sense of things lost—is but the prelude to the play, for the very just Providence who delights in causing pain has decreed that the agony shall return, and that in the midst of the keenest pleasure.

More stories

This was a digression; a new volume of the stories that suited his genius came out the same year, and another two years later. Not a great proportion of those in his earlier collections are worth many re-readings. The young journalist was rather "a snapper-up of unconsidered trifles," and his brilliant handling often made a success of something that one does not want to hear about again. That brilliance, however, was not of a sort to draw attention to itself: quite the reverse. Kipling's first stories, in *Plain Tales of the Hills* and its satellites, looked like rough, impromptu accounts of things witnessed or heard about, jotted down off-hand, without the least care how they would strike the reader, with very little effort to make the situation clear and define the issues or forecast the probable upshot. Kipling made none of the usual concessions to the reader, who was called upon to watch things taking place and perceive their implications for himself. But this apparent heedlessness was only a disguise for the subtlest art. Kipling knew very well there is nothing that convinces like an air of unstudied candour. No doubt, he meditated long enough over many a seemingly haphazard train of incidents, before deciding at what point in the course of events he should strike in, how much could be taken for granted, what should be explained in detail, and what deliberately left vague, or deliberately, though as if by an oversight, left for the reader to fill in from some casual allusion.[1] What looks like an oversight may prove the safest imaginable warrant for what without it would sound incredible.

His concrete method

The fact is, in his story-telling Kipling displayed all the craft and subtlety of Kim and Mowgli's dread acquaintance, the Python. He realized in his own art the efficiency which he was to inculcate as the most valuable quality in a man. Actually, no one could be more precise and lucid in the vital points of a story, or know better what is gained by leaving certain things and certain characters impenetrable. He may have lacked Conrad's magical power of weaving an atmosphere, of compelling the reader to experience all the sensations of some overwhelming situation or physical state of things, like the prolonged struggle with sea and cyclone, in "Youth," or "Typhoon," or *The Nigger of the "Narcissus,"* or the sinister mysteriousness of the equatorial forest, in "Heart of Darkness." The atmospheric tension that breaks all at once into the hurricane was not his mark. But when it came to vivid description or to retailing a story, Kipling was not to be matched, and certainly had no need of Conrad's elaborate system of testimony and corroboration. That was the supreme virtue of his method of working entirely in the concrete, the rationale

[1] As Maurois notices (55–56), Kipling will pretend not to know all the circumstances of some odd incident himself, such an innocent attitude being a conclusive guarantee of his honesty.

of which has been seen already, for instance, in such summary contrasts of character and disposition as Mrs Hauksbee and Mrs Reiver, or the perfect definition with which his privates, his subalterns, and any other individual, no matter what his order, race, or caste, stand out distinct, and speak and act just as that one and no other would act and speak. Each is seized as a whole, a person reacting with all his individuality to the situation whatever it may be. In that which is visible he reveals all that is going on within.[1] This was how Kipling's imagination worked, always in the concrete. Not his business to study and analyse. He identified himself with Mulvaney, or Ortheris, or Learoyd, or any of his adopted children, the well-loved progeny of a penetrating imaginative knowledge, down to the native clerks and servants and coolies, the instant one of them was called upon for speech or act or gesture. He is inside all the time, though he seems to be outside; his heart beats in unison. Thus he is able to plunge into the very crisis of a tale, and, without portrayal or explanatory prelude, show such a strange being as the Pathan in "Dray Wara Yow Dee" doing precisely what a man of that stamp would do. The wild soul of him is seized in a flash; and, no matter how the reader's sanity or dread of anything that might disturb his mental routine may shrink and dissent, he cannot help realizing for himself the barbaric thirst for vengeance. *Life's Handicap* (1891) and *Many Inventions* (1893) may on the average be finer stories than the older ones; but Kipling had not changed his method, only refined it by use and experience. How well he was aware of his differences, and also of the difficulties of his undertaking, is shown by that interesting gloss on the realism of his accomplished elders, "A Conference of the Powers," in *Many Inventions*, where the famous novelist of

[1] Roz is particularly good on Kipling's realism. "On a comparé son œuvre à un cinématographe. Soit; mais il faut ajouter que ces tableaux manifestent la vie intérieure des personnages et suffisent à la manifester, parce qu'elle y tient tout entière et ne les déborde pas" (193). Later he remarks, "Il a, dans le domaine limité où il excelle, ce don merveilleux d'un Shakespeare ou d'un Balzac qui dispense de patience et épargne le temps: il voit et dévine, plutôt qu'il n'observe. Son imagination est précise, rapide, concrète. Nul écrivain n'est moins 'intellectuel.'" In short, he comprehended everything by intuition, and compelled the reader to do exactly the same.

manhood and action is dumbfounded and humbled at the terrific experiences these beardless boys, officers on frontier stations, have gone through—and yet they listen to him with bated breath. In the talk with Gobind, also, which forms the preface to *Life's Handicap*, there are sidelights on the writer's task in these sophisticated days, when the precept no longer holds good, "A tale that is told is a true tale as long as the telling lasts." There, too, it is on record that "the very best" in the book were given to Kipling by his father.

"Soldiers Three" again

The first three are three of the finest, and two are among the most intimate stories of his chosen heroes: "The Courting of Dinah Shadd" is Mulvaney's love-story and "On Greenhow Hill" is Learoyd's. Both, with all their muscularity, are grave and touching revelations of two who do not wear their hearts on their sleeves. What a cunning extra touch of art is the dovetailing with Learoyd's narrative of the stalking of the sniper by Ortheris! And not irrelevant either:

> "That's a clean shot, little man," said Mulvaney.
>
> Learoyd thoughtfully watched the smoke clear away. "Happen there was a lass tewed up wi' him, too," said he.

And "His Private Honour," in *Many Inventions*, telling how Ortheris vindicates his self-respect against the young lieutenant who had in a moment of irritation flicked him with his cane, is an eloquent sequel to "The Madness of Private Ortheris" already quoted from *Plain Tales*. Ortheris had learned long ago what a man must put up with:

> "My right!" Ortheris answered with deep scorn. "My right! I ain't a recruity, to go whinin' about my rights to this an' my rights to that, just as if I couldn't look after myself. My rights! 'Strewth almighty! I'm a man."

The didactic or moralizing turn in the new stories is no novelty; but nowadays Kipling is more downright and undisguised about it:

> "Did you iver have onendin' devilment an' nothin' to pay for it in your life, sorr?" asks Mulvaney in "The Courting of Dinah Shadd."
>
> "Never, without having to pay," I said.

"That's thrue! 'Tis mane whin you considher on ut; but ut's the same wid horse or fut."

Far off they hear the voice of the senior subaltern of B Company uplifted in a sentimental song.

"For all we take we must pay, but the price is cruel high," murmured Mulvaney when the chorus had ceased. It is always the old orthodox doctrine of the nemesis awaiting on a misspent life, with this desponding affix. Still more barefaced is the didacticism in that faultless masterpiece, "Love-o'-Women," in *Many Inventions*—a preachment if ever there was one—Kipling never does anything by halves. But how infinitely tragic is the colloquy of the seducer and the woman damned to hell on earth! Mulvaney is a true philosopher, and his wisdom is not of the platitudinous, catch-penny order.

"But whin was a young man, high or low, the other av a fool, I'd like to know?" said Mulvaney. "Sure, folly's the only safe way to wisdom, for I've thried it."

Kipling himself was some time in attaining to Mulvaney's sobriety and tolerance. His grudges and antipathies were so many and so fierce, and make such demands on the reader's concurrence or forbearance, that it is impossible in reviewing him to avoid considerations that have little to do with art. There are glaring examples in this volume of his technical accomplishment used for extraneous and illegitimate purposes. "The Head of the District" is almost a tract, exposing the folly of deferring to the desires of the people "by appointing a child of the country to the rule of that country." The imbecility, conceit, and cowardice of Mr Grish Chunder Dé, M.A., are easily made to point the moral, to the detriment of a powerful story about devoted English commissioners who do perform their tasks, even at an exorbitant cost to themselves. So, too, the side-hits at "the Member for Lower Tooting" and at "vestrymen" of that kidney, in "Without Benefit of Clergy," have nothing whatever to do with this pitiful story.

But it is in "The Man who Was" that blatant jingoism, a muscularity as crude as Guy Livingstone's, and Kipling's ineradicable Russophobia, turn a promising yarn into a *"The Man who Was"* caricature of itself. It is the tale of the poor wretch who finds his way back to the regimental mess, and proves to be an officer who disappeared after Sebastopol, as the glib and unremorseful Dirkovitch confirms. "It was an accident; done because he did not apologize to that our colonel."

"What an infernal shame! Insulted one of their colonels, and was quietly shipped off. Thirty years of his life wiped out."

A first-rate story in itself, but the trimmings are of the cheapest and vulgarest dye.

> The great beam-roofed mess-room of the White Hussars was a sight to be remembered. All the mess plate was out on the long table, etc., etc.
>
> The servants in spotless white muslin and the crest of their regiments on the brow of their turbans waited behind their masters, who were clad in the scarlet and gold of the White Hussars, and the cream and silver of the Lushkar Light Horse. . . .
>
> The talk rose higher and higher, and the regimental band played between the courses, as is the immemorial custom, till all tongues ceased for a moment with the removal of the dinner-slips and the first toast of obligation, when an officer rising said, "Mr Vice, the Queen," and little Mildred from the bottom of the table answered, "The Queen, God bless her," and the big spurs clanked and the big men heaved themselves up and drank the Queen upon whose pay they were falsely supposed to settle their mess-bills. That Sacrament of the Mess never grows old, and never ceases to bring a lump into the throat of the listener wherever he be by sea or land.

At the end of the ritual, the native officer who has played for the Lushkar team is brought in. "He could not, of course, eat with the mess, but he came in at dessert,[1] all six feet of him, with the blue and silver turban atop, and the big black boots below." The fuddled captain of Cossacks from the back of beyond was meanwhile "fraternizing effusively" with the rest. Such are the manners and sentiments of that era which Kipling applauds.

[1] It might perhaps be pleaded that as a Mohammedan he was forbidden to eat with infidels. The Russian was a different matter.

From a sense of humour so defective as is evident in this Ouidaesque lyricism nothing very refined in the way of comedy was to be expected. Kipling's wit and humour show best in his workaday prose, into which he would breathe a sly vivacity, helped by an athletic command of words, the verb especially, which resulted in a style more supple and sprightly than any in English fiction since Meredith's. Here is a piece with nothing to show for itself except this pleasant faculty for characterizing anything, even a broken-down steamer. This is how "The Devil and the Deep Sea" begins, in *The Day's Work*; and what could be more pungent or hit the nail on the head more elegantly?

Kipling's farces

Her nationality was British, but you will not find her house-flag in the list of our mercantile marine. She was a nine-hundred-ton, iron, schooner-rigged, screw cargo-boat, differing externally in no way from any other tramp of the sea. But it is with steamers as it is with men. There are those who will for a consideration sail extremely close to the wind; and, in the present state of a fallen world, such people and such steamers have their use. From the hour that the *Aglaia* first entered the Clyde—new, shiny, and innocent, with a quart of cheap champagne trickling down her cutwater—Fate and her owner, who was also her captain, decreed that she should deal with embarrassed crowned heads, fleeing Presidents, financiers of over-extended ability, women to whom change of air was imperative, and the lesser law-breaking Powers. Her career led her sometimes into the Admiralty Courts, where the sworn statements of her skipper filled his brethren with envy. The mariner cannot tell or act a lie in the face of the sea, or mislead a tempest; but, as lawyers have discovered, he makes up for chances withheld when he returns to shore, an affidavit in either hand.

When, however, Kipling exerted himself to be funny, the best he could compass was a mighty farce, such as "Lungtungpen," or an uproarious extravagance like the overture here, "The Incarnation of Krishna Mulvaney." It is an elementary form of humour, neither satirical nor ironical, but a plunge into sheer absurdity for its own sake. One of the best of his tomfooleries is "Brugglesmith," tale of the sinful old ruffian who compels the respectable author to wheel him in an ambulance by night from Thames-side in the City right down to Hammersmith. It is carried off by its irresistible momentum. In his big farces, the secret was to contrive a crescendo of effects, climax overtopping climax, up to the overwhelming finale, as in "The Village that voted the Earth was Flat," that gigantic hoax which is at the same time a skit upon democracy. Kipling is as inventive and indefatigable as his music-hall impresario.

"It cost Bat Masquerier two thousand," Ollyett replied. "D'you think he'd let any one else in on that? . . . He had Huckley posted in three colours, 'The Geoplanarians' Annual Banquet and Exercises.' Yes, he invented 'Geoplanarians.' He wanted Huckley to think it meant aeroplanes. Yes, I know that there is a real Society that thinks the world's flat—they ought to be grateful for the lift—but Bat made his own. He did! He created the whole show, I tell you. He swept out half his Halls for the job. . . . There was a girl in the blue brake. . . . She told Huckley how she had suffered for the Cause as a governess in a rich family where they believed that the world is round, and how she threw up her job sooner than teach immoral geography. That was at the overflow meeting outside the Baptist chapel. She knocked 'em to sawdust! . . . But Lafone! Lafone was beyond everything. Impact, personality—conviction—the whole bag o' tricks! He sweated conviction. Gad, he convinced *me* while he was speaking! (Him? He was President of the Geoplanarians, of course. Haven't you read my account?) It is an infernally plausible theory. After all, no one has actually proved the earth is round, have they?"

A finer humour

A more delicate humour is exploited in "The Disturber of Traffic," first of *Many Inventions*, about the lighthouse-keeper in Flores Strait, whose eyes were magnetized by the streaky water—"Those streaks, they preyed upon his intellecks," he thought they were made by the ships, "instead of by the tides as was natural." He half knows he is mad, yet cannot fight down the delusion. So he buoys the channel, and makes the steamers and junks go round, until they discover his mania and send him home. And even then "he never got rid of that suspicion that he'd sunk some ships a-cause of his foolishness at Flores Straits; and now he's a wherryman from Portsmouth to Gosport, where the tides run crossways and you can't row straight for ten strokes together." Later in the day, Kipling reverted to his farces and hoaxes and elaborate waggishness, and in *Traffics and Discoveries* and *A Diversity of Creatures* launched upon a gratified world as master of the ceremonies his Mr Emanuel Pyecroft, who helps to fool the British Army in "The Horse Marines" and scores heavily off two fleets seriously engaged in mimic war in "Their Lawful Occasions." It is only a superlative form of buffoonery; but it would be unfair to label Pyecroft a mere buffoon, his humour is too peculiar, and he is such a masterly raconteur that the full flavour of these colossal jokes comes out only in his own idiomatic account and spicier commentary. One ingredient of Kipling's narrative style that gave it singular vivacity, as is evident in the last two pieces quoted, is the adroit and suggestive misuse of words. He was a master of the art of catachresis. When he lets Mr Pyecroft take up the parable, he gives this subtle form of humour full fling. Mr Pyecroft is the child of his bosom, who lisps in malaprops for the malaprops come. Hear him explaining the plan of campaign before the obsolete "two-funnelled craft of a type—but I'm no expert—between the first-class torpedo-boat and the full-blooded destroyer" slips in disguise among the modern destroyers, and manages to torpedo half-a-dozen first-class cruisers according to rule:

"Our Mr Moorshed done his painstakin' best—it's his first command of a war-canoe, matoor age nineteen. . . . But be that as it may, His Holiness Frankie is aware of us crabbin' ourselves round the breakwater at five knots, an' steerin' *pari passu*, as the French say. . . . If he'd given Mr Hinchcliffe, our chief engineer, a little time, it would never have transpired, for what Hinch can't drive he can coax; but the new port bein' a trifle cloudy, an' 'is joints tinglin' after a post-captain dinner, Frankie come on the upper bridge seekin' for a sacrifice. We, offerin' a broadside target, got it. . . ."

The "blasphemious" first-class engine-room artificer who,

"if you hand 'im a drum of oil an' leave 'im alone . . . can coax a stolen bicycle to do typewriting"; Jules, "on leaf from a French cassowary-cruiser," who is found "cruisin' on his own . . . in company of copious lady-friends"; and Mr Leggatt, who "drew the line at the girls—loud and long he drew it," and goes "fair homicidal on the subject" of the damaged paint-work, are as good as the dazzling exploits in which they engage, especially when they are full of "*juice de spree.*"

Black and White again

There is some overflow from *In Black and White* in *Life's Handicap*, which contains several tales of natives and that piece of deliberate and grimly significant word-painting, "The City of Dreadful Night." It is a famous piece, to which admiration cannot be grudged; yet somehow it fails to penetrate as it ought. Not a line or shade is missed that eye or ear or the other senses perceive; Kipling has the right pigment for every stroke. But not the touch that sets the imagination working in concert—the feel of it is missing. Normally, he describes by way of narrative; the highly efficient mechanical procedure is the same in both. Take, for instance, the tale just cited, "Their Lawful Occasions," the brilliant snapshots of the rough-and-tumble drive down Channel in the sham torpedo-boat, the wild-and-whirling rush through the big seas and the big ships, the touch-and-go and the narrow squeaks—nothing could be more vivid, quite apart from the salt and savour of Mr Pyecroft's running remarks. Here he secures almost the same atmospheric effects as Conrad's, but by means utterly different. Why was he never commissioned to write a primer of science? How graphic and lucid, and how beautifully educative it would have been! The tales of mathematical and mechanical marvels soon to appear show that convincingly. But when the outwardness or the inwardness of native life is in question, it is better to turn to some piece with a story in it, even such a trifle as "On the City Wall," last of those *In Black and White*. Nothing grandiose here, and not a line of set description. It is only some thirty pages about Lalun, one of the "heterodox women," "a member of the most ancient profession in the world," in her dainty chamber on the city wall, where English and Mahommedans meet and talk, and the young newspaper-man sits taking notes, or looks down on the terrific riot when the Hindus fling brickbats at the Moslem procession and the troops are called out. Yet the many sides of Indian life, and the past as well as the present, are focused there, the tragedy of now and the romance of then. And the art of the young novelist has at last achieved a form as sensitive and expressive as Lalun's sayings, and apparently as unstudied.

Stories of the occult

The stories that touch upon the supernatural begin with Kipling's usual realism, if they travel far beyond it, the starting-point being a personal experience or what otherwise purports to be fact. That calm explicitness which was the mark of the great realist may not be a master-key to the realms of mystery, but it was more effective than a magician's wand in compelling belief and in numbing with fear and horror. And the very absence of a suggestive penumbra often intensifies the initial or, it may be, the ultimate sensation, which is that of a physical shock. A good many of these stories actually go no further, they are shockers, pure and simple. "The Return of Imray" or "Beyond the Pale," for instance, does not trench upon the supernatural, or the sham-supernatural, though the creepiness and the violent blow on the nerves are of the same nature as the ghastly final incident "At the End of the Passage." There are shapes and shocks of dread and repulsion in plenty in "The Strange Ride of Morrowbie Jukes" and "The Man who would be King"; but these likewise keep well on this side of the curtain. It is Imray's dead body that returns. He had mysteriously disappeared, and the shrivelled corpse is found above the ceiling-cloth in the bungalow. His old servant Bahadur Khan confesses the deed; it was in vengeance for the death of his little son, whom he averred Imray had bewitched. "Bertran and Bimi," tale of the "devil-animal," the great orang-outan "dot thought he was a man" and out of jealousy tore his owner's wife to strips, vies with any of the ghost-stories in gruesomeness. And, for that matter, Kipling was able to get all the agonies and frightfulness he wanted out of a mere slum-story. "The Record of Badalia Herodsfoot" would have filled Gissing with envy if he did not find it too horrifying, though it is redeemed from crude ghastliness by the sublimity of Badalia's meek heroism. Tales dealing frankly with black magic differ in an essential particular, even though the set purpose, to give readers the creeps, may be practically identical. As far back as *Plain Tales*, there was "The Bisara of Pooree," of the talisman that brings luck once, but if you keep it "you will be sorry that you had not killed yourself in the beginning." The thaumaturgy in "The House of Suddhoo" is only ventriloquism; the trick is exposed, so far as the witness and the reader are concerned. But Kipling has not the least compunction in palming off on the trustful reader things quite as bad. If it would be going too far to charge him with false pretences when in "The Mark of the Beast" he affirms that the vengeance of the insulted Indian god upon the rowdy lieutenant, who ground out the ash of his lighted cigar on the forehead of the sacred image, is a fact, at any rate, the wicked implication "At the End of the Passage" that Spurstow saw the image of the devil from hell on the dead man's retina—and photographed it—is, surely, stealing a march on poetic faith. It is all the more flagrant here inasmuch as we have entered only too feelingly into Hummil's haunted insomnia, and descended with him in our souls "into the Dark Places." It is too much like hitting us when we are down. As to "The Phantom 'Rickshaw," it would be irrelevant to ask whether the phantom vehicle with the figure of the dead woman in it which haunts the man who drove the poor thing to her untimely end is an hallucination or something else. This is a good orthodox ghost-story, with the details that ask and receive poetic belief; and thrills all the more in clinching so neatly the moral import. Very different but making the same appeal to the mesmerized imagination is "The Lost Legion," in *Many Inventions*. The wraiths of the dead regiment, cut up long ago by Afghans, still infest a valley among the rocks, and join in the night attack on the Afghan village.

Poetic fantasies

But there is a third group of fantasies in which the hard-headed realist lets poetic fancy play freely with his sense that the other world is never far away, such tales as "They," "The Brushwood Boy," "The Wish House." At least half the credit for "The Finest Story in the World" must go to W. E. Henley, whose stanza printed at the head of it gave the creative hint:

> Or ever the knightly years were gone
>   With the old world to the grave,
> I was a king in Babylon
>   And you were a Christian slave.

It is a tale of metempsychosis, cunningly attested by little bits of realistic detail, like the young bank-clerk's remembrance of the line of water topping the bulwarks when the rammed galley went down. "'What did it look like?' I had my reasons for asking. 'It looked just like a banjo-string drawn tight, and it seemed to stay there for years,' said Charlie." Even more transporting, perhaps, than the images called up of Romans and Vikings in furious action is the thought of the mental possibilities into which we have taken such a plunge. There is a magical charm in the two later stories, "The Brushwood Boy" and "They"; but the sentimentalism that reinforces the magic, the ecstatic lyricism, is too unblushing: a second reading rubs off the glamour.[1] A young fellow and a girl, in the one, have dreamed the same dream and know the same queer song, and at last they meet—a pretty idea, but—! In the other, a motorist wanders into a nook in the South Downs, where a blind lady is living in a lovely old house, with a swarm of children flitting about and playing among the flowers and trees. "They" are departed little ones, who have come back to revisit their own. She has "neither borne nor lost"; love alone gives her the right to know them near. Charming; but only compare it with Charles Lamb's "Dream Children." "The Egg" is mere abracadabra. Later still is "The Wish House," a bucolic idyll in broad Sussex in which is unfolded a finer conception of self-immolating love than perhaps anywhere else in Kipling, homely and humble as the

[1] It is only fair to remember, however, that in writing "They" Kipling had had a narrow escape from death by pneumonia himself, and had lost his elder daughter. The *Just-so Stories* and "They" were a memorial to that loved girl. From this sad time may indeed be dated a general surrender to didacticism, which meant a steady decline in his art.

characters are. The touch of supernaturalism is justified as a symbol of superhuman unselfishness, for the sake of love—yes, and of love despised.

> 'Tis a motion of the Spirit that revealeth God to man
> In the shape of Love exceeding, which regards not taint or fall,
> Since in perfect Love, saith Scripture, can be no excess at all.

This snatch is from "Rahere," the poem affixed as comment or parable, as was now Kipling's regular wont.

"The Jungle Books"

In the two *Jungle Books* (1894–1895) Kipling invented a new literary form, absorbing such ancient species as the beast-fable and the allegory, and, with the plastic force of an imagination radically poetical and a sympathetic insight that knew no bounds, he brought even the mysterious life of the tropical forest into what is essentially a kind of novel. Later on, in a spirit of unconstrained fantasy and with Lear's nonsense-rhymes before him, he was to evolve a bold variant in his *Just-so Stories*; and then go on to a further feat, in the new kind of fairy-lore and history reinterpreted of the Puck story-books. The rhymed rubrics and mottoes and inset verses were thoroughly in keeping, and in such a context could hardly be considered a poetic licence. Already he had told many a tale of beast as well as of man in India; there were several in *Life's Handicap* and *Many Inventions*. "Moti Guj" was an almost Dickensian character-study of the whims and eccentricities, and the craftiness, of a petted old elephant. A more redoubtable specimen nearly gets Mulvaney in "My Lord the Elephant." Those lively sketches of horses and their idiosyncrasies, "A Walking Delegate" and "The Maltese Cat," were to come later; but Kipling had practically started, or at least laid the first stone for *The Jungle Book*, when he told the story "In the Rukh," and begat Mowgli, the little Hindu,[1] fosterling of the wolves and free companion of the jungle-folk, most charming and debonair of all his characters—an original imaginative creation, which must needs be beautiful. Old Muller feels that.

[1] We must not lose sight, however, as M. Chevrillon reminds us, of the hard fact that Mowgli is English, and the law of the jungle is that imposed on India by its overlords. "Même Kim, même la Jungle, qui passent pour les deux livres proprement indiens de Kipling, sont de cette pure essence anglaise" (*Kipling*, 104).

"Now I tell you dot only once in my service, and dot is thirty years, haf I met a boy dot began as this man began. Und he died. Sometimes you hear of dem in der census reports, but dey all die. Dis man haf lived, and he is an anachronism, for he is before der Iron Age, und der Stone Age. Look here, he is at der beginnings of der history of man—Adam in der Garden, und now we want only an Eva! No! He is older than dot child-tale, shust as der *rukh* is older dan der Gods. Gisborne, I am a Bagan now, once for all."

The new Mowgli and the beasts

But the Mowgli of *Many Inventions* is not quite the Mowgli of *The Jungle Book*: he is too knowing and well-spoken in his contacts with the civilized—he is a wood-god who has been to a public school. Kipling saw he had hit upon an idea far too good to be wasted; he took it back and remoulded it. The result was the complete history told in the two *Jungle Books*; and, from the night when Mother Wolf refuses to give up the man's cub to Shere Khan, the tiger, to the day when he bids a loving adieu to old Baloo, the bear, and his friend Bagheera, the panther, and the Master of the Jungle goes forth with his human wife on a new trail, there is not a false note, not a single improbability, nor any undue strain in the translation of this other half of the animate world into a language we can understand. For this is no representation of human beings masquerading as beasts. The anthropomorphic device is only a literary pretence used from of old for satiric, didactic, or merely playful purposes. This is a story of real life translated, and is entirely free from the conventions sacred to apologue. It is as dramatic, exciting, and moving, and makes the same appeal to our feelings and our sense of probability as the most realistic story of human beings that Kipling ever wrote. The primary assumption is that the mentality of the lower creation, at least on its upper levels, is not so rudimentary as science makes out; that beyond instinct, which we share with them in some degree, the beasts have feelings and intelligence, likes and dislikes, moods and whims and eccentricities, analogous to if not the same as those of human beings. Whether they have personality or any self-consciousness, Kipling prudently leaves an open question: Baloo is the bear, sober, frugal, and sedate; Kaa, the serpent, old and wary; Shere Khan, the tiger, ravenous and ruthless; and the Bandar-Log are the monkey-tribe of scamps, mountebanks, braggadocios, cowards —no doubt a satire on the self-dubbed intellectuals and emancipated of this and other ages.[1] Now and then, the animals throw up a genius. Thus the White Seal is a non-human Mowgli, even as Baloo is a philosopher and the elephant Kala Nag has earned the name of "the old wise Black Snake." Kipling's prized virtue is intelligence. Our misfortunes and our unhappiness are due to lack of intelligence, or to the neglect of it. The animals dare not neglect it, else like the seals they will be led off to be poleaxed. Each in his own walk learns as his first lesson to be wideawake, to understand what lies around him, and recognize what is good and what bad, or suffer the penalty; they know their business and attend to it, and in this respect are a shining example and a rebuke to mankind.

The Law of the Jungle

And the jungle has its morality; that has been forced upon it by sheer necessity—the rule of life between instinct and appetite and the dangers lying in wait on every side. Law, order, restraint, obedience, efficiency are the vital need here as in the human world.

Now these are the Laws of the Jungle and many and mighty are they:
But the head and the hoof of the Law and the haunch and the hump is—Obey!

But, over and above a merely prudential legalism, the virtues of affection, comradeship, trust in one's fellow, have due honour. It is as if Kipling were presenting another world to redress the balance of the one we know. He finds order even in the jungle; it is the law of all life—the lesson he is always deducing. Hence some will call it all didactic, as if he wrote to inculcate a maxim rather than to enjoy and communicate his delight in a happy vision. Mowgli is, surely, that one of his creations which he loves best; he loves him as himself; perhaps it is himself, at any rate it is an impersonation of his

[1] See Roz, 203.

far-reaching insight and sympathy with all things alive. Whence the touching farewell scene, the like of which was never penned in all the books of all the fabulists:

"Listen, dearest of all to me," said Baloo. "There is neither word nor will here to hold thee back. Look up! Who may question the Master of the Jungle? I saw thee playing among the white pebbles yonder when thou wast a little frog; and Bagheera, that bought thee for the price of a young bull newly killed, saw thee also. Of that Looking Over we two only remain; for Raksha, thy lair-mother, is dead with thy lair-father; the old Wolf-Pack is long since dead; thou knowest whither Shere Khan went, and Akela died among the dholes, where, but for thy wisdom and strength, the second Seeonee Pack would also have died. There remains nothing but old bones. It is no longer the Man-cub that asks leave of his Pack, but the Master of the Jungle that changes his trail. Who shall question Man in his ways?"

"But Bagheera and the Bull that bought me," said Mowgli. "I would not——"

His words were cut short by a roar and a crash in the thicket below, and Bagheera, light, strong, and terrible as always, stood before him.

"*Therefore*," he said, stretching out a dripping right paw, "I did not come. It was a long hunt, but he lies dead in the bushes now—a bull in his second year—the Bull that frees thee, Little Brother. All debts are paid now. For the rest, my word is Baloo's word." He licked Mowgli's foot. "Remember, Bagheera loved thee," he cried, and bounded away. At the foot of the hill he cried again long and loud, "Good hunting on a new trail, Master of the Jungle! Remember, Bagheera loved thee."

"Thou hast heard," said Baloo. "There is no more. Go now; but first come to me. O wise Little Frog, come to me!"

"It is hard to cast the skin," said Kaa as Mowgli sobbed and sobbed, with his head on the blind bear's side and his arms round his neck, while Baloo tried feebly to lick his feet.

"The stars are thin," said Gray Brother, snuffing at the dawn wind. "Where shall we lair to-day? for, from now, we follow new trails."

"*Stalky & Co*"

After *Captains Courageous* (1897), which tells of the rough life of the Nova Scotia fishermen and the regeneration of a spoilt boy from a comfortable and over-respectable home, appeared another story-book, *The Day's Work* (1898), and then *Stalky & Co.* (1899), the history of Kipling's school-life at Westward Ho! Such an anthology of pranks, hoaxes, and truculent escapades at the expense of schoolfellows and masters might have been put together as a counterblast to *St Winifred's*, *Eric*, and all the other pious classics "of that ilk." But, though selection had been at work, it proved to be only a singularly unreticent and unblushing account of the doings of Kipling and his three chums, who were a law to themselves, with a faithful portrait of the actual Head, Cormell Price. Stalky's original supplied the proof of this, in Major-General L. C. Dunsterville's *Adventures of Dunsterforce* (1920) and *Stalky's Reminiscences* (1928). *Stalky & Co.* is a book much disliked by the orthodox schoolmaster, a tribute to its veracity.

"*Kim*"

And now *Kim* (1901) arrived, that survey of India and its marvels in a story having the scale and some vestiges of the form of a novel. But, though it keeps on plunging into the moving panorama of Indian life, this is not a novel, for it does not move of itself. As Dixon Scott said, "Kim never grows up," and the other figures, unmistakable individuals as they are, likewise never change a hairbreadth; they are fixtures, cleverly shifted about, but always doing or saying the same sort of things.[1] At all events, it was a brilliant device, that intermingling of ancient and modern, holy and profane, the Lama's search for the river, the Fountain of Wisdom, with the Great Game, the secret service for the security of all those myriads against their lurking enemies. "Truly, it runs like a shuttle throughout all Hind." Kipling meant something

[1] "Mulvaney, Ortheris, and Learoyd live long but never alter; Kim never grows up" (*Men of Letters*, "The Meekness of Mr Rudyard Kipling," 58). "And so, in this way and in that, the actual words which he wrote joined in the conspiracy to keep him toiling on hopefully after that *ignis fatuus* of fiction. Until at length he made his supreme effort, fitted all the lore he had gathered—the sharp-set scenes, the well-cut dialects, the crisp impressions of life—into a single ingenious zoetrope—set it whirling on one of the spindles of the Indian machine, the secret spindle called the Great Game—and so created that spirited illusion of a novel which we know as *Kim*" (*Ibid.*, 60).

by the K in his young hero's name: Kim is like the little Kipling at Lahore. He is also another Mowgli, the same kind of boy, with a different stage and a different part. Every man idealizes his own gifts; and again it is intelligence, alertness, insight, which are the primary endowments: loyalty and endurance were to be learned as he grew up. "There is no sin so great as ignorance," Colonel Creighton tells him. "Remember this."

Kim is sent to the *madrissah*, where, as Mahbub impatiently puts it, "they take the best years of a man to teach him what he can only learn upon the road. The folly of the Sahibs has neither top nor bottom." At length he joins his partners in the Game. The patient old Lama, "coming and going across India as softly as a bat," has thought it well worth while to wait for such a *chela*. Lovely is the bond of affection between them.

"A day and a half have I waited—not because I was led by any affection towards thee—that is no part of the Way—but, as they said at the Tirthankers' Temple, because, money having been paid for learning, it was right that I should oversee the end of the matter. They resolved my doubts most clearly. I had a fear that, perhaps, I came because I wished to see thee—misguided by the red mist of affection. It is not so. . . . Moreover, I am troubled by a Dream."

That simple, wise, venerable figure is one of Kipling's most adorable creations, and pairs beautifully with his young disciple. "Never," he says, "never was such a *chela*. Temperate, kindly, wise, of ungrudging disposition, a merry heart upon the road, never forgetting, learned, truthful, courteous. Great is his reward." For they end their pilgrimage together, and the Lama enters into his rest. "He crossed his hands on his lap and smiled, as a man may who has won Salvation for himself and his beloved."

Native types

It is a tale that never flags in the varied interests that absorbed the two sides of Kipling's brain—the mystic soul of the East and the ordering intelligence of the West are symbolized in a story that holds the least initiated reader in the grip of its kaleidoscopic romance. Creighton Sahib and our old acquaintance Strickland are of a now familiar stamp; but the swarms of Orientals in their inexhaustible variety are hit off with unfailing individualizing touches. Kipling is all but a humorist in the scenes with the old lady of Kulu and the Woman of Shamleigh and her submissive husbands; but the reader is inclined to make friends with Hurree Chunder Mookerjee in spite of the quizzing of his "Babudom." It is Hurree who tracks down and discomfits the pair of Russian agents who have mapped out the terrain for a coming invasion by the Tsar, an exciting story, admirably told, if only another fine frenzy of Kipling's Russophobia. He hated the Russians as fiercely as Conrad did; and when he is credited with having foreseen the Great War it should be remembered that it was Russia he was most afraid of. Many stories that do not seem so were alarmist admonitions. "The Russian shindy," as someone says in *The Story of the Gadsbys*, was always "ready to come to a head at five minutes' notice."[1] A more sub-substantial pendant to the farcical Hurree is the great horse-dealer Mahbub Ali,[2] "whose caravans penetrated far and far into the Back of Beyond," and who as one of the most formidable players in the Great Game might have upon him at any moment documents in cipher compared with which "dynamite was milky and innocuous." But "Mahbub had no particular desire to die by violence, because two or three family blood-feuds across the border hung unfinished on his hands, and when these scores were cleared he intended to settle down as a more or less virtuous citizen." It is up among the hills on the edge of Tibet that the later episodes have their setting, and Kipling's pen transmits the very sensations

[1] One of the Russians heavily pronounces on the loquacious Hurree: "He represents *in petto* (*sic*) India in transition—the monstrous hybridism of East and West. . . . It is we who can deal with Orientals" (chap. xiii.). Of course, lots of people believed in "The Russian bogey" then. H. W. Nevinson says (*Fire of Life*, 155), it "had distracted our foreign policy for fifty years," and it was not till about the epoch of the Russo-Japanese war that it proved "but an illuminated turnip," and the Russian steam-roller "would neither steam nor roll." But Kipling was looked upon as a first-hand authority, and certainly ought to have known better.

[2] Mahbub Ali, in "The Ballad of the King's Jest" (*Barrack-room Ballads*) observes:

"I sought a word of a Russian post,
Of a shifty promise, an unsheathed sword
And a grey-coat guard on the Helmund ford."

of those colossal depths and heights. When the Ao-chung man throws the empty whisky-bottle out of the window—"'No need to listen for the fall. This is the world's end,' he said, and swung off. The lama looked forth, a hand on either sill, with eyes that shone like yellow opals. From the enormous pit before him white peaks lifted themselves yearning in the moonlight. The rest was as the darkness of interstellar space." In the village clinging to Shamleigh hill it was "like sitting in a swallow's nest under the eaves of the roof of the world." There are many such vignettes, caught, as it were, in a crystal beam of unrefracting light.

The Puck stories

Puck of Pook's Hill (1906) and its sequel, *Rewards and Fairies* (1910), were, if not a new kind of literature, a new amalgam of history with the magic that transfigures and interprets. It is not historical romance, but imaginative re-creation, inspired by a patriotic love of the very soil. The drama of the past is called up again in all its vivid actuality by the bold and simple device of letting Puck and old Romans and Danes, Saxons and Normans, gods and heroes, kings and queens, walk into the play which Dan and Una are performing in their little rustic theatre under Chanctonbury Ring, in a region drenched with history and legend.[1] Kipling goes back right to the Stone Age, and tells of the rout of the beast when man invented the knife of iron. He comes down to the dawning nineteenth century. And everything is didactically expounded according to his own simple philosophy, prejudices and all. The Norman conquest was just a friendly coalition with the Saxons. Henry VII was simply one of those men who cannot help doing the wrong thing. There were trade unions even in his days, which would not let men do an honest day's work. Says Mr Springett, in the same story, "The Wrong Thing," "If a man has his private spite laid up against you, the Unions give him his excuse for working it off." Kipling's ethical creed is writ large throughout; and one of the inset poems, "If—," is a famous and inspiring outburst:

[1] *Rewards and Fairies* was hailed when it was new by Dixon Scott as the possible forerunner of a new kind of fiction perfectly and incomparably suited to Kipling ("The Meekness of Mr Rudyard Kipling," 1912, *Ibid.*, 60–61). Hubert Bland thoroughly disliked both the Puck books (*Essays by Hubert*, 48).

If you can dream—and not make dreams your master;
    If you can think—and not make thoughts your aim,
If you can meet with Triumph and Disaster
    And treat those two impostors just the same;
If you can bear to hear the truth you've spoken
    Twisted by knaves to make a trap for fools,
Or watch the things you gave your life to, broken,
    And stoop and build 'em up with worn-out tools . . .

And yet, in his simple exposition of Norman economics—"This is craft and cunning such as I love"—Kipling cherishes and exalts those very material interests which Conrad denounced as the bane of our civilization. He is a thorough Anglo-Norman, with his guileless version of a conquest which is still going on. And, as in "The Man who would be King" and many more of his Indian stories, he is a good Freemason; in "The Winged Hats," for instance, he traces back the secret Word to Roman times at least—"the Word that belongs to the degree of Gryphons in the science of Mithras my God." [1]

Later stories—the machine

A leading feature of the stories in and after *The Day's Work* (1898) is that so many are about modern machinery and those constructive works which are parallel examples of orderliness and working efficiency. It is the same in his poetry. Kipling was tending more and more to identify the virtues most to be prized in mankind with the mechanical qualities of precision and efficiency. In verse or in prose, the gospel he taught was a gospel of action: his ethics were fundamentally a matter of the adequacy and effectuality of the action performed. Man must above all be efficient; order, discipline, obedience are for the sake of efficiency. Wherefore it is his first duty to be intelligent, observant, enduring, and honest towards his fellow-workers. The idle classes hardly count—"those first-class passengers" of "M'Andrews' Hymn." But Kipling would never have admitted that the classes he revered were without their appointed task. Whatever that task might be, he envisaged it as a piece of constructive work allotted by the Deity:

[1] His stories are full of direct or indirect allusions to the Craft. Perhaps it was Freemasonry, into which he had been initiated at Lahore before he was twenty-one, that gave him his liking for symbolism—in the esoteric more than the poetic sense.

Who, lest all thought of Eden fade,
Bring'st Eden to the craftsman's brain—
Godlike to muse o'er his own Trade
And manlike stand with God again![1]

He was a firm believer in progress. This was the great age of machines, and so the great age of progress. Observe the air of almost personal triumph when he introduces some new invention, wireless or aeroplanes, or some vast display of organized force, like the two great fleets in "Their Lawful Occasions." Machines to him were the most romantic thing in modern life, as he avows in the oft-quoted "Romance brought up the Nine-fifteen." But the great point was that machinery exhibits the highest form of what he most desiderated, efficiency. And how? Through its perfect subordination to the purpose for which it exists. So the machine gave him a measure and a rule for mankind. Let them be as orderly, obedient, and hence as efficient, and the ultimate good is assured. It is an ethic, not so much of conduct, kindness, goodness, regard for one's fellows, as of action, in the material sense. This, as much as anything, was the basis of his imperialism: the English were to show modern efficiency at its highest pitch of development, and extend its blessings by persuasion or, if need be, otherwise, to the rest of the world. It may have been the basis of his religion; for after we have laboured well for a life-time,

We shall rest, and, faith, we shall need it—lie down for an æon or two,
Till the Master of All Good Workmen shall put us to work anew![2]

Such is the refrain of the great canticle "M'Andrews' Hymn."

I mind the time we used to serve a broken pipe wi' tow.
Ten pound was all the pressure then—Eh! Eh!—a man wad drive;
An' here, our workin' gauges give one hunder fifty-five!
We're creepin' on wi' each new rig—less weight an' larger power:
There'll be the loco-boiler next an' thirty knots an hour!
Thirty an' more. What I ha' seen since ocean-steam began
Leaves me no doot for the machine: but what about the man?
The man that counts, wi' all his runs, one million miles o' sea:
Four times the span from earth to moon. . . . How far, O Lord, from Thee?

[1] "My New-cut Ashlar" (*Life's Handicap*). [2] L'Envoi to *Barrack-room Ballads*.

It is the apotheosis of order, precision, discipline, efficiency.

Fra skylight lift to furnace-bars, backed, bolted, braced an' stayed,
An' singin' like the Mornin' Stars for joy that they are made;
While, out o' touch o' vanity, the sweatin' thrust-block says:
"Not unto us the praise, or man—not unto us the praise!"
Now, a' together, hear them lift their lesson—theirs an' mine:
"Law, Orrder, Duty an' Restraint, Obedience, Discipline!"
Mill, forge an' try-pit taught them that when roarin' they arose,
An' whiles I wonder if a soul was gied them wi' the blows.

The exploits of a steamer, in "The Ship that Found Herself," of a locomotive, in "·007," of an engineer on his beam-ends, in "The Devil and the Deep Sea," [1] of the English in India engaged in vast enterprises and fighting against incompetence, superstition, and what almost seems the malice of nature, in "The Bridge-Builders" and many another story, in *The Day's Work* or elsewhere, keep up the parable. The last-named story goes off into vision, which would have enforced Kipling's reiterated lesson much better had it been less laboured and pragmatical. "William the Conqueror," a twofold story of which the titular hero is a woman, is of English fortitude and devotion in a cholera epidemic. "I like men who do things," says William. These are the obscure, overworked and badly paid, unhonoured toilers, who are the ones that keep the Empire going. There are more tales of like inspiration in *Traffics and Discoveries* (1904), including "Steam Tactics," "Wireless," and "The Bonds of Discipline," in which the comic side comes uppermost and Mr Pyecroft resumes his drolleries. "The Army of a Dream" is a militarist "Utopia"; Kipling prescribes universal service as the cure for all social ills.

Kipling's gods

Kipling recognizes and salutes all the gods, the gods of every tribe and nation; for God to him is simply the source and sustainer of the law. "When man has come to the turnstiles of Night," he says in the preface to *Life's Handicap*,

[1] "Surely the limit of what may be termed *allegorical realism* is passed in the story of 'The Ship that Found Herself,' where there is an indiscriminate endowment of life and personality on every individual bolt and rivet" (James Oliphant, *Victorian Novelists*, 237). It is put rather ponderously, not to say ungrammatically, but there is something in it. Kipling did not foresee that the machine age led ultimately to the state of decivilization satirized in Aldous Huxley's *Brave New World*.

"all the creeds in the world seem to him wonderfully alike and colourless." And in *Kim* there is that ingenuous conversation with Mahbub:

"What am I? Mussulman, Hindu, Jain, or Buddhist? That is a hard nut."

"Thou art beyond question an unbeliever, and therefore thou wilt be damned. So says my Law—or I think it does. But thou art also my little Friend of all the World, and I love thee. So says my heart. This matter of creeds is like horse-flesh. The wise man knows horses are good—that there is profit to be made from all; and for myself—but that I am a good Sunni and hate the men of Tirah—I could believe the same of all the Faiths. . . . Therefore I say in my heart the Faiths are like horses. Each has merit in its own country."

So even the Red Gods of the Indians have their call for the young men.[1] Poseidon is for the Greek mariner:

"Mariner," said he,
"Behold a law immutable I lay on thee and thine,
That never shall ye act or tell a falsehood at my shrine." [2]

In "The Children of the Zodiac," as long ago as *Many Inventions*, he had symbolized the commerce between the less implacable of the celestial powers and man, whereby the latter learns to live his life in defiance of death, by virtue of fraternal loyalty. In "They," and "The Brushwood Boy," and "The Wish-House," he leads the way into a region of our spiritual consciousness to which he seems to attribute objective reality, though he makes no pretence of unravelling its mysteries. Neither one nor the other, the European nor the Oriental mind, had secrets for Kipling. He reveals the soul of the Eastern mystic by joining in his dreams, facing the ultimate mysteries which remain inscrutable. The reader goes hand in hand with him to the ultimate limits of the intelligible, to the point where further questioning is vain. For Kipling never tries to rationalize a universe which, beyond the sphere where law and obedience suffice for man's guidance and render

[1] "The Feet of the Young Men" (*The Five Nations*).
[2] "Poseidon's Law" (*Traffics and Discoveries*).

existence orderly and fruitful, cannot be understood. In contemplating that outer region "there is nothing to hold by except submission and resignation." The knowingness of his precocious youth did not shut his eyes to the vastness of man's ignorance; he acknowledged the limits and bowed before the unknowable. Man himself is intelligible; but man is involved in a world of inscrutable forces and surrounded by impenetrable darkness. So we must accept a "Grand Overseer" who sanctifies such a mode of life as makes the best of our limited nature and is the likeliest way of securing the available good, whatsoever that may prove to be. So far his philosophy of life coincides with Browning's doctrine of steady work:

> And the sin I impute to each frustrate ghost
> Is—the unlit lamp and the ungirt loin,
> Though the end in sight was a vice, I say.

The Lord of Hosts

In war-time, our prayers will be to the Lord of Hosts. Kipling, at the dramatic moment, could be as pious as anyone; he could feel and display the right fervour and unction in the terms of a national creed. And this without a jot of insincerity. Hence the mighty success of his "Recessional," written at the Diamond Jubilee, a solemn admonition to the "chosen people" to beware of pride and self-confidence.[1] It was the time when the first Chamberlain was enjoining upon them to "think imperially." But there was no hint that it might perhaps not have been by divine behest that they were singled out for an imperial lot—"Dominion over palm and pine." It appealed to devotees of hymnology by qualities more akin to Moody and Sankey than to poetry.[2] Kipling was a veteran myth-maker,

[1] "A poem in which Kipling's humility, even, is noticeably dictatorial" (A. C. Ward, *The Modern Short Story*, 119). Cp. Chevrillon, "une si orgueilleuse humilité."

[2] "This feeling culminated in the Jubilee of 1897, which was a corroboree in adoration of the great god Jingo. The chief priest was Kipling, whose tales and poems were glorifications of the soldier, intermixed with exhortations to 'give hell' to those who, like the wicked animal, had the impudence to defend themselves when attacked. At the same time, it is true, the high priest did not disdain to play the part of warning prophet. No sooner was the frantic revel over than he urged us not to forget the God in whose service and by whose help these conquests had been won. But that he spoke in English, and spoke of God instead of Allah, he might have been a Mahommedan imam crying to the true believers to go forth and offer the infidel the choice between the *Koran* and death. It was useless for another poet to point out that most of the conquests had been made

as so many of his stories, as well as his poems, have shown: he was prepared to draw upon any of the mythologies, according to the country and clime in which he found himself. His gods are symbols of energies and laws that he perceives at work everywhere:

> My brother kneels, so saith Kabir,
> To stone and brass in heathen-wise,
> But in my brother's voice I hear
> My own unanswered agonies.
> His God is as his fates assign,
> His prayer is all the world's—and mine.[1]

Bow down, then, and obey; and what will you earn? Heaven—immortality? As to that, there is no answer from Kipling. But you will have a chance of worldly prosperity, and you will achieve yourself. Perhaps you will make good a soul, where, as Browning put it, "a soul can be discerned." But, come what may, if you have waited and trusted and borne trials and injustices as was required of you in "If—," then—

> Yours is the Earth and everything that's in it,
> And—which is more—you'll be a Man, my son![2]

His last story-books

There was no falling off in craftsmanship in Kipling's ultimate collections of stories; what they suffer from is rather that the craftsmanship is too obtrusive: some of those, for instance, in *Debits and Credits* (1926) are, so to speak, technique *et preterea nihil.* But the style that he had made for himself, constructed out of elements hardly to be found elsewhere, is as accomplished as ever. He was still living in Sussex. This,

when we forgot, or for others to remark that 'the lesser breeds without the law' were hardly likely to accept the Bible from the conqueror's left hand when they saw the sword in the right. We were the Chosen People, the 'lesser breeds' were, if not Amalekites to be slaughtered, yet Gibeonites to be our hewers of wood and drawers of water: and they ought to jump at the privilege" (E. E. Kellett, *As I Remember*, 167–168).

[1] "The Prayer" (*Kim*).

[2] A brief but searching study of Kipling's fundamental unbelief, by Professor Denis Saurat, appeared in *Marsyas* (February, 1936, p. 864): "Il a exploité des thèmes littéraires sans aucune honte, sans que quiconque, dans l'œuvre d'art finie, puisse découvrir une seule paille révélant le vide intérieur. C'est dire qu'en tant qu'artiste il a atteint la perfection—à ce niveau. Son scepticisme foncier et total, il l'a mis dans *l'homme qui voulut être roi*, et dans *Kim*, et dans beaucoup d'autres récits; ce n'est qu'en méditant ceux-là que nous découvrons la perfection des autres, de ceux où, artiste suprême, il nous fait presque croire ce qu'il ne croit pas."

in fact, was the period of "They," the two Puck story-books, and a good deal of verse telling of the fine old world he had discovered there. Sussex is the site of "An Habitation Enforced," the first item in *Actions and Reactions* (1909). This is, as it were, the obverse to "An Error in the Fourth Dimension," in *The Day's Work*, which brought out, almost in the manner of Henry James, American incapacity to comprehend the English point of view. Here, also, American and English manners, mentality, and ruling ideas, appear in all their astronomical opposition.

"My dear," says the sympathizing Englishwoman, and the compelling tone dropped to a soothing gurgle, "d'you suppose I don't know how it feels to come to a strange county—country I should say—away from one's own people? When I first left the Shires—I'm Shropshire, you know—I cried for a day and a night. But fretting doesn't make loneliness any better."

The millionaire and his wife somehow fit themselves into the new order, all which is very amusing; but the further proposition, that they have by pure chance happened upon the very estate which the ancestors of one of them came from, may do in a fantasy like "The Brushwood Boy," but is surely "enforced" too violently here. The beatific wonders of modern invention are carried forward to the year A.D. 2000 in "With the Night Mail"; Kipling never discovered triteness in that theme. Psychical imaginations in "The House Surgeon" are perhaps less moving than the simple statement of a common event in "An Habitation Enforced":

Iggulden sat in his chair by the fire, a thistle-spud between his knees, his head drooped. Though she had never seen death before, her heart, that missed a beat, told her that he was dead. She did not speak or cry, but stood outside the door, and the dog licked her hand. When he threw up his nose, she heard herself saying: "Don't howl! Please don't begin to howl, Scottie, or I shall run away!"

Then, Mulvaney, Ortheris, and Learoyd make a new appearance in "Garm—a Hostage," and have not changed a feature in all these years; and Kipling's old divination of the un-commonest shapes of idiosyncrasy is shown once more in the mighty slave-dealer, in "A Deal in Cotton." Stalky and Beetle return to life in *A Diversity of Creatures* (1917), together with Sikhs, Gurkhas, and other Indian natives recalling *Kim*; and the occult looks in again, in two or three stories. But the great feature of this volume is the series of elaborate farces. In *Debits and Credits* (1926) the Great War is always in the background, even when it is not the actual theme; it gave even Kipling his fill of fighting and patriotic self-sacrifice. Besides "The Wish-House," there is a characteristic piece of other-worldly experiences stated and actualized in terms of the vulgarest realism, "A Madonna of the Trenches." The story is extracted in spasmodic bursts of confession from a shell-shocked, hysterical boy under chloroform, and the hideous and ghoulish surroundings of corpse-lined trenches and abandoned dug-outs give a strange force by their incongruousness to a flaming conception of romantic love. The boy had seen the woman's ghost at the very moment of her tryst with the man who slew himself to be with her. Now he knows "what reel things reelly mean!" To go back to life and his commonplace sweetheart as if he had not had that glimpse of heaven and hell is unthinkable. It is here that occurs Kipling's fine criticism of Jane Austen, the little story called "The Janeites." But his cleverness plainly overreaches itself several times in *Limits and Renewals* (1932); the intricate technique and the encyclopædic knowledge get in the reader's way and clog the threads. "Dayspring Mishandled" is about the hoax on a Chaucerian scholar, who is made to believe that he has discovered a new text. In "The Woman in his Life," a dog fascinates an overworked inventor, and cures him of hallucinations set up by his life in the trenches. Then, in "The Church that was in Antioch," vivid scenes are reconstructed of early Christian and Jewish feuds, in which Paul and Peter and a young Roman police-officer figure. "The Manner of Men" is of the same era. Kipling reverts to farce in "Aunt Ellen," which, however, is so intricate and recondite that it provokes the demand whether he had a normal sense of humour at all.

From first to last, Kipling was a journalist. Be it said

Still a journalist

without the slightest depreciation of his literary genius. It was the peculiar form which that genius took. The realism which first brought him notice was that of the highly proficient reporter, who succeeded in making his public see and feel the things described.[1] In a word, it was realism of the sensational kind. From his first years to his last, he could give his readers the nearest possible duplicate in words to the rage and blood-thirst of the hand-to-hand combat, the filth and horrors and ghastly unburied carnage of the battlefield, the wellnigh unimaginable terrors of a haunted soul. He retails it all as sheer hard fact; it is always as if he had seen and been thunder-struck by the phenomenon himself. Whatever the subject, the impression is that he knows all about it, and so what he states has instant acceptance. The very glibness of his narrative style is corroborative evidence. Though he tried more complicated modes of story-telling in his later work, these characteristics never failed; they were the cogent qualities of his realism. Nor did he ever drop the absorbed attention to current affairs, to public events, that is, which is second nature to those of the profession. Half his stories, at least, are in this sense a "criticism of life." Even the excursions into history are a comment on the present. Until his death, he was an oracle whose views were sought at times of crisis, or who communicated them spontaneously in a poem or a public speech. The Great War came, as he had foreseen; and he confessed his apprehensions of further war with Germany in his last poem, "The Cyclone," in 1932.

The common man

The journalist writes for the man in the crowd, and is presumably most interested in him. Kipling assuredly was. Whilst other novelists were going out of their way to explore and depict abnormal products of civilized or uncivilized existence, complex minds, subtle and unstable temperaments, the over-sensitive, the morbid, the aberrations from the common order, Kipling shunned the uncommon and abstruse, and, even more than such contemporaries as Arnold Bennett and Galsworthy, demonstrated the ample and sufficing interest

[1] "En ce temps de sa jeunesse, Kipling écrit parfois comme sous l'impulsion d'un démon" (Chevrillon, *Kipling*, 40).

of the ordinary man. There is not a single character in his stories who is incredible or hard to fathom. Even the wildest and most outlandish are types, not, like most of Conrad's, rare and anomalous beings, and perhaps unique. The strangeness that he aimed at was in the circumstance and the ways of life or the extraordinary incidents. Whilst he fought shy of exceptional characters, like most experts in the short story he revelled in exceptional concatenations of events. It was the common and even the primitive man that he preferred to represent, and oft-times vulgarity thoroughly pleased with itself was depicted by Kipling without a hint of disapproval. His figures are so lifelike they are recognized at sight—a sign of their commonness. Yet, with all their commonness, those among them in whom interest centres are complete personalities, and, without any self-assertion, have a dignity all their own, and show an integrity of character and a loyalty to their duty and their fellows that stamp them as peculiarly his. Those three privates and the Stricklands and other unpretending heroes of the harassed civilian services are not people of temperament or rare intellectual gifts. Theirs are essentially the simple virtues; but Kipling was a judge of what is sterling, and knew what he was doing in putting them into his triptych and into his most memorable stories, not once but over and over again.[1] And, though he never seems to be attending to their inner life, he knows by a sort of divination grounded in fellow-feeling exactly what their thoughts are, and without any visible effort constrains the reader to think and feel the same. Hence, in spite of the contrast between his method of characterization and Hardy's or Conrad's, it is fallacious to regard these creations of his as superficial. George Moore's saying, "That which is firmly and clearly imagined needs no psychology," does not of course mean that what he calls "psychology" is omitted or ignored. The great art is to

[1] Mr Dobrée calls them aristocrats, they realize their own values with such a hearty disdain for the appreciation of others. "It is that kind of individuality, that kind of integrity, proud and secure in its own fortress, which constitutes the aristocracy which alone is worth while, which alone can play the Great Game of actuality. An aristocrat is, for Mr Kipling, one who, whatever his race or caste or creed, has a full man within him" (*The Lamp and the Lute*, 50).

convince that it is working punctually and infallibly without saying a word about it.

Journalistic failings

At the beginning, his precocity, combined with an aptness at hitting the nail on the head and saying the very thing required, his magical, unerring craftsmanship, and assured application of the moral, seemed the obvious marks of one of those rare geniuses who appear now and again to electrify the world and help to change the current of history. These were his characteristics right to the end. Undoubtedly, he did make history or at least help to shape it. Some results of his mighty appeal to his age, however, must now be regarded with misgivings. There is always a latent bias in the mind of the journalist; that was why C. E. Montague and Cunninghame Graham were only minor men of letters. The journalist has a case to make out. Kipling's was the British Empire; a big one, but not one of the universals of art. Hence the absurdity of comparing him to Shakespeare. His bias happened to be the popular one, and so it passed unrebuked, and indeed almost unremarked. So, too, his belief in progress and his craze for machinery corresponded with almost everybody's of his period. Production, production—to what end? To ensure more production. The one obvious result is that man is machine-ridden, and the great majority are tending to be machine-made. Paradoxically, his appeals were often based on grounds which misled himself. As Chesterton pointed out, the militarism that he preached was derived, not from "the idea of courage, but the idea of discipline" [1]; and his patriotism was only an extension of the same thing: "He admires England because she is strong, not because she is England." It was the Empire as a heaven-sent instrument for disciplining the entire globe that engaged his devotion, and put his into quite a different category from the patriotism of the Boers or the Irish fighting against foreign domination.[2] The result of all his admonitory eloquence was to make the Britisher more satisfied with himself. The pharisaic conviction of his "Song of the English" and "The White Man's Burden" is scarcely

[1] *Heretics*, "On Mr Rudyard Kipling and making the world small" (44–45).
[2] *Ibid.*, 48–49.

mitigated by the penitential attitudinizing of the "Recessional." Both directly and indirectly, Kipling is largely responsible for the reduced esteem and even jealousy and indignation felt towards us now by the "Gentiles." It is his poetry chiefly that has done us this disservice; but his fiction, though not so full of quotable aphorisms, is almost as plain a statement of this aggressive attitude. Many of his stories could not have been more polemical and irritating to the "lesser breeds" if they had been deliberately framed as pamphlets—in truth, some allowance might then have been made for their controversial nature. He is usually arrogant and very rarely urbane in his remarks on the inferior races.

Limits of his comprehension

Kipling, in fact, was a much narrower-minded person than he looks at the first glance. His interests were far-reaching; but his thinking was not so penetrating and infallible as he and his more fervid admirers believed. He had the gifts of the heaven-born journalist, with something superadded; which was, however, not the universality of the philosophic mind but the quickening imagination of the poet. Prejudices can be forgiven to a poet, together with some lacunæ in the argument. Swift comprehension of whatever strikes upon an alert eye was the secret of his realism. Unfailing intelligence was Mowgli's secret and also Kim's, the two of his creations that embody most of himself. Both are born with it; both, even as infants, are wideawake, receptive, shrewd; they see everything that is going on, and learn with a rapidity that astounds their elders. Kipling's swift, wide-angled vision, to which no subject or object came amiss; his generous attitude towards all things and all varieties of men, so long as they refrained from hostilities, give the impression of a more humane philosopher than he really was. His was a practical philosophy, and hence almost necessarily a shallow one. He reiterates a few simple ideas, with great force but often small insight. He had, in fact, more foresight, which is a practical talent, than insight; even *Kim* and the *Jungle Books* would hardly disprove this. As Chesterton observed, he fails to perceive the real significance of much that rivets his attention; hence many a false note, of praise or reproof. Versed in the wisdom of the ages, he treasured most those maxims which enable man to keep his head in a world of doubts, mistrusts, and bitter regrets, and still find something to live for. Acceptance, never revolt; submission to the powers that be and that have been consecrated by ages of respect: this is his set policy. His superlative common sense and his sureness of touch have very naturally credited him with a vision far more searching. At all events, he was honest to himself. He was well aware of the paradoxes of existence, and that man cannot help being haunted by the spectre that all is vanity. If those who are hot for certainties will not recognize his fundamental scepticism, it is not from any insincerity on Kipling's part. And the affirmative articles of his creed, his faith in duty, loyalty, and service, were at any rate a wholesome doctrine to embody in such enthralling shapes.[1]

[1] For severe but not unjust criticism of Kipling's failings, especially the circumscribed nature of his vision and his fanatical glorification of the unregenerate Britisher, see "Rudyard Kipling" (*The Lamp and the Lute*, by Bonamy Dobree) and "The Decadence of Rudyard Kipling" (*Essays by Hubert*, by Hubert Bland). His "boy-scout mentality," jingoism, and idealization of everything English, in comparison with which foreigners are almost always blackguards and their works detestable, are rudely stripped of their pretences by Philip Henderson (*The Novel of To-day*, 248–249). For the actual truth, the reader is referred to Lester Hutchinson's *Conspiracy at Meerut*, or Mulk Raj Amand's *Untouchable* and *The Coolie*. "As a glorified detective-story, *Kim* is entertaining enough; as a picture of life in India it is quite fantastic."

CHAPTER IV

THE SCOTS GROUP AND SOME IRISH

MacDonald and the "Kailyard School"

KIPLING and Conrad and the more elderly Henry James, Hardy, and Stevenson, were all competing at the circulating libraries when, for a season or two during the eighteen-nineties, they were dislodged from favour by a group of Scottish writers nicknamed, only half in disrespect, the "Kailyard School." For the chronicling of the pathos and humour of domestic life in the Scottish lowlands was an established branch of fiction. It was as old as the modern novel, dating from Smollett and Mackenzie in the eighteenth, and from Scott, Galt, Moir, and Susan Ferrier at the beginning of the nineteenth century. A gap was always perceptible when no one of eminence appeared to carry on the tradition. This time, there was no long hiatus, for whilst the last four were still alive and publishing books, George MacDonald (1824–1905) was born, who must be greeted as the immediate progenitor of the latest group, even if at the time his paternity went all but unrecognized in the fuss made over Crockett, Barrie, and "Ian Maclaren." He was Gaelic on both sides, and a descendant of some of those MacDonalds who escaped from the massacre of Glencoe. Brought up for the ministry, he won some university distinctions and took charge of a Congregationalist chapel. But he speedily rebelled against the narrow dogmas of Calvinist theology, and threw up his post, though he continued most of his life to preach as a layman in various pulpits. He was poor; and he turned to writing as a means of livelihood, supplementing it with lecturing, preaching, and other work of that kind, till after a strenuous life hampered by ill-health he died at an advanced age. After two volumes of poetry having some affinity to Browning's, came his first prose work, *Phantastes, a faerie romance* (1858), which like Meredith's *Shaving of Shagpat* of three years before, but without the humour and the Oriental extravagance, teaches a lesson of courage and self-control. His fairy-stories, for this was followed at intervals by the tragic love-tale *The Portent, a story of second sight* (1864), the more playful though by no means frivolous story-books for children, *The Light Princess* (1867), *At the Back of the North Wind* (1870), and *The Princess and the Goblin* (1871), and similar things in prose or verse or in both, are, with his poems in common English or in broad Scots, the clearest expression of his spiritual view of the world and of his war with materialism. The Celtic element is as evident in them as it is in the old Celtic romances afterwards collected or reconstituted by "Fiona Macleod," or the Irish myths and legends given a more glorious lease of life by W. B. Yeats and his collaborators. But MacDonald's versions of the ancient legends are more didactic, if at his best he is as gracefully and unobtrusively so as Hans Andersen himself. To him, the love and beauty to be perceived in human existence and in external nature were the symbols and the gateway to the ultimate spiritual beauty. The religion which he preached and which brought him into collision with the authorities was a very practical religion: one must live Christianity, not merely believe it. A mysticism akin to Crashaw and Vaughan's is set forth in such a poem as "The Diary of an old Soul." The gem among the stories is "The Golden Key," albeit that of the redemption of the vampire-woman Lilith is fuller of his deepest thought. *The Princess and the Goblin* and *The Princess and Curdie* have the lightness and playfulness of the fairy-tale at its best and most serene. Barrie may have owed not a little to MacDonald for the quaint fancy and charm of *Peter Pan* and the more sophisticated fantasias that link on with it. But the genealogy of that engaging sprite and of the elfin strain generally in Barrie goes back to Hogg, the historian of Bonnie Kilmeny, and to still older poets and adepts in fairy lore.

When he started novel-writing, George Eliot was at her

meridian, and MacDonald adopted the same manner of showing causation and the same solid and ponderous structure, notably in that powerful spiritual biography *Robert Falconer* (1868), which is the fullest manifesto of his beliefs and a criticism of the obtuse dogmatism and spiritual blindness, not merely of Calvinism, but of all the churches. What he was driving at is summed up in the little girl's exclamation, "He's Jesus Christ!" MacDonald contended that Providence will do all that is best for us if we put our trust in God. But the reader cannot help feeling that the contrivances by which the situation is so often saved are not less improbable than many of the events of a different tendency with which Thomas Hardy enforces an exactly opposite view. Dooble Sammie, with his love for his old fiddle, and the Calvinist grandmother, brimming over with affection which she thinks it her duty to repress, and many others too, are appealing figures, though Shargar turns out to be little more than a reflection of Robert. In *David Elginbrod* (1863) and *Alec Forbes of Howglen* (1865), MacDonald had already delineated the humble villagers and engaging humours of Aberdeenshire, in a manner that set the pattern for the future "Kailyarders," though a vein of mysticism and of ethical teaching predominated. The latter novel was indeed a kind of Pilgrim's Progress. He followed Scott and Galt in the humorous use of dialect, erring perhaps on the side of literal reproduction. It was the same with the more romantic *Malcolm* (1875) and its sequel, *The Marquis of Lossie* (1877), with *Thomas Wingfold, Curate* (1876), telling of a conversion from mere lip-service, and a sort of sequel to this, *Paul Faber, Surgeon* (1879). Perhaps, *Sir Gibbie* (1879) and *Heather and Snow* (1893) are the best of his subsequent novels.

The novels

It should not be forgotten that the prolific, very unequal, but far from negligible Mrs Oliphant (1828–1897) was of Scottish birth and began her long career with a brace of novels in a milder and tenderer version of the manner of Galt, *Passages in the Life of Mistress Margaret Maitland* (1849) and *Lilliesleaf* (1856). They were praised by Jeffery, and were followed by *Katie Stewart* (1856), a tale of Fifeshire about the

Some other Scots

time of the Forty-five.[1] That old favourite of childhood, Mrs Molesworth (1839–1921), was also Scottish; and Charles Reade, who ought to have known, said, "Any chapter of *The Cuckoo Clock* or the enchanting *Adventures of Herr Baby* is worth a shoal of the very best novels dealing with the characters and fortunes of mere adults." [2] William Black (1841–1898), fashionable at the circulating libraries, hardly counts as a faithful delineator of northern characters and manners; and James Grant (1822–1887) forgot his Scottishness in spinning romantic military tales that might begin with Killiecrankie or Sauchieburn, Covenanters or Jacobites, but usually flitted off to the Continent or even the Orient. Enough has already been said about Stevenson, perhaps; here it need only be added that *Kidnapped* and its sequel and *The Master of Ballantrae* are thoroughly Scottish novels, "Thrawn Janet" is a masterpiece in broad Scots; and, at the very time Barrie and "Ian Maclaren" were thrilling and seducing the English and American public, he retaliated upon their amiable sentimentalities with his tragic *Weir of Hermiston* (1896), and its pictures of old Edinburgh and the moorlands dark with memories of martyred Cameronians. Neil Munro, too, was almost as good at drawing a Lowlander and making him speak his right vernacular as at a Highlander of his own breed, as his *Ayrshire Idylls* (1912) show. Then such natives as Henrietta Keddie (1827–1914), who wrote under the name of "Sarah Tytler," author of *St Mungo's City* (1885) and *Logie Town* (1887), cultivated the "Kailyard" before it became classic ground, and in fact went on doing so when the nickname had gone out of fashion. Scottish novelists are remarkably long-lived and keep going right to the last. One who was not a novelist except as a diversion, the learned Sir John Skelton (1831–1897), author of *Maitland of Lethington and the Scotland of Mary Stuart* (1887–1888), *Essays of Shirley* (1885), and *The Table-Talk of Shirley* (1895–1896), included in this latter miscellany, which he called as a variant "Summers and Winters at Balmawhapple," some

[1] Later, she wrote *The Minister's Wife* (1869), *The Ladies Lindores* (1883) and *Kirsteen* (1890); the last is discussed by Henry James in *Notes on Novelists* (1914). Mrs Oliphant is treated at length in Chapter V (see p. 199 *et seq*).

[2] *Miscellanies*, 294.

semi-historical tales and character-studies of the Border which entitle him to a place beside his more popular compeers for both their truth and raciness and their literary grace.

J. M. Barrie

The chiefs of the "Kailyard School" were James Matthew Barrie (1860–1937), Samuel Rutherford Crockett (1860–1914), and the Rev. John Watson (1850–1907), better known as "Ian Maclaren." Barrie, the only one of the group whose work has much chance of survival, created his delectable village of Thrums out of memories of his birthplace, Kirriemuir, in Forfarshire; Crockett's particular domain was Galloway, and Ian Maclaren's "Cranford" was the village of Drumtochy, somewhere on the border of Lowlands and Highlands. Barrie's pre-eminence was due to a genius which transcended local and personal interests, in his later novels and in his plays. He became the ultra-modern exponent of an older and more specific order of fiction, the novel of sentiment, founded by Sterne, whose devoutest disciple was Barrie's countryman Henry Mackenzie, author of *The Man of Feeling*. The whole group made a cult of sentimentalism; this was their outstanding quiddity, and their excesses eventually made them a byword. But Barrie was able to outgo the mere sentimental idyll, and with a finer art handle a more subtilized affair, the comedy of sentiment. He handled it so well because he was himself a sentimentalist: of that he makes no secret and tolerates no reproach. The favourite child of his genius, Tommy Sandys, just like himself as biographer of his mother Margaret Ogilvy, says things freely that an Englishman would never utter aloud, even on the rack of acutest personal suffering. And what he does is often enough incomprehensible to the Southron. It is a commonplace that every true satirist, from Juvenal down to Thackeray, has been more than suspect of a leaning towards the vice that he is most given to rebuking; as to comedy, there could be no such thing without some positive sympathy. His creator certainly loves Tommy, loves him as his own offspring, a bit of himself—he is perfectly candid about it. It is not only in *Margaret Ogilvy*, the history of his mother and himself, that it is impossible to separate the man from his books. Few who have not written avowed autobiography, and not so very many who have, were ever such bountiful self-revealers.[1] Those of his characters which are chips of his own personality are recognized at sight, if only through his always being too hard on them; others, too, have the marks of being sketched from real life, and the reader flatters himself that he could point out the very place where personal experiences have been worked into the story. Here lies, in fact, the pitfall of this very personal and intimate kind of art. It is a delightful study to watch an author finding his material and transmuting it in the alembic of his brain into literature. But what if the product is not properly alembicated? What if crude chunks of life are mingled with that which has been refined and reshaped by the processes of art; what if raw facts are included, with no literary metathesis beyond that of the journalist's effort to be smart and amusing whatever the price? A training in the higher journalism is not always to the benefit of genius.

Barrie's early work

In *Margaret Ogilvy* (1896), Barrie tells how he and his mother used to read the books from the penny library, and when they had exhausted the stock he had a glorious idea—why should he not write the tales himself? So he "commenced author." In *Better Dead* (1887), an amusing fantasia on a theme like that of De Quincey's *Murder as one of the Fine Arts*, a pushful young Scot, Andrew Riach, weaver, fortified with diplomas from Scottish universities and testimonials from the "unco guid," comes to London with an empty pocket to take the Cabinet by storm, appoint himself private secretary to the Prime Minister, and in due course become a minister himself. These are his fixed intentions; he does not actually carry them out, for it suited his creator to find him a different destiny. Next year, in *When a Man's Single* (1888), Rob Angus, a saw-miller from Thrums, also comes up to town, with overwhelming credentials in the shape of a literary reputation, local but superlative; batters on the doors of editors, and in a remarkably brief space of time, from being without a penny to bless himself

[1] The special thesis of *J. M. Barrie* by W. A. Darlington (1938) is that it was the spurious elements in his nature that fascinated Barrie—"Tommy is Barrie's Mr Hyde" (82).

with, is in receipt of a handsome salary as leader-writer to a principal London daily.

In *Tommy and Grizel*, Tommy, aged sixteen, walks into the sanctum of a popular novelist, after the recognized pilgrimage from Thrums, and announces his intention of taking a post that has been advertised. The duties have not been disclosed; but whatever they are, Tommy peremptorily asserts his unique qualifications therefor, and is duly installed as amanuensis to the noted Pym, which is his own introduction to literature. Pym is a study in the Dickens vein of a serial novelist of the old school: he had already appeared under an alias in *When a Man's Single* in the rougher sketch of Noble Simms, the celebrated writer. Tommy's duty is occasionally stretched so far as to continue those parts of a story which do not require the peculiar and inimitable touch of his employer. The born sentimentalist falls in love with Pym's heroines. For him they are real women. To Pym's dismay, it transpires one day that Tommy has been exceeding his commission, and turning the machine-made heroines and damsels in distress into human beings—a thing no reader of mass-produced fiction can possibly stand. Pym has to sit down to his desk and cut out all Tommy's embellishments. But Tommy saves the discarded padding, especially the screeds of noble sentiment, the brilliant sayings, and the philosophic musings on women and love, and publishes them in a book of his own. That is how Tommy, who came to London penniless at sixteen, is a writer of world-wide fame at twenty-one. The same programme is carried out in the play *What Every Woman Knows*, giving the surprising career of John Shand, the studious railway porter. Now this is not mere repetition through lack of inventiveness. Andrew Riach, Tommy Sandys, and the rest of them, are Barrie himself; and, in truth, so is Peter Pan, under another disguise, just as that motherly young woman Wendy is the patient Grizel reduced to the scale of a children's comedy. It was Barrie's way. He takes his mother in *Margaret Ogilvy*, and paints one of the finest portraits in Scottish literature, a literature rich in the most delicate traits of the home affections. He looks round at his old acquaintances at Kirriemuir, sketches them just as

Tommy Sandys, etc.

he sees them, though the amiable optimist sees only the brighter side of human nature, and so begets the charming old cronies and gossips of Thrums. Then, as his imagination grows stronger on the wing, he sails off on higher flights and brings back rarer beings, the finest of which are the man of imagination and insight, Sentimental Tommy, his own type of the artistic temperament, and that peerless woman, so subtly and pathetically drawn in his two best novels, Grizel McQueen. His leading gentlemen are seen starting as poor young fellows of humble origin but acknowledged brilliance at Thrums, coming up to London, conquering and to conquer, and returning in glory to their native home. It is his own career, perfunctorily diversified rather than disguised.

At length a novel

"He was so fond of being a boy that he could not grow up," he says of Tommy; "in a younger world, where there were only boys and girls, he might have been a gallant figure." But it is clear to any who read between the lines that Barrie attached great virtue to this art of not growing up. "What is genius?" he asks. "It is the power to be a boy again at will." A manly Tommy might have cut a better figure beside the dour but sterling Dr David Gemmell, but it would have been at ruinous expense to the comedy of sentiment. The precocious statesman John Shand is one who must needs remain a boy: this is the secret of which his wife, who certainly has not failed to grow up, understands the importance, in *What Every Woman Knows*, not the jocular discovery that woman was made out of man's funny-bone, not his rib. Nevertheless, Barrie grew up perceptibly, in literary tact as well as skill, from the date of his "Society for doing without some People," in *Better Dead*; though he never outgrew his joy in extravaganza and in pure whimsicality, such as the allusion to actors, as a sex by themselves, like curates. Clever as was the journalism in his early books, they were good only in parts: sentimentalism was apt to run riot, as in the gratuitous death of a sweet little child of four which makes the first part of *When a Man's Single* (1888) distressing. And the humour does not rise far above mere facetiousness, as about the hammock "whose one flaw was that it gave way when any one got into it"; which is on a par with the characterization of Gilray, in *My Lady Nicotine* (1890), who falls in love, and being rejected tries vainly to appear desolate. Much of the jocularity of *Auld Licht Idylls* (1888) and *A Window in Thrums* (1889) is on this level. It is the pawky use of dialect as much as anything that carries off such pleasantries as Tammas Haggart's scheme for geniuses:

"I'm thinkin' 'at if there was a small chairge for admission the Home could be made self-supportin'. Losh! to think 'at if there had been sic an institootion in his time a man micht hae sat on the bit dyke and watched Robbie Burns danderin' roond the——"

But there has been enough said about Robbie Burns, and they shut him up. Even *Margaret Ogilvy* reads like a Barrie novel, so full is it of these sallies, for instance Margaret's tirade about clubs when her son proposes to join one:

"Thirty pounds is what he will have to pay the first year, and ten pounds a year after that. You think it's a lot o' siller? Oh no, you're mista'en—it's nothing ava. For the third part of thirty pounds you could rent a four-roomed house; but what is a four-roomed house, what is thirty pounds, compared to the glory of being a member of a club? Where does the glory come in? Sal, you needna ask me; I'm just a doited auld stock that never set foot in a club, so it's little I ken about glory. But I may tell you if you bide in London and canna become member of a club, the best you can do is to tie a rope round your neck and slip out of the world."

Why Barrie likes to pitch his stories two or three generations back he explains in *Margaret Ogilvy*. His mother's father was the one hero of her life, and she loved to tell tales of her girlhood.

I soon grow tired of writing tales unless I can see a little girl, of whom my mother has told me, wandering confidently through the pages. Such a grip has her memory of her girlhood had upon me since I was a boy of six.[1]

[1] A clue to Grizel's haunting by the little girl that she once was: Grizel was drawn from Margaret.

How like is this tenderness, and also the drollery, to *The Vicar of Wakefield*, which, bear in mind, Galt declared to be his chosen model in *The Annals of the Parish*, however much critics may scent the stronger bouquet of Smollett. We shake hands with Tibbie McQuahatty, who objects to "run line" in singing the Psalms, and regularly withdraws outside the kirk whilst the canticles are chanted in this paganish fashion; with Tammas Lunan, with his passion for funerals; with sarcastic Tammas Haggart, and the schoolmaster who acted as judge at a beauty-show, and had the effrontery to award the prize to his plain daughter; and finally with the Little Minister, Gavin Dishart, who, however, was to be touched up considerably before he appeared in the novel named after him. Here he is in *Auld Licht Idylls*:

Never was there a man more uncomfortably loved than Mr Dishart. Easie Haggart, his maid-servant, reproved him at the breakfast-table. Lang Tammas and Sam'l Mealmaker crouched for five successive Sabbath nights on his manse wall to catch him smoking (and got him). Old wives grumbled by their hearths when he did not look in to despair of their salvation. He told the maidens of his congregation not to make an idol of him. His session saw him (from behind a haystack) in conversation with a strange woman, and asked grimly if he remembered that he had a wife. Twenty were his years when he came to Thrums, and on the very first Sabbath he knocked a board out of the pulpit. Before beginning his trial sermon, he handed down the big Bible to the precentor, to give his arms freer swing. The congregation, trembling with exhilaration, probed his meaning. Not a square inch of paper, they saw, could be concealed there. Mr Dishart had scarcely any hope for the Auld Lichts; he had none for any other denomination. Davit Lunan got behind his handkerchief to think for a moment, and the minister was on him like a tiger. The call was unanimous. Davit proposed him.

Auld Licht Idylls and *A Window in Thrums* form a random chronicle of courtings, weddings, christenings, funerals, great snows, great floods, new ministers, labour troubles among the weavers, and so on: it is a Wilkie-like picture of a Forfarshire village early in the nineteenth century. Barrie the playwright may be discerned already in many of the talks; "Preparing to receive company" and "How Gavin Birse put it to Mag Lownie" were dialogues that pointed to the five-minute dramas of a few years later. In *The Little Minister* (1891), Thrums humour and pathos are dexterously worked up for the enjoyment of the novel-reading public, and woven into a romantic story having the trade-marks of a "best-seller," which was easily reduced afterwards to the melodramatic form of a popular play. There are some authentically humorous scenes in the book, adroitly blended with Barrie's most seductive sentimentalism. But there is less of the footlights and more of the genuine Thrums—if that can be termed genuine which belongs at least as much to dreamland as to reality—in the two parts of one long story, *Sentimental Tommy* (1896) and *Tommy and Grizel* (1900). Barrie apparently thought himself a realist and a serious critic of life, in his novels and tales of Thrums, fondly conceiving that imaginary township to be a faithful replica of Kirriemuir. He had not yet put forth his full strength as a creator of cloud-cuckoo-towns, though he had nearly finished his apprenticeship. But he evidently had misgivings that he had been allowing sentiment too free a rein; and now, if only half deliberately, he set himself the task of an anatomy of sentimentalism, which would reveal the fatuity of one who was completely its slave. Was he conscious, also, that it must needs be a vivisection of himself? For Tommy is composed out of his own fibre, and his efforts to look at Tommy from the point of view of a detached spectator continually betray his inability to see truly. Such were the lenses in Barrie's eyes that he never saw the world with unrefracting vision. He could not be a realist. In his novels and in his plays, it is evident that a good half of the world which he thought he was contemplating lay entirely outside his roseate ken. Consummate stage-craft—in both—blinded the critics to the futility of his "criticism of life." And he must have suspected that he suffered from some such disability, or he would never have been so hard on Tommy when he caught him in the act of self-deception, as, to choose one out of scores of instances, in the affair of the glove:

"Sentimental Tommy" and "Tommy and Grizel"

The abject one found a glove of Grizel's that she did not know she had lost and put it in his pocket. There it lay unknown to her. He knew that he must not even ask them to bury it with him in his grave. This was a little thing to ask, but too much for him. He saw his effects being examined after all that was mortal of T. Sandys had been consigned to earth, and this pathetic little glove coming to light. Ah, then, then Grizel would know! By the way what would she have known? I am sure I cannot tell you. Nor could Tommy, forced to face the question in this vulgar way, have told you; yet whatever it was it gave him some moist moments. If Grizel saw him in this mood her reproachful look implied that he was sentimentalising again. How little this chit understood him.

Whether he wrote no more novels after he and his corrivals had their extravagances exposed in *The House with the Green Shutters* because he now realized his shortcomings, or simply that he was now too busy writing plays, must remain an open question. At any rate, he did not reach the heights of humour Sterne attained in the total incapacity of the Shandy brothers to comprehend each other in spite of their more than brotherly affection, which made that incapacity the more pathetic; though, on the other hand, he did not flounder into morasses of sentimental affectation over a dead ass or the wretched idiot, Maria of Moulines. Tommy Sandys is a sort of Laurence Sterne; he is a sentimentalist who loves to write on moving subjects and never even tries to stand aloof and efface himself. He is wrapt up in his own fine feelings, and keeps importuning the reader to admire them.

The new book, of course, was *The Wandering Child.* I wonder whether any of you read it now. Your fathers and mothers thought a great deal of that slim volume, but it would make little stir in an age in which all the authors are trying who can say Damn loudest. It is but a reverie about a little boy who was lost. His parents find him in a wood singing joyfully to himself because he thinks he can now be a boy for ever; and he fears that if they catch him they will compel him to grow into a man, so he runs farther from them into the wood and is running still, singing to himself because he is always to be a boy. That is really all, but T. Sandys knew how to tell it. The moment he conceived the idea (we have seen him speaking of it to the doctor) he knew that it was the idea for him. He forgot at once that he did not really care for children. He said reverently to himself, "I can pull it off," and, as was always the way with him, the better he pulled it off the more he seemed to love them.

"It is myself who is writing at last, Grizel," he said as he read it to her.

She thought (and you can guess whether she was right) that it was the book he loved rather than the child. She thought (and you can guess again) that in a subtle way this book was his autobiography. But she did not say so. She said it was the sweetest of his books to her.

Sterne was a large figure to put into a novel. Barrie drew similar effects of humour and pathos from Tommy's fatal inability to appreciate such a woman among women as Grizel. But he was certainly not Sterne's superior. He shared Sterne's foible, and was rather afraid of it; he was never quite sure of hitting the mark.[1] Hence Tommy and his sister are only half real. They are rather like adventurous sentimentalists playing at infancy, in *Sentimental Tommy*; and the Thrums people have degenerated into mere sentimental connoisseurs, a chorus of inquisitive and admiring or captious spectators. And Grizel herself, meant to be the antipodes of all that, is a sentimentalist like the rest when she nurses the dyspeptic plant, because if it droops she will know that Tommy is ill, and again when she carries his love-letter about with her unopened, to save up the ecstasy of reading it. There is nothing left for Barrie at last but to get rid of his pseudo-hero, by means too summary and unceremonious to be very artistic, and write his epitaph in the

[1] Dixon Scott says *à propos* of this passage and Tommy's or Barrie's dive into sentiment: "Now why did he dive? . . . Because he feared sentiment. And if you press me further and ask why he was afraid of sentiment, I am afraid I must just make a clean breast of it, fellow-countryman though I am, and confess that it was because he was a Scot. But do not misunderstand this: do not take it to mean that he shrank from sentiment because, as a Scot, he hated it. It was the opposite of that: Barrie feared sentiment because, being a Scot, he loved the seductive thing too well" (*Men of Letters*, "The Ambitions of Sir James Barrie," 68). Mr Darlington carefully points out, "In all his early writings the most characteristic of these three elements, sentiment, is rigorously excluded" (p. 40). The other elements, of course, were satire and humour.

literary Press. The story becomes the tragedy of the patient Grizel.

Barrie and other critics of sentimentalism

As a treatise in artistic form, the only novel to be compared with this two-volume study of sentimentalism is Meredith's anatomy of a kindred vice, *The Egoist*. Sentimentalism, as Meredith was always pointing out, is simply one of the forms which egoism instinctively takes. The sentimentalist sees everything through his emotions. Real values escape him. What things are in themselves he neither knows nor cares, but he enjoys the luxury of the feelings they evoke. Grief, remorse, pity—especially self-pity—give him a pleasure that he does not admit even to himself. He loses his grip on realities, but the shadow yields him a superior satisfaction. Tommy is so wrapt in fold upon fold of sentimental illusion that there is no way of getting to the essential Tommy. Few novelists, indeed, have ever succeeded in holding themselves aloof and exposing sentimentalism to the very quick. Those who may think themselves George Eliots usually settle their problems by a clandestine appeal to sensibility, and dignify this to their consciences as an appeal to poetic justice. Thackeray repeatedly fell into the snare, although he framed plausible definitions of certain kinds of sham sentiment, for example in his summary of Blanche Amory, in *Pendennis*:

> This young lady was not able to carry out any emotion to the full, but had a sham enthusiasm, a sham hatred, a sham love, and a sham grief, each of which flared and shone very vehemently for an instant, but subsided and gave place to the next sham emotion.

But this is not the kind of sentimentalism dissected in a Barrie novel. Nor is Barrie's anything like the lyrical sentimentalism of Pierre Loti, unless it be that of Loti's decadence, when he has grown aware of it and fondles his idiosyncrasy. The nearest resemblance will be found in the kinds of sentimentalism anatomized by Meredith, when he was showing up those who "fiddle harmonics on the strings of sensualism." In *Sandra Belloni* he distinguishes the various grades. There are the three Miss Poles, representing the Fine Shades and the

Nice Feelings; there is Sir Purcell Barrett, who commits suicide because the realities of life are too gross for his sensitive soul; and there is the arch-sentimentalist Wilfrid Pole, who philanders with a girl and jilts her, and then falls helplessly and hopelessly in love when he finds that other men think her worth pursuing. Tommy Sandys is such another, more amply and complacently developed, drawn more to the scale of a Sir Willoughby Patterne. He, too, is an egoist; but egoism must not be confounded with crude selfishness. There is nothing selfish about Tommy, nothing commonplace; everybody loves him, except one person here or there of preternatural insight. He has by nature a charming disposition; and his exploits in downing two burglars single-handed [1] and rescuing a little boy from the torrent before he has learned to swim prove his physical courage. But the point is that he exploits his personality as a work of conscious art, he himself being the artist. "I'm near the greeting," he admits on one occasion to his sister Elspeth, "but I'm no sure what about." As Barrie explains, "His sympathy was so easily aroused that he sometimes cried without knowing exactly why." "It's because you're so good," Elspeth told him; but Grizel is not so unillumined. To put it bluntly, all his emotions and other mental experiences fascinate him as so much copy, so much material for his next book.

Tommy and Grizel contrasted

Tommy never falls in love, but he is always in love with the idea. As soon as the critical point approaches, he is terror-stricken and shudders at the dreadful consequences. This is the tragi-comedy. Sentimentalism has such a grip of him that will-power—and he is endowed with "a magerfu' will"—grows weak and flabby. Those emotional passages of his with the sympathizing widow Mrs Jerry might have been done by Sterne:

> She was a wealthy widow, buxom, not a day over thirty when she was merry, which might be at inappropriate moments, as immediately after she had expressed a desire to lead the higher life. "But I have a theory, my dear," she said solemnly

[1] Characteristically, when he has secured them, he lets them out, with two shillings apiece, because their family histories are so touching.

to Elspeth, "that no woman is able to do it who cannot see her own nose without the help of a mirror." She had taken a great fancy to Elspeth, and made many engagements with her and kept some of them, and the understanding was that she apprenticed herself to Tommy through Elspeth, he being too terrible to face by himself, or, as Mrs Jerry expressed it, "all nose." So Tommy had seen very little of her, and thought less, until one day he called by passionate request to sign her birthday-book, and heard himself proposing to her instead.

For one thing it was twilight, and she had forgotten to ring for the lamps. That might have been enough, but there was more; she read to him part of a letter in which her hand was solicited in marriage, "and for the life of me," said Mrs Jerry, almost in tears, "I cannot decide whether to say yes or no."

This put Tommy in a most awkward position. There are probably men who could have got out of it without proposing, but to him there seemed at the moment no other way open. The letter complicated matters also by beginning "Dear Jerry" and saying "little Jerry," farther on, expressions which stirred him strangely.

"Why do you read this to me?" he asked, in a voice that broke a little.

"Because you are so wise," she said. "Do you mind?"

"Do I mind!" he exclaimed, bitterly. ("Take care, you idiot!" he said to himself.)

"I was asking your advice only. Is it too much?"

"Not at all. I am quite the right man to consult at such a moment, am I not?"

It was said with profound meaning, but his face was as usual.

"That is what I thought," she said, in all good faith.

"You do not even understand!" he cried, and he was also looking longingly at his hat.

"Understand what?"

"Jerry," he said, and tried to stop himself, with the result that he added "dear little Jerry." ("What am I doing!" he groaned.)

She understood now. "You don't mean—" she began, in amazement.

"Yes," he cried, passionately. "I love you. Will you be my wife?" ("I'm lost!")

The gloss on this occurs later, when Tommy goes through the same kind of performance with Mrs Jerry's wideawake daughter, Lady Pippinworth, and afterwards apologizes.

Her eyes opened to their widest, so surprised that the lashes had no time for their usual play.

"Was that what you call making love, Mr Sandys?" she inquired.

"I call a spade a spade."

"And now you are apologizing to me, I understand."

"If you can in the goodness of your heart forgive me, Lady Pippinworth."

"Oh, I do," she said heartily, "I do. But how stupid you must have thought me, not even to know! I feel that it is I who ought to apologize. What a number of ways there seem to be of making love, and yours is such an odd way."

As they have grown up together, and Tommy has valiantly defended her against the innuendoes thrown at her mother, that factitious figure of tragedy the Painted Lady, it would be perfectly natural for Tommy and Grizel to fall in love. He is in love with the experience of being in love, and he is one of those jealous beings who take it as a personal grievance when a lady falls in love with someone else. Though, as a sentimental egoist, he never is and never can be in love with Grizel, it would drive him desperate if she did not fall in love with him. She makes no response to these queer demands upon her heart, and he chews the cud of bitter-sweet reflection over her glove. She finds the glove in circumstances that make the seeming fact of Tommy's hopeless worship break upon her in all its pathos. And now he has to live up to the part that he has created. But that is a feat beyond even his magerfu' will.

Ah, if only Tommy could have loved in this way! He would have done it if he could. If we could love by trying, no one would ever have been more loved than Grizel. "Am I to be condemned because I cannot?" he sometimes said to himself in terrible anguish, for though pretty thoughts came to him to say to her when she was with him, he suffered anguish for her when he was alone. He knew it was tragic that such love as hers should be given to him; but what more could he do than he was doing? Ah, if only it could have been a world of boys and girls!"

Grizel's tragedy

Grizel is as large-hearted as her ancient namesake, and much more attractive. She stands for natural feeling, honesty and unselfishness, "noble strength on fire," as Meredith would have put it, when she loves; and Meredith would have approved her—she has a mind. It was inevitable that the keen-eyed Grizel should perceive sooner or later that Tommy was only toying with love, and that the discovery should break her heart. How she hears that Tommy is desperately ill; how she journeys across the Continent to the Alps, and by a fatal coincidence overhears the infatuated idealist declaring his passion for another woman, is a long and far-fetched story. Her mind is unhinged; and Tommy, never so noble as when there is a call for showy self-sacrifice, devotes his days and nights to nursing her back to happiness. He still tries to persuade her and himself that he is in love like an ordinary healthy man. But it is impossible to wring genuine feeling out of a confirmed sentimentalist. Such is Grizel's tragedy. That of Master Thomas Sandys is of a more sardonic kind. He falls a self-devoted victim to an incredible type of man-killer—a siren who feasts on the bones of her lovers. His death would be an ignoble one for the most depraved of sentimentalists. Both Meredith and Barrie had one immense advantage over Sterne, not Sterne the humorist but Sterne the novelist of sentiment. When *Tristram Shandy* was written, such a thing as passion was inconceivable; the human soul had not been discovered—or, rather, rediscovered—nor passion as a state of the soul. As Meredith was able to contrast Wilfrid and the three Poles with Vittoria, who is passion incarnate, so Barrie shows up Tommy by placing him over against Grizel.[1] Hence there is something beyond the range of Sterne in such a chapter

[1] As Miss Amy Cruse reminds us (*After the Victorians*, 175–176), Barrie as a young man of twenty-eight wrote an article on Meredith in *The Contemporary Review* (1888) pointing out that, in spite of the jargon, he was "one of the great intellects of the age."

as "How Tommy saved the Flag," in which the expert in woman's feelings, out of an impulsive and specious magnanimity, convinces Grizel that she has not been humiliated, when her pride has just received its death-wound.

His plays like his novels

When Fielding became a novelist, his plays went into oblivion; with Barrie it was the other way about, the novels and the portfolios of tales and sketches were forgotten in admiration of the playwright. These plays are brilliant fantasies of a world that is no more like reality than Thrums is like Kirriemuir. They consist of the same finished dialogue, in which every rejoinder is a bit of pretty irony that never hurts—an exchange not of sentiments but of sentiment. There is not much essential difference between the plays and the stories. Charming little scenes and conversations held together by a thread of incident, the plays in their published form are just as readable, so liberally are they fitted out with stage-directions and asides by the author, which not merely describe the setting and the people, but carry on the story and interpret it.[1] Thus *The Old Lady shows her Medals* (1917) is a tale requiring more explanation than a playbill would give, and on the stage it is bereft of many asides on the author's part, though Barrie saw to it that the acting should convey all he meant. It is about the old charwoman who sends presents to a namesake in the Black Watch, then at the front, and lets her cronies believe he is her son. When Kenneth turns up at last, she prevails on him, after some cautious flattery, to adopt her as his mother in real earnest, the happiness of the childless woman and the good nature of the rough soldier-boy making an agreeable mixture. Long before this, *Quality Street* (1901) might have been a study after *Cranford*, the spinster ladies of Waterloo times recalling Miss Matty and her friends, with their ladylike refinements, especially the exquisiteness of Phœbe. There is even a Mr Brown, not however a conjurer nor known as Signor Brunoni. It is Captain Valentine Brown, who failed to propose to Phœbe before he went to the wars. When he comes back, Phœbe and her sister Susan, like Miss

[1] Many of these were added after he had seen the plays presented, or at any rate rehearsed.

Matty again, have lost their money and have to keep a school. Phœbe is indeed ten years older, but she has not lost her youthful spirit; and to avenge herself on the laggard captain she passes herself off as her own sprightly niece, who flirts with the middle-aged hero. But he spoils her game, and will not be fascinated by the counterfeit Livvy. He is in love with the Phœbe who has grown old, so that the end may be guessed. A whimsical piece of make-believe is so skilfully wrought, that the extravagances are carried off, even when the lover, in the character of a physician, has to spirit away the mythical Livvy in his arms, to avoid a scandal if Phœbe's escapade leaked out. It is all complacent, sugary sentiment, not free from mawkishness—too many lollipops, a sweet cake too heavily iced. There is always the chance of a good cry, a cry because things are so much better than we deserve.

More plays

The Admirable Crichton (1902) was his next success. The idea of the butler who by dint of his intrinsic superiority to the aristocrats he is used to wait upon becomes ruler of the desert island on which they are cast away, gave many the impression that it was meant for a criticism of the present regime; but to Barrie, no doubt, it was simply something amusing for the public and himself. Entertainment is the prime object, still more in his plays than in his novels. And he loved nothing better than to sport with ideas. But, though he liked being credited with a magical insight into certain human failings, he was never safe from ruining a sound idea by some contrariety or wild exaggeration. His plays, in particular, look more original than they are, in the sense of revealing new truths, because of his topsy-turvy way of tricking out a situation that has not escaped attention already. *What Every Woman Knows* (1908) starts with one of his topsy-turvydoms. John Shand the railway porter is caught burgling the Wylie mansion in order to read the books which form the owners' ornamental library. They let him off on condition that he marries the plain but admirable Maggie, in six years' time, after finishing the education which they agree to pay for. In the second act, he has made good and become a popular M.P., and in due course he marries the lady. By her aid and advice, though he is blissfully unconscious of the debt, he wins his way into the Prime Minister's favour and has every prospect of a brilliant career. But he makes no secret of his tepid regard for Maggie, who gives in to an old understanding that he is to be free if he falls in love with someone else. He thinks he has found his Egeria in Lady Sybil Tenterden. Maggie contrives that he and Sybil shall be thrown together, for Egeria to see what she can do with him. It is a complete fiasco. Left to himself, Shand cannot even prepare the big speech that he is to deliver at the Prime Minister's great meeting. It was Maggie who used to put in the "delicious little touches," the Shandisms that always brought the house down.

Every man who is high up loves to think that he has done it all himself; and the wife smiles, and lets it go at that.

It is the first joke John Shand ever saw in his life. He is a serene, conceited ass, the sort that get on, if they have an able wife. His discomfiture gratifies everyone. Maggie, like all Barrie's finer women, owes her existence to Margaret Ogilvy; her name would identify her, were it necessary. Still more deadly in their ironical humour are that small masterpiece, *The Twelve-pound Look*, and *The Will.* But he preferred to take a not-unfamiliar moral idea and illustrate it in a charming way of his own, which somehow evaded unwelcome implications, as in *Dear Brutus* (1917), a poetic fantasy in which a crowd of people, who in their various ways have made a mess of life, enter the enchanted wood on midsummer night and are given their second chances. Lovers are changed into husbands and wives, and vice versa, their old handicap being cancelled and their private longings fulfilled. Yet all retain their old propensities and weaknesses, and come to grief again in much the same way. Shakespeare had summed it up:

> The fault, dear Brutus, is not in our stars,
> But in ourselves, that we are underlings.

In *Mary Rose* (1920), he marries the old Celtic myth of the "*Mary*
Otherworld, Tir nan Og, Hades or Avalon, the Land of Heart's *Rose*"

Desire, the "land of thought" to which Thomas the Rhymer and Hogg's Kilmeny were carried off, to our familiar sphere of actuality. Mary Rose is rapt away to a lonely Hebridean isle, the abode of spirits, and comes back after twenty-five years to find her son a grown man. What will she make of the world, and what will the world make of her? And also, what will she have to tell of the wonderland where she has been? Barrie has no definite answer to any of these questions. Mary Rose endures various kinds of earthly agony, and then the curtain falls. In the last act, she is nothing but the ordinary country-house ghost that is thrown in with the other effects by the estate agent. The beautiful Celtic magic has dissolved into vulgar spiritualist occultism, intertwined with another case of the person who never grows up. For Mary Rose stopped growing when the fairies carried her off; and when she becomes Simon's wife it is her childishness, not her otherworldliness, that provides the fantasy Barrie required. That he handled such a situation with the finest dramatic skill goes without saying; but the ambiguity is not conjured away.

Fantastic novels

The truth of the matter is, of course, that there was a part of Sir James Barrie that never grew up[1]; and to this the world owes his charming pranks with fanciful ideas or sheer, ingenious nonsense, not only in his theatre for children but even when he was aiming at realism on the stage or in novel or story. He did not mean it as extravaganza when Mary Rose came back as a young woman to sit on her grown-up son's knee, when John Shand committed burglary to read in a rich man's library, Phœbe masqueraded as her own niece, or Tommy sprained his ankle on purpose, just to show Grizel that he had not been shamming. The apparent impishness which led him to make elaborate foolery out of that which on another side may be infinitely tragic originated, perhaps, in a sort of duality

[1] "It is a fascinating thing, this progress of Tommy—I mean Barrie: the way he has diffidently (but oh, how obstinately!) worked and wriggled along his form until at length he reached his proper place. The fashionable thing to say about him now is that he has 'never grown up.' It is intended for praise, but it is a terribly tame version of the actual process which lies behind his career. The amazing thing about him is that he *has* grown, grown incessantly; but instead of growing up, has grown down. His case is like Alice's" (Dixon Scott, *Men of Letters*, "The Ambitions of Sir James Barrie," 66).

forced upon him by a sense of frustration in his own life. Did he half-consciously evade the issues implied in *Mary Rose* and *Dear Brutus*, because he shrank from honestly facing them? Were his lapses from realism in general due to his recoil from actualities too painful to dwell upon? It is matter for serious speculation. Now he seems to be surrendering his mind to the new current; he claims to be, and sometimes is, a realist. Then, in a moment, he yields to the obsessing lure of make-believe, in both his chosen mediums. He was always mingling the romantic or the absurd with his matter of fact. And the pathetic entered into the combination just as easily. When Reddy dies, what melts Reddy's mother at last to tears is the sight of Tommy waiting for the little friend who had been dead for a month. But Barrie cannot dispense with the comic anticlimax.

> When Tommy knew that Reddy was a deader he cried bitterly, and the man said, very gently, "I am glad you were so fond of her."
>
> "'Tain't that," Tommy answered with a knuckle in his eye, "'tain't that as makes me cry." He looked down at his trousers, and in a fresh outburst of childish grief he wailed, "It's them!"
>
> Papa did not understand, but the boy explained. "She can't not never see them now," he sobbed, "and I wants her to see them, and they has pockets!"

A divided mind—"Peter Pan"

Pathos and humour are often said to be not far apart. In Barrie's case, a certain ambiguity of feeling and hence of meaning hampers him continually. He had a divided mind; and, when he surrendered to a current of ideas or of artistic attitudes, it was a halting surrender. *Sentimental Tommy* is not meant to be sustained burlesque; yet as often as not the only substitute for ironical raillery of the sentimentalist is pure extravagance or journalistic facetiousness of the cheapest dye.

> About ten o'clock Ballingall's cat was observed washing its face, a deliberate attempt to bring on rain. It was immediately put to death.
>
> A more tragic figure was Francis Crabb (one and sevenpence), who, like a mad, mad thing, had taken all his money

to the fair at once. In ten minutes he had bought fourteen musical instruments!

Barrie could always revel in the most childish forms of pretence and masquerade. He never seemed to realize the responsibilities of grown manhood; and, when he dealt with ideas, they amused rather than absorbed him. *Peter Pan* and its progeny of tales, presumably for children, *The Little White Bird* (1902), *Peter Pan in Kensington Gardens* (1906), and *Peter and Wendy* (1911), present the same kind of ambiguity, which is apparent also in his many inconclusive conclusions. *Peter Pan*, by virtue of irresponsible fantasy, became a national institution. Its charm nobody can deny. But, as Chesterton said, "No one can be really hilarious but the serious man." *Peter Pan* is full of paradoxes having no ulterior significance; the nonsense is often singularly irrelevant. Peter Pan himself is as spontaneous a creation of Barrie's mind as was his more realistic predecessor Tommy Sandys. Both are boys that never grow up, and they are the counterpart of a great deal in Barrie that never grew up, that also produced the drollery which shoots its flowery branches through the whole fabric of his novels and stories. Barrie can be brilliant, but somehow it always seems the brilliance of precociousness. These tales were told for and even enacted by a lot of real children, in the pine-woods of Barrie's woodland home near Farnham. It is a medley of long-remembered pranks and of new ones invented on the spot.[1] But it is not merely that the element of literal fact does not blend perfectly with the inner autobiography, the story of frustration shadowed forth allegorically; there is often some confusion between the plane of actuality and that of imagination—realities are somewhat out of place in fairyland.

Peter Pan in a book

Peter Pan comes on the stage in *The Little White Bird*, the scene of which is Kensington Gardens, turned for the nonce into a land of enchantments. *Peter and Wendy* is the children's comedy itself converted into a novel. It might be truer to

[1] See Darlington (19) for the games of the pirate crew at the Dumfries Academy, who enacted "a sort of Odyssey that was long afterwards to become the play of *Peter Pan*."

say that they are dilutions of the play. Both contain some of Barrie's most inimitable fooling; but a good deal of it in *The Little White Bird* is the kind of fooling that a mere child would not understand. The other story is not quite free from this drawback, but it does enable the reader to see what there actually was in the famous play. The result for some is disillusioning. There was a tendency long before Barrie's death to regard him exclusively as the creator of Peter Pan, and ignore his books. Critics did not hesitate to put what was undoubtedly a brilliant play for children on a level with comedy of the highest intellectual scope. It was the time when society, after centuries of negligence, began to make a cult of the child, lift him up to a pedestal and regard him as the peculiar genius of the age. There is so much affectation and morbid pretentiousness about, that, when we come across an example of healthy nonsense, we are apt to mistake it for the profundity of wisdom. Every healthy mind should be able to appreciate nonsense; it is only the fool that cannot enjoy good fooling. The mistake about *Peter Pan* and *The Blue Bird* was to forget what they really are, plays for children, and to venerate them as oracular utterances of divine truths. It was as if the child could be seen trailing his clouds of glory. The best to be said of *Peter Pan* is that it is exquisite childishness, true on the whole and unfailingly charming: these are high merits, and they are to be found in the stories as well as in the plays from which these are drawn. But the very finest of stories for children are so fine that the maturest mind can fling off the burden of maturity and recapture the childish bliss of imagination—without worrying over hidden meanings or anything not plain to the child as well as to maturity. Any healthy mind can revel without restraint in Hans Andersen, or Lewis Carroll, or Kipling of the *Jungle Books*. But in the tales of Peter Pan fantasy is again only an escape from sentimentalism—and the disillusionment which is its inevitable concomitant. Barrie is only half laughing at Wendy, who is sentimentalism to the marrow; he makes more fun of the self-consciousness and conceit of the clever artist, Peter Pan. All that about good form is twaddle:

"Is it quite good form to be distinguished at anything?"

"Most disquieting reflection of all, was it not bad form to think about good form?"

"Has the bo'sun good form without knowing it, which is the best of all?"

Conclusion

Barrie's children's stories are pretty good, his character-sketches and full-length portraits from Thrums entitle him to a place among the novelists of real life; but it is his anatomy of sentimentalism, especially in *Tommy and Grizel*, that puts him not far below Sterne and Meredith. Sterne committed excesses, when he let sentimentalism have a grip of him. Barrie was likewise, and is sometimes led further astray by his weakness for paradox and hyperbole. Tommy's sprain is one instance, Grizel's emulation of Isabella and the pot of basil is one again, her wild pursuit of Tommy and incredible discovery of him in the hotel garden in the Alps is yet another. There are similar exaggerations and errors of judgment in the plays: he was not self-critical enough to be safe from blundering. Barrie evolved two notable characters, one made out of himself, one out of his mother. Tommy Sandys, Peter Pan, Rob Angus, and his other heroes, are himself, the man of imagination who never grew up, never even divested himself of the journalistic foible for being always and at all costs amusing. Grizel and Wendy and Mrs Shand and all the rest of them, the womanly women, the Philistines, the Scots moralists, the tender-hearted and caustic mothers, lovers, and wives, are Margaret Ogilvy.[1] He cannot get his young men to grow; he really did not want them to, for he has a theory that men are always boys. In *Mary Rose* he tried to picture a girl who never grew up, forgetting that women always do grow up and are marvellously quick about it. He gave her an extra dose of childishness, or otherworldliness, which rendered her pretty and distinctive; but the result was not a success. His claims to greatness will have to rest on his exposure of the comedy and tragedy of sentimentalism in *Tommy and Grizel*.

[1] He said himself, "If readers discovered how frequently and in how many disguises she appeared in my books—the affair would become a public scandal" (*Margaret Ogilvy*, ix., "My Heroine").

Crockett and "Ian Maclaren"

Barrie's success at the libraries soon roused competition. His rivals were a man of the same age, Samuel Rutherford Crockett, and a Scots minister, ten years older, the Rev. John Watson, who as a writer of fiction called himself "Ian Maclaren." He had delighted and multiplied his readers with *The Little Minister*, and was busy winning new laurels in the theatre, when the former entered the lists with a set of tales of Galloway villagers, *The Stickit Minister, and some Common Men* (1893), and the latter arrived—in every sense of the word—with a batch from his parish on the Highland border, *Beside the Bonnie Brier Bush* (1894). Both employed a closer form of Lowland vernacular; both actually outwent Barrie in the direct appeal to sentiment. The pastor, like others before him, found the Scots tale of lowly suffering and submission such a ready instrument of edification, that for some years, between the demands of literature and those of platform and pulpit, he was one of the busiest men in Britain, and his readings brought tears to the eyes of immense audiences in the United States. For the time being he eclipsed both his rivals; but in the end it was plain that neither "Ian Maclaren" nor Crockett had the lasting qualities of Barrie. Crockett deliberately held up his "Stickit Minister" as a shining example of patience and altruism; the humour of his stories, so he claimed, was "near the Fountain of Tears." Probably the most unconscionable display of sentimentalism, simple and unabashed, in the work of all the school, was his love-story *The Lilac Sunbonnet* (1894). But Crockett had the journalistic talent for exploiting his native vein in any direction that offered returns in popularity and sales. Just now, historical romance was all the rage, and he followed the lead of Stevenson at his most profligate in *The Raiders* (1894), a story of moss-troopers, smugglers, and gipsies, on the Border two centuries ago, and again in *The Men of the Moss-Hags* (1895) and *The Grey Man* (1896). But Dumas rather than Stevenson or Scott was his guiding star in a long string of semi-historical romances of Scotland and of the Continent, from *Lochinvar* (1897) to *The White Plumes of Navarre* (1906). Crockett let himself go in the incidental love-making, and struck out another line of sentiment in such novels as *Cleg Kelly* (1896) and *Kit Kennedy* (1899), with street arabs for his heroes who are angels in disguise.

"*Beside the Bonnie Brier Bush*"

But the most popular of all the Kailyard books was *Beside the Bonnie Brier Bush*. "Ian Maclaren" was a salvationist, and probably never wrote a story that was not calculated to save a soul or two in this world and the next. His optimism must have made as strong an appeal as his sentimentalism, which revelled in scenes of pathos and loved to dilate on what most people find too sacred to talk about. Poetic justice never fails in any of his stories. There is something almost materialistic in an ethical doctrine which invariably shows good deeds well paid for—one way or another. "Ian Maclaren" was half-aware of it himself. His "General Practitioner," who is "accoucheur and surgeon" for all the glens, "oculist and aurist," "dentist and chloroformist," "chemist and druggist," and other things as well, and no skinflint for his fees, lays up for himself so much treasure that it almost looks as if he had his eye on the main chance above—

> "A've often thocht oor doctor's little better than the Gude Samaritan, an' the Pharisees didna think muckle o' his chance aither in this warld or that which is tae come."

It is possible to believe in Drumsheugh, who stints himself and gets the reputation of a miser, to help the man who married the girl he himself loved to make ends meet; but not so easily in Dodson, the good fairy who sends a cheque on the quiet to save a firm from bankruptcy, and in the same clandestine manner pays for a widow's son's education, the minister's holiday, or for a people's playground, knowing all the while that he is being cursed as a close-fisted curmudgeon. On the other hand, the pharisaical newcomer who criticizes the Auld Kirk though he considers it better than the Free, and is too holy to be improved by the minister's sermons, yet has a reputation for cheating at cards, is rather too gross an example of trust in faith not works. But he is converted when, after a terrible illness, all the Drumtochty folk, whom he has cheated and chidden, come and plough his fields. This gentleman appears in *The Days of Auld Langsyne* (1895), with cynical Jamie Soutar, Burnbrae, Milton the pharisee, Domsie the schoolmaster, and other worthies, all connoisseurs of points of doctrine, a good sermon, or local vices and virtues. *Kate Carnegie and those Ministers* (1896) introduces another saintly original, Rabbi Saunderson; and *Afterwards, and other stories* (1898) tells of Domsie's death and other tearful events.[1] Marget, Kirsty, and several others show that the women are not better or more soft-hearted than the men, and for that matter not more addicted to reticence. But it is incredible that the taciturn Drumsheugh should reveal to an old crony the love he has always harboured for William Howe's wife. If he did, why tack on "Drumsheugh's Reward," in which the friend breaks his confidence, Marget hears of her debt to Drumsheugh, and in an affecting scene thanks him for his great and faithful love? "Afterwards" tells how a bereaved husband, sorting out his wife's treasures, comes across the six purses for housekeeping and charity, and Christmas and birthday presents, proofs of the way she had slaved and sacrificed for his ungrateful self. But the didactic sequel is as overstrained as that which asks one to believe that Lachlan Campbell would stand up in public and confess his misdeeds:

"And there iss something that I must be asking of the elders, and it iss to forgive me for my pride in this Session."

The Drumtochty people held the old doctrine that obtrusive prosperity was an irresistible provocation to the higher powers, and that a skilful depreciation of our children was a policy of safety.

"'Lat weel alane,' says I to the Dominie; 'ye'll bring a judgment on the laddie wi' yir blawing.' . . . Ay, ay, it's an awfu' lesson, Marget, no to mak' idols o' our bairns, for that's naethin' else than provokin' the Almichty."

[1] Ian Maclaren's enormous vogue, even among people who thought themselves cultivated and intelligent, is a significant episode in the history of popular taste. One remembers the resentment and indignation with which a flippant remark was received by the critics, that his favourite and most telling chapters were those about death-beds.

But the humour in "Ian Maclaren," though overstrained, runs very thin, as in the report of Macfee's sermon:

"There will be many wonders in the latter day; but this is the greatest of them all—the voice of the turtle shall be heard in the land. This marvel falls into two parts, which we shall consider briefly and in order.

I. A new posture evidently implied, when an animal that has gone upon its belly for ages shall arise upon its hind legs and walk majestically through the land, and

II. A new voice distinctly promised, when a creature that has kept silence from generation to generation will at last open its mouth and sing melodiously to the people."

The farce and practical jokes in the tale of his own school-days, *Young Barbarians* (1901), made poor amends for such heavyhandedness.

Gabriel Setoun, "Fiona Macleod," G. D. Brown

Barrie was the sole humorist who counts in this group, which included beside those who had so many thousands of readers far beyond their own country such minor collaborators as Henry Johnston, who wrote *Chronicles of Glenbuckie* (1889) and *Kilmallie* (1891), "Gabriel Setoun" or Thomas Nicoll Hepburn, author of *Robert Urquhart* (1896) and *The Skipper of Barncraig* (1901), and the more versatile Sarah Macnaughtan, whose pleasant novels of South African and Anglo-Indian life had been preceded by some spirited sketches of character in *The Fortunes of Christina M'Nab* (1901) and *The Three Miss Graemes* (1908). There had always been room in Scottish literature for the amateur of local manners and collector of idiosyncrasies, even when there was no hope or intention of emulating Scott and Stevenson. The intimacies of domestic life were a traditional subject in other branches also of the national art. But an eye for the ridiculous was as necessary as any other sensibility in the delineator. A finer sense of humour, or in this case one that was more wideawake, would have saved even Barrie from many excesses, and would have been a priceless advantage to some of the others. It would have saved "Fiona Macleod," whose Highland romances belong, however, to a radically different branch of literature, from some absurdities, as for instance when, in *The Mountain*

Lovers, she—or, rather, he—makes Oona say, in reply to Nial's fear that he could not manage a soul of the ordinary size, "No, no, Nial, bigger than mine, *really*, *really*—yes, and—fatter." [1] The standing complaint against the Kailyard school was that they might paint accurately enough the things that pleased them, but they ignored or falsified the rest. It comes to the same thing at bottom—too fond a feeling for the pathos of life, with a defective sense of the perpetual comedy. Crockett and "Ian Maclaren," not to mention the less noted, were all in the same boat, when a stalwart realist, "George Douglas" or G. D. Brown (1869–1902), arose in his wrath and smote them in *The House with the Green Shutters* (1901), that grim reversal of their sentimental values. It depicts in their right colours the hatreds and jealousies, the hypocrisies, slanders, and sheer brutalities, which a merciless eye finds to be the actual and ineradicable traits of the supposed "worthies" in a small Scottish township. The tragedy of the Gourlay household is worked out on severe classical lines, though half the characters in the drama are a libel on human nature. It was a terrible exposure, and there has never been a Kailyard novel written since that is worth criticizing.[2]

The Irish novelists

The Celtic movement of which "Fiona Macleod," or, to give her the right name and sex, William Sharp (1856–1905), was self-appointed champion in Scottish letters did enormously more in Ireland to reawaken the native genius, and led to a great literary revival. But, though a number of those who took a strenuous part in this were novelists, not for a long while, not, in fact, till very recently, did the Irish novel show definite signs of entering upon a new epoch: it is in the work of James Stephens and James Joyce, both born in 1882 and both still writing, that something like a revolution in the art and craft of fiction has to be studied. George Moore learnt

[1] For "Fiona Macleod," *i.e.* William Sharp, see Vol. IX. 336.

[2] Somehow, one tends to think of that very masculine north-country novelist Alfred Ollivant (1874–1927) in association with the Scots novelists—not those of the Kailyard, however. His *Owd Bob, the Grey Dog of Kenmuir* (1898), was a story of the Cumberland dalesmen (who have so much in common with their northern kindred), and of their doughty tykes. The dogs are characters just as much as their masters, the shepherds on the fells. His *Danny, story of a Dandie Dinmont* (1903), and his subsequent historical and other novels do not compare.

his "art based on science" elsewhere. But he became a recruit of the movement, writing a play, *The Bending of the Bough* (1900), for the Irish Literary Theatre, and collaborating with W. B. Yeats in another, *Diarmuid and Grania* (1901). This was the time when he came back and settled in Ireland for ten years. As already said,[1] *The Untilled Field* (1903) and *The Lake* (1905) showed that he had saturated himself with the atmosphere that exhales from a purely Irish soil, and modulated his style to catch the music and raciness of the peasant speech. These two novels, however, are almost all that can be put forward to redeem the fiction of this period from a singularly barren look, in comparison with the activity of the Scottish novelists; and still more, as is much more relevant, with the great period of Irish fiction which began with the effort to do for Ireland what the Waverley novels had done for Scotland, the period of the two Banims, Griffin, William Carleton, Lever and Lover, and also of the belated gothicism and lurid mystery-mongering of C. R. Maturin and Le Fanu.[2] But a still better comparison would be with the creative outburst, already imminent, in poetry and drama, of which Yeats and Synge, G. W. Russell, or "A.E.," and John Eglinton, the mystics, and Lady Gregory and Edward Martyn, were the protagonists, together with the scholars who had prepared it by disinterring the ancient Gaelic literature and salving current folklore. Some future historian of the Irish novel will have to add the names of Stephens and Joyce, and of Padraic Colum, Shan F. Bullock, Lord Dunsany, Conal O'Riordan, and perhaps others, to the list of novelists co-operating in the work of renewal and making fiction once more an utterance of the thought and imagination of the age, and will doubtless be able to write a worthy sequel to the chapter containing the names of Carleton and his associates. The truth of the matter is stated by E. A. Boyd in his survey of the Irish Literary Renaissance:

Anglo-Irish literature has been rich in poetry and drama, but the absence of good prose fiction is noticeable, when it

[1] See Vol. IX. 180–188.
[2] See Vol. VII. chap. i. For Le Fanu, see Vol. VIII. 216–219.

is remembered that the romances of O'Grady were the starting-point of the revival.[1]

It comes to this, that the immediate predecessors of Stephens and Joyce did very little indeed to make history. Respectable journey-men, or journey-women, with a fair knowledge of the world about them and an attentive eye for native and local traits, but with small creative power and no ideas, they kept the Irish novel just alive whilst more or less designedly toning down or at least accommodating the picture to the tastes of English readers. The critic just cited is no doubt right in hinting that the mediocre quality of their work was due as much to their having to accept the standards of an industry, provision of the articles on demand at the libraries, as to want of talent or of inspiration.[2] For Jane Barlow, Katherine Tynan, and Emily Lawless, to take but three, were poets of some genuine accomplishment; but they must rarely have put the best they were capable of into their fiction.

Origins of the revival

More than a generation before, Sir Samuel Ferguson and the poet Mangan had done much, according to their lights, to revive interest in the old Gaelic literature. The work they did, valuable in its day, was continued in a more scholarly and systematic fashion by Standish Hayes O'Grady and Dr Whitley Stokes, the *Silva Gadelica* (1892) of the former being a rich treasury of ancient texts, of historical or semi-historical legends and all sorts of early lore. With the establishment of a School of Irish Studies at Dublin by Dr Kuno Meyer, the transcription and translation of the huge corpus of old literature was put upon a scientific basis, and the work went on steadily. Dr Douglas Hyde, Eleanor Hull, Lady Gregory, T. W. Rolleston, A. P. Graves, George Sigerson, and others, edited the texts and provided translations in a literal or a modernized form. Besides the heroic sagas and romances, the resuscitated literature comprised lives of the saints, humorous and satirical tales, and an abundance of narrative and lyrical verse, this last in particular being largely of a

[1] Boyd, 375.

[2] A vast quantity of purely "circulationist" fiction must be laid to the charge of Irish writers. Much of it is frankly added as a "side-line" to their literary activities; some of it is doubtless intended as a contribution to literature (*Ibid.*, 375).

mystical trend. All of it had a profound effect upon the poets and novelists, and the influence is still working. In Yeats, for example, the humour comes to life again, and no merely archaic life, in that little morality-play, *Cathleen ni Houlihan*; the myths and fairy-lore, kept alive among the peasants, are preserved and transfigured with a new gramarye in two sets of prose versions, *The Celtic Twilight* (1895) and *The Secret Rose* (1897), and given fresh import in his lyrical play, *The Shadowy Waters*; whilst the dramatic grandeur of the old epics is seized and developed anew in his tragedies, *On Baile's Strand* and *Deirdre*. Writers of comedy such as Synge and Lady Gregory, though their characters had to resemble sufficiently the people of their own day, were none the less indebted to the older literature and to the folklore which has roots as primeval. The Irish literary renaissance was in truth based, like the English Romantic movement, on a resurrection of the past, even of the Middle Ages and times still more remote. In the novel this is particularly evident, for the man who roused general interest in the great stories from the ancient literature and who has even been hailed as "the Father of the Literary Revival in Ireland,"[1] was another Standish O'Grady, whose two volumes of a *History of Ireland*, vol. i., *The Heroic Period* (1878), and vol. ii., *Cuculain and his Contemporaries* (1880),[2] had a huge circulation, and were followed by a long series of romances and novels, retelling the heroic legends in a simple but adequate epic style and dressing up in attractive colours famous episodes of Elizabethan and Jacobean times in Ireland.

Standish James O'Grady

Standish James O'Grady (1846–1928) was not one of the exact and highly scrupulous scholars, such as his namesake and the other redactors and translators mentioned. The job to which he applied himself was to stir up popular interest in his

[1] Boyd, 54. Father Stephen Brown pays him a similar tribute (*Ireland in Fiction*, 202–203).

[2] Only the first volume appeared of O'Grady's *History of Ireland, critical and philosophical* (1881), in which he alludes to these earlier volumes as "portions of a work in which I propose to tell the history of Ireland through the medium of tales, epical or romantic . . . the work of which the present is the first volume belongs to an altogether different order of historical composition, and is critical, not constructive or imaginative."

country's past. His work is finished and done with now; but, at any rate, he did it at the right moment, and the result was an awakening of the racial consciousness and of patriotic feeling. In his first work of fiction, *Red Hugh's Captivity* (1889), he appeared in the role of a Malory; this was his picturesque account of Hugh Roe O'Donnell's kidnapping and captivity in Dublin Castle in 1591. But it was rather as an Ossian that in *Finn and his Companions* (1893), *The Coming of Cuculain* (1894), and its sequel, *In the Gates of the North* (1901), he reduced the confused story in the old epics to a form suited for common reading. He rewrote his story of Red Hugh in *The Flight of the Eagle* (1897), one of his most vivid evocations of the past, though *Ulrick the Ready* (1896) falls little short of it, and his nine stories of Elizabethan times, *The Bog of Stars* (1893), had been a stirring example of his historical realism, always richly seasoned with romance. He returned to the heroic age and knit all together in *The Triumph and Passing of Cuculain* (1919). Irish writers had long been addicted to historical fiction; it was this lively and popular style of his, and the vivifying light he shed over the national past, that outdistanced these laborious predecessors, and made such a definite mark upon his time. Thus, there was Charles ffrench Blake-Forster, who in *The Irish Chieftains* (1872) gave his countrymen a learned account of the Williamite wars and of the part played by the O'Shaughnessey and Blake-Forster clans, all well documented in an appendix. And there was the prolific Miss M. L. O'Byrne, the best of whose half-dozen careful historical studies was *The Pale and the Septs* (1876), a circumstantial and thoroughly anti-English account of the subjugation of Ireland in the sixteenth century. But neither these earnest statements of a case in the form of fiction, nor the numerous historical romances intended simply to amuse, are likely now to be read again; they are scarcely works of literature. And forgotten now, for other reasons, are a handful of novels by the Fenian journalist, Charles Joseph Kickham (1826–1882), who was sentenced to fourteen years' penal servitude, and broken in health and spirit found relief in these lifelike and both humorous and touching stories of the small farmers and peasants of his native Tipperary. The best of them, *Knockagow* (1879), appeals to some Irish critics as "one of the greatest, if not the greatest, of all Irish novels." [1]

Emily Lawless

More of a novelist than O'Grady, and as good an historian without so much romanticism, the Hon. Emily Lawless (1845–1913) knew the western peasantry, and had the historical imagination to paint some circumstantial and infinitely affecting pictures of the grimmest phases of the English conquest, without undue bias towards either side, though as a refined Victorian lady she was liable to depict the common people of long ago as little better than savages. But she by no means minimized the atrocities wreaked by the English in their campaigns against the guerrillas and their policy of merciless reprisals. Her worst faults appear in her first novel, *Hurrish* (1886), in which she tried sincerely to be just and kind to the peasants of County Clare, but felt at the same time that she must show up the dark deeds of the Land Leaguers. And she always had difficulties with the brogue. She knew the Aran Isles, and her next peasant novel was written in a mood of tenderness and idealism: *Grania, the story of an island* (1892), may stand beside the finer of her Irish poems. In between these novels, she wrote what was intended to be a realistic narrative, *With Essex in Ireland* (1890), in what she supposed to be Elizabethan English, of the abortive attempt to put down the rebellion of 1599 in Tyrone. It was an able effort at historical reconstruction, and better on the whole than her next, *Maelcho, a sixteenth-century narrative* (1894), an appalling record of barbarities and horrors, every one of them said to be an historical fact, the aftermath of the Desmond revolt. Miss Lawless drew nearer to the peasants, and she showed a kindlier understanding of their warm but reserved humanity and incalculable vagaries, and a graphic pen for the scenery of Connemara and the extreme south-west, in a miscellany of tales, some semi-historical, *Traits and Confidences* (1898), and her story of a boy, *The Book of Gilly* (1906). She also wrote a book in conjunction with Shan F. Bullock, *The Race of Castlebar* (1913), in which a very matter-

[1] Brown, *Ireland in Fiction*, 131.

of-fact Englishman describes as an eyewitness the French invasion of Ireland in 1798, and the famous rout of the English forces at Castlebar, with the subsequent savage chastisement of the rebellious Irish. The authors founded their story on a contemporary relation by Joseph Stock, Protestant Bishop of Killala. Emily Lawless was good at a ballad, and many will remember her "Fontenoy":

> Send us, ye western breezes, our full, our rightful share,
> For Faith, and Fame, and Honour, and the ruined hearths of Clare.

Jane Barlow and other ladies

Jane Barlow (1860–1917), also, was a poet; and the first of her volumes of peasant stories in verse, *Bogland Studies*, appeared the same year as her first collection of prose tales, *Irish Idylls* (1892). In both, she made extensive use of dialect, and native critics were of opinion that she never quite mastered either the peasant idiom or an accurate rendering of the pronunciation. They also refused to recognize the more humorous of her figures as anything more than the traditional types current in fiction ever since Lever. At any rate, many are entertaining enough; and the pious old folk, whether peasants or broken-down gentry, bearing their lot with a simple dignity and unfailing charity towards their even poorer neighbours, are drawn with an infectious kindliness. It is impossible to avoid a comparison with the Kailyard group: these are sketches of the same class of people, but in this case not by one of themselves. Miss Barlow shows the familiarity of a friend and intimate; but her appreciation of lowly virtues is not always free from an air of condescension. She has been censured also for ignoring such regular appurtenances of an Irish village as the priest, the gombeen-man, and the agitator, and indeed for showing no awareness of the darker realities in the background of Irish life. Her talent was for the simple little tale, the idyll as she called it, dwelling on the more admirable aspects of human relations; and she knew very well therewith how to convey the charm of an Irish landscape. *Strangers at Lisconnel* (1895), *Maureen's Fairing* (1895), *Mrs Martin's Company* (1896), *From the Land of the Shamrock* (1901), *By Beach and Bogland* (1905), and *Irish Neighbours*

(1907) show the same general complexion and the same refined qualities of English prose as the *Irish Idylls* with which she began. When she exceeded her range and tried to sustain interest in a novel of full length, as in *Kerrigan's Quality* (1893) or *The Founding of Fortunes* (1902), she failed somehow to make it hold together properly.

Katherine Tynan, and Somerville and Ross

Another who was fertile in minor verse and in the early years of the revival was regarded as full of promise, in spite of a hankering after Rossetti's Pre-Raphaelitism, was Katherine Tynan (1861–1931), who married the novelist H. A. Hinkson. The best of her work is in *Ballads and Lyrics* (1891), and, like her fiction later on, is devoutly Catholic in feeling. For she turned novelist, and had great vogue as a purveyor of stories and novels of the light drawing-room order, the kind of thing indicated in such titles as *The Dear Irish Girl* (1899), *She Walks in Beauty* (1899), *A Girl of Galway* (1901), and *The Handsome Quaker* (1902)—this last is a set of peasant stories. Story-tellers of an entirely opposite cast were those productive friends, Miss Edith Œnone Somerville and the late Violet Martin, who called herself "Martin Ross." *Some Experiences of an Irish R.M.* (1899) and *All on the Irish Shore* (1903) were followed by a long series of yarns and anecdotes of the hunting-field, the gentry, and the peasants, the sparkling and unforced humour of which is very catching, and is calculated to provide a holiday from more serious fiction. Without apparent effort, they hit off the lineaments of peer and peasant, and even elicit humour from dogs and horses. It is Lever all over again, but with distinct modern improvements. The local colour, for instance, of Connemara and County Cork is both vivid and accurate.

Other novelists and story-tellers

Most novelists of the other sex were seriously intent on realism, and may safely be regarded as authentic witnesses of character and ways of life. Shan F. Bullock, for example, already mentioned as a collaborator with Emily Lawless, went on from such sketches of his native district on the borders of Fermanagh and Cavan as *Ring o' Rushes* (1897) and *Irish Pastorals* (1901), to painstaking studies of character and the trials of life, in full-length novels, such as *The Barrys* (1899),

The Squireen (1903), and his history of a self-made man from America, *Dan the Dollar* (1906). On the whole, he is more serious than Seumas MacManus, who was professedly doing much the same thing for Donegal, but overdid the regulation humour and the brogue, except perhaps in *A Lad of the O'Friels* (1903), dealing with the complex stresses of lowly life in a poor hamlet, at the time O'Connell was agitating. The Rev. Patrick Augustine Sheehan (1852–1913), parish priest of Doneraile, likewise took the precaution to enliven with humour his treatment of various basic problems, such, for instance, as confront even a comparatively humble person, the fresh arrival who proposes to be a new broom in a sleepy parish, in *My New Curate* (1900). Later novels deal thoughtfully and idealistically with certain moral dilemmas. In *Luke Delmege* (1901), probably his best, it is the public and the private bearings of a parish priest's routine of duties. *Glenanaar* (1905) opens with that notorious affair, the Doneraile conspiracy of 1829, and claims some allowances for tainted heredity in the third generation for one of the later informers. In *Lisheen, or the test of the spirits* (1907), the idea of a landed proprietor undertaking to live as a labourer is obviously borrowed from Tolstoy's *Resurrection.* Another very earnest study of ethical and social issues is *The Blindness of Dr Gray, or the final law* (1909). Few Irish novelists ventured on themes of such momentous scope; it will, on the contrary, have been noticed that they were often content with the slightness of mere sketches, having considerably less even than the substance and significance of a story. Thus, the Ulster novelist Archibald M'Ilroy (1860–1915) is almost summed up in two small story- or sketch-books, *When Lint was in the Bell* (1897) and *By lone Craig-Linnie Burn* (1900), which are intrinsically not much more substantial in their idyllism than is the old-fashioned but evergreen humour of Edmund Downey, author of *Anchor-Watch Yarns* (1884) and of a nautical novel, *Dorothy Tuke* (1905), not quite so well known. One Nationalist writer followed older usage by putting famous historical episodes into a form that so readily pressed home his own convictions. This was Matthias M'Donnell Bodkin, author of *Lord Edward*

Fitzgerald (1896) and its sequel *The Rebels* (1899), and of a new reading of the story of Robert Emmet, *True Man or Traitor* (1910). No kind of fiction lends itself more readily to disguised pamphleteering.

Lady Gregory

As to the translations of the ancient literature, little of this mass of fiction from an earlier world comes into consideration here, except as offering imaginative ideas and suggestions and requickening the national genius. The Hydes and Sigersons and the rest of them were propagandists as much as preservers of a precious heritage. Eleanor Hull's collection of stories entitled *The Cuchullin Saga in Irish Literature* (1898), or the versions she made for young people, *Cuchulain, the Hound of Ulster* (1909), or Dr Hyde's editions of *The Adventures of the Lad of the Ferule* and *The Adventures of the Children of the King of Norway* (1899), or his collection of Gaelic folk-tales, *Beside the Fire* (1891), belong to the history of the revival but only indirectly to the history of the Irish novel. It is not quite the same with the best of the collateral work produced by Lady Gregory, for she wished her *Cuchulain of Muirthemne* (1902) and *Gods and Fighting Men* (1906) to be read by a public that was normally content with the ordinary novel; and to a large extent she succeeded. She thought it "more natural to tell the stories in the manner of thatched houses . . . than in the manner of the slated houses" where she had not heard them. It was an archaic, but not a dead language that she used; Yeats called it "the beautiful speech of those who think in Irish." By choosing the example of Malory rather than of those who censured her for not observing the strictness of scientific scholarship, she probably did more for the greater purposes they all professed than any except the creative poets Yeats and Synge.

Donn Byrne

Though born in New York, Bryan Oswald Donn Byrne (1889–1928) was the son of an Irishman and thoroughly Irish by genius and education, and his right to a postscript to this chapter is not to be questioned; he loved his country with a passion that is obtrusively lacking in the mere Anglo-Irish. He was a student of Dublin University, and used to spend his holidays in Antrim with Ada McNeill when she was organizing festivals and rousing enthusiasm for music, dancing, and the native language. Two negligible novels, the second, *The Foolish Matrons* (1920), a review of the garish excesses of so-called advanced society in New York, were followed by an Irish one, *Messer Marco Polo* (1921), first conceived as a poem but eventually thrown into the form of a folk-tale, and put in the mouth of an aged peasant. It tells how the great adventurer journeys across the ghoul-infested deserts of central Asia to the court of Kubla Khan, whose daughter he marries. Then came something more ambitious and more hazardous, *The Wind Bloweth* (1922), a romantic novel of the sea in the last great days of sailing-ships, centring in the outer and inner life of a young officer, a Campbell of Antrim. He blindly seeks his fate through a series of idylls, each ending in what he sees to be illusion; but at last, after wandering between hell and paradise, he hammers out a philosophy: "Success is in yourself, not outside yourself," and further, "There is a great Master and there is a Plan." There is something here of that hybrid thing, the problem novel, which has a certain rough logic; but a problem romance is, after all, only romance. This one hovers between prose and poetry; and the old legends give concrete shape to the travails of soul, and bring out the spiritual import of love between man and woman. Beauty and heroism move Donn Byrne to lyrical outbursts, while he renders the sordid things of life with a very plain-spoken realism.

The historical element

Blind Raftery and his wife Hilaria (1924) reverts to the saga style, the rhapsodical prose breaking now and again into musical verse. The old poet wanders about Connaught singing his songs, in the times of the South Sea Bubble—a full century out, but what odds? A villainous Welshman palms off his concubine on the sightless bard. But the shame of the innocent woman defiled by her foster-father is redeemed by her candour and devotion, and signally avenged by Raftery's scorching invective. Donn Byrne was a master of atmosphere, of picture and mirage: it is in large measure the evocative rhythm of the language, half-way to balladry, that works the miracle. *Hangman's House* (1925) challenges comparison with Moore's *Untilled Field* and *The Lake*, but only to result in utter contrast.

It is a romance of sporting life in County Dublin a century ago. Glenmalure, the grim Lord Justice's mansion, is virtually the protagonist in the drama. *An Untitled Story* (1925) and *Brother Saul* (1927) belong to the same genre as George Moore's last books. The one is the story of a nun who runs away with an Irishman, and finally has to obey the inner voice bidding her return to the cloister; the other is that of St Paul, from his youth at Tarsus to the end at Rome. *The Power of the Dog* (1926) might be called an historical novel, with its background hewn out of the Napoleonic era, and its unflattering effigies of Castlereagh and others. The situation between the loyal Irishman on Castlereagh's staff and his wife whose father was a rebel is one of those that always put Donn Byrne on his mettle. He was ever exploring the odd recesses of the Irish soul, and illustrating some vital concept in life and action. There is an historical element in all his stories; for, as he said of Shane Campbell, "It wasn't his past that was dead. The past lived. It was he was dead, he, his present, his future." Thus, it would be easy to affix dates to such a tale as *Crusade* (1928), in which claimants to the throne of Jerusalem and famous paladins figure. But what it does conjure up is the magic of an eternal past, inhaling which the reader comprehends why the Irish knight, who joined the crusade full of ardour and idealism but found the great heroes engaged in shabby intrigues and ruthless barbarities, turns in loathing to the Saracens, who had treated him as a captive with courtesy and chivalry, and rather than lose the beautiful daughter of the sheikh embraces Islam. Irish dislike of Norman greed and arrogance and Norman unscrupulousness is not yet dead. Says the Arab, flushing red with anger at the least innuendo of treachery, "There are some customs we have not yet learned from the Christians."

CHAPTER V

SOME WOMEN NOVELISTS

To group the women novelists of a period together is not intrinsically more illogical than to do so with Scottish or Irish novelists. The woman of letters has peculiarities that mark her off from the other sex as distinctly as peculiarities of race or of ancestral traditions. Whatever variety of talent, outlook, or personal disposition may be discernible in any dozen women writers taken at random, it will be matched and probably outweighed by resemblances distinctively feminine. So that it would be perfectly feasible to consider Jane Austen, Mrs Gaskell, George Eliot, and the Brontë sisters as forming a group, and contrast them as novelists with those of the opposite sex; but it would be absurd to try to do the like with Dickens and Thackeray, Meredith and Hardy.

Mrs Oliphant

There is no better example of the truth of this generalization than that industrious writer Mrs Oliphant, whose early novels in the manner of Galt and her other countrymen have already been mentioned.[1] Margaret Oliphant (*née* Wilson, 1828–1897) sent her first novel into the world in 1849, and kept up a steady supply of the same sort of fiction, interspersed with works of travel and biography, nearly to the end of the century. She was born the same year as Meredith and Rossetti, and so was senior to William Morris, Swinburne, and Hardy. In fact, her earlier novels belonged to the age of Spencer, Mill, Huxley, Ruskin, Carlyle, Tennyson, and the Brownings. Her Carlingford novels (1861–1876),[2] which hold the same place in her work as the Barchester novels in Trollope's, began well before the end of his famous series. It was the year of *Romola*, and the year between Meredith's *Evan Harrington* and *Sandra*

[1] See above, p. 159.

[2] They began in "Maga" (1861)

Belloni. Mrs Oliphant was a decade younger than George Eliot; but her fiction is as much of George Eliot's time as of that which followed. In truth, the novels of domestic life by her and her like belong to no particular era, even if incidents and social and religious embarrassments here and there such as could not have occurred at any other period give some of them a date. She is not to be ranked as anything more than a minor novelist, though her quiet humour gave her another distinction than that of the honoured veteran in a crowd of sister novelists some of whom are still alive. She is a clear-sighted woman looking archly at the human comedy, as it proceeds on the stage of a small country town—a Mrs Gaskell who has learned a good deal from Dickens [1] and still more from Trollope. But Trollope, Mrs Gaskell, and Dickens were too original and too self-willed to be unduly hampered by the laws and regulations of the novel of commerce.

The three-volume regime

Mrs Oliphant cheerfully submitted to the ordinance that the novel must be a composition of a certain length, with a mystery or some exciting complication in it, and a denouement, in other words a happy ending, in the third volume. Her own interest was in manners and characters. But she always had to devise a story, to hold the fabric together; and this evidently went against the grain, though when there was nothing more to say she still had to go on and fill the allotted span. The result was that her novels almost always begin with a sprightly and arresting and by no means hackneyed round-up of the characters destined to cross each other's paths, and of the incompatibilities, jealousies, and petty feuds which are bound to bring them sooner or later to the most entertaining loggerheads; but ere long there are baffling signs of some artificial imbroglio, through the mazes of which the reader has to thread his way, praying for a winding-up the general shape of which he has long ago learned to foresee.[2] *Miss Marjoribanks*

[1] Although she did not like Dickens and was repelled by *Edwin Drood* and other late novels.

[2] The passing of the three-volume novel was an historical event, but mainly in the annals of minor fiction. A tradition ruled of ample proportions and lavish furniture, of which writers were afraid not to take advantage. Terseness was unheard of as a virtue; it would have been mere parsimony. Subscribers must

is a glaring instance. Nothing could be more diverting than the advent of the widowed doctor's capable young daughter and the revolution she brings about in Carlingford society; but the sequel is not merely an anticlimax, it is lame and humdrum. The comedy has been played out; yet Mrs Oliphant must observe the conventions and arrange a marriage for her heroine, which she does with a suitor who has been dismissed as a blockhead in the earlier pages—and a good riddance too! What with a weakness for repeating a good joke when she thinks of one, and labelling her characters with their pet phrases, like Lucilla's in this same novel, when anyone suggests that she ought to think of getting married now that she has done the grand tour and made a conquest of society, "If it had been *that* I was thinking of, I need never have come home at all, you know; and my object in life is just what it has always been, to be a comfort to papa," what with all this diffuseness, it is no wonder that Mrs Oliphant is as long-winded as any of her school.

The Carlingford novels

In Carlingford proper there is no trade, no manufactures, no anything in particular, except very pleasant parties and a superior class of people, indeed, to anything one expects to meet with in a country town, which is not even a county town, nor the seat of any particular interest. It is the boast of the place that it has no particular interest—not even a public school: for no reason in the world but because they like it, have so many nice people collected together in those pretty houses in Grange Lane—which is, of course, a very much higher tribute to the town than if any special inducement had led them there. But in every community some centre of life is necessary. This point, round which everything circles, is, in Carlingford, found in the clergy.

get their money's worth, at all events in quantity. The most importunate demand of the three-volume regime was for "poetic justice," *i.e.* a happy ending. Then there came a sudden halt; a shock went through both authors' and readers' minds: the paralysing question had arisen—Is justice a literary duty? Must art chastise sinners? The ship lay tossing, with engines reversed, in the grip of a fearful dilemma. No one had doubted the obligation that lay on the novelist to carry out that impeccable retribution which is so rarely attained in life—whatever may happen hereafter. It was only the greater novelists who were not much disturbed by the situation, when the happy ending and the whole doctrine of poetic justice were seen to be an offence against truth.

One can see from this preamble to *The Perpetual Curate* that it was not by accident both she and Trollope employed the clerical gambit, the latter with *The Warden* and *Barchester Towers*, Mrs Oliphant with *Salem Chapel*, *The Rector*, and *The Perpetual Curate*, not to mention disturbances between clergy and their patrons or critics of their orthodoxy in the later novels of both. Trollope had the wider outlook, but both had much the same sort of aims. Class distinctions, or, as Mrs Oliphant put it, "the perennial inequality between the two halves of mankind," and the heart-burnings as well as the spites and affectations of which they are the source, furnished in the last analysis half the efficient motives in the novels of both. Questions of doctrine or of conscience are of less importance, especially in Trollope, than the nice gradations between the higher dignitaries and the humble minister of the gospel. But the main point in the novels of either, whether the clash is between High and Low Church, Church and Chapel, or over the succession to a living or the prerogatives of a rector in his own parish, inevitably brings affairs into the public arena. The individual has his private troubles; but, as he stands peculiarly in the eye of his neighbours, the drama soon involves everybody in Carlingford, down to the maid-servants and errand-boys. It is remarkable what a large part is played by mere gossip in Mrs Oliphant's novels, right to the last. This it is, or its equivalent, being sent to Coventry, that drives the heroine of *The Cuckoo in the Nest* (1892), to take a late example, to change her mind and at a stroke provide a denouement satisfactory to everyone. She is the astute daughter of an innkeeper, and manages to become the legal wife of a baronet's weak-willed son and inherit the great house and the estate when they both die. But her old friends desert and the gentry ignore her, and she is glad to renounce her ill-gotten gains and marry the once-despised sweetheart who is now a champion cricketer. In *The Perpetual Curate*, it is nothing more than the baseless gossip of the town that threatens disaster to the heroic incumbent and the girl who loves him. It is much ado about absolutely nothing, and Mrs Oliphant seems to be clumsily making bricks without a blade of straw. But the ironical satire must not be missed, on the bent for scandal even in those who pride themselves on their goodness of heart, though it often leads her into exaggeration. It is at any rate much more telling than Trollope's attempts at the sardonic; and she went on applying it in her renderings of people's follies and absurdities still longer, with an industry not to be beaten even by his.

"Salem Chapel"

In *Salem Chapel* (1863), first of the Carlingford series, the tragi-comedy upsets the quiet routine of a Nonconformist congregation and the humble and somewhat smug society of "greengrocers, dealers in cheese and bacon, milkmen, with some dressmakers of inferior pretensions and teachers of day schools," belonging to the connexion. A new minister, Mr Vincent, fresh from the theological college, has succeeded old Mr Tufton, and arrives full of ideals and trust in human nature, only to find everything different from his expectations. He is a great preacher, but his flock do not respond; those who are impressed by his oratory are estranged by the reserve of a man who drapes himself in the mantle of his divine office. He suffers acutely, but all his efforts only make matters worse. When the crisis comes, he is manfully defended by Tozer the deacon; but it is of no avail. The minister has unhappily laid himself open to various misunderstandings through sheer extravagance of feeling, and throws up his pastorate.[1] The truth is, he is one of those leading masculine figures of Mrs Oliphant's whom she drew from her inner consciousness rather than from knowledge of the world. He is the sort of man that only a woman would have depicted, and his morbid sensitiveness and even his idealism are at bottom feminine qualities. Tozer and his brother deacons are much more true to life; but by far the best characters are the women: old Mrs Vincent, "quite the lady," gentle and self-effacing, but with a genius for social diplomacy, in fact, the one heroine in the book; Mrs Tozer and Phœbe and Mrs Pigeon the "deaconess," and

[1] Mrs Oliphant has repeatedly been compared to "Mark Rutherford" (see Vol. IX., chap. iii.), mainly on the strength of this delineation of a little world of Dissenters and "the revulsion of the young pastor" from its narrowness and intolerance (see, *e.g.*, *Cambridge History of English Literature*, xiii. 430–431). Her point of view, however, is totally different.

also the lachrymose Mrs Tufton and her cynical Adelaide. One of the best of those scenes in which Mrs Oliphant was wont to make her heterogeneous characters show themselves off to advantage, or disadvantage, is where Mrs Vincent deals with Mrs Pigeon and the sentimental Phœbe and handles Deacon Tozer with her usual unfailing tact. All this is recounted in such a lively style, and such spontaneous dialogue, that it seems to be going on before the eye; the old-established method of story-telling does not seem old-fashioned in the hands of Mrs Oliphant, especially as it affords full scope for her pungent but not unkindly irony. To Mr Vincent, and possibly to his creator, the ordeal he went through was a case of conscience. Actually, it is one of temperament, and as such came well within her range. As to the melodramatic business annexed to the main affair, Colonel Mildmay's attempt to seduce Susan Vincent and the attempted murder, this was the usual concession to the supposed expectations of the reading public, the sort of thing that was to mar a good half of Mrs Oliphant's fiction.

"The Rector," "The Perpetual Curate," etc.

In *The Rector* (1863) and *The Perpetual Curate* (1864), the situation is roughly parallel to Mr Vincent's, but the scene of action is the church and the parish, and society in the fullest Carlingford sense takes an active part. In the one, a learned Oxford don is appointed to the living; but his fervent "Low Churchism" makes no appeal to those habituated to "the old-fashioned orthodox way of having a great respect for religion and as little to do with it as possible." He does himself no credit, though he amuses the reader, in his bouts with the liberal-minded Archdeacon Beverley; and eventually he retires to the haven of his college. More like the Vincent case is that of Mr Wentworth, the perpetual curate of St Roque's, who is imbued with High Church principles, has a surpliced choir, and, aided by sisters of mercy, carries on a vigorous missionary campaign among the porters and bargees of the disreputable Wharfside. The new rector, Mr Morgan, violently resents both the ritualism and what he considers an unauthorized intrusion upon his own territory, the parish of Carlingford. The war between the two obstinate clerics comes to a head in the scandal made out of Mr Wentworth's blameless patronage of a giddy young woman. All this is very entertaining, though a little hard to swallow; and it leads up to a bit of first-rate comedy, the "bed of justice," on mediæval lines, in which the curate is tried by his peers, the best people of Carlingford, and triumphantly acquitted. But, again, Mrs Oliphant must complicate matters with her mysterious stranger, who turns out to be the swindling son of one of the curate's best friends, and the long-lost brother of the girl he wants to marry. The Rev. Frank Wentworth is another woman's man, a charming young fellow of the loftiest principle but far too good to be true. Mrs Oliphant goes deeply into the heart-searchings of his brother Gerald, who sacrifices his rectory and his family to join the Church of Rome; but such questions were evidently beyond her. Her proper line was to show how such persons as the fanatical Aunt Leonora were affected by these controversies. The spectacle of this dragonish lady, who has in her gift a well-endowed living that would have saved her nephew from all his troubles, torn between family affection and a stern fidelity to the purest Evangelicalism, is a recurring occasion of quiet mirth. "The Last Chronicle of Carlingford" was *Phœbe Junior* (1876), which follows the amiable Mr Beecher, who succeeded Mr Vincent and married Phœbe Tozer, to London and a fashionable chapel near Regent's Park. Their daughter, Phœbe Junior, has been to a superior school and is altogether a modern young woman. She enlightens and rather frightens her parents with her advanced ideas, and makes herself a central figure in very different spheres of society from those of Nonconformist Carlingford, though not less fertile in the human characteristics congenial to Mrs Oliphant.

"*Miss Marjoribanks*"

Ten years previously had appeared *Miss Marjoribanks* (1866), which might have been the masterpiece of the series had Mrs Oliphant only known when to stop. Its subject is the impact of a domineering young woman on a society that badly wants enlivening, and the delicate situations in which she finds herself in the course of her campaign. When, in the second part, Mrs Oliphant turns aside to the history of Lucilla's heart, an organ not previously heard of, it is really a change of subject that dislocates the book. Lucilla comes home from abroad determined to be a comfort to the bereaved Dr Marjoribanks, who does not feel in the least bereaved and does not want to be comforted. Nevertheless, next morning,

She was down to breakfast, ready to pour out the coffee, before the Doctor had left his room. He found her, to his intense astonishment, seated at the foot of the table, in the place which he usually occupied himself, before the urn and the coffee-pot. Dr Marjoribanks hesitated for one momentous instant, stricken dumb by this unparalleled audacity; but so great was the effect of his daughter's courage and steadiness, that after that moment of fate he accepted the seat by the side where everything was arranged for him, and to which Lucilla invited him sweetly, though not without a touch of mental perturbation. The moment he had seated himself, the Doctor's eyes were opened to the importance of the step he had taken. "I am afraid I have taken your seat, papa," said Miss Marjoribanks, with ingenuous sweetness. "But then I should have had to move the urn and all the things, and I thought you would not mind." The Doctor said nothing but "Humph!" and even that in an undertone; but he became aware all the same that he had abdicated, without knowing it, and that the reins of state had been smilingly withdrawn from his unconscious hands.

When Nancy made her appearance the fact became still more apparent, though still in the sweetest way. "It is so dreadful to think papa should have been bothered with all these things so long," said Miss Marjoribanks. "After this I am sure you and I, Nancy, can arrange it all without giving him the trouble. Perhaps this morning, papa, as I am a stranger, you will say if there is anything you would like, and then I shall have time to talk it all over with Nancy, and find out what is best,"—and Lucilla smiled so sweetly upon her two amazed subjects that the humour of the situation caught the fancy of the Doctor, who had a keen sense of the ridiculous. He laughed out, much to Nancy's consternation, who was standing by in open-eyed dismay. "Very well, Lucilla," he said; "you shall try what you can do. I daresay Nancy will be glad to have me back again before long;

but in the meantime I am quite content that you should try."

So, good-bye to the little bachelors' dinners, for which the Doctor's house was famous; a new epoch commences in its history and that of Carlingford society. For Lucilla soon prevails upon her father to have the house refurnished, in a style new to Carlingford; and in the now well-appointed drawing-room she purposes to entertain the immaculate inhabitants of Grange Lane and those of the county people who are near enough to drive in when there is a moon. Such was the origin of Lucilla's Thursday evenings, which speedily became a regular institution and made Carlingford a different place. Having brought the Doctor to heel, she had to do the same with various other recalcitrant persons, and do so with a grace and ease that left the most redoubtable perfectly speechless. Hence a series of inimitable scenes. The Rector, incited by a circle of female friends, finds a companion for the lonely young lady, who would have scorned the very idea of a chaperon: "My dear Miss Lucilla, now you have come home, who stand so much in need of a mother's love, we must try to find someone to fill her place":

Lucilla uttered a scream of genuine alarm and dismay; and then she came to herself, and saw the force of her position. She had it in her power to turn the tables on the Rector, and she did not hesitate, as a weaker woman might have done, out of consideration for anybody's feelings. "Do you mean you have found someone for him to marry?" she asked, with a look of artless surprise, bending her earnest gaze on Mr Bury's face. As for the Rector, he looked at Lucilla aghast, like a man caught in a trap. "Of course not, of course not," he stammered, after his first pause of consternation; and then he had to stop again to take breath.

The schemes of the anxious friends are brilliantly outwitted. But Lucilla surpasses herself in the great scene, long and carefully prepared, when she both literally and metaphorically corners the Archdeacon, with his dangerous knowledge of the real facts of the case between Mr Cavendish and the widow whom he is supposed to have done out of her legacy; and not only saves the naughty Cavendish from an exposure that would not have suited her book, but actually patches up a marriage between the Archdeacon and the lady. The cross-purposes of the different parties called upon her for the utmost ingenuity, but she rose to the occasion.

She had to frighten the Archdeacon with the idea that Mrs Mortimer might marry the impostor, and she had to keep the widow in the profoundest ignorance of this suggestion, and she had to manage and guide the impostor himself, to save his position, and deliver him from his enemies, and make his would-be prosecutor for ever harmless. If by chance she should forget herself for a moment, and say to Mr Beverley what she meant for Mr Cavendish, or betray her mode of dealing with either to the third person interested, then farewell to all her hopes. But when all that was required was skill and self-possession and courage, Miss Marjoribanks knew herself too well to be afraid.

Her only defect, which she herself acknowledges, but only as a strange singularity, is that she has no sense of humour. But she supplies humour unfailingly, when she makes her guests the unconscious instruments of her entertainments; when she stupefies Mr Cavendish's sister, who hopes and trusts he has proposed to her, by imploring her to send him back to flirt with the young ladies—"As for flirting, I have always said he was the only man that knew anything about it"—and when she urbanely carries him off under the very nose of the girl who is trying to entrap him. This young woman, Barbara Lake, is not a likeable person, and Mrs Oliphant obviously does not love her a bit. Hence it is the more significant of Mrs Oliphant's powers of characterization that, after Lucilla, she makes her minx the most interesting study of a female personality in the book. Barbara is utterly wrong-headed, and resents Lucilla's efforts to bring her out in Carlingford society, merely that her fine contralto voice may be heard in duets with that young lady's soprano.

Barbara was quite unscrupulous, for at the bottom she could

not but feel that anyone who was kind to her was taking an unwarrantable liberty. What right had Lucilla Marjoribanks to be kind to her? As if she was not as good as Lucilla any day! And though it might be worth her while to take advantage of it for the moment, it was still an insult, in its way, to be avenged if an opportunity should ever arise.

The scandalous behaviour of Mr Cavendish at the Thursday evenings makes excellent comedy; but the mystery and melodrama of his more serious delinquencies are as usual trumpery stuff: Mrs Oliphant was a bad hand at roguery.

Later novels

She never reached these high standards again; her kindness of heart tended to stifle her irony, although she tried harder and harder to be an uncompromising realist and draw characters just as they are, without undue indulgence and without satire, as in the case of the sordid vulgarian in *Old Mr Tredgold* (1896), which appeared a year before she died. Hers is an expurgated edition of life; like most of the novelists of the domestic sphere, she calmly and perhaps unwittingly shunned the more serious realities. Her characterization is not much more than skin-deep. Though she was not content even to begin with stock characters and stock situations, her originality did not survive middle age, and she went on repeating herself at last. It is a woman's view, and it is only the women that are drawn with thorough comprehension and adequate but not excessive sympathy, though Mrs Oliphant was no friend to the women's movement of her day. The established test of such a writer's thoroughness is the way she deals with love between her men and women. Mrs Oliphant seems to have accepted her duties in this ticklish matter as part of the regular routine of novel-writing, and acquitted herself with her usual conscientiousness but a perfunctoriness indicating a considerable lack of interest. There are plenty of love-affairs in her novels, but there is no genuine love-making. People propose and are accepted, and the engagements are announced, and sometimes are a factor in the trend of events. But Mrs Oliphant treats love with much the same indifference as does Lucilla Marjoribanks, her perfect criterion of a well-regulated mind, one of whose pet phrases is that fortunately her "affections were not engaged," and so no harm was done when Mr So-and-so did not offer himself as her friends expected. On the other hand, the clandestine affairs with little Rosa in *The Perpetual Curate* and between Barbara and Mr Cavendish in *Miss Marjoribanks* are so silly and incredible, that they can be described only as prudish make-believe for eking out the prescribed melodrama. Mrs Gaskell had not shrunk from the truth, and the Brontë sisters had boldly faced the ugliest facts. It is hard to realize in reading Mrs Oliphant's hollow versions of the commonest event in the drama of life that she was writing after the date of *Adam Bede* and of *The Mill on the Floss*.

Novels of the occult

She revealed an unexpected talent about the middle of her career, in a set of spiritual romances. *A Beleaguered City* (1878) had the long sub-title, "A narrative of certain recent events in the city of Semur, in the department of the Haute Bourgogne: a story of the seen and the unseen." It is the mayor of Semur who recites the plain facts of the dread visitation, in the manner for which Defoe had long ago supplied the precedent. A spectral twilight falls on the city, followed by a darkness that can be felt, and the inhabitants flee under a compulsion stronger than fear. It is the dead who have expelled the living, obliged them "to yield their places, which they had not filled aright, to those who knew the meaning of life, being dead." *A Little Pilgrim in the Unseen* (1882) and *The Land of Darkness* (1888) tell of the life after death, as a very simple-minded woman awakes to envisage it.[1]

Anne Thackeray and Rhoda Broughton

The quiet, delicate, meditative novels of Thackeray's daughter, Anne Isabella Thackeray, afterwards Lady Ritchie (1838–1919), pleased one generation, but their popularity did not survive it, and they were thrown into the shade, even in her own day, by the far from quiet and delicate love-tales of Rhoda Broughton, two years her junior. It would seem, perhaps, indiscreet to couple such contrasts together, had not Trollope already done so, when he remarked of the latter that

[1] Mrs Oliphant is cautiously summed up by Henry James, in *Notes on Novelists*. He regretted that "her singular gift was less recognized, or at any rate less reflected, less reported upon, than it deserved."

she "does take the trouble to make her personages stand upright on the ground," which the "lazy" Miss Thackeray often failed to do.[1] Portraiture of common average character, and musings on those defects and perversions of will which affect the happiness of others as well as oneself, form the gist of *The Story of Elizabeth* (1863), *The Village on the Cliff* (1867), and *Old Kensington* (1873). The man in the first, a prey to indecision, who falls in love with the daughter of the woman who has loved him for twenty years; the poor governess in the second, who loves without return, and then marries one who could never be her true mate; and the prig, Robert Henley, and the gentle, idealizing heroine, in the third, are all examples of such calamitous results of egotism or error. She adapted a well-known theme to the same effect in *Blue-beard's Keys* (1874), and in *Miss Angel* (1875) and *Mrs Dymond* (1886) placed her little moralities in a framework of historical manners: Reynolds and Angelica Kauffmann are the prominent figures in the one, the other dwells on the sad lot of the women and children when the Germans had France at their mercy.

Rhoda Broughton

Trollope went on as to Rhoda Broughton (1840–1920), "And she has the gift of making them speak as men and women do speak." There is nothing wooden about her novels. "But they are not sweet-savoured as are those by Miss Thackeray, and are, therefore, less true to nature. In Miss Broughton's determination not to be mawkish and missish, she has made her ladies do and say things which ladies would not do and say." [2] So fierce was her revulsion from the conventionalism of most novelists of her sex, and from the reticence which she would have called prudery of such as Miss Thackeray and Mrs Oliphant, that she took her revenge by writing of nothing but love, and writing with an unrestraint that was too much for the stiff decorum of the sixties and seventies. But there was nothing really dreadful in her effusive displays of amorous emotion, though, as she said in old age, she was like a Zola to the times when she began, and a Charlotte Yonge to her contemporaries later. "It's not I that have changed, it's my fellow-countrymen." The story goes, apropos of her first

[1] *Autobiography*, chap. xiii., "Modern English Novelists." [2] *Ibid.*

novels which were anonymous, that her father strictly forbade her to read them. The very titles indicate what they are: *Not Wisely, but too Well* (1867), *Red as a Rose is She* (1870), *Good-bye, Sweetheart* (1872), *Doctor Cupid* (1886). But the contents are not utterly frivolous, unless a lively fancy and genuine humour are frivolous things. Under all the effusiveness and the flippancy, a sharp penetration will be recognized: a pretty wit will not allow it to escape detection. She may deify passion—and those whose magnificent physique rather than any finer qualities evoke it in the gentler sex—and regard the world simply as a theatre for erotic perturbations. At any rate, she is not a crude sentimentalist; and Trollope did no more than justice to her artistic qualities, over-lenient though he was to the lapses from good taste and the overstrained use of the present tense which were the accompaniments of her sprightliness and her determination to be lifelike whatever the expense. He was hardly qualified himself to criticize her style. In *Not Wisely, but too Well*, Dare, who is on his deathbed, says to his sorrowing beloved:

"O child, to-night I'm going somewhere, or"—with a pause—"who knows?—nowhere!"

A spasm of agony crossed her face. "Don't talk that way," she said, with a gesture of despair; "it kills me to hear you. Oh, my poor dear fellow, you *are* going somewhere indeed! Oh, I wonder is it anywhere good!"

A dreadful innuendo; but Rhoda Broughton's candid heroines do say such things. Her general programme appears in her first novel, *Cometh up as a Flower* (1867), where the innocent, impulsive girl loves a handsome soldier, but has to marry a rich husband for the sake of the family finances. The heroes that follow are of the Guy Livingstone stamp; the heroines as a rule have more heart than head. But in *Second Thoughts* (1880) she presents a very tolerable taming of a shrew.

"Belinda," etc.

And then came what is probably her best novel, *Belinda* (1883), a more complicated story, with a number of caustic sketches bordering on caricature. Outwardly, Belinda is cold and impassive; but her nature is as ardent as that of her predecessors, and she is saved only just in time from the wages of folly. Her "fierce shyness" is a little overdone. "Is it her fault that all strong emotion with her translates itself into a cold, hard voice, and a chill, set face?" Of course, it is, if it will cost her the man she passionately loves. But she never cures herself of meeting her lover's timid—too timid—advances with a chilling reserve that seems like the maiden bashfulness of the sentimental novelists reduced to absurdity. The upshot is, she puts Rivers to flight, finds herself presently the wife and bond-slave of a pachydermatous professor, and is saved at last from "infamy" by the sudden death of her husband at the very moment that she has nerved herself to run away. In *A Beginner* (1894) and *A Fool in her Folly* (1920) Miss Broughton put on the stage a novelist as unsophisticated and indiscreet as she herself was supposed to have been in her youth. The Beginner writes a novel that is branded as improper, to the dismay of her relatives, friends, and lovers. In the other, a posthumous book, a lady of eighty relates how she wrote, as a girl, the daring novel "Love," and subsequently encountered the lover whom her youthful imagination had glorified, and he turns out to be a thorough-paced scamp. One of Rhoda's admirers, Helen Mathers (1853–1920), made a hit with *Comin' thro' the Rye* (1875), a novel published anonymously which was put down at once to the author of *Not Wisely but too Well* and *Good-bye, Sweetheart*.

The Problem Novel

But the women's novels having widest vogue in the middle years of Victoria's reign were written, and also read, in a graver mood. The authors took themselves and their duties as seriously as if they were George Eliots; and their readers seem to have preferred them, forasmuch as they provided cut-and-dried solutions of the most harassing riddles. For they narrowed their vision so as to see life as made up of problems, which is as much as to say that they reduced it to a series of abstractions. Fiction almost ceased in their hands to be an art concerned with the concrete material of the human world. They are, indeed, a phenomenon of social rather than literary history, and interesting here only as further examples of the readiness with which a facsimile of the novel can be applied to the purposes of controversy and didacticism. One of the most influential of these counsellors and expositors was Mrs Lynn Linton (1822–1898), who wrote what purported to be novels, bearing such titles as *Grasp your Nettle* (1865), *Sowing the Wind* (1867), *Under which Lord* (1879). The alternative indicated in this last is between a woman's husband and the priest. One of her successes was a parallel to the scriptural story, *The True History of Joshua Davidson, Christian Communist* (1872). She was a rabid opponent of the women's movement, which she satirized in *The Rebel of the Family* (1880) and *The Autobiography of Christopher Kirkland* (1885). Even a meek and harmless caterer for the schoolgirl and older lovers of sentiment, "Edna Lyall" (Ada Ellen Bayly, 1857–1903), wrote a problem novel, *Donovan* (1882), which is a shallow study of agnosticism in Bradlaugh's time.

Lucas Malet, etc.

But the lady who called herself "Lucas Malet" (Mary St Leger Harrison, 1852–1931) was read and earnestly discussed by people who called themselves intellectuals. *The Wages of Sin* (1890) and *The History of Sir Richard Calmady* (1901), the one on the most hackneyed of themes and the other the moral history of a self-tormenting baronet, as rich as Crœsus but a cripple from birth, were long a topic of solemn conversation and of sermons that struck while the iron was hot. "Lucas Malet" was a daughter of Charles Kingsley; but, as Abel Chevalley observed, tried too much to rival Mrs Humphry Ward. Mrs William Kingdon Clifford, wife of a well-known scientist, found her favourite subjects in cases of morbid psychology as much as in ethical dilemmas, as in *Mrs Keith's Crime* (1885) and *Aunt Anne*[1] (1892). But for several years the novel that focused debate was *The Heavenly Twins* (1893), by that champion of woman's freedom, "Sarah Grand." And this soon had to bear the brunt of competition with *A Superfluous Woman* (1894), by Emma Frances Brooke, and Grant Allen's bold and hardly serious manifesto, *The Woman who Did* (1895). Another lady who had a good innings was Mary Cholmondeley, who wrote melodramatic novels of fashionable society, with a great display of the psychology of motive, the

[1] "La 'Mère Goriot' du roman anglais" (Chevalley, 189).

most notorious of which was *Red Pottage* (1899). Beatrice Harraden (1864–1936) worked hard for social reform and women's suffrage; but she refrained from controversy in her most popular book, *Ships that Pass in the Night* (1893), about the people at an Alpine health resort who come within hail and comfort each other on the the voyage of life.

A bare mention must suffice for Mrs Dudeney (1866–1930), *A few others* who, if she did not concentrate on problems, was given to contrasting modern types and manners and morals with those of a bygone age, and for Mrs Lizzie Allen Harker, a minor Mrs Gaskell, writing charming stories and novelettes of and for children and the domesticated people who never cease to love them. Mrs Hubert Bland (1848–1924), who often wrote under her maiden name of Edith Nesbit, was another who excelled in this sphere. *The Story of the Treasure Seekers* (1899) was followed by several others of the delightfully mischievous Bastable family. One batch of stories with a curious appeal was *The Literary Sense* (1903): the trouble arises in every single case from the fact that nearly everyone in these days has read far too many novels, and is liable at any moment to commit some fatal error through subconsciously trying to live up to the style of someone in a book. Another of the ladies who made a disturbance for a time was Ellen Thorneycroft Fowler (afterwards Mrs Felkin, 1860–1929). *Concerning Isabel Carnaby* (1898) and *A Double Thread* (1899) had the charm of witty dialogue and slashing contrasts of manners. The ingenious plot of the second was also a nine days' wonder. Miss Fowler came from Wolverhampton, and was particularly good at bringing out the humours and recapturing the pithy table-talk of Methodist society in the Midlands, especially the Black Country. Turn then to a novelist of a wider geographical range. But for the misfortune that she had to compete with Rudyard Kipling, Mrs Flora Annie Steel (1847–1929) might have been accepted as the standard Anglo-Indian novelist. She was of Scottish birth, and her *Red Rowans* (1895) and *In the Tideway* (1897) were about Scots characters. But already, in her conventional first novel, *Miss Stuart's Legacy* (1893), there had been incidental sketches of native Indian types, and the eight tales in the contemporaneous *From the Five Rivers* (1893) evinced an intimate acquaintance with native life in the Punjab, and even a power of throwing herself into the attitude of an Eastern raconteur. Folk-tales and more elaborate stories afterwards alternated with novels or romances, *Tales of the Punjab* and *The Flower of Forgiveness* (1894) and *In the Permanent Way* (1897) with a novel of the Mutiny, *On the Face of the Waters* (1896), and one of Akbar, the Great Mogul, *A Prince of Dreamers* (1908).

"John Oliver Hobbes"

Of more formidable calibre than most of these women was Mrs Pearl Mary-Teresa Craigie (1867–1906), who wrote under the style of "John Oliver Hobbes." She might have been included among the problem novelists; she was provocative enough. But she did not deal much with the commoner problems; rather did she excel in propounding some moral conundrum quite out of the ordinary, and resolving it in a manner entirely her own. In reading her, do not overlook the fact that she was American by birth,[1] though she received her education on this side of the Atlantic, and no one was better versed in the externals of fashionable society in London and also in the uglier features of its under side. She was one of those who have found an escape in fiction from the anguish of their own experiences. Her stories are charged with an intense personal emotion, only half disguised by the air of cynicism; and the twofold novel giving the career of Robert Orange indirectly lays bare the whole mental process that led her ultimately, through the stages of abnegation and moral austerity, to Roman Catholicism.

Tales

Four stories that had already made some noise are brought together in *The Tales of John Oliver Hobbes* (1894). The first sentence of *Some Emotions and a Moral* (1891) strikes this significant keynote:

"Ideals, my dear Golightly, are the root of every evil. When a man forgets his ideals he may hope for happiness, but not till then."

[1] See the *Life of John Oliver Hobbes, told in her correspondence, with a biographical Sketch* by her father, John Morgan Richards (1911).

At the end, Golightly, who has been philandering with another woman, finds out that his nearest friend has seduced his wife and has now committed suicide. The tragedy of marrying the wrong woman and loving and missing the right one is the burden of *The Sinner's Comedy* (1892). Anna is the pearl thrown to a swine, who amuses himself with it, whilst the man who knows the value of the treasure cannot touch it. But the tone is cynical; it is a wry comedy.

"My love for you," he said, "is a power outside myself. I cannot control it—*it* controls me. It is for you to decide whether for good or evil." Dimly it occurred to him that he had said something of the kind once before—to Anna. "I will try to be worthy of you," he added. She was a very pretty woman. He stooped and kissed her hand.

"Yes? A man may give his whole life to a woman, and it won't mean so much to her as if he had once jawed her out of neuralgia!"

"And a woman," said Emily, "may give her soul for a man, and he won't think so much of her as if—she had jilted him for somebody else."

A Study in Temptations (1893) and *A Bundle of Life* (1894) are to much the same purpose. "If the gods have no sense of humour they must weep a great deal." All four are condensed novels rather than mere stories, with numerous characters and all the rest of the paraphernalia. The characters for the most part are remarkable not for their individuality, but for their situations and emotions; many of them might be interchangeable. In fact, a certain shallowness is imputed; they are mostly beings "with many emotions but no heart, with ideas but no thoughts," as Mrs Craigie describes one of them. It all sounds very clever; but the cleverness is chiefly in the dialogue, which is often a continuous display of pyrotechnics. Chesterton was at fault, however, in putting down this overstrained brilliance to the assumption of the novelist of the "Smart Set" that these people are "distinguished, not only by smart dresses, but by smart sayings." [1] Mrs Craigie had a wit of her own, which she could not, anyhow at first,

[1] *Heretics*, "Smart Novelists and the Smart Set" (199–200).

keep under proper control. It was partly her disillusionment, her resentment, the pessimism that finds no relief but in gibes at everything, in perverse ejaculations. In her mature work—she was only thirty-nine when she died—wit and wisdom wed in many a fine aphorism; in these early pieces she seldom soared beyond epigrammatic smartness, hitting out at things in general but at nothing in particular. She hardly aimed at realism; she was not trying to execute a close copy of life. She was intent, rather, on finding for herself answers to certain insistent questions; and she sought moral rather than purely intellectual satisfaction. So she set little dramas going in an imagination only too full of apposite material, and worked out her sums in terms of what she had experienced of human nature. It required only a minimum of realistic detail, no elaborate circumstantial setting, and merely enough accuracy in such matters as Chesterton discusses not to stultify the inquiry. An art having this restricted range can with impunity take a great deal for granted.

"Robert Orange"

After a dubious and rather meretricious story of a man who finds that the woman he has just married has been a wanton, *The Gods, some Mortals, and Lord Wickenham* (1895), and the stronger and deeply pathetic "fantasia," *The Herb Moon* (1896), in which two unspotted beings love each other but are sundered by the fact that the woman's husband still lives, though in an asylum, Mrs Craigie bent her energies to a larger task. *The School for Saints* (1897) and *Robert Orange* (1900) are virtually one book, and it is a pity she did not keep this history of a man, or rather, of a soul, within such limits. There are too many characters, too wide an embrace of those religious, political, and social events that disturbed even the chancelleries of Europe in the period 1868–1870, and the analysis of states of mind determining the various transitions in her hero's career is needlessly elaborate. For in this case Mrs Craigie was profoundly serious, and renouncing her cynical pose traced the progress of two or three persons living on a higher spiritual plane than that of ordinary humanity to a state of certainty and peace. The main incidents in Robert's life, and some of them are very dramatic, mark the stages in his development of a philosophy. "Early in life, he had shaken his mind through the Hegelian sieve," a discipline that leaves no one unaltered. It was a potent influence even in his love-affairs—"Orange loved madly, passionately; but he knew it." His ceaseless self-scrutiny and the tragic crosses of his love for Brigit so react upon this son of a Dominican, that at last he fulfils the presage of his soul and becomes a Catholic priest. Meredith, whose influence is written large on the book, would have made it a more cogent and symmetrical whole, as he would have made some of the beautiful letters, including those supposed to be written by Disraeli, more beautiful still. It is evident also that Mrs Craigie had read Henry James; she had claimed to belong to the same school.[1] But her more particular model in this instance was Disraeli; the plot is like that of *Henrietta Temple*, the religious issues correspond to those of *Lothair*—there are three ladies here too who exercise no trifling influence over the hero's destinies.[2] And one of them, Pensée Fitz Rewes, eclipses in charm the heroine Brigit. Disraeli is, further, the oracle of the book: he is consulted, he gives advice, he moralizes on Robert's acts at the chief crises, and finally his general estimate of Monsignor Orange forms a sort of appendix to the book. A Whig's idea of the great statesman is quoted: elsewhere more respect is paid.

"Consider Dizzy. He won't be fully appreciated till every man jack of this generation is dead. He's too brilliant—he makes us all feel very dull dogs and very lame ducks. And he isn't an Anglo-Saxon—another crime. To be sure, we call him clever—*infinitely clever*—and we listen to his wit—as we watch a comedian—with amusement, which, however, we should be sorry to derive from anyone who had better claims to our society! We are so jealous of his statesmanship that we wouldn't even govern Europe by his influence. Lord! how he must despise us! That is why I like him."

Mrs Craigie not merely admires and emulates, but adopts

[1] *Life*, 106.

[2] To verify her resemblances to Disraeli as a novelist, see Vol. VII., chap. iii., especially pp. 147–148, 153, 159, 175, and 179.

Disraeli's general plan and many of his technical methods. Like him, she is a critical spectator of high society, reproducing its lively conversations and barbing them with epigram, and presenting her dramatis personæ in the same kind of pithy summaries of traits and tendencies rather than in dramatic action. Without falling short in the mundane picture, she shows herself, however, much more aware of the deeper issues, of the eternal rather than the merely earthly meanings. The life of Robert Orange is indeed a spiritual dialectic in action, as his journal abundantly illustrates.

Prayer has recently been defined as a *reference to one's higher self!* But one's "higher self" is the soul, and the soul belongs to God—and a man must save his soul because God will call him to account for it. *Individuality* is the new soft name for our secret sins.

That Mrs Craigie had her own case in view all the time is attested by her remarks on creative work as being autobiography in essence:

the rapid changes of mood, the disordered views, the storm and violence which are characteristic of every artist whose work is a form of autobiography rather than a presentment of impersonal forms and effects.

Of the conflict of ideas in Disraeli's novels it was said that there was no finality.[1] So it is also with Mrs Craigie's, not because ideas are exhausted, but because the contest does not end here. Orange says to Lady Sara, "Most lives have no denouement—so far as lookers-on are concerned." But he says elsewhere, more significantly, "If this life were all, it would be different." The denouement is not in this present existence. He "knew the claims which the world to come has upon us." As Disraeli puts it in his summing up, "It was his faith to believe that salvation rests on the negation and renunciation of personality." In the long journey to this destination there is a vast range of changing prospects and dramatic ups and downs, the most poignant of which is the

[1] See Vol. VII. 180.

long hoped-for marriage with Brigit, ruptured on the brink of the honeymoon by the fatal intelligence that she is still legally tied to the wretched Parflete. This is the grand climacteric, and the scene has great beauty, in spite of the tortuous casuistry that precedes and follows. In the four more of her riper novels finished before her untimely death there is the same explicit criticism of life in lieu of genuine presentation of it, especially in the pointed but too discursive conversations. *The Serious Wooing* (1901) was another "heart's history" like those with which she began; *Love and the Soul Hunters* (1902), another international novel of a shadier world than that traversed by Robert Orange; *The Vineyard* (1904) showed dull provincialism in a very distorting mirror, and *The Dream and the Business* (1906) was hardly more charitable towards various circles of suburban Nonconformists.

Mary Webb

One temporary result of Hardy's novels was a cult of the primitive mind: in those of Baring-Gould, the lady calling herself "Zack," Mr Eden Phillpotts, and some others, rustic life appeared to be a regular stage for ungovernable passions, culminating in crimes or tragic errors which had to be expiated by suffering, often on the part of the innocent.[1] A later hierophant of this cult of the primitive was the Shropshire novelist, Mary Webb (1883–1927), born Meredith, who was hailed as a genius by Edwin Pugh, G. K. Chesterton, Earl Baldwin, and other voices of some weight, and was awarded the Femina Vie Heureuse prize in 1926. For some years, *The Golden Arrow* (1916), *Gone to Earth* (1917), *The House in Dormer Forest* (1920), *Seven for a Secret* (1922), and *Precious Bane* (1924), along with her poems, made a deep impression on various grades of critical opinion. Then she went into eclipse; and the question now is whether her vogue was not as spurious as the quondam infatuation of comparatively sane people for Martin Tupper, to say nothing of such impostors as Marie Corelli and Hall Caine who were idolized by the uncritical mob. One cannot read her now without noticing that her work is a synthesis of many influences that easily combine, the result of much reading. Some called her a second Thomas

[1] See Vol. IX. 94–96.

Hardy, but that was a missfire. There is more of George Eliot in her composition, and even of Mrs Gaskell, than of Hardy, though Hardy is by no means ignored. But Charlotte and Emily Brontë, Mrs Humphry Ward, and other novelists, also contributed; and her poetical philosophy of life is Wordsworth's, annotated by Meredith, with a strong infusion of Blake. Fiction in the hands of Mary Webb is a highly self-conscious affair. Her eye was constantly on the great exemplars; she borrowed shapes and omitted to put anything inside them; and she had reflected so much on the inner meanings of her predecessors, that she could not help thinking more of the doctrine to be illustrated than of the concrete drama to be set afoot. Hence a lack in her books of the liveliness and assuring feel of reality; they have not the sterling qualities of less pretentious fiction. She was as much as Hardy a votary of local colour, and went even further in making it symbolical of a moral climate or of all that thwarts good intentions. Folk-lore, ancient rites and superstitions, quaint ways of speech, picturesque customs, sinister old buildings, woods, crags, and the like—the house in Dormer Forest, or Gillian Lovekin's Farm, or the mere in *Precious Bane*, which drowns Jancis and her babe and gets Gideon at last—these are a sort of code for her ulterior implications. Hence the story is often told in pictures, so to speak. Much of the dialogue is for the sake of dialect, and there are pieces of description that seem to be there chiefly to bring in obsolete words.

Echoes of George Eliot

All the characters that matter in *The Golden Arrow* are two pairs of lovers and their fathers and mothers; the true love of Deborah and Stephen, symbolized in the title, has its foil in the other couple. Lily is a second-hand Hetty Sorrel, and a second-hand George Eliot can be heard moralizing over "the slave of sex":

> Lily had never looked so frail, so provocative. . . . Lily was genuinely pleased . . . the compact little house was delightful . . . she thought how easy the work would be. She was not meant for the hardy magnificence of manual labour. . . . But here she felt a decided impetus in the direction of domesticity, because for the first time it was picturesque; for the first

time she saw herself in a romantic setting of shelves, cupboards, clean paint and flowers. She had a vision of the vicar's wife alluding to her as "Joe Arden's pretty wife who makes such good jelly."

The heroine's strong points and the foolish young woman's weaknesses are carefully underlined, and the extra information is dropped: "Joe was unaware (in his lover's rhapsodies) that Lily had barely begun to cultivate a heart." George Eliot would never have been as crude as that. As to the other pair, the author thinks an explanation necessary which is really an exposition of her theory of fiction, didactic fiction, that is to say.

If other lives could have been hindered from impingeing on those of Deborah and Stephen, they might have worked out their destinies in the swift way of great lovers. But Mrs Arden with her definite morality, Joe with his obstinate and straitened view of sex, Eli with his ranting dogmatism, and the world in general with its terror of nonconformity—all these came round them as stealthily as the tide round a promontory, and (some of them with the best intentions) brought about tragedy. The only person to utter no word was John, for he had no moral code. Those that dwell in the lands of the sun do not need fires.

John, of course, is the mouthpiece of Mary Webb's pantheism; the pharisaic Eli a too neat compendium of Welsh religiosity:

His plain living, his long prayers, his loud confessions of sin, his harsh treatment of himself and his unquestioning meekness to the God he believed in (a vengeful, taloned replica of himself) all these things had to be paid for by someone. . . . A few times in the year, when things had gone wrong, the lust of torture came upon Eli, and the contemplation of a deferred and somewhat problematical torment of the wicked (*i.e.* the not-Eli) in hell-fire could not slake it. At these times he exhibited the subtlety of a woman in finding weak points wherein to stick pins—a subtlety inherited by Lily.

Mary Webb is interested in the problem of evil, and discusses it in the same abstract way, except in one violent episode. Her Stephen perceives ugliness and malice in the rugged landscape that fills John with a sense of peace and trust. He is haunted by the spirit lurking in the Devil's Chair. The world looks black and evil, and at last he can stand it no longer and takes flight. Not, however, before his obsession has become monomania, and he tries to blow up the baleful rock with dynamite.

Superstitious tremors began to make themselves felt in Stephen's nerves; and because he had neither Deborah's naturalism, nor John's deep, pantheistic Christianity, nor Joe's stolidity, nor the indifference of a shallow nature, he had nothing with which to combat them.

But the conflict is not resolved. After having a bad time knocking about the world, he comes back to throw himself on Deborah's breast, in an orgy of sentimentalism. It is as if George Eliot had wedded her Maggie to Stephen Guest after all, or Hardy had united Clym and Eustacia to be happy ever after, to the joy of the soft-hearted but not of the hard headed reader.

Of Blake and Hardy

The contrast between the bigoted, materialist family of *The House in Dormer Forest*, with their subservience to convention, the religion of the herd, and the free-livers, the children of Nature, who are like the forest, is something learned from Blake, who would have agreed—

that when law is put before love and the material before the spiritual there is nothing left wherewithal to combat evil; that the commonplace is the soul's peril; that a person with low aims, paltry pleasures, and an inability to love or hate passionately is more dangerous than any beast of prey.

Mary Webb had noble conceptions of human nature, but she could not clothe them with life; the moulds are sound, but the material poured in is too thin to set. And she uses the same material over and over again in different novels—always the plain, despised woman, who has a life of her own to lead, and is saved at last from wasting her sweetness by the arrival of the ideal man, the child of Nature, with a true sense of values; and always, on the other side, divers sordid, egotistic, spiteful characters, whose great object is to repress and ridicule the saner view. The former invariably triumph in the long run; but her happy endings are far from inevitable. Gideon Sarn, in *Precious Bane*, is another Mayor of Casterbridge, a one-idead egotist, blind to everything but the ambition of exploiting his little property of Sarn, in the days of Waterloo and Corn Laws, making money, and buying a squire's house and a place in county society. Perhaps he is still nearer to Heathcliff—a natural force, a blind instinct, a devouring passion, a Troll. When "the mighty hand was upon him, striving with him to make him go widdershins to what he was, to what Father had made him, and Grandad, and all of them, back to Timothy, that had the lightning in his blood," he stands for the usual antagonism, evil versus the good element in Nature and man. There is an obvious reminiscence here of *Wuthering Heights*, whilst the plain heroine, the narrator with the hare-lip, Gideon's sister, recalls Jane Eyre. The story of Gideon's dogged and almost superhuman fight with destiny and his final overthrow is clumsy and even childish in places, especially in the doings of the astrologer Beguildy and the fantastic raising of Venus. Who believes in all that business of Gideon's attempt to forestall Beguildy's objection to his daughter's marriage, by sending him off on a wild-goose chase from which he returns to find the lovers established in his house? Mary Webb's strength is in the evocation of homeliness and peace in the bosom of nature. Nature and humanity may live together in a divine harmony. The peace that is beyond understanding descends upon life; man is brought into immediate touch with eternity.

It was pleasant to be in the warm, glowing kitchen, full of the good smell of bread, and to look out at the grey-white fields and woods, cold and lonesome, and then to draw the curtain, and kindle the rushlight, setting the table and putting the tater pie to get hot on the gledes, and knowing that in a little while all those I cared for would be comfortable for the night. The fowl had been shut up since the first dusk, the cows and sheep were folded, Bendigo littered-up, Pussy by hearth, Mother with a bit of fire in her room and the warming-pan in the bed, and now Gideon was on the way back to his supper. The oven being still hot, I put in a batch of mince-pies, for Gideon liked a bit of good fare as well as anybody, though he'd growl times, and talk about ruination, and where'd our house be and the silver plate and all? But though I did as he said all the year round, with a bit of bread and cheese and a tater for a meal, at Christmas time I went by my own road, and we had our merrymaking almost like other folks. And since, after all, that came to pass, I've been more glad of that bit of disobedience to Gideon than of anything in our lives then. For I can say, "anyway, they had *that*, whatever else they didna have."

The rapture that falls on Prue Sarn when "a fair, lovely look" comes over things, one "gleaming morning after rain," is like the sense of being called and dedicated which Wordsworth records in *The Prelude*. Nevertheless, the question cannot be evaded whether all this is fiction at all, or only the well-meant attempt of a rustic philosopher to express her views in the forms of the great artists who have excited her admiration. Mere abstracts of human nature and abstracts of human life do not make a novel, however interesting they may be as a commentary. The historical interest of Mary Webb is that at a certain date this could pass as genuine novel-writing. Unfortunately for her, the very next writer to be considered, Katherine Mansfield, is a supreme example of the fiction that has all the essentials of the art which are to seek in Mary Webb, and confronts the reader with an indefeasible version that amuses or holds in suspense, horrifies or transports, like a direct view of life through the eyes of a superhuman observer compared with whom he is purblind.[1]

Katherine Mansfield

Kathleen Beauchamp (1889–1923) took the name of Katherine Mansfield when she began to write—her grand-

[1] The farcical extravaganza, *Cold Comfort Farm* (1932), by Stella Gibbons, is a skit on Mary Webb and other exponents of the emotional and fatalistic novel of rustic life. "Mrs Starkadder was the curse of Cold Comfort. Mrs Starkadder was the Dominant Grandmother Theme, which was found in all typical novels of agricultural life (and sometimes in novels of urban life, too). It was, of course, right and proper that Mrs Starkadder should be in possession at Cold Comfort; Flora should have suspected her existence from the beginning. Probably it was Mrs Starkadder, otherwise Aunt Ada Doom, who had sent the postcard with the reference to generations of vipers. Flora was sure that the old lady was Aunt Ada Doom, and none other." *Cold Comfort Farm* gained for its author the very prize, the Femina Vie Heureuse, previously awarded to her victim. Was it from a sense of "poetic justice"?

mother's name was Margaret Mansfield Dyer. She took the name of the Burnells, a family of children and their elders vividly drawn in a number of early stories, from that of her mother, Annie Burnell Dyer.[1] Born in New Zealand, she came twice to England for her education, and decided to stay in this country and devote herself to literature, but was driven by the small encouragement she received into a hand-to-mouth Bohemian existence. Her genius was presently recognized by competent judges, more particularly by J. Middleton Murry, whose wife she became, and by the novelist D. H. Lawrence. She was reckless about her health, and the latter part of her life was spent in feverish efforts to work, and to outstrip a galloping consumption. She died of hæmorrhage of the lungs at the age of thirty-four. She left a *Journal* (1927), which is one of the most poignant and revealing autobiographies ever penned, and five collections of stories, of the highest rank in any literature, though they must be regarded as only fragments of what she would have achieved, had she been blessed with normal health and a fair span of life. Of these collections, the first published, *In a German Pension* (1911), stands apart from the rest, not merely for an immaturity which she herself recognized, but for other reasons. She said, "It's not what I mean; it's a lie," and refused to republish it. It consists of a dozen sketches of the people observed during her stay in a Bavarian health resort, greedy, bloated, mannerless Germans, always talking about their symptoms and their appetite for food, which are often illustrated with physical demonstrations only too graphic. As in a story of very different quality published later, "The Little Governess," Katherine Mansfield betrays that she has a grudge against Germans; these are not merely crude snapshots, but often little more than skits, and it is no wonder that she felt it would be unworthy to issue them again whilst the war was going on. One alone, "The Swing of the Pendulum," is so much as a story. It is the account of a mere incident, but it is handled with much

[1] Her father was a cousin of the Gräfin von Arnim (*née* Beauchamp, afterwards Countess Russell), author of *Elizabeth and her German Garden* and other novels or fictitious memoirs.

of that insight and that sureness of touch which were to be her characteristics later on. A girl in a rebellious mood, yearning for "passion and love and adventure," is for a moment fascinated by a man who tries to take advantage of her incautious freedom. She turns him out of the room; and the victory restores her spirit which had been flagging at the long-continued silence of her lover.

Stories of New Zealand

The scene of many of Katherine Mansfield's stories, both early and late, is pitched in New Zealand surroundings; they are reminiscences of her childhood and youth.[1] No doubt, some had their original shaping on the spot, and were polished and perfected, and often completely transformed, as she acquired dexterity. But to single out any as autobiographical would be only to lay undue emphasis on the recognizability of some of the facts embodied. In some degree, all her work was autobiographical, inasmuch as it was all based on her own vivid experiences, and often on experiences in which she was the chief person concerned. The German sketches are an instance; but there are historical proofs that "The Voyage," which appeared in *The Garden Party, and other stories* (1922), and "An Indiscreet Journey," written off-hand in 1915, are both transcripts of personal adventures, and that "Mr Reginald Peacock's Day" was made up from observations of her neighbours; there is internal evidence of a similar origin for a great many more. She filled note-books with her daily memoranda of what she saw going on; she put more into her letters to friends and relations. When she was deliberately practising writing, she worked all this up into what she called "vignettes," many of which survive, in the original or a refurbished form, a form she often found fully adequate, right to the end. For a "vignette" by Katherine Mansfield is by no means a still life; it is as dynamic as one of her stories. And now, since a fair number of the experiences afterwards used as material are on record in her life or her journal, and in

[1] This is not the place to go into the question of the bitterness of her memory of New Zealand, where she experienced a sense of separateness and solitude, of being "the outlaw of the family," or the view that her resentment against New Zealand was, as it were, the symbol of her resentment against life itself, discussed in the *Life* by R. E. Mantz and J. Middleton Murry (p. 2, etc.).

some cases more than one version of a story are extant, it happens that the progress of her art to its ultimate felicity can best be studied in her stories of New Zealand. But only if the passages relating to her incessant effort are read in conjunction with the finished stories, and some comparison is made with those remaining unfinished which are included in *The Doves' Nest, and other stories* (1923). Another posthumous volume, *Something Childish* (1924), is a gathering-up of her earliest and her latest work, the first four items dating from before her first book published, *In a German Pension.* The earliest of all, "The Tiredness of Rosabel," the sensations and dreams of a girl in a huge millinery establishment," is commonplace for Katherine Mansfield. But it was written when she was only nineteen. The New Zealand stories in the two volumes named after "Bliss" and "The Garden Party," published in her lifetime, and "The Doll's House," published with "The Doves' Nest," satisfied Katherine Mansfield herself; they expressed all she had in mind, and had that perfection of form which she attained by the elimination of all formality, as well as other extraneous elements. She records in the *Journal* what trouble it cost her to write "The Aloe," the original version of "Prelude." Her dearly loved brother, killed at the front shortly before, was always now in her mind's eye; and she tells him how she is "getting down to the New Zealand atmosphere," has been "in dreadful places," has seen the mists rising; but at last "it is made plain," and no matter how often she may have had to write and rewrite "the book shall be written and ready."[1] "Prelude" introduces the Burnells, a family of children and grown-up people to be identified with Katherine Mansfield's home-circle at Wellington, Anikewa, Karori, and other places of sojourn in New Zealand; it is all about their removal to a new home in the country, and the reader sees everything through the eyes of the youngsters or of their worried mamma, Linda Burnell—of course, she herself was one of them. Never any regular specification of a character; and yet at the end they have been read each one like a book. The nearest she comes to any sort

[1] *Journal*, 45–48.

of likeness or outline is in such a miniature as this of tiny Kezia's sensations:

Kezia liked to stand so before the window. She liked the feeling of the cold shining glass against her hot palms, and she liked to watch the funny white tops that came on her fingers when she pressed them hard against the pane. As she stood there, the day flickered out and dark came. With the dark crept the wind snuffling and howling. The windows of the empty house shook, a creaking came from the walls and floors, a piece of loose iron on the roof banged forlornly. Kezia was suddenly quite, quite still, with wide-open eyes and knees pressed together. She was frightened. She wanted to call Lottie and to go on calling all the while she ran downstairs and out of the house. But IT was just behind her, waiting at the door, at the head of the stairs, at the bottom of the stairs, hiding in the passage, ready to dart out at the back door.

Lottie is still tinier. She pricks up her ears when she hears the name Charlotte Crescent; "she always felt that Charlotte Crescent belonged specially to her. Very few people had streets with the same name as hers."

"Look, Kezia, there is Charlotte Crescent. Doesn't it look different?" Now everything familiar was left behind. Now the big dray rattled into unknown country, along new roads with high clay banks on either side, up steep, steep hills, down into bushy valleys, through wide shallow rivers. Further and further. Lottie's head wagged; she drooped, she slipped half into Kezia's lap and lay there. But Kezia could not open her eyes wide enough. The wind blew and she shivered; but her cheeks and ears burned.

"Do stars ever blow about?" she asked.

"Not to notice," said the storeman.

"We've got a nuncle and a naunt living near our new house," said Kezia. "They have got two children, Pip, the eldest is called, and the youngest's name is Rags. He has to feed it with a nenamuel pot and a glove top over the spout. He's going to show us. What is the difference between a ram and a sheep?"

"Well, a ram has horns and runs for you."

Kezia considered. "I don't want to see it frightfully," she said. "I hate rushing animals like dogs and parrots. I often dream that animals rush at me—even camels—and while they are rushing, their heads swell e-enormous."

They are taken off to bed; "Isabel and Lottie lay in a room to themselves, Kezia curled in her grandmother's soft bed."

"Aren't there going to be any sheets, my granma?"

"No, not to-night."

"It's tickly," said Kezia, "but it's like Indians." She dragged her grandmother down to her and kissed her under the chin. "Come to bed soon and be my Indian brave."

"What a silly you are," said the old woman, tucking her in as she loved to be tucked.

"Aren't you going to leave me a candle?"

"No. Sh-h. Go to sleep."

"Well, can I have the door left open?"

She rolled herself up into a round but she did not go to sleep. From all over the house came the sound of steps. The house itself creaked and popped. Loud whispering voices came from downstairs. Once she heard Aunt Beryl's rush of high laughter, and once she heard a loud trumpeting from Burnell blowing his nose. Outside the window hundreds of black cats with yellow eyes sat in the sky watching her—but she was not frightened. Lottie was saying to Isabel:

"I'm going to say my prayers in bed to-night."

"No you can't, Lottie." Isabel was very firm. "God only excuses you saying your prayers in bed if you've got a temperature." So Lottie yielded.

And now there is lots of exploring to be done and famous discoveries to be made, before everybody, including the elders, settles down in their new surroundings. Mr Burnell has to adapt himself to the long drive from town; but "it was splendid to live in the country—to get right out of that hole of a town once the office was closed." The children have the Trout boys to play with; and there are people to tea.

"Oh, Alice," said Miss Beryl. "There's one extra to tea, so heat a plate of yesterday's scones, please. And put on the Victoria sandwich as well as the coffee cake. And don't forget to put little doyleys under the plates—will you? You did yesterday, you know, and the tea looked so ugly and common. And, Alice, don't put that dreadful old pink and green cosy on the afternoon teapot again. That is only for the mornings. Really, I think it ought to be kept for the kitchen—it's so shabby. Put on the Japanese one. You quite understand, don't you?"

Oh, Alice was wild. She wasn't one to mind being told, but there was something in the way Miss Beryl had of speaking to her that she couldn't stand. Oh, that she couldn't. It made her curl up inside, as you might say, and she fair trembled.

"If you please, Mrs Burnell," said an imaginary Alice, as she buttered the scones, "I'd rather not take my orders from Miss Beryl. I may be only a common servant girl as doesn't know how to play the guitar, but . . ."

Meanwhile, the posturing Miss Beryl sits writing a letter in her room, and has a look inside her own self.

In a way, of course, it was all perfectly true, but in another way it was all the greatest rubbish and she didn't believe a word of it. No, that wasn't true. She felt all those things, but she didn't really feel them like that. It was her other self who had written that letter. It not only bored, it rather disgusted her real self. "Flippant and silly," said her real self. Yet she knew that she'd send it and she'd always write that kind of twaddle to Nan Pym. In fact, it was a very mild example of the kind of letter she generally wrote.

Here and in later stories Beryl is a problem to herself, and her modern young woman's self-consciousness is a trial to other people. She looks in the glass. "Yes, my dear," she says to the charming image, "there is no doubt about it, you really are a lovely little thing."

At the words her bosom lifted; she took a long breath of delight, half closing her eyes. But even as she looked the smile faded from her lips and eyes. Oh God, there she was, back again, playing the same old game. False—false as ever. False as when she'd written to Nan Pym. False even when she was alone with herself.

There is Katherine Mansfield's method in a nutshell. She

seems to put everything in, important or unimportant, as if to her everything was important; but, actually, she has sifted and resifted till only the bare essentials are left, and a perfect illusion of life. A house-moving, a casual talk set down verbatim, a brown study, a day-dream, domestic fusses over next to nothing—inventoried thus it all sounds trivial, almost banal. But it is nothing of the kind. She makes it clear that these seeming futilities and inconsequences are anything but trivial; they are the stuff of which life is composed. This impressionism through different ages and temperaments is life caught on the wing. Nor is it by any means undramatic or unexciting. There seems little at stake in these domestic episodes; yet not only is there the stir and incessant movement of real existence, but an intensity that holds the reader spellbound. Katherine Mansfield never deals in the melodramatic of commerce; but she can, at any moment, evoke suspense and keep the reader's heart in his mouth waiting for what will happen next. When a great deal is at stake, as in such stories as "Bliss," where the happy wife finds that she has been betrayed and the bliss turns to gall, or "The Little Governess," of the ingenuous girl who falls into the clutches of the bestial old German, the tension verges on the unendurable.

"The Garden Party." etc.

There is another tale or simple vignette of little children, "Sun and Moon," in the same volume, in which the boy and girl are exquisite individuals though hardly more than babes. Then the first story, "At the Bay," in the one with "The Garden Party," returns to the Burnells, who are holidaying at Crescent Bay. It is the same sort of thing, except that it is all quite new, and deals with what she called "more difficult relationships"; and it is one of Katherine Mansfield's finest pieces. Yet "The Garden Party" is more memorable, for the simple reason that it is one of those stories which have a denouement. The men are putting up the marquee, the band is expected, and all the good things, the flowers, and the fruit, are ready for the Sheridans' garden-party, when the cook tells Laura of a horrible accident; a young chap from the little cottages just below has been killed. "He's left a wife and five little ones."

"Jose, come here." Laura caught hold of her sister's sleeve and dragged her through the kitchen to the other side of the green baize door. There she paused and leaned against it. "Jose!" she said, horrified, "however are we going to stop everything?"

"Stop everything, Laura!" cried Jose in astonishment. "What do you mean?"

"Stop the garden-party, of course." Why did Jose pretend?

But Jose was still more amazed. "Stop the garden-party? My dear Laura, don't be so absurd. Of course we can't do anything of the kind. Nobody expects us to. Don't be so extravagant."

"But we can't possibly have a garden-party with a man dead just outside the front gate."

But her mother is worse than Jose in refusing to take Laura seriously. "You are being very absurd, Laura," she said coldly. "It's not very sympathetic to spoil everybody's enjoyment as you're doing now."

"I don't understand," said Laura, and she walked quickly out of the room into her own bedroom. There, quite by chance, the first thing she saw was this charming girl in the mirror, in her black hat trimmed with gold daisies, and a long black velvet ribbon. Never had she imagined she could look like that. Is mother right? she thought. And now she hoped her mother was right. Am I being extravagant? Perhaps it was extravagant. Just for a moment she had another glimpse of that poor woman and those little children, and the body being carried into the house. But it all seemed blurred, unreal, like a picture in the newspaper. I'll remember it again after the party's over, she decided. And somehow that seemed quite the best plan.

The party is a great success; and when it is all over Laura has one of her brilliant ideas. Why should all those sandwiches, cakes, puffs, all uneaten, be wasted? She makes up a basket and goes down to the little cottages. A woman with an oily voice lets her in. "Em! It's a young lady."

She turned to Laura. She said meaningly, "I'm 'er sister, miss. You'll excuse 'er, won't you?"

"Oh, but of course!" said Laura. "Please, please don't disturb her. I—I only want to leave——"

But at that moment the woman at the fire turned round. Her face, puffed up, red, with swollen eyes and swollen lips, looked terrible. She seemed as though she couldn't understand why Laura was there. What did it mean? Why was this stranger standing in the kitchen with a basket? What was it all about? And the poor face puckered up again.

But the sister insists on her seeing the dead man. "'E looks a picture. There's nothing to show. Come along, my dear." Laura came.

There lay a young man, fast asleep—sleeping so soundly, so deeply, that he was far, far away from them both. Oh, so remote, so peaceful. He was dreaming. Never wake him up again. His head was sunk in the pillow, his eyes were closed; they were blind under the closed eyelids. He was given up to his dream. What did garden-parties and baskets and lace frocks matter to him? He was far from all those things. He was wonderful, beautiful. While they were laughing and while the band was playing, this marvel had come to the lane. Happy . . . happy. . . . All is well, said that sleeping face. This is just as it should be. I am content.

At the corner of the lane she met Laurie. He stepped out of the shadow. "Is that you, Laura?"

"Yes."

"Mother was getting anxious. Was it all right?"

"Yes, quite. Oh, Laurie!" She took his arm, she pressed up against him.

"I say, you're not crying, are you?" asked her brother.

Laura shook her head. She was.

Laurie put his arm round her shoulder. "Don't cry," he said in his warm, loving voice. "Was it awful?"

"No," sobbed Laura. "It was simply marvellous. But, Laurie——"

She stopped, she looked at her brother. "Isn't life," she stammered, "isn't life——" But what life was she couldn't explain. No matter. He quite understood.

"*Isn't* it, darling?" said Laurie.

"Her thoughts were always in a minor key, even as a child,"

said Katherine's father, Mr Beauchamp.[1] Nearly everything in this volume is in a minor key, even if a tender mockery softens the chagrin of the young man in love with a girl who cannot help laughing at him, as in "Mr and Mrs Dove," [2] or laughter follows the crying, as in "The Singing Lesson." It is said that the unutterable dreariness which is the lot of the two old sisters, in "The Daughters of the Late Colonel," expressed Katherine Mansfield's overwhelming mood at the time it was written.[3] Gissing certainly never concentrated so much human misery and so much meek endurance into a few pages as she into her "Life of Ma Parker"; disillusionment was never bantered more compassionately than in "Miss Brill." These are pages torn from life, and still raw and bleeding.

"The Doll's House," etc.

Another masterpiece to set beside "The Garden Party," with a sting of irony in lieu of the tragic envoy, is "The Doll's House," as to the remote origin of which there are "recollections of childhood" in the *Journal*.[4] The Burnells have had a marvellous doll's house sent them, with a porch and real windows, dining-room, drawing-room, kitchen, and bedrooms, all complete. But the chief wonder is a little lamp on the dining-room table, with something in it that looks like oil, ready for lighting. The children in the neighbourhood troop in to see it, all but one family. For, though they all went to the same school, there were distinctions that must be observed: "the line had to be drawn somewhere. It was drawn at the Kelveys." They were the children of a hard-working washerwoman, whose husband, it was whispered, was probably in prison.

Many of the children, including the Burnells, were not allowed even to speak to them. They walked past the Kelveys with their heads in the air, and as they set the fashion in all matters of behaviour, the Kelveys were shunned by everybody. Even the teacher had a special voice for them, and a special

[1] *Life*, 27.

[2] In the *Journal* (p. 184) she says, alluding no doubt to the girl's revulsion of feeling at the end, "I have a sneaking notion that I have, at the end, used the Doves *unwarrantably*. . . . I used them to round off something—didn't I?"

[3] *Life*, 27.

[4] Pp. 49–52.

smile for the other children when Lil Kelvey came up to her desk with a bunch of dreadfully common-looking flowers.

Kezia begs to be allowed to show them the doll's house just once; but it is no use. She is told to go away; and the other children jeered at the girl who was going to be a servant, and whose father, for all they knew, was in prison. But the Kelveys only stand humble and shamefaced. Then one day Kezia sees two dots coming along the road; they are the Kelveys, and she cannot resist the impulse to let them come in and see the doll's house.

"There it is," said Kezia.

There was a pause. Lil breathed loudly, almost snorted; our Else was still as stone.

"I'll open it for you," said Kezia kindly. She undid the hook and they looked inside.

But at that instant Aunt Beryl appears. "How dare you ask the little Kelveys into the courtyard?" said her cold, furious voice. The little pariahs run away, and when they are out of sight sit down at the roadside and look dreamily about. "What were their thoughts?"

Presently our Else nudged up close to her sister. But now she had forgotten the cross lady. She put out a finger and stroked her sister's quill; she smiled her rare smile.

"I seen the little lamp," she said, softly.

Then both were silent once more.

It is a model of the story told and all the meaning conveyed without a syllable of comment. Katherine Mansfield is never didactic, never has anything to do with abstractions. But here, as in scores of other instances, her scale of values is as clear as daylight: the story is her comment on life. This is how fiction ought to be written. "The Woman at the Store," "Ole Underwood," and "Millie," in *Something Childish*, paint rough and pretty ugly life in the New Zealand bush, with a realism that reminds most readers of Kipling's, never mincing the foul language and all the other hideousness. The art is as fine and subtle as ever. All that has baffled the two wayfarers in the behaviour of the woman at the store is revealed when the spiteful child draws the picture that her mother told her she never was to. "The kid had drawn the picture of the woman shooting a man with a rook-rifle and then digging a hole to bury him in." She had killed her husband. Kezia, in "The Little Girl," is not Kezia Burnell; but this is as poignant a glimpse as any of the foregoing into the dim workings of a little child's mind. It is another of those intimate revelations of the terrors and shapeless agonies that haunt these infant souls.

How did she learn her art? Katherine Mansfield seems to have made up her mind in early girlhood that her role was to be a writer, and she can be seen still practising in the mature pages of her *Journal*. The swift thumbnail sketches are studies for vignettes; little incidents expand into episodes in somebody's life; such a harrowing narrative as "The Cook's Story" [1] might have gone, just as it stands, into one of her regular collections. For this, like many casual impressions, she thought worth recasting, till she got it just right. She would make a note of anything, a taking sentence, for example: "One never knows when a little tag like that may come in useful to round off a paragraph." [2] The art of these New Zealand stories is so unlike that of most writers of short stories, Kipling, for instance, or Maupassant, or Turgenev, or Gorky, that it is tempting to declare outright that this is an art entirely her own. Even Chekhov, whose affinity strikes everyone, though his outlook is very similar, is different in manner and method. But she did not grow up and develop her talent in sheer independence of other writers. From the beginning, she lived in an atmosphere of literature, modern literature especially. She is known to have been pretty familiar with the work of Ibsen, Maeterlinck, Oscar Wilde, who fascinated her for a long while, of Arthur Symons, Dowson, Baudelaire, Verlaine, H. G. Wells, Bernard Shaw —all having the common tendency, to liberate from time-worn restraints. In her latter years she was continually reading and reinterpreting Shakespeare, who is always modern. And she was well read in the great exemplars of the short

[1] *Journal*, 112–116. [2] "Je ne parle pas Français" (*Bliss*, etc.).

story, Maupassant and the Russians. Turgenev was "wonderfully talented," but "such a poseur, such a hypocrite!" [1] She knew that she was "streets ahead" of such as Gorky.[2] Dostoevsky sometimes bewildered her; but as to his insight into women, "it's profound, profound."[3] "Ach, Tchehov! why are you dead?" she exclaims in one place,[4] and in another notices that one of his stories read to herself seemed nothing, "but read aloud, it was a masterpiece." [5] She found pleasure in Colette, and the author of *Erewhon* was "dear, dear Samuel Butler." There is probably not a single one of them from whom she did not learn something; and another might be added to the list, Elizabeth Robins. The way so many of her stories end abruptly, and yet leave the conviction that as a particular view of life it is complete, that everything essential has been stated, inevitably calls to mind such an ending as Chekhov's in "A Dreary Story." That breaks off at a point the significance of which is not emphasized or definitely explained, when the superannuated professor shows himself impotent to appreciate the immeasurable sympathy of big-hearted Katya, who flees to the Caucasus to escape from the baseness and horror of the human world. Katya was a favourite character to Katherine Mansfield, who was of the same spiritual kith and kin: Mary Webb might have recognized in them the free-livers whom she extolled, those who are great enough to live by impulse, not by law. Chekhov's is the same in essence as Katherine Mansfield's fiction; both exemplify Blake's "ultimate identity of Christianity and Art." [6] But there are large differences in their technical procedure, and in the span of their vision. Chekhov is more explicit on the introspective experiences of his characters; her method was to show what is going on before the eye, and make it reveal what is going on under the surface. She actually went a stage further in liberating fiction from the old-established requirements of the

[1] *Journal*, 15. [2] *Ibid.*, 14.

[3] *Ibid.*, 61–62. She reviewed *An Honest Thief* by Dostoevsky, in the *Athenæum* (*Novels and Novelists*, 111–114), and was rather afraid she had been over-confident in pronouncing his influence on the English intellectuals to be now on the wane. But she still finds in him that mysterious relationship, that "sense of sharing," that "togetherness," which was inherent in his and Chekhov's fiction—and in hers.

[4] *Journal*, 91. [5] *Ibid.*, 230. [6] *Life*, 7.

novel, and thus came closer still to everyday routine. A story of hers looks like an artless and unstudied outpouring of personal impressions, without plot or any conventional feature whatever. She never wrote a novel, except a juvenile performance that was not published, though some of her stories are long, and often several are about the same people. Yet they rarely or never form a serial whole. In such fiction as she aimed at, there is no call to invent brilliant characters and put them in anomalous situations or make them undergo exciting haps and adventures. The object is to bring out the intense and absorbing interest that every day and every minute has for those of adequate insight and imagination. There need be no problem, no climax or central incident, no wager—nothing at all at stake, except everything, which is always at stake.

Insight matched by the art

The symmetry is all internal, perfect coincidence of matter and meaning. Often the form is less pattern than rhythm, like that of music, but felt rather than definable. For this clear, unerring, comprehensive vision is matched by the art with which the results are presented, in a way that seems simple and spontaneous, a swift reproduction of all that has been seen and felt. But this apparent facility and spontaneity is the final result of a long process of brooding, arranging, sorting-out and suppression, till nothing remains but the bare essentials. Katherine Mansfield prayed for a transparent soul, a vision crystal clear—"May I be found worthy to do it! Lord, make me crystal clear for thy light to shine through!" [1] Her genius for seeing things, the ecstasy of her "glimpses" [2] had to be subjected to an arduous discipline, a process of self-examination and self-purification, which ensured clarity through "a complete abeyance of the self." [3] Sometimes she sees with such transports that it sounds almost neurotic. But intensity was her aim, as much as anything [4]; and there are

[1] *Journal*, 197.

[2] *Ibid.*, 148: "What is it that happens in that moment of suspension? It is timeless. In that moment (what *do* I mean?) the whole life of the soul is contained," *et seq.*

[3] *Life*, 7.

[4] *Journal*, 152, "there is a real danger of forgetting *that kind* of intensity, and it won't do."

numberless instances in both the diary and the tales of her rapture in experiencing and recording the full pitch of some sensuous impression, or of human felicity, sadness, longing, or blank bewilderment. Whatever it might be, it had to be rendered in its completeness, with all the mental reactions and the sensuous feel of everything around. It must be put in the right perspective, all must be in focus. "The worst of it is," says the husband in "A Bad Idea," "I can't get this thing into focus—if you know what I mean. I just feel in a muddle—in the hell of a muddle." This is one of her unfinished pieces, meant probably to develop into something like "The Wife," by Chekhov, a husband's involuntary diagnosis of those intangible incompatibilities which ruin married life, in a story that amounts to a gloss upon Paul's great sermon on charity, the thirteenth chapter of first Corinthians. It is one of the many in which Katherine Mansfield came nearer than anyone to the great Russians; as already said, she was something more, or something less, than an English Chekhov. And concomitant with the need to get all into focus was the need for elimination of every redundancy. Only the truly significant must be left, the truly significant which requires no emphasis. Instances enough have been cited already of the force of her reticence, such as "The Garden Party" or "The Doll's House." The small schoolchildren imbibing the disease as it were at their mother's knee, and the ostracism of the sad little victims, are more illumining than all the Books of Snobs and the other diatribes. The story is again the comment; there is no particular point, because it is all point. So with "The Fly," or with "Sixpence," of the father who whipped his little boy. You watch a man doing an involuntary thing, making an unconscious gesture; and that man's inner nature is laid bare, more completely than if he had been stretched on the operating-table in a clinic. Suffering was an integral part of the discipline to purify her insight and perfect her art: here again she is at one with the Russians. The agony it cost her appears in "The Confession."[1] "I do not want to die without leaving a record of my belief that suffering can be overcome. . . .

[1] *Ibid.*, 163–165.

One must *submit*. Do not resist. Take it. Accept it fully. Make it *part of life*. . . . To live—to live—that is all. And to leave life on this earth as Tchehov and Tolstoi."

Other significant stories

Her sense of humour was always alert, but humour or satire was never a definite object. The humour was in her way of seeing things, one of the factors that kept her vision in focus, not to mention its preserving her from the least particle of sentimentality. There are no little farces among her stories, hardly any miniature comedies, mainly because she does not make them turn upon some droll point or paradox, or hit out at some vice or foible. "The Doll's House" was not a fling at snobbishness. The raillery of a girl's sentimentalism in "Taking the Veil" is not meant for satire; nor again in "Violet," where the young woman exclaims, "Don't you find that the Russian novelists have made an upheaval of all your conclusions?" and loves to "go down into the depths with them, for the sake of that wonderful upward spring on to the pinnacle of happiness." "Mr Reginald Peacock's Day" may be welcomed by some as a scathing anatomy of an egoist, of the artistic breed; but it was not meant so. No doubt, Katherine Mansfield laughed at many of the people whom she turned almost inside-out; but she did not write their stories in order to ridicule or expose them, but to enjoy and make others enjoy such marvels of actual life. There is no malice, as there is no didacticism; she steers clear of burlesque or caricature. It was the truth she wanted, and if the truth amused, she hit off a character or an incident with the playfulness that suited it, or the sardonic, wry-mouthed humour that is not very far from tears. Hence it would be a mistake to pronounce the word "cynicism" when the broken-down but eternally hopeful contralto, in "Pictures," after her feverish day of hunting for a job at the halls or the picture-houses, goes off so distressingly with the stout gentleman. And it would be absurd to say it of the story that chaperons "Bliss," one so exquisitely unfolded in its desultory phases that it seems to tell itself, "Je ne parle pas Français," which is put in the mouth of a pimp; or of the conclusion of "Marriage à la mode," where the giddy wife, who has been justly reproaching herself as "vile, odious, abominable, vulgar," cannot resist the philandering pals who jeer at hard-working William, away at the office. "Psychology," a sequence of impalpable moods, and "Revelations," both in the same volume with "Bliss," are further masterpieces of the art of reticence. One of the unfinished, "The Doves' Nest," gives the title to another volume, rightly, for the tenderness and delicacy of the humour make another masterpiece of the little group of timid ladies at the Mediterranean plage entertaining the glossy American. Here too are "Honeymoon," revealing, like several others, the two sides, the different moral aspects, of mutual incomprehension; and "The Canary," trying to define the sadness that is "there, deep down, deep down, part of one, like one's breathing": they are both remarkable feats of reticence. And, no small feat, she can take a theme as old-fashioned as that of "Her First Ball" or the idyll of the two young innocents in "Childish but Natural," and recapture the charm of all her predecessors with never a touch of the hackneyed. Katherine Mansfield fell often enough below the level she set herself; but her standard of accomplishment was so high, in a form of the art which was such a new departure in English, that to discuss her in a smaller allowance of pages has proved impossible.

CHAPTER VI

SATIRISTS AND UTOPIANS, REVOLUTIONARIES AND EVOLUTIONARIES

Samuel Butler and his age

SAMUEL BUTLER (1835–1902) actually came before the public, though rather unobtrusively, as early as 1872, with the original edition of *Erewhon, or over the range*, a work which had some temporary success, chiefly because it was rumoured to be by Lytton, whose utopian novel, *The Coming Race* (1871), preceded it through pure coincidence by a few months. The book was anonymous, and the name of one so unknown as Butler on the title-page would certainly not have helped it. This was the year of *Middlemarch*, *Under the Greenwood Tree*, and *The Eustace Diamonds*. But the right chronological place in history for Butler is at the beginning of the twentieth century, when a revised edition of *Erewhon*, accompanied by *Erewhon Revisited* (1901), recalled attention to it, and with the novel that soon followed, *The Way of all Flesh* (1903), had drastic effects on the minds of a great many readers and fellow-writers, now better prepared for such revolutionary ideas. In between, he had published a number of books that made no great stir at the time, in which he propounded a very liberal attitude to religion, criticized and corrected Darwin's theory of evolution, made out a case for supposing the *Odyssey* to have been the work of a woman, and recounted his wanderings and artistic discoveries in the Italian Alps—books which have had a profound appeal for the thoughtful and have helped to elucidate certain disputable points in his three works of fiction.

Bernard Shaw's illustrative plays

Mr Bernard Shaw was one of the few who read Butler before general interest was excited by the new *Erewhon* and *The Way of all Flesh*. After Butler's death, he assumed the office of interpreter of the long-ignored oracle, and made it no secret that his own views of society and progress were assimilated to a very large extent at the feet of Butler. In *Man and Superman* (1903), his version of the Don Juan legend, he set forth the new attitude to sex, the doctrine that woman is the prime agent, the love-maker, and thus fulfils her natural function; the *Revolutionist's Handbook* appended was largely a repository of social maxims derived from Butler, identifying the life-force or will to live, the moving spirit of evolution, with the Holy Ghost. The long preface to *Back to Methuselah* (1921) was a concise history of the successive theories of evolution, and described how Butler had been ostracized by the Neo-Darwinians for his criticism of Darwin, but had succeeded in establishing his rectified theory of a self-creative process, and in refuting the hypothesis that what Shaw called "circumstantial selection," the mechanical elimination of the unfit, has been the sole agency in the progress of organic life. Butler's contention that illness is a misdemeanour is adopted as an axiom in *The Doctor's Dilemma* (1906); and the Bishop in *Getting Married* (1908), preaching the "Gospel of Laodicea" in this overture for a friendly accommodation between marriage and parenthood, may be identified as either Butler or Butler's disciple and spokesman. Butler's ideas on heredity and the relations of parents and children appear in *Misalliance* (1910), and his use of topsy-turvy situations, the old Gulliverian device, to show what things are in themselves, is eminently characteristic of Bernard Shaw's plays. They do not profess to hold a faithful mirror up to nature; they submit an artificial projection, throwing objects into clearer definition by detaching them from the usual confusing perspective.

Influence on novelists

In fiction, the influence of the modern Socrates has not been avowed with such candour; nevertheless, in this province also of creative art it has been as potent on a number of the most thoughtful writers as that exercised on the previous generation by Flaubert, the Goncourts, Maupassant, and Zola. Several who were following steadily in those footsteps now found an example closer at hand of facing and reporting the truth with uncompromising frankness, in *The Way of all Flesh*, at the same time as they gained a new outlook on the world in general from Butler's teaching. In *Erewhon* and *Erewhon Revisited* he had enunciated his doctrines in ways meant to startle readers and compel them to scrutinize and probably amend rooted convictions. In *Life and Habit* (1877), *Unconscious Memory* (1880), and *Luck or Cunning?* (1887), life as a process of evolution always going on was discussed in more orthodox fashion, established views being thoroughly investigated and the evidence reinterpreted. Then Butler took a relevant case, which happened to be his own, and told the story of his life in *The Way of all Flesh* as a piece of natural history. It is the typical bad example of a child's nature perverted and his life ruined by an unenlightened system of education, the main object of which is to reduce individuality to an approved pattern by the facile method of stereotyping in a mould. It was, in short, an exposure of the modes of parental upbringing consecrated by usage, and a chief weapon of the satire was Butler's irradiating irony which unmasks the most specious pretences.

Psychological fiction

But, as a biologist dealing with a specific case, he employed methods more like the analysis of a psychologist than the imaginative treatment of familiar experience by a George Eliot. As he always insisted that the mental phenomena that matter were commonly not those which leave plain traces on the surface, he explored the instincts, the temperamental dispositions, likes and dislikes, obstinate impulses, of which the individual himself is not more than half aware. His followers also paid more attention to the unconscious than to the conscious realm of mind and motive; it is there, they believe, that the decisive conflicts are fought out, and insignificant events lead ultimately to failure or success, misery or happiness, or rather, as they would put it, to disease and sickness or health and vigour. The human being is considered as an organism, a union of body and mind, rather than as a moral entity or character, in the old dramatic sense. There is a distinct bias towards pathology: many a character that rivets attention may be described as a "case" [1]; morbid or at least abnormal

[1] Butler himself was a "case"; else he would never have had to wait for posthumous recognition, and his influence would have been direct, instead of through more self-confident disciples, such as Bernard Shaw.

mentalities preponderate. There is continual insistence on heredity and on very early influence; a character's life is traced from childhood to puberty, to its collision with the facts of sex, and to crime much oftener than would average out in ordinary life. A favourite case has been the "inferiority complex," which was the trouble with Butler's select example in *The Way of all Flesh*. These tendencies were strengthened by what the novelists learned from Freud and Jung and Adler on psycho-analysis. The result has been a large group of novelists dealing with the phenomena of mental and moral disturbances, with conflicts, complexes, inversions, and cognate disorders. It would be taking too much for granted to call them Butler's school; but at any rate they have followed his lead in a direction that has given new vitality to realistic fiction. With the exception of D. H. Lawrence, who stands apart as possessed of, or possessed by, an innate and almost mystical clairvoyance, they are still alive and working, and it is happily requisite here only to enumerate the leading names, those of H. G. Wells, Somerset Maugham, J. D. Beresford, Oliver Onions, Frank Swinnerton,[1] Gilbert Cannan, Sir Hugh Walpole, May Sinclair, "Rebecca West," Clemence Dane, E. M. Delafield, Dorothy Richardson, Virginia Woolf. They represent such a variety of talent that it is as much by negative as positive attributes they for a moment form a group. Katherine Mansfield would have to be included with them, if her Russian affinities had not set her apart. To what extent Arnold Bennett and Galsworthy should be linked with this crowd of emancipated students or professors of what is now almost as much a school of research as a school of art, will perhaps appear from the later chapters dealing with their work.

An age of satirical and controversial fiction

Erewhon was a composite book put together from papers written during the previous ten years, such as the article "Darwin among the Machines," and the serio-comic disquisitions on the World of the Unborn, the Musical Banks, and the trial of the man guilty of being a consumptive; these

[1] Mr Swinnerton avers (*The Georgian Literary Scene*, 297) that he has "never read *The Way of all Flesh*," though he is very wide awake to the effect of Butler on the "younger novelists."

were made into a continuous narrative, with a picturesque beginning and end, in the introductory adventures and the story of the escape from the amazing country when it was growing too dangerous to stay there. Satire is always in fashion in England, and the self-complacent Victorian period was no exception, though there had been none so devastating, and none that went like this to the root of the matter, since *Gulliver's Travels*. The only satirical work of the slightest importance exactly of the same date was Calverley's *Fly-leaves*, the humour of which is so kind-hearted that the sting almost escapes attention. But a good many that were unequivocally satiric, or, which is next-door to it, utopian, were coming out about this time. Matthew Arnold had tossed his *Friendship's Garland* at the Philistines the year before, two years after *Culture and Anarchy*. One year earlier, also in the outwardly innocuous shape of fiction, and fiction of the homeliest brand, had appeared and done no small execution that skit on the benevolent agencies of the time, *Ginx's Baby, his birth and other misfortunes*, by J. E. Jenkins (1838–1910), scarifying the philosophers, politicians, and poor-law ministers, who went on theorizing and debating whilst the wretched infant waited for someone to look after it. Disraeli had not finally laid down his satirical pen, and Lewis Carroll was still splitting the difference between the higher mathematics and the glory of nonsense, when Laurence Oliphant fired off his whiff of grape-shot at society, in *Piccadilly* (1870), and a farewell salvo in *Altiora Peto* (1883).[1] Mallock, in *The New Republic* (1877) and *The New Paul and Virginia* (1878), was at once parodying and disputing the views of prominent scientists and sociologists, including several who belonged to the same school of thought that Butler was challenging. He was as ponderous and as devoid of a sense of humour as his younger collaborator in polemical fiction of a Tory bias, Mrs Humphry Ward. Such heavy-handedness was more than counterbalanced, however, by the punning *Punch* facetiæ of F. G. Burnand (1836–1917), aimed at any glaring eccentricity or exaggeration, from the gush of Rhoda Broughton to the

[1] See Vol. IX, 225, n.

solemn pretences of the æsthetes, the Pre-Raphaelites, and the self-dubbed decadents, all of whom were being turned to derision in magazine and newspaper, in Gilbert and Sullivan's operas, and anywhere that common sense and philistinism were hand in glove.[1] Oscar Wilde, at once dilettante and cynic, sustained the parts of both victim and scoffer. He wrote satire, and he accepted it with imperturbable grace. He probably did more than he intended, and the authors of *The Green Carnation* and *The Autobiography of a Boy*, and humorists of range as different as Max Beerbohm,[2] Barry Pain, "F. Anstey," and "Grant Allen" did as much as they could, to laugh down contemporary shams and extravagances. Satire to them was indeed one of the useful arts, which they applied to the good work of the abatement of nuisances. Butler, with his interest in Greek antiquities, had a high opinion of the erudite wit with which Dr Richard Garnett (1835–1906) travestied the Prometheus legend in *The Twilight of the Gods* (1888), and in the "other tales" accompanying it satirized decadent Byzantines or burlesqued superstitions creeping in long ago from the Orient. Academic humour like this was, however, too remote from present-day absurdities to have any wide appeal. On the other hand, the defect of *The New Antigone* (1887) and the rest of the descanting and romancing upon the opposite ethical and religious standards supposed to be polarizing the world, by the Rev. William Barry (1849–1930), was the absence of genuine satire. Barry was interested enough to write on "Samuel Butler of Erewhon" in the *Dublin Review*[3]; but there is no evidence that Butler paid attention to the Irishman's heavy handling of some of his own problems. Such satire as there was in *Three Men in a Boat* (1889) and the other farcical novels of Jerome K. Jerome (1859–1927) was subservient to the milder purposes of low comedy; Jerome was no more a satirist than Edmund Downey was,[4] or Mr W. W. Jacobs. There was in fact more

[1] *Ibid.*, chap. vi., "Æsthetes and Eclectics," especially pp. 224–226.

[2] Max Beerbohm's caricatures with their humorous letterpress are perhaps the finest of that sort of combination ever done; they are the work, however, of a great jester rather than a satirist.

[3] October, 1914.

[4] See above, p. 195.

that could rightly be called satirical in the works in which Mark Twain and Bret Harte were habituating the English reader to new modes and broader criteria of humour. Satire has a legitimate place in the novel, but only when it keeps within the bounds of comedy. Many of the current exposures of injustices, anomalies, and social vagaries simply applied the machinery of fiction to their own purposes, which might be polemical or propagandist, or merely the castigation of fools and delinquents. There was plenty of satire of fools and delinquents in Dickens and Thackeray; but even the *Book of Snobs* was a comic and not a reformatory work; its aim and end was the merriment of the world, though it happened to do the world good, like many another example of a spontaneous and disinterested art. The great ones, the Merediths, Hardys, Jameses, kept satire in its place. Conrad's bitter ironical humour and moral aversion for people of a certain stamp, and Kipling's penetration through all disguises and every subterfuge, prompted them ever and anon to scathing exposures. But their sardonic view of some furtive iniquity or repulsive fact was, like their relish of some rich human absurdity, only one of the ways of their æsthetic reaction to the world. Arnold Bennett, also, will prove to be a serene and appreciative humorist, responding genially to foibles and aberrations as well as to the kindlier traits of his fellow-men. But he will be chargeable with a fit of aberration himself when, in *A Great Man* or *The Regent*, he writes a lampoon and calls it a novel. This may be good journalism, and at the time it was a good day's work; it is nothing higher; and the same reproach often attaches to the gall poured out by Cunninghame Graham and the sarcasms of C. E. Montague, on what they would contend is falsely called civilization. But satire was mending its wings for higher flights, and even putting forth new ones; and, surely, it was Butler's fearlessness and cheerful irreverence, and his telling combination of unorthodoxy and common sense, in *Erewhon* and *Erewhon Revisited*, with *The Way of all Flesh* revealing further possibilities, that as much as anything gave its impetus to the revival, which began almost simultaneously with the new century. Butler, though he was wary enough to justify everything he did by unexceptionable precedents, was anything but old-fashioned. He was as inevitably a satirist as Swift; his mordant humour was just as personal and instinctive. There were rooted errors and absurdities that he could point to when he burlesqued the English system of public school and university education in the Erewhonian colleges of unreason, or mocked at our treatment of delinquency by making his Erewhonians regard ill-health as a legal offence and immorality as a case for medical attention. But his satire never oversteps the bounds of pure comedy. In a memorable letter to Darwin,[1] he said that he developed his idea of the machines "for mere fun and because it amused me and I thought it would amuse others." Though his subsequent novel was largely an account of what he had suffered at the hands of a stupid and spiteful father, his mode of retaliation was to turn it all into ironical comedy, which gave himself and his readers the same sort of fun. *Saeva indignatio* was never the motive or the keynote of Butler's satires.[2] Nor is there animus in Barrie's humorous fantasies; his fortuitous caricatures, even when an actual original can be found, charm by their far-fetched absurdities. They are comedy, transcendently. Chesterton, again, was far too much in love with laughter, no matter whence it arises or whither it is directed, to be tempted beyond the frontiers of comedy, though his paradoxes and flights of apparently irresponsible extravagance were a definite criticism of life, satirizing cherished commonplaces and illusory modernisms from the empyrean of pure ideas—or from a judgment-seat reinstated after the lapse of half a millennium. Whether he owed anything to Butler, beyond the urge and audacity inspired by such an example, may be discussed later on. Humour was visibly renewing itself, as it must if it is to keep alive; without novelty and surprise it would perish. Butler, Barrie, and Chesterton had the largest share in this renewal.

As to utopias, whether of the Gulliverian, the satirical kind

[1] *Life*, i. 156.

[2] He apologized for any inadvertent betrayal of "the sense of wrong" that he felt with regard to Pauli, the Darwins, and his father. To ventilate it in his writings was far from his intention (*Life*, ii. 1).

The utopians

or the Platonic and Baconian, the constructive and truly utopian, there had been a truce ever since Bage's *Hermsprong* (1796), which contrasted man as he is with the beauties of an idealistic colony planted in the wilds of North America, until Lytton, in *The Coming Race*, told of his lost community with their superior civilization in a remote subterranean region, and Butler simultaneously brought news of his Erewhon. Butler's utopia, it should be noticed, was a blend of the two traditional kinds; the Erewhonians were a caricature of the English, and their eccentricities were placed in the most comical light; yet they had a sanity of their own which was a corrective for people who cherished irrational practices and beliefs simply because they had inherited them from the past and no one of any consequence had called them in question. Butler's was a cunning blend of the mock-serious with serious mockery. Swift had kept his parody of the English and his vision of a superior race in separate compartments, though in the final book he put his Houyhnhnms side by side in contrast with the repulsive Yahoos. Perhaps it was some secret uncertainty as to where exactly the satire ended and the idealism began that accounts for the indifferent success of the original *Erewhon*. It called for more thought than the average reader was inclined to bestow. As already said, it was a book dovetailed together out of various earlier pieces; whereas *Erewhon Revisited* was thrown off at a heat; "he wrote this book more easily than any other of his books," no doubt "because the idea had been in his mind for so many years" [1]; and so it presents no uncertainties or ambiguities. *The Coming Race* was a poor affair, and *Erewhon* at first made very little noise. It is doubtful whether a double event that passed off so quietly had much to do with the extraordinary proliferation of utopias during the eighteen-eighties. These were mostly of the speculative sort, earnest thinkers solemnly drawing up programmes of social and moral advance, satire being almost entirely in abeyance. Besant's *Revolt of Man* and *All Sorts and Conditions of Men* (1882) were, the one merely an elaborate

[1] *Life*, ii. 353. It is remarked earlier that it was the "least rewritten" of his books. See the *Note-Books* (288–296) for the material Butler had been accumulating.

jest on the woman question, the other a serious dream of social betterment.[1] *After London* (1886), by Richard Jefferies, and *A Crystal Age* (1887), by W. H. Hudson, were the visions with which two great worshippers of Nature solaced their dejection at human shortcomings.[2] Two very diverse excursions of sociological fancy came out at the same date as Garnett's *Twilight of the Gods* (1888), the American Edward Bellamy's *Looking Backward*, picturing a Socialist millennium, and *The Island*, by Richard Whiteing, author of that searching study of poverty, *No. 5 John Street*.[3] William Morris's *News from Nowhere* (1891) was another Socialist dream, whereas *A Traveller from Altruria* (1894), by W. D. Howells, was mainly an arraignment of the monstrous social inequalities of American life by one who had studied them under the microscope. Howells brought back an inhabitant of Altruria, and castigated them again in *Through the Eye of a Needle* (1907). Meanwhile, Mr H. G. Wells had begun his long series of scientific romances, contrasting the present with the future or life on this planet with that of Mars or some imaginary region. At least half his novels have some such utopian framework, though the contrast is rather between different ages and states of knowledge and civilization than different worlds. It was a scheme for fiction that suited Wells the programme-maker, and there are vestiges of it even in his satires, *Tono-Bungay* (1909), *Mr Polly* (1910), and *The Autocracy of Mr Parham* (1930). The utopian element in *The Martian* (1898) of Du Maurier amounted to nothing more than the artist's yearnings for a comelier race of men. But even a writer of propagandist novels for the Church of Rome, Monsignor R. H. Benson (1871–1914),[4] could not refrain from the fashionable utopianism. His *Lord of the World* prefigures the reign of Antichrist (1907), and *The Dawn of All* (1911) an era when all controversies have come to rest and the Church is at length omnipotent. His brother, Mr E. F. Benson, has been content to give a fantastic turn to some of his realistic vistas of life in this or a less humdrum country,

[1] See Vol. IX. 295.
[2] For Jefferies, *ibid.*, 91; for Hudson, above, pp. 86–94.
[3] See Vol. IX. 234.
[4] See also Vol. IX. 334.

for the sake of mockery or of frank sensation, and to take his David Blaize through the blue door into Wonderland. The other namesake, A. C. Benson (1862–1925), put only a spice of the utopian into his "imaginary portraits" and forecasts of a finer and more unworldly mode of existence, in *The House of Quiet* (1903), *Beside Still Waters* (1907), and the rest of his philosophic musings in a form approximating to fiction. One who had shown himself a disciple of Butler in *The Invisible Event* (1915), Mr J. D. Beresford, employed a variation of the utopian device in *Goslings* (1913), making room in Europe for new developments by sweeping it almost bare of male inhabitants with a strange pestilence from Russia. It might be urged that the partiality of so many writers for historical romancing, and for seeking far-off environments for dramas in which moral values are the chief stake, should be ascribed to this same craving for the purity and absolute justice to be found—nowhere. That is the thought suggested by the predominantly spiritual interest of such novels as the earlier ones of "John Ayscough," Monsignor Count Bickerstaffe-Drew (1858–1928)—*Marotz* (1908), *Dromina*, *San Celestino* (1909), *Hurdcott* (1911), and *Faustula* (1912). This may seem to be travelling a long way from the satires of actuality and the utopias giving the converse of actuality which have now been reviewed; but it is only further evidence how speculative and subversive thought was now permeating fiction. The novel was becoming more and more an arena for general ideas. This is strikingly evident in the case of Butler.

Samuel Butler

Samuel Butler happened to be the offspring of a typical family of the comfortable higher middle classes of the Victorian epoch, those whose immutable orthodoxy and spotless respectability made them, in their own and many others' estimation, the backbone of the English social system. He was the grandson of a famous headmaster of Shrewsbury, afterwards Bishop of Lichfield, and son of Canon Thomas Butler, whose candid portrait is painted in Theobald Pontifex, in *The Way of all Flesh*, a novel that gives the pith of Butler's inner history, and is an indispensable document on the influences that shaped his mind and bred the spirit of rebellious mockery animating a good half of his written works, not excepting his correspondence. Butler went to Shrewsbury School, and afterwards to St John's, Cambridge; and in spite of a system of teaching that he detested he did well in classics. But from boyhood onwards he was in silent and then articulate revolt against a social order and a discipline the implicit aim of which was to compel first the boy and then the adult "to see things as his neighbours see them," [1] and stamp out any dangerous sign of individuality. In the two books on Erewhon and in *The Way of all Flesh*, Butler caustically lays bare the world of strict observances and repressions in which he found himself. The discipline applied at home and at school was ostensibly based on morals, but actually on the need for maintaining a rigid class-system. The religion publicly recognized and forming a compulsory item in the programme of education amounted to little more than a professed belief in the literal accuracy of everything stated in the Scriptures. In *The Fair Haven* (1873), an ironic defence of Christian evidences, Butler showed it up as a tissue of sanctimonious pretence and subterfuge. The religion that actually governed the lives of respectable people was worship of the national goddess, Ydgrun, Mrs Grundy. The great rule of life was to keep thought and imagination under strict control; to this the favoured classes owed their self-complacency; it was heretical and wicked even to harbour the possibility of alternative modes of living or thinking. The name free-thinker was a word of abuse. The situation of one who asked the most obvious questions going to the root of things is depicted in Butler's Ernest Pontifex. Butler, who not only asked questions but actually saw the answers, found himself more and more at odds with his pastors and masters. When the

[1] *Way of all Flesh*, xxxv. "You've been real bad brought up, and I don't think you have ever had so much as a chance yet," says Mr Shaw (*Ibid.*, lix.) "His education had been an attempt, not so much to keep him in blinkers as to gouge his eyes out altogether" (*Ibid.*, lxi). The real Mr Shaw, *i.e.* G.B.S., says flatly, "The vilest abortionist is he who attempts to mould a child's character" (*The Revolutionist's Handbook*, 230). Ernest says, when he looks back on his time at Roughborough (Shrewsbury), "I am glad Skinner could never get any moral influence over me; I am glad I was idle at school, and I am glad my father overtasked me as a boy—otherwise, likely enough I should have acquiesced in the swindle, and might have written as good a copy of Alcaics about the dogs of the monks of St Bernard as my neighbours," etc. (*Ibid.*, xliv).

time arrived, he firmly refused to take Holy orders, and his parents were nonplussed. He was not without talent. He was no mean musician, and he had a gift for painting. They let him make a futile start at teaching. But it was eventually decided that he should go to New Zealand and take up sheep-farming. Accordingly, he went out to the Canterbury Settlement, and remained there five years (1859–1864), coming back then to England and studying art more seriously for a few years. It was while in New Zealand that he published the articles, including "Darwin among the Machines" (1863), which he afterwards embodied in *Erewhon*. Three years later he abandoned painting as a career [1]; and henceforth his main occupation was literature, though he was well enough off to travel and enjoy the pleasures of quiet life and reading and the social give and take that he loved in a small circle of chosen friends.

His works

Butler was at his ripest and mellowest in those episodic works, *Alps and Sanctuaries of Piedmont* (1881) and *Ex Voto* (1888). But the most important of the books he published between the original and the later *Erewhon* were his critical studies of Darwin's theory of evolution; they need be touched upon here only so far as they illuminate passages in his fiction. Butler admired Darwin's work, and accepted it with certain reservations. He aimed at correcting Darwin's undue insistence on "natural selection" as the all-sufficient agency of evolution; and in many a passage in his three novels, as well as in these critical and controversial works, he illustrated with both lambent wit and dialectical skill his opposite doctrine of an unconscious memory in living organisms, by virtue of which they solve their vital problems, and so, by "intelligent striving" rather than "the uninspired weeding-out by natural selection," progress in complexity and variety.[2] His blows were aimed

[1] Butler had several pictures hung on the line at the Academy. His best was "Mr Heatherley's Holiday," a view of the artist's studio where he worked. It was given after his death to the Tate Gallery. On calling there recently to have another look at it, I found it had gone on tour and was now in New Zealand, a most appropriate place of sojourn.

[2] It is noteworthy that W. H. Hudson agreed with Butler without mentioning him. He remarks in *Far Away and Long Ago* (1918), after reading *The Origin of Species*, that "Darwin had to my mind only succeeded in disproving his own

at the neo-Darwinians more than at Darwin.[1] He was more severe on the professional scientists even than he had been on the professional upholders of religious orthodoxy. "The spirit behind the Church is true," says Mr Overton in *The Way of all Flesh*, "though her letter—true once—is now true no longer. The spirit behind the High Priests of Science is as lying as its letter." [2] It is not to be wondered at that the author of so many gibes was boycotted by the adherents of both orthodoxies. Butler was a devout lover of truth, and only too outspoken in affirming what he held to be the truth, in season and out of season and in the most uncompromising terms, although he was fond of enjoining upon others that fibbing was the better part when a downright statement of facts might do more harm than good. He was a very straightforward and essentially a simple-minded man himself, but painfully aware of the duplicity of the world; often disillusioned, he was curiously ready to be deceived again. He showed supreme common sense in his books and in advice to his friends, but not much in the management of his own affairs. It is a byword how he let himself be victimized by Pauli,[3] the man whom he befriended in New Zealand, brought home to London, and allowed a regular income to make ends meet when the rascal was actually in receipt of a larger income than himself. In life and in some of the ideas he maintained, Butler often appears singularly wrong-headed.[4] But his

theory with his argument from natural selection. He himself confessed that no new species had ever been produced in that way." Later on he says, "Insensibly and inevitably I had become an evolutionist, albeit never wholly satisfied with natural selection as the only and sufficient explanation of the change in the forms of life." Both quotations are from the final chapter, "Loss and Gain." The Darwinians would have objected that Hudson and Butler were not trained scientists: they would have retorted, "So much the better!"

[1] As Bernard Shaw pointed out (Preface to *Back to Methuselah*, xlv.), Darwin "was not a Darwinian, but an honest naturalist working away at his job," etc. He did not repudiate all other explanations than the one put forward by himself, viz. circumstantial selection.

[2] "To him the professional man of science, with self-conscious knowledge for his ideal and aim, was a medicine-man, priest, augur—useful, perhaps, in his way, but to be carefully watched by all who value freedom of thought and person, lest with opportunity he develop into a persecutor of the worst type" (Marcus Hartog, in his introduction to *Unconscious Memory*, 1910).

[3] How deep was the personal fascination exercised by Pauli on Butler is shown by the attractive figure of Towneley in *The Way of all Flesh* (*Life*, ii. 8).

[4] A dictum of the late J. Arthur Platt, Professor of Greek at University College,

mistakes were rather to his credit than otherwise. There was a good deal of the crank in Butler; that must be admitted, but it must also be affirmed that he was a crank of genius. His life and letters and the evidence of his friends testify to a character in which modesty and a dignified self-esteem were admirably blended, together with a benevolence and a genial humour that shines very clearly in his books, which are the best extant evidence of the frequent impishness of that humour. This was the one of his qualities that he failed to transmit to the child of his brain and heart, Ernest Pontifex, who in his mature years is otherwise the very image of Butler. He and this offspring of his both inculcated a refined Laodiceanism as the wisest rule of life. For Butler, in spite of his many attacks on the professed pietists, was truly religious, if the Broad Church which he recommended existed only in his own earnest desires. There is a memorable passage in *Erewhon* contrasting "the many very godly people who have had a great knowledge of divinity, but no sense of the divine"; and he adds, "Mention but the word divinity, and our sense of the divine is clouded." [1] He believed in "the omnipresence of a mind and intelligence throughout the universe to which no name can be so fittingly applied as God." [2] "We may not always know very clearly what is meant by God, and things may not always work together for the particular kind of good that we desire; but there is 'a something as yet but darkly known which makes right right and wrong wrong,' and no man can ultimately fail who obeys the dictates of that voice which we can all hear within us if we will but listen." [3] The "Dedication" chapter in *Erewhon Revisited* is a noble statement of his "modest pantheism." [4] On the scientific value of Butler's

London, who described Butler as "the Galileo of mares'-nests," may be put down chiefly to the account of *The Authoress of the Odyssey* (1897). The *mot* appears in an amended form, "The Columbus of mare's-nests," in an article on Butler in the *Independent Review*, by Mr Desmond MacCarthy.

[1] Chap. xvii.

[2] *Life*, ii. 41.

[3] *Ibid.*, 16. Butler's is at least the basis for a spiritual view of the world, since he maintains that life is not the sport of chance and natural accidents, but self-determined—an affair of self-development, of ultimate realization of all the possibilities inhering in the germ.

[4] "The universe is instinct with the mind of God. The mind of God is in all that has mind throughout all worlds." "If we speak ill of God in our ignorance,

rectifications, as he regarded them, of the Darwinians, which were corroborated by the subsequent theories of Hering, Haeckel, and others, but are still questioned on the ground of the absolute separation of the germ-cells and the impossibility of the transmission of acquired characters, it is not for a layman to pronounce. But, like his Laodiceanism and his rich humanity, they were views that appealed to the thinker. There was a boom in Butlerism in the years following his death, and his influence on mental attitudes has been powerful and lasting. Not the least effective was his appeal for tolerance. For this was the basic motive even of his satire, though, paradoxically, he was so often driven to excesses of sarcasm and intolerance by the intolerance of his adversaries.[1]

"*Erewhon*"

Butler was not a young man when he wrote *Erewhon* (1872), or the articles which he revised and incorporated in it. Very adroitly, he combined these dialectical items with other interests, and produced what was not unlike an ordinary novel, with the three regular ingredients, picturesque adventure, a love-affair, and a romantic escape with the lady. Nor is there any lack of amusing character; Mr and Mrs Nosnibor are delectable creatures, quite apart from their satirical value, and Arowhena would do credit to any select gallery of heroines.

it may be forgiven us; but if we speak ill of His Holy Spirit indwelling in good men and women it may not be forgiven us" (chap. xv.). It is rather a pity that Butler, in *God the Known and God the Unknown* (1879), undertook to explicate to himself and others what this God of his should be identified with, more definitely than he had done in *Erewhon Revisited*, where he says, "There is no God but the Universe, and man in this world is His prophet." He is not content with the idea of "the Spirit and the Life which creates, governs, and upholds all living things," "a single Being or Animator"; his God, being a person, must have a body, must be corporeal, else we cannot imagine Him as existent—"an immaterial God" is "Atheism in another shape." However inadequate most will find Conrad's religion, which knows nothing conscious outside and beyond the soul of man, it has a richer spiritual content. As an able critic puts it, "Butler drew a sharp line of division between the organic and the inorganic, but soon after, he came to see that this was wrong" (Rattray, 109). Butler was too early to welcome recent views, such as Eddington's argument "for volition in the unit of matter" (*Ibid.*, 112), though he said that "Matter and motion are functions one of another" (*Note-Books*, 74). As Rattray points out, he anticipated Freud and others (Rattray, 143), including much that is summed up by A. N. Whitehead (*Nature and Life*, 1934) on the baselessness of a "sharp division between mentality and Nature."

[1] Half a dozen "Erewhon dinners" were organized by Butler's surviving friends and took place in London in the years subsequent to his death—the seventh and last was in 1913. It was noticeable that the company always consisted almost entirely of authors, journalists, musicians, and the like, *i.e.* the intelligentsia.

Butler made good use of his acquaintance with New Zealand, in the Defoe-like account of his hero's life on the sheep-farm and the curiosity, and hopes of making his fortune, that led him to undertake his expedition to the mysterious region beyond the mountains, with Chowbok, his man Friday, who deserts and leaves him to continue the perilous journey alone up to the pass guarded by the mysterious statues. All this is first-rate romance, stamped real and unforgettable by the man's plain tale of his sensations. He is a mixture of simplicity and shrewdness; and Butler makes excellent use of both these qualities in the matter-of-fact account of the strange country in which his hero finds himself. As already said, *Erewhon* is a satirical utopia, though not devoid of idealistic elements; it presents a world as imperfect as ours, and in many features still more absurd. Some of Butler's paradoxes are simply truths put in a startling shape; but he also loved to turn familiar things inside out, so as to show the preposterousness of much that we accept as rational. The result is a humorous amalgam of specious sophistry with truths that badly needed enforcing. Along with the cutting absurdities, he brings in things that are worthy of emulation, such as the good nature and urbanity of the Erewhonians, who put in practice Butler's own principles of forbearance and compromise in social and intellectual intercourse, and their avoidance of excessive earnestness. Priggishness and bigotry are taboo in Erewhon. Man should not be righteous overmuch. Often it is obvious that the argument which sounds nonsensical to the simple-minded narrator is a statement of Butler's own views: there is an obvious instance in "The Book of the Machines," in the "one serious attempt to answer" the learned professor of hypothetics, who had persuaded the government to put a ban on machinery.[1] In the course of it is expounded an idea on which

[1] In his abstract of the professor's treatise, Butler makes his usual mixture. He slurs over certain fallacies, and then shows, by a cogent process of reasoning from premises that are not so general as they look, that, if we are not careful, machines will soon be our masters instead of our servants. The mock parallel with crude Darwinism in the evolution of machinery is very neat. Natural selection, *i.e.* the mechanical operation of external circumstance on living organisms, is shown at work in man's deliberate selection of better and still better machines; and it is hinted that if the real explanation be, as of course it is, that machinery progresses

Butler rather prided himself, that organs and limbs are simply the mechanical appurtenances by which vital needs are fulfilled. "The lower animals keep all their limbs at home in their own bodies, but many of man's are loose, and lie about detached, now here and now there, in various parts of the world—some being kept always handy for contingent use, and others being occasionally hundreds of miles away. A machine is merely a supplementary limb; this is the be all and end all of machinery." Of the same sort are the views which Mr Higgs, to give him the name not disclosed before his revisit to Erewhon, finds so shocking, on the alleged immorality of the belief in a future state:

When I asked how it could be immoral, I was answered that, if firmly held, it would lead people to cheapen this present life, making it appear to be an affair of only secondary importance; that it would thus distract men's minds from the perfecting of this world's economy, and was an impatient cutting, so to speak, of the Gordian knot of life's problems, whereby some people might gain present satisfaction to themselves at the cost of infinite damage to others; that the doctrine tended to encourage the poor in their improvidence, and in a debasing acquiescence in ills which they might well remedy; that the rewards were illusory and the result, after all, of luck, whose empire should be bounded by the grave; that its terrors were enervating and unjust; and that even the most blessed rising would be but the disturbing of a still more blessed slumber.

Obviously, there is much to be said for considering disease a crime, and theft and other immoralities as disease. Observe that malefactors do not escape punishment: moral ailments are very severely treated by the straighteners.[1] Butler tends, however, to weaken his case by making ill-luck penal. The dig at the medical profession must, of course, be taken much more than half seriously.

Were the severity of the law or the current feeling of the country to be relaxed never so slightly, these abandoned

through the purposive effort of mind, then we must look for a purposive impulse bringing about natural evolution.

[1] Mr Bernard Shaw's views on the penal system obviously owe a great deal to Butler.

persons, who are now compelled to practise secretly and who can be consulted only at the greatest risk, would become frequent visitors in every household; their organization and their intimate acquaintance with all family secrets would give them a power, both social and political, which nothing could resist. The head of the household would become subordinate to the family doctor, who would interfere between man and wife, between master and servant, until the doctors should be the only depositories of power in the nation, and have all that we hold precious at their mercy. A time of universal dephysicalization would ensue; medicine-vendors of all kinds would abound in our streets and advertise in all our newspapers.

Butler's irony

Butler's irony was at its gentlest, which, as usual, was its deadliest, in his satire on religious formalism and moral indifference, under the charming conceit of the Musical Banks and the two currencies—the coin of the realm which, as the faithful would insist, was dross in comparison, and the clerical coinage, grace, piety, good works.[1] Butler's method requires close attention, if his own opinions are to be recognized through the deliberate sophisms, and his favourite device of showing what is the truth by turning the picture upside down. He continually changes his point of view. Now he is depicting a better state of society as a pattern, and now as a sarcastic contrast, and then, again, he is engaged in caricaturing existent things. Often the three methods or points of view alternate or even combine. Swift employed different kinds of satire in the four books of *Gulliver's Travels*, but never mixed them. Swift was a perfect

[1] Butler did not so much attack or try to destroy religion as put it in its proper place, just as Swift did. Mr Bernard Shaw used to be always citing Butler, "in his own department the greatest English writer of the latter half of the nineteenth century," on the religious and other social questions, and complains of our neglect of the teachings of *The Way of all Flesh*, and that "when . . . I produce plays in which Butler's extraordinarily fresh, free and future-piercing suggestions have an obvious share, I am met with nothing but vague cacklings about Ibsen and Nietzsche," etc. This is from the preface to *Major Barbara*, where he is continually echoing Butler, as in the just tirade, "We frantically scatter conscience money and invent systems of conscience banking, with expiatory penalties, atonements, redemptions, salvations, hospital subscription-lists and what not, to enable us to contract out of the moral code." Remember also Shaw's saying, "Beware of the man whose god is in the skies." Hypocritical ecclesiasticism is the foe. Higgs reflects, "Indeed, the recollection of the many falsehoods which I was then obliged to tell, would render my life miserable were I not sustained by the consolations of my religion."

master of irony; irony was sometimes the master of Butler. Irony is a double-edged weapon, and Butler often cuts himself. He must have his fling. The chapter "Birth Formulæ" is largely mere fooling, except the hits at baptism and at original sin. The Erewhonians are at times most admirable people, at other times quite the reverse. Not all their absurdities are to be taken ironically.[1] The summing-up is clear: "Indeed I can see no hope for the Erewhonians till they have got to understand that reason uncorrected by instinct is as bad as instinct uncorrected by reason." [2]

"Erewhon Revisited"

Butler was an old man when he wrote his sequel to *Erewhon*. Though *Erewhon Revisited* (1901) is largely another exercise in hypothetics, there is no shifting now of the point of view; Butler knew exactly what he wanted to say, and said it without ambiguity or hesitation. He was a firm disbeliever in the miraculous Ascension; and it is not strange that he could not resist the temptation afforded by the denouement of the previous novel, the escape in a balloon, to exploit this as a satire on that venerated dogma of the literalists. Higgs comes back on a visit to Erewhon, and is distressed to find that the Erewhonians were so wonder-struck by his miraculous ascent into the heavens, that a canonical account is now prescribed to be read in churches, differing materially from the facts; that his sayings are treasured, in amended forms, and divers worthless relics are piously preserved; and that Sunchildism has been grafted on their old religion and is now the orthodox creed. It was not Butler's intention, however, to be irreverent. It has been seen that he had the deepest respect for religion, though he had no mercy for those professional exponents who insist upon such marvels as the chariot and horses which were said to have carried their messiah aloft in triumph, but neglect the spiritual ideal which is the divine truth contained in it.

[1] It is possible that Butler indulged in some of his ambiguities and equivoques on purpose, to make his readers think out for themselves what he was driving at, at the cost of thinking themselves fools. He was impish enough, anyhow.

[2] Why on earth did Meredith "turn down" *Erewhon*? Butler himself answered that question. He did not think it strange, "for I should probably have condemned his *Diana of the Crossways*, or indeed any of his books, had it been submitted to myself. No wonder if his work repels me that mine should repel him" (*Life of Meredith*, by S. M. Ellis, 207).

Hence there is no scurrilous mockery of the virgin birth in the discovery that Yram, daughter of the jailer, who fell in love with Higgs when he was a prisoner, subsequently had a son George, who is generally accepted as the child of her husband, the mayor of Sunch'ston, but is believed by others to have had no earthly father. On the contrary, the meeting with Yram, and the colloquies with the estimable and charming young man whom he must not claim as his son, are among the most touching incidents in Higgs's story. Butler succeeds in giving *Erewhon Revisited* genuine human interest. Yram took good Mrs Humdrum's advice and told her husband the truth, and in due season she tells her son, begging him to forgive her.

"How much does not all this explain," said George, smiling but very gravely. "And you are going to ask me to forgive you for robbing me of such a father."

"He has forgiven me, my dear, for robbing him of such a son. He never reproached me. . . . Your having light hair and eyes made things more difficult; for this, and for your being born, almost to the day, nine months after Higgs had left us, made people talk—but your father kept their tongues within bounds. They talk still, but they liked what little they saw of Higgs, they like the Mayor and me, and they like you the best of all; so they please themselves by having the thing both ways."

There is beauty as well as pathos in the parting of father and son at the statues; and, no anticlimax, but the same with a difference, when the narrator, Higgs's son, bids his newly-found brother farewell at the same spot.

Satire from another angle

It should be noticed, however, that Higgs in this book is a very different man from the primitive Nonconformist of *Erewhon*: he is much more like Butler himself, whose theological position he expounds with admirable humour.

Sukoh and Sukop were two pretty men,
They lay in bed till the clock struck ten.

The man who is forbearing towards Mr Balmy, but exposes the charlatanism of Professors Hanky and Panky, is not the one who hoped that by converting Chowbok to the true faith he "might in some degree compensate for irregularities and shortcomings" in his previous life, and whose cheeks burned with excitement at the thought that the inhabitants of Erewhon might be the lost ten tribes of Israel. It might be objected, also, that Bishop Kahabuka, who tells so many pious falsehoods, is hardly recognizable as even a much matured Chowbok; but to a satirist much can be forgiven. The feats of honest or fallacious dialectic are as brilliant as ever. Hanky and Panky are a couple of vitriolic caricatures of pharisaic humbug. Nor is there any falling-off in the aphoristic side-hits, whether they are to be taken ironically or to the letter. It would not be easy to say off-hand from which book come such dicta as those on historians and eye-witnesses: "It has been said that God cannot alter the past, historians can"; "Nothing is so misleading as the testimony of eye-witnesses." Butler no doubt had a rich store of such sayings ready for use, as the posthumous *Note-Books* confirm (1912). These are as good as his hit at art critics and at public statuary. A convict in Erewhon, if he be a gentleman and unable to earn his living, "must pick oakum, or write art criticisms for a newspaper." In old times, the Erewhonians allowed their streets to be infested with statues of dead worthies, until it was enacted that every one should be broken up after fifty years, unless it were spared for another fifty by a large majority of a special jury. The result was that many statues were not ordered, whilst sculptors, "knowing their work to be so ephemeral, scamped it to an extent that made it offensive even to the most uncultured eye."

Hence before long subscribers took to paying the sculptor for the statue of their dead statesman, on condition that he did not make it. The tribute of respect was thus paid to the deceased, the public sculptors were not mulcted, and the rest of the public suffered no inconvenience.

The witty logic of the longer discourses, which in the previous book were directed mainly at the problems of evolution, now chiefly elucidates more spiritual questions. Dr Gurgoyle's pamphlet "On the physics of vicarious existence" is the richest in Butler's paradoxical wisdom: it is a sermon on genuine immortality. The Sunchild used to talk, sometimes a little tediously, about a great poet, whose name, he said, was Shakespeare.

"Whilst he was alive, very few people understood his greatness; whereas now, after some three hundred years, he is deemed the greatest poet that the world has ever known. 'Can this man,' he asked, 'be said to have been truly born till many a long year after he had been reputed as truly dead? While he was in the flesh, was he more than a mere embryo growing towards birth into that life of the world to come in which he now shines so gloriously? What a small thing was that flesh and blood life, of which he was alone conscious, as compared with the fleshless life which he lives but knows not in the lives of millions, and which, had it ever been fully revealed even to his imagination, we may be sure that he could not have reached?' . . . Who would not go cheerfully to block or stake if he knew that by doing so he could win such life as this poet lives, though he also knew that on having won it he could know no more about it? Does not this prove that in our heart of hearts we deem an unfelt life, in the heaven of men's loving thoughts, to be better worth having than any we can reasonably hope for and still feel?"

This brings Dr Gurgoyle to the question of faith:

"Faith does not consist, as some have falsely urged, in believing things on insufficient evidence; that is not faith, but faithlessness to all that we should hold most faithfully. Faith consists in holding that the instincts of the best men and women are in themselves an evidence which may not be set aside lightly; and the best men and women have ever held that death is better than dishonour, and desirable if honour is to be won thereby."

Higgs lays down Butler's acceptation of the spirit but not the letter of Anglicanism in the oft-quoted passage:

"You Musical Banks people bear witness to the fact that beyond the kingdoms of this world there is another, within which the writs of this world's kingdoms do not run. This is the great service which our church does for us in England, and hence many of us uphold it, though we have no sympathy with the party now dominant within it. 'Better,' we think, 'a corrupt church than none at all.'"[1]

"*The Way of all Flesh*"

Butler was the first of the Victorians to come to his full senses,[2] and *The Way of all Flesh*, begun in 1873, finished in 1884, and published in 1903, a year after his death, is the record of this awakening. It must be read both as his inner biography and as a practical illustration of his views on creative evolution.[3] Like a biologist, he traces the pre-natal influences that moulded the germ-plasm of his hero: before coming to Ernest himself, he investigates the family history on both sides for several generations.

> If a man is to enter into the Kingdom of Heaven, he must do so, not only as a little child, but as a little embryo, or rather as a little zoosperm—and not only this, but as one that has come of zoosperms that have entered into the Kingdom of Heaven before him for many generations.

Butler is to be recognized in the historian Mr Overton, and also in the subject of the memoir, Ernest Pontifex; the one understands what is perplexing to the other, and thus the pitfalls of autobiography are avoided; and with some allowance for a laxity here and there, as when Christina's thoughts and feelings are read like an open book, the realism is straightforward and conclusive. Butler knew nothing of the scrupulous technique of modern realism, and cared less. There is a frank disregard for any artistic niceties in his ingenuous procedure. The facts are stated without the least show of authenticating them through someone on the spot. And he kept so close to actual events that he could insert raw chunks of fact from elsewhere, on the principle that human nature never varies, without any incongruity showing. He knew he was "an unimaginative person," and preferred to insert any genuine incident or any document that came in handy, rather than

[1] Cp. "The irreligion of orthodoxy—We do not fall foul of Christians for their religion, but for what we hold to be their want of religion—for the low views they take of God and his glory, and for the unworthiness with which they try to serve him" (*Note-Books*, 350).

[2] Meredith could hardly have done so when he boggled at *Erewhon*.

[3] As it were, almost undesignedly and unwittingly, it is also a very great novel. See the admiring analysis by Mr Orlo Williams, in *Some Great English Novels* (1926).

rely upon invention.[1] Later on, in *Erewhon Revisited*, he was to borrow that part of Professor Hanky's sermon which dealt with Sunchild evidences almost word for word from a letter in *The Times* in support of the Christian Evidence Society. Both the father and the mother of Ernest Pontifex are drawn in the exact likeness of Butler's own parents; confessedly, the portraits were "as accurate as he could make them, with no softening and no exaggeration."[2] If the Rev. Theobald was the least shade worse than Canon Butler, there was no conscious misrepresentation; the son honestly did his best to keep down his resentment and see his father as he truly was. Nor is it for the reader interested in all types of humanity, unless he is a confirmed sentimentalist, to brand such candour as unfilial. This would be to condemn all that Butler inculcated on the honest facing of vital facts, howsoever unpleasant. As to Christina, his mother's vagaries and romantic reveries were notorious in the Butler family circle. To reproduce seemed so much better than to try and invent that some of Theobald's most egregious epistles, on the boy's "folly and wickedness," and others that gave the man away completely, are verbatim transcripts of the elder Butler's letters to his son Samuel, with merely the necessary alterations of names and circumstances. Many other persons are drawn straight from life, Dr Skinner, for instance, from the famous Dr Kennedy of Shrewsbury. Butler was too infernally serious in this book to be humorous very often, though Mrs Jupp is a great creation and there are scenes of high comedy between Theobald and Christina: he was not writing now to amuse himself or anyone else, as in *Erewhon*. In fact, as in reading the life by Festing Jones, one smiles or winces as much sometimes at Ernest Pontifex, or Samuel Butler, as with him. This is a book that had to be written, call it confession, self-defence, exposure, what you will. The account of his upbringing and his father's tyrannical efforts to eradicate the self that was in him is the most literal

[1] *Life*, ii. 354.

[2] *Ibid.*, i. 19. Many have censured Butler for inserting his mother's sentimental letter before the birth of her third son, almost verbatim, as Christina's to her "two dear boys" (chap. xxv.). Unquestionably, he did so after due deliberation. Ernest says (chap. lxxxiv.) it was "because my mother would have wished it published."

version of the facts. After that, some of the experiences were Butler's own, but more were from his memoranda of incidents he had heard of or places that he knew. He never went to prison, or, so far as he was aware, had any illegitimate children.[1] But he makes Ernest, in spite of his false start, settle down at length to the same placid existence as his own, cultivating the same tastes, and accepting the world with the same calm recognition of its frauds and imperfections. Both Ernest and Mr Overton are mouthpieces of their author's philosophy, and even let fall the germs of some ideas to be developed in *Erewhon Revisited*. Such is Ernest's belief in a College of Spiritual Pathology, or Mr Overton's suggestion that professorial chairs of speculation might be established at Oxford and Cambridge, and that speculation masters should be attached to every school. He considered the handling of money a subject of supreme importance, and even of ethical importance, in the conduct of life.[2] Both here and in his reported conversations, Butler seems often to take up a very cynical attitude in what are usually regarded depreciatively as matters of mere self-interest. In his notes for the Pontifex novel,[3] will be found two pithy articles of his creed:

> That God *is* a respector of money, whether he respects persons or no and he seldom goes behind ye money.
> If a man sins agst money it is ye sin agst ye H.G.

Worldly wisdom was an intrinsic part of his philosophy of life, but was in no wise at variance with the lofty benevolence and refined conscientiousness that Butler exhibited again and again in his life. Many of the dicta in the *Note-Books* sound still more dangerous, if not interpreted in the spirit that prompted them. Butler's bark was often worse than his bite. Ernest, at the end of *The Way of all Flesh*, is much more like the Butler who was over-generous to Pauli, and who scrupulously paid back out of his own pocket the shares his friends lost in a company which he had recommended. He contended more than once that "a man's best peers" were "his safest

[1] *Life*, ii. 8–13.
[2] His views on money are illustrated in Mr Shaw's *Major Barbara*.
[3] *Ibid.*, ii., Appendix, 470.

moral guide"[1]; but his own conscience and that of Ernest Pontifex were of their own make, simply checked and corrected by that criterion. Hence the complete and lovable personality in which the Rev. Cuthbert Creighton always discerned "something of what I conceive to be saintliness."[2]

The legacy of Butler

Some who have been disciples or at any rate vitally affected by Butler have been mentioned already; the great proselyte is Mr Bernard Shaw, who helped him early in 1901 to find a publisher for *Erewhon Revisited* and the revised *Erewhon.*[3] He succeeded Butler in the role of our chief satirist and challenger of rooted opinions; but as a master of dialogue and repartee chose to write didactic and propagandist plays rather than pamphlets disguised as novels. The earlier influence of Nietzsche and Ibsen is often as apparent as that of Butler, for instance in *Man and Superman* (1903). Butler, however, is avowedly the Socrates to his Plato in a long series of plays hingeing upon the same topsy-turvy, Gulliverian situations, for the purpose of the same stereoscopic exposure of realities, illustrating similar ideas in similar ways, and carrying on the same war with uncompromising pertinacity. The explosive free thought, the criticism that strips shams and insincerities naked, the inversions of current dogmas, and the maxims with a sting in them, are all Butler or glosses upon Butler. Mr Shaw took up the same position in what was known as the conflict of science and religion, the general assault on the Victorian compromise. He had no more faith than Butler, or Meredith and Conrad, in the simple-minded doctrine of progress, or any more belief in mere machinery. Progress is an illusion, he maintains in *The Revolutionist's Handbook.* Like them, he lays the stress on immaterial values, and calls for an inner change—of desires, aims, character. Neither he nor Butler was indifferent to religion. The preface to *Back to Methuselah* is a denunciation of "the infidel half century." Religion is a matter for this present world; it is a personal and social issue, and a vital one. Their objection to the conventional God is that He is not a God. They have too much reverence

[1] Letter to editor of the *Spectator*, discussing certain points in a review of *Erewhon* (*Life*, ii. 375).
[2] *Ibid.*, 180.
[3] *Ibid.*, 339–341.

as well as ethical scruples to believe in a capricious being made up of sentiment and vindictiveness. "What's this game that upsets our game?" asks Blanco Posnet, and presently discovers the God which is within us. *Androcles* is a drastic exposure of vicarious salvationism, and likewise affirms a God not of Death but of Life. The doctrine of *laissez-faire*, cut-throat competition, survival of the fittest to survive, is radically immoral and irreligious. The Great War, which was the great try-out of the principle, showed what inevitably came of it. The veteran disciple of Samuel Butler reiterates that neo-Darwinism is an inadequate theory, and that the human race must have a religion, and one not at variance with the facts of science. Myths might do for uneducated peasants. But for every advance in intelligence religion has to be remade: Butler had indicated the lines on which this was to be done. Shaw did not disapprove of "the Gospel of Laodicea" preached by Butler; "there is no more dangerous mistake than the mistake of supposing that we cannot have too much of a good thing." [1] To the recoil of the two Roman Catholic reactionaries Chesterton and Hilaire Belloc, the double-headed monster "Chesterbelloc," from this alleged worldliness, and their appeal to the primitive, to the dark ages, to the mystical, the reply was that, on the contrary, it was this that made the world itself divine and attested that man proceeded from the spiritual substance of God. Shaw's function on the stage was much the same as Butler's had been in *Erewhon* and the other works; and he prided himself that "Comedy, as a destructive, derisory, critical, negative art, kept the theatre open when sublime tragedy perished." [2]

G. K. Chesterton

Gilbert Keith Chesterton (1874–1936), a much younger man than either of them, was on the other side, and his views were very different; but his fiction was in the same full measure a statement of views, the expression of philosophic ideas in

[1] *Getting Married*, preface, 125–127.

[2] *Back to Methuselah*, preface, "The infidel half century," p. 82. *God the Invisible King*, by H. G. Wells, expounds a similar gospel, whereas *The Interpreters* of "A.E." and the poems, essays, stories, etc., of Walter de la Mare are in their different ways more mystical, or at least dependent upon some rarer sensibility. The agnostic religion of the last-named, his recognition of the Unknowable, the divine element in life, constitutes a different reconciliation of knowledge and faith, science and spirit.

the artistic form of a story. In the strict æsthetic sense, he was no more a novelist than Butler was or than Shaw is a dramatist: for all three, the dialectic is the primary element; the realistic portrayal of life is solely of instrumental value, and only to that extent subject to criticism. And Butler had set an example of fearless and outspoken criticism, of facing facts and then setting them in a light that was satire in itself, which Chesterton found as congenial as Shaw had done. In startling antitheses and paradoxes that threw everything into new perspectives he often outwent even Butler, though not with the same infallibility or his senior's demure air of sanity and composure. Chesterton was a man of vast and picturesque physique and great conversational prowess, as formidable in lecture and debate as in his writings. In fact, those writings, even the poetry and fiction, show the marks of the debater, in the mediæval sense; for he was a born fighter, happiest in the stress of battle, though one of the warmest-hearted and most genial of men. "The Wild Knight," the title of his first book, a collection of poems (1900), evidently describes himself. He was conservative from innate antipathy to everything new, a man to whom progress was anarchy, modern thought heresy, modern science the deceits of Satan, and most modern distempers, pessimism for instance, the work of the same foe. His poems are chiefly rhetoric, meant to be shouted: "You that have snarled through the ages, take your answer and go." That is the first and the last line of "The Pessimist." The swinging, crashing lines of "Lepanto," masterpiece of the style, are obviously begotten of and meant to excite the same berserk fury.

> *Vivat Hispania!*
> *Domino Gloria!*
> Don John of Austria
> Has set his people free!

Some analogies with Butler —and contrasts

He was as versatile as Samuel Butler. A student of the Slade School, he started his journalistic career as an art critic, and several times illustrated his own works. He was a brilliant essayist; at any rate, an admirable proportion of his essays count as first-class literature. He was a stimulating critic, and even an historian of literature; his monographs on Dickens, Browning, and G. F. Watts aimed at defining the basic meaning of each of these men of genius, and, within limits, brilliantly succeeded. Jester, satirist, and philosopher, in his novels, he was all three again when he transformed detective fiction. Chesterton hated progress, not like Butler and Shaw, as a fallacious deduction from disputable premises, but from what Butler would call pre-natal tendencies; he preferred regression to a fabulous past age of virtue and happiness, though not of peace. "Progress" is an unmeaning term "without the previous definition of a moral doctrine." The free-thinking of Shaw and H. G. Wells, and such modern concepts as "the economic man" and the "superman" appeared to him inhumane; the latter showed the trail of the serpent Nietzsche. Both truth and falsehood work ruin in Ibsen's plays: "there are no cardinal virtues of Ibsenism." All these, together with Kipling's glorification of discipline, organization, imperialism, and his lack of true patriotism, are the modernist sophisms diagnosed in *Heretics* (1905). George Moore, Whistler, the æsthetes, the Omarians, the neo-pagans, and even the slum novelists, devoid of a real sense of fraternity, come under the same ban. The mighty optimist was to go on fulminating against all the decadents and preachers of despair, from Wilde and Hardy to Rose Macaulay and Aldous Huxley. He sets forth his own opposite views in *Orthodoxy* (1908), which is virtually his acceptance of the Roman or mediæval Church, though he was not formally received within it till 1922. "Materialism leads men to complete fatalism"; "the determinists come to bind, not to loose. They may well call their law the 'chain' of causation." This is not so far from the arguments of Butler and Shaw in their refutation of materialism and determinism. They, too, saw no place for a God in a system of mechanical evolution which denied free will and the working of mind and spirit. But Chesterton soon goes off in other directions. Not intelligence, not faith in their own potentialities, but mysticism is what keeps men sane. Each must understand everything "by the help of what he does not understand." "Reason is itself a matter of faith." The universe "may be a miracle with a supernatural explanation; it may be a conjuring trick, with a natural explanation." The latter supposition has never satisfied him. "The thing is magic, true or false," and he finds it true. "It was Huxley and Herbert Spencer and Bradlaugh who brought me back to orthodox theology. They sowed in my mind the first wild doubts of doubt." *Orthodoxy* makes his position clear, and should be read as the preface to Chesterton's novels and stories.

His extravaganzas

Butler and Shaw had used realism, with a plunge now and then into hypothetics, as the vehicle of their philosophic argument in novel or play. Chesterton inclined to romance, with merely a corroborative touch of realism here and there; and oftenest to romance in its extremest form, fantasy and extravaganza. Paradoxy would be the nearest name for it. His first essay, *The Napoleon of Notting Hill* (1904), is not meant merely as brilliant nonsense, for in the last pages it is urged that even a joke may suggest things which are "real and passionate." The brain has two lobes; wherefore any man may again and again be called mad. The fanatic without humour gropes; the humorist may in dark days be stripped of "the joy of gravity." Both the pure fanatic and the pure satirist are necessary; between them they may lift the commonplace of our modern existence into poetry. Hence this vision of a London suburb, only half a century from now, transformed into an independent city, with fortified walls, provost, and pageantry, and of the sanguinary war that breaks out when its rights and autonomy are threatened by modernizing neighbours. Democracy is visibly played out; bureaucracy supersedes it: why not then make one of the bureaucrats king? All are much alike; no one will be allowed at this stage of civilization to become a tyrant; so let the election be by lot. The king revives mediæval usages, and through the folly of certain boroughs which take offence hostilities break out. Chesterton's delight in primitive colour, pageantry, heroism, bloodshed, has full fling. He revels in the ecstasy of warfare, as he does in the blessings of romance. It is a poet's serio-comic dream, to be taken as he means it. The one revolver does not go off; halberts and swords are the weapons for the real business. *The Club of Queer Trades* (1905), which followed, is fantasy in the manner of *The New Arabian Nights*, but curiously abstract as well as paradoxical: the point is always a philosophic idea. Modern life is dull; so the Adventure and Romance Agency is established to furnish excitement—to make life like fiction. Every member of the Club has to invent a new way of earning his living. One starts as a professional butt for amateurs of repartee. A naturalist sets up as a house agent, and of course runs a line of villas in trees. It is elaborate tomfoolery, with perhaps a side-hit at Sherlock Holmes.

Chesterton's style

Chesterton's style, which is as personal and distinctive as his mode of thought, was now fully developed; *Orthodoxy* (1908) and *Tremendous Trifles* (1909), the latter a book of essays from the *Daily News*, show it at its best, and not so often as later books at its worst. It was primarily a way of thinking, and secondarily a method of vivid and forcible expression. Like his two predecessors, he aimed at the overthrow of conventional illusions and hereditary fallacies; he wanted unprejudiced definitions—"We lose our bearings entirely by speaking of the 'lower classes' when we mean humanity minus ourselves." He wrestles with fundamental terms of thought, and strives to break away from the vague significations which they have acquired in the wear and tear of easy-going, unreflecting converse. There is a merely superficial resemblance between him and those whose antitheses are rather a vivacity of writing than a mode of thought. His incessant effort to bring out exact meanings by comparing opposites is a rough-and-ready application of Hegel's dialectic—the resolution of contraries. He thinks in contradictions instead of affirmations. He shows up by showing both sides of the shield. "There is nothing that fails like success." "There is but one step from the ridiculous to the sublime." [1] "Folk-lore means that the soul is sane, but that the universe is wild and full of marvels. Realism means that the world is dull and full of routine, but that the soul is sick and

[1] Cp. the ironical "It takes some time to prepare an impromptu" (*Magic*, 50).

screaming. . . . In the fairy-tales the cosmos goes mad; but the hero does not go mad. In the modern novels the hero is mad before the book begins, and suffers from the harsh steadiness and cruel sanity of the cosmos."[1] Both paradox and antithesis, it is evident, are essential to such a manner of reasoning, or of narrative, which to him was the same thing; this is how he envisages everything, how he approximates to the truth. But with Chesterton, the commonest common sense must be enlivened by hyperbole; nothing can be true or of much significance that does not shape itself spontaneously into an epigram. The instrument becomes a walking-staff, and he leans upon it far too persistently. Contradiction becomes a habit; he keeps it up when he should be going quietly straightforward, like a man in a state of hypnotic excitement. He cannot write like an ordinary man, any more than the ordinary man can write like him. And it follows that he has no use for the finer shades of meaning; he gets after all only a rough approximation to reality, which is not to be taken by storm.[2] Thus for him, "Exaggeration is the definition of art."[3] And he lets out at a venture, "By simply going on being absurd, a thing can become godlike."[4] The mental contortions grow wearisome to sober readers; it is tiring to see only by flashes of lightning—after all, one moment of illumination was enough for St Paul. An epigrammatist should never write a book, unless he has the discretion of a Samuel Butler, who left the bulk of his for others to garner in the *Note-Books*. A book that is all paradox is sure to be intolerable, like several of Chesterton's, in spite of the padding with which he is obliged to relieve it. His poetry is full of the same athletic sporting with words and ideas, apart from the initial paradox of the sedentary writer —William Morris and R. L. Stevenson were not so very different—finding vicarious recreation in fierce hand-to-hand combat and unlimited bloodshed—on paper.

1 "The Dragon's Grandmother" (*Tremendous Trifles*).

2 "But the moment we begin to believe a thing ourselves, that moment we begin easily to overstate it; and the moment our souls become serious, our words become a little wild" (*Charles Dickens*, 1906, pp. 18–19.

3 *Ibid.*, 18. Characteristically, he qualifies this later on—"Exaggeration is almost the definition of art—and it is entirely the definition of Dickens's art" (p. 49).

4 *Ibid.*, 21.

There lives one moment for a man
    When the door at his shoulder shakes,
When the taut rope parts under the pull,
And the barest branch is beautiful
    One moment, while it breaks.
. . . . .
And the heart of the locked battle
    Is the happiest place for men;
When shrieking souls as shafts go by
And many have died and all may die;
    Though this word be a mystery,
        Death is most distant then.[1]

From first to last, his was a primitive mind cherishing its simplicity, and recognizing at sight the sophistry and self-contradictions of the intellectuals. He called their logic paradoxes, his own are plain common sense. Intellectualism was the foe, rationalism a foolish attempt to abolish the romantic, the mysterious, the magical, which to him were the basic truths.

More fantasias

After the header into mock mediævalism and pure extravagance, Chesterton indulged in what he called a nightmare, but a reassuring one, for it removed his fears of "the airless vacuum of science."

> The first was the old fear that any miracle might happen, the second the more hopeless modern fear that no miracle can ever happen. But he saw that these fears were fancies, for he found himself in the presence of the great fact of the fear of death, with its coarse and pitiless common sense.

Such is the enlightenment granted to Syme, in *The Man who was Thursday* (1908), when he has to fight a duel and realizes that his adversary is a terrible fighter. This is an allegory of the central mystery that the Almighty allows evil to flourish, for what ends? Ancient illusions are overturned and cherished convictions changed to their opposites with bewildering rapidity. The Rabelaisian fun is fast and furious. The oracles masquerade as clowns and harlequins; wisdom flashes out in star showers. What could seem more absurd than the tale of a club of anarchists in a plot to destroy the world, six of whom,

[1] "The Harp of Alfred."

after terrific efforts to run each other to earth and foil their deadly schemes, turn out to be police officers in disguise? What fancy more light-hearted than this of a corps of "policemen who are also philosophers," whose mission is to detect and thwart the subtle machinations of the pessimists, impressionists, hedonists, and all the artistic people who are steadily corrupting the soul of the common man? Story and dialogue are Chesterton's mode of reasoning, and he flings the lines of his discourse through illimitable space; they describe curves that reach through heaven and hell; but he proves his theorem, if it is to be proved. Each sleuth has tracked the others down, and found them to be friends. The little band are fighting with their backs to the sea against a countless mob led by the secretary of the Anarchist Council, when the secretary himself proves to be on the side of the law. There remains only the president, Sunday, the enormous man with the back of an animal and the face of a god. He is the mystery.

"When I see the horrible back, I am sure the noble face is but a mask," says Syme. "When I see the face but for an instant, I know the back is only a jest. Bad is so bad, that we cannot but think good an accident; good is so good, that we feel certain that evil could be explained."

It is the dilemma that drives some to Manicheism. The pursuit of Sunday, mounted on the biggest elephant at the Zoo, with the sham anarchists racing after him through the streets of London, is the maddest scene of all. At length, the oracle speaks. Sunday was the chief detective, sitting invisible in the darkness, who had given each man his commission.

"You heard the voice in the dark, and you never heard it again. The sun in heaven denied it, the earth and sky denied it, all human wisdom denied it. And when I met you in the daylight I denied it myself."

In the everlasting struggle of order with disorder, virtue with profligacy, man cannot distinguish friends from enemies, right from wrong; the whole basis and the ultimate sanction of his faith remains an enigma. At length Syme sees everything clearly:

"Why does each thing on the earth war against each other thing? Why does each small thing in the world have to fight against the world itself? . . . For the same reason that I had to be alone in the dreadful Council of the Days. So that each thing that obeys law may have the glory and isolation of the anarchist. So that each man fighting for order may be as brave and good as the dynamiter. So that the real lie of Satan may be flung back in the face of this blasphemer, so that by tears and torture we may earn the right to say to this man, 'You lie!' No agonies can be too great to buy the right to say to this accuser, 'We also have suffered.'"

Chesterton used the weapons that suited him. "Moderate strength is shown in violence, supreme strength is shown in levity." He certainly found in a pretence of levity the better part.[1]

"The Ball and the Cross"

The Ball and the Cross (1910) is not so neat in the conjunction of fable and thesis. The opening is a rather irrelevant burst of fireworks; and the fairy-tale would have been better abandoned at an earlier stage, not because of improbability, since in apologue and the like mere probability must be kept in its place, but for the slenderness of the links between it and the ensuing logomachy. Professor Lucifer arrives in an airship, and disembarks on the ball of St Paul's a holy man from Bulgaria, who is the apostle of old tradition, faith, mistrust of rationalism, and speaks in parables. "You begin by breaking up the Cross; but you end by breaking up the habitable world." For everything is irrational—an argument tending now to fall a little flat. There is lots of fighting, muscular or verbal. But Turnbull, the materialist, is a poor debater, and much too easily put down by MacIan, who demonstrates incidentally that the Ibsens, Zolas, and Shaws have not got even so far as "realizing that a man is a man." Some shrewd hits befall at silly conventions. Someone uttered the word "God." "Be quiet," said the magistrate angrily, "it is most undesirable that things of that sort should be spoken about—a—in public, and in an ordinary Court of Justice.

[1] W. L. Knox (in the study of Chesterton in *Great Catholics*, ed. Father Claude Williamson) compares this effort of his to "rewriting the *Pilgrim's Progress* in the style of the *Pickwick Papers*."

Religion is—a—too personal a matter to be mentioned in such a place."

Father Brown, detective

In the new-fangled kind of detective story beginning with *The Innocence of Father Brown* (1911), and continued in *The Wisdom of Father Brown* (1914), *The Incredulity of Father Brown* (1926), and *The Secret of Father Brown* (1927), Chesterton introduced two novelties into the established genre—a simpler but more surprising method of solving the good old problems, and a cunning manipulation of the general lighting, so that the dullest and vulgarest backgrounds looked weird and portentous, just as in the apocalyptic romance of *The Man who was Thursday*. It was the former that seemed to his readers the great stroke of originality, the old priest's uncanny insight into the recesses of a man's conscience, a faculty trained in the confessional and now become second nature and wellnigh automatic.[1] One mystery after another foils all the resources of the profession, but is quietly unravelled by the calm, ungullible intelligence of this fat little commonplace *curé*, who never gets excited, never loses his head, and if he does not have an instantaneous intuition thinks hard till he has reconstructed the whole imposture, as if he had got inside it. "In such moments he put two and two together and made four million." Father Brown is a captivating personage, and his genial reflections on the rogueries and blood-curdling atrocities which he thrashes out—for as usual Chesterton is not sparing in horrors—impress with an air of wisdom and broadmindedness which is not, however, as infallible as it looks. He is not less optimistic than his creator. Thus Father Brown appeals to the good instincts even of the desperado Flambeau, and begs him for the sake of his own peace of mind to restore the stolen diamonds: "I want you to give them back, Flambeau, and I want you to give up this life." It must be a very guileless reader who is not taken aback when Flambeau penitently drops his hard-earned booty. The first three in the first

[1] *E.g.*, the duplicate parcel, in "The Blue Cross"—"an old dodge, Father Brown—a very old dodge." "Yes," said Father Brown, and passed his hand through his hair with the same strange vagueness of manner. "Yes, I've heard of it before." "Well, I mustn't tell you his name, of course," said the little man simply. "He was a penitent, you know."

book, "The Blue Cross," "The Queer Feet," and "The Secret Garden," are as good as any in the whole series; the ghastliness of the last-named is paralysing, even though the mechanical explanation rather damps the effect. "The Scandal" is how a journalist thinks he has caught the good priest condoning a wife's runaway affair with a poet. His first report gets printed; and, though the corrected version follows immediately, it never quite catches up the "tale of the Brown Scandal, or Priest Ruins Potter House." "The Blast of the Book" is a good story of a magical volume into which if anybody looked he instantly disappeared from human ken. It comes out that the stodgy clerk in Mr Pringle's office is an accomplished humorist, who has played a trick on his own employer and the expert in psychic phenomena, Professor Openshaw. The best item in the fourth and last collection is "The Purple Wig," with its satire, strangely characteristic of such a conservative as Chesterton, on aristocracy, especially aristocratic snobbishness. The Duke of Exmoor to-day is Isaac Green, who swindled his principal, the late duke; and, having the property, managed to get the title revived in his own favour. The wig does not conceal the elfin ear which was the ancestral birthmark and the sign of mystery and terror in the family history, but the absence of it.[1] It is a wildly improbable tale, and the paradox far-fetched; but it can be enjoyed on its own account, with no questions asked. Scientific evidence is mocked at in "The Mistake of the Machine." "You always forget," says Father Brown, "that a reliable machine always has to be worked by an unreliable machine." "Why, what do you mean?" asked the detective. "I mean Man," said Father Brown, "the most unreliable machine I know of." His particular crony and repeatedly his coadjutor is Flambeau, ex-criminal and now detective himself, who, it goes without saying, is often the most surprised of anybody at his old friend's unerring flair. And yet, the frauds and mysteries, however dumbfounding and no matter how long they defy the reader's

[1] As the narrator explains, "it is the practice of journalists to put the end of the story at the beginning and call it a headline." This is necessary here, to get the effect.

conjectures, always turn out to be manufactured complications, with the solution ready made, and obviously constructed for the very purpose of being solved by Father Brown. The explanation may be the last thing that would occur to the ordinary mind; but, since it was evidently all thought out beforehand, the surprise tends to fall flat. Constructing such riddles is soon perceived to be an ingenious but purely mechanical operation; with a little practice, it would be as easy as cat's-cradle. It is, of course, the congenital defect of the police-novel, which only a few great writers have evaded by amplifying or sublimating the interest. Since Chesterton's time, there has been an extravagant output of the article, and the bulk of it seems to have no higher object than to compete with crossword puzzles and other antidotes for mental vacuity. Though Chesterton was largely responsible for this overwhelming revival, he would now probably be violently in favour of a moratorium for detective fiction.

The romantic atmosphere

But the Father Brown stories surely owe much more to Chesterton's talismanic power of shedding a magical light on surrounding objects, and giving a commonplace spot the air of being somewhere in fairyland or in heaven or hell, than even to the unfailing clairvoyance of the little priest. The bar of a low public-house, a restaurant cloakroom, a dingy street in Camden Town, or a dull square at the back of Victoria, becomes as romantic as a mountain-top or the edge of a stormy ocean. Fairyland, it is revealed in his little three-act play *Magic* (1913), is "either nowhere or it's wherever you are." There is magic everywhere. Old women tell you "that the fairies are too small to be seen. But I tell you that the fairies are too mighty to be seen." "They are the Elemental Spirits, and any one of them is larger than the world." So the walled-in garden behind the old house on the Seine in Paris is inevitably a haunted place, and the nook under the bank on the Norfolk Broads where they moor the boat in the gloaming brings up in both men simultaneously "a reminiscence of childhood, of the elfin and adventurous time when tall weeds close over us like woods." A spell, or at least something inscrutable, excites undefinable apprehensions in a corner of Hampstead

Terrace rose above terrace, and the special tower of flats they sought rose above them all to almost Egyptian height, gilt by the level sunset. The change, as they turned the corner and entered the crescent known as Himalaya Mansions, was as abrupt as the opening of a window; for they found that pile of flats sitting above London as above a green sea of slate. Opposite to the mansions, on the other side of the gravel crescent, was a bushy enclosure more like a steep hedge or dyke than a garden, and some way below that ran a strip of artificial water, a sort of canal, like the moat of that embowered fortress. As the car swept round the crescent it passed, at one corner, the stray stall of a man selling chestnuts; and right away at the other end of the curve, Angus could see a dim blue policeman walking slowly. These were the only human shapes in that high suburban solitude; but he had an irrational sense that they expressed the speechless poetry of London. He felt as if they were figures in a story.[1]

Chesterton draws his settings in lines that seem to quiver and suggest something beyond, as if they were the borderlines of space and time. As in a Dream-Fugue of De Quincey's, you are led to infinite horizons. A novel or story was for him the junction where you change for other worlds. A sense of the bizarre, the macabre, of some overwhelming hostile force, grips the two men who have climbed the church tower, in "The Hammer of God."

Immediately beneath and about them the lines of the Gothic building plunged outwards into the void with a sickening swiftness akin to suicide. There is that element of titan energy in the architecture of the Middle Ages that, from whatever aspect it be seen, it always seems to be rushing away, like the strong back of some maddened horse. This church was hewn out of ancient and silent stone, bearded with old fungoids and stained with the nests of birds. And yet, when they saw it from below, it sprang like a fountain at the stars; and when they saw it, as now, from above, it poured like a cataract into a voiceless pit. For these two men on the tower were left alone with the most terrible aspect of the Gothic; the monstrous foreshortening and disproportion, the dizzy

[1] *The Innocence of Father Brown.*

perspectives, the glimpses of great things small and small things great; a topsy-turvydom of stone in the mid-air. Details of stone, enormous by their proximity, were relieved against a pattern of fields and forms, pigmy in their distance. A carved bird or beast at a corner seemed like some vast walking or flying dragon wasting the pastures and villages below. The whole atmosphere was dizzy and dangerous, as if men were upheld in air amid the gyrating wings of colossal genii; and the whole of that old church, as tall and rich as a cathedral, seemed to sit upon the sunlit country like a cloud-burst.

"Man-alive"

Such things cannot be classified with ordinary novels and stories; they are a unique kind of facetiæ, like his articles and essays, radiant with flashes of sudden insight and revelation. Superlative nonsense in *Manalive* (1912) proves, often if not always, to be transcendent wisdom. Much of it is preposterous, in the etymological sense of the word. But he is a master of that irrelevance which always hits the mark, none the less for continuing to sound absurd. At the same time, Chesterton never doffs the role of journalist; whatever the risk, he must show off his supreme cleverness. Hence the incessant epigrams are often iridescent bubbles that will not hold even air more than a couple of seconds. In the extravaganza that followed this, *The Flying Inn* (1914), he repeatedly came to grief in this way. It is one of his polemics against those who would refuse us any more cakes and ale. The puritans have made drinking and the sale of liquor an indictable offence, so two champions of freedom and joviality set up a peripatetic tavern to outwit Malvolio. But it is only the snatches of Rabelaisian verse that save the joke from dullness. *Manalive* is a romantic apology for the romantic attitude: we must never cease regarding the most hackneyed and wearisome things as if they were perpetual novelties, everlastingly calling out our capacities for heroism, affection, passion—though Chesterton sedulously avoids that last word. The scene of events is one of those towering structures near Swiss Cottage described in "The Invisible Man." It is a very decorous boarding-house, and into the garden one windy day, amid a party of bored men and girls, alights like a bolt from the blue a fellow named Smith, who is supposed to be touched in the upper story. Everybody else finds life intolerably dull; not so Smith. "It looks as if he could turn into a sort of wonderland any minute by taking one step out of the plain road." He has a method of his own, "a method of the most daring ingenuity. He is popular wherever he goes, for he invades every house as an uproarious child. People are getting suspicious of all the respectable disguises for a scoundrel; so he always uses the disguise of—what shall I say—the Bohemian, the blameless Bohemian. . . . He goes in for eccentric good nature. . . . You expect a humbug to behave like Sir Charles Grandison; because (with all respect, Miss Hunt, for the deep, tear-moving tenderness of Samuel Richardson) Sir Charles Grandison so often behaved like a humbug. But no real red-blooded citizen is quite ready for a humbug that models himself not on Sir Charles Grandison but on Sir Roger de Coverley. Setting up to be a good man a little cracked is a new criminal incognito, Miss Hunt." He arrives among the house-party by a flying leap over the shrubbery. It appears later that when he goes home he habitually comes down the chimney. Before long, he has bored two holes with his revolver in the tall hat of the most respected gentleman at the boarding-house, and with the muzzle at his ear he compels the most irreverent of the pessimists to go down on his knees and eat his own profanities. But Innocent Smith is not only acquitted of attempted murder, for he has such a record for straight shooting that he could not have missed the warden had he meant to; he proves to be the beneficent revolutionary, and the one creative genius in the whole crowd of their acquaintances.

The truth is that when people are in exceptionally high spirits, really wild with freedom and invention, they always must, and they always do, create institutions. When men are weary they fall into anarchy; but while they are gay and vigorous they invariably make rules. . . . Even the wild authority of the harlequin Smith was still authority, because it produced everywhere a crop of crazy regulations and conditions.

Michael Moon explains that Smith visits Beacon House as a physician, to cure their maladies, most of which are melancholic. Someone tells him he has some bad habits.

"All habits are bad habits," said Michael, with deadly calm. "Madness does not come by breaking out, but by giving in; by settling down in some dirty little self-respecting circle of ideas; by being tamed."

Enjoyment of life, however, must not be confused with the Will to Live: "That's German, and German is High Dutch, and High Dutch is Double Dutch." Smith soon disposes of the pessimistic professor's show of reasoning. "The academic mind reflects infinity and is full of light by the simple process of being shallow and standing still." Smith's theory is very unacademic. "Though not an optimist in the absurd sense of maintaining that life is all beer and skittles, he did really seem to maintain that beer and skittles are the most serious part of it. 'What is more immortal,' he would cry, 'than love and war? Type of all desire and joy—beer. Type of all battle and conquest—skittles.'" The most awkward charge against Smith was one of unblushing profligacy. He was paying marked attentions to Miss Grey of Beacon House; but it came to light that he had already gone through the marriage ceremony with a certain Polly Green, and also with a Miss Brown and a Miss Black. What was the meaning of this curious coincidence of colours? The meaning is plain to anyone who knows his Chesterton. Smith had been "in the habit of taking the woman whom he loved with a permanent loyalty, and leaving her about (so to speak) at schools, boarding-houses, and places of business, so that he might recover her again and again with a raid and a romantic elopement. He seriously thought by a perpetual recapture of his bride to keep alive the sense of her perpetual value, and the perils that should be run for her sake."

Chesterton was a fanatical denouncer of the doctrine of evolution; yet it is pretty certain that Butler would have read him, not only with gusto, but also with no small measure of agreement. As humanists, they were not quite at opposite poles.[1]

The present and future

This chapter, happily, must remain unfinished. The school or group, or set of near and distant relations, are still alive and very active. The process of creative evolution in their art, and in their outlook on life through their art, is working more steadily. They are not so lawless and insubordinate as Butler or so freakishly revolutionary as Chesterton, who wasted his brilliance in trying to apply an exploded philosophy to a stage of knowledge and spiritual conditions for which it had no vital relativity. They keep their philosophy in its right place, not too much in the foreground and not in the background, but in the foundations and the solid framework of the structure, as a system of values shedding a steady light for the interpretation of an unintelligible world. Satire is still flourishing. The veteran is Mr Hilaire Belloc, who will require some day at least as many pages as Chesterton has appropriated. But, though Belloc started ten years earlier, Professor L. P. Jacks, who is ten years older, must not be overlooked simply because his satire is so peculiarly philosophical. His range is wider than it looks at first sight, though it may not seem to have the actuality of Mr Laurence Housman's Jingalo stories or anything like the encyclopædic pertinence of Mr Aldous Huxley. And the realists show in varying measure a like emancipation from the ordinances and restrictions and the fixed scales of values that weighed upon their predecessors, as will be no less apparent in the work of Arnold Bennett, Galsworthy, and D. H. Lawrence, than it is in the living novelists already mentioned.[2]

[1] "That man of genius has often reminded me of a village-pump, which on festal occasions may run wine, and ordinarily runs first-rate water; but never knows whether it is running wine of the best or water of the best or liquid mud or nothing at all, but always wears the same alluring look of promise" (H. W. Nevinson, *Fire of Life*, 214).

[2] See above, p. 247.

CHAPTER VII

ARNOLD BENNETT AND GALSWORTHY

Fiction as social history

ARNOLD BENNETT and Galsworthy, both born in 1867, are eminently examples of those novelists who by their intensive study of large segments of the surrounding world, and their honesty and accuracy, leave a record of their time which is, intentionally or not, of genuine value as social history.[1] Both would have repudiated the name of sociologist, for if they criticized or satirized ever so slily, they had no specific doctrine to preach; they were not propagandists, like H. G. Wells and Bernard Shaw, who have reviewed the latest stages in modern civilization in order to expose its shams and absurdities and the need for radical reconstruction, a programme for which they have ready to hand.[2] In novel after novel, however, they showed life going on through long tracts of time. They differed in their temperaments and their attitudes and outlook, and in their aims in writing. Bennett was so fascinated by the spectacle of all that was happening around him that he was amply content to depict what he saw, without much effort to bring into daylight the invisible complex of motive which would explain the working of cause and effect. He understood all that instinctively, and left it to be understood, often at the cost of the same uncertainty as prevails in actual life, and

[1] Bennett liked to earn "plenty of money and the praise of the discriminating," but said "I cannot conceive that any author should write . . . for posterity" (*Journal*, 28th January 1897).

[2] Sheila Kaye-Smith will have it that Galsworthy is a propagandist, because he raises a "barrier of ideas" between himself and those who might otherwise read him (*John Galsworthy*, 13–14). Such fiction as his is science as well as art; a theory of life, a philosophy, or at least a personal view, is always implicit in serious fiction. Galsworthy's is permeated with ideas; but so are those of Hardy, Conrad, etc., dealt with in the same series, whom it would be absurd to call propagandists.

sometimes even of misapprehension on the part of those who do not go all the way with him. He thought it only a matter of tact and common sense to interpret the unseen by the seen, the mind by the features, character and motive by behaviour. But he was apt to trust too recklessly to that common sense of his, which may have been infallible, but only when he took the trouble to exert it seriously. His craftsmanship, at any rate, his ability to maintain a hypnotizing semblance of actuality, was not to be surpassed, when once he had got into his stride. Contrariwise, Galsworthy's eye was centred on those very factors which underlie the visible drama. His sensibility and his feeling of responsibility were so acute that he had to get down to the mainsprings, and he thrashed out his problems with the zeal and minuteness of a sociologist. He was a thinker, a philosophic observer, urged by compassion for his brethren's lot to investigate prevailing conditions; who put anxious questions to himself, embodied those questions in his portrayal of life, and pleaded for an answer from the world. Inevitably, he was an idealist, though by no means with any tendency to optimism; and his picture of what exists always implied a contrast with what existence might be. Their mental constitutions, their conception of life and society, their scales of values, were so different that a comparison of the results brings out more oppositions than correspondences. But it is as if two complementary sets of the qualities required for the perfect sociologist were separately bestowed on these two: in one, eager curiosity, unerring vision, and the faculty of exact and lifelike registration: analysis, generalization, theory, and criticism, in the other.

Their treatment of time

Perhaps the key to the differences in their vision and their rendering of what they beheld is to be found in their different ways of dealing with time and with life as a process of continual change. It is illuminating to compare *The Old Wives' Tale* or the Clayhanger series with *The Forsyte Saga*. Narrative, the medium by which life is represented or interpreted in fiction, has to include characters and sentiments as well as actions and events. And the question at once arises, is the reality that we apprehend as life to be represented in this fictitious history as a series of states, succeeding each other from moment to moment and related by the operation of cause and effect, the only way in which intelligence can grasp it, or as a continuous movement, as we are aware of it in consciousness? The mind tends to assimilate time or duration with space, two modes of homogeneous extension, the one in a vertical direction, so to speak, the other horizontal. Both can be set out diagrammatically, in charts and tables. Science takes cross-sections of the ever-changing reality, which it cuts up into successive states, viewing things in their simultaneousness. It draws maps of things coexisting, the present resulting from their previous state and subsequent changes depending on conditions now. Life, to the intellect, appears as a succession of states, it may be an extremely rapid succession, nevertheless each is distinct. Each moment is predecessor to the next, and holds in itself the reasons for what is about to be, and so on. This is the intellectual, the analytical, the scientific mode of viewing time and reality, and it is Galsworthy's mode. He sees the passage of time as such a steady progression, each moment containing the germs of the next, the present being, not the instant that is gone as fast as it is here, but simply that space of time in which the past is in the act of disappearing and the future arriving. *The Forsyte Saga* is a vast series of these cross-cuts, vignettes, panels, episodes—the Forsytes seen in typical phases of the gradually changing fabric of existence, each leading imperceptibly but inevitably to the next, a continual progress in which there is never any real surprise, since nothing strange and unexpected can insert itself into the unwinding chain of causation. Everything is the result of what has gone before. It is a closed system of determination.[1] Yet consciousness tells us that the continuity does not break up into separate moments, that the sequence of definite states is only a convenient fiction; we are in the midst of incessant

[1] Galsworthy was a firm believer in free will: "However certain it was from the beginning that a man shall act in such a way, it is never known by that man in what way he is going to act until after he has acted. Hence, there is no deadening of the springs of individual action in a philosophic Determinism" (cited in a letter from Mrs Galsworthy). The Forsytes were free to choose how they would act, but it was determined for them already how they would exercise their freedom.

change, the process is one and indivisible. Imagination seizes it as a perpetual becoming; art puts itself at the centre and heart of life and shares in the creative activity. There is something in life beyond the ken of science; there are irrational elements that science would fain ignore. Life continually surprises those who watch it most intently. All the efforts of biochemistry, physiology, and the rest, to predict the future of a living organism are liable to be overthrown by what actually occurs. Life is ceaseless activity, perpetual change. Bennett was one of those who do not break up and analyse, but comprehend by intuition: he was not a rationalist, like Wells and Shaw and Galsworthy. Instinctively, such as he put themselves inside the movement; they take part in the time-process, identify themselves with life, as this process of incessant change. They rely on their natural insight, which is tantamount to saying that they have creative imagination adequate to all emergencies. Dip at random, practically anywhere, into their respective books, and this fundamental contrast stares you in the face: Bennett absorbed in the moment that has arrived, thrilled with "the miraculousness of life," and staring expectantly at the future; Galsworthy judicially scanning the present as the melancholy resultant of an infinitely complicated past, the fated sequel to what has been studied on an earlier page. It is a distinction that divides all novelists into two great classes—those such as Meredith, Hardy, D. H. Lawrence, Dostoevsky, on the one side; those like George Eliot, Gissing, Balzac, or Zola, on the other.[1]

Arnold Bennett

Enoch Arnold Bennett (1867–1931) was born at Hanley, one of the "Five Towns" in the Potteries region of Staffordshire, which are now incorporated in what is almost the metropolitan city of Stoke-on-Trent. The growth and modernization of this congeries of manufacturing towns is an intrinsic part of the story told in one large group of his novels and tales. He came partly of people employed in the local industries and

[1] In this attempt to elucidate basic differences, it is probable that various concepts and even turns of expression may have been derived from recent expositions of the philosophy of Bergson, in particular *The Philosophy of Change* (1914), by H. Wildon Carr, to which acknowledgments are due.

partly of agricultural stock, farmers on the borders of Wales and Cheshire. His parents were chapel folk, and he long resented the repressive puritanical instruction to which he had to submit, and the religiosity cloaking an intense materialism which he was to caricature in *Anna of the Five Towns* and other novels. After working a few years as a clerk in the office of his father, a local solicitor, reading law and acquiring an invaluable familiarity with business methods, he took a similar place at a low salary in London, and devoted his spare hours to self-education. His ambition was to be an author, and success in various prize competitions led to his becoming sub-editor of a woman's magazine, and then editor. He was reviewing books for *The Academy* and other journals, collaborated with Eden Phillpotts in some light plays, and published two novels that made no great mark, *A Man from the North* (1898) and *Anna of the Five Towns* (1902). He was still acquiring experience, principally of London life, but also in occasional trips abroad, once as far as South Africa. Bennett established himself in Paris early in 1903, where he wrote away industriously and at the same time laid the foundations of a thorough and discriminating knowledge of French literature. He was living near Fontainebleau when he finished *The Old Wives' Tale* (1908), the long work that brought him recognition as our leading realist. He had married a Frenchwoman in 1907, but the union ended in a separation fourteen years later. In 1911 Bennett settled down in a quiet spot in Essex. Next year saw the success of his best play, *Milestones*, in which he had a collaborator in Edward Knoblock. *Clayhanger* (1910) was a novel of the same order as *The Old Wives' Tale*; but its two sequels did not reach that standard, and the farces, melodramas, and lighter pieces of realism, which alternated with these fine novels and with the only one that stands comparison with them, *Riceyman Steps* (1923), seemed so unworthy of his great abilities, that he is now often said to have wilfully sacrificed artistic integrity to mere opportunism. He believed in meeting the preferences of readers half-way, he inculcated "the judicious compromise," and urged that "the artist of genuine vocation . . . can mysteriously put himself into a pot-boiler."[1] But the probability is that he was simply taking a holiday from his exhausting labours when he wrote such novels as *Buried Alive*, *The Card*, and *The Regent*, and put the more frivolous and exuberant side of himself into farce and extravaganza, without troubling his head whether he was acting up to his own artistic creed or ignoring it. His literary principles and their applications to himself and others may be studied in his vade-mecums, *How to become an Author* (1903) and *The Author's Craft* (1914). There is good journalism and occasionally something superior in his collections of articles, *Books and Persons* (1917) and *Things that have Interested Me* (1921–1926). For a time during the war, Bennett held the post of Director of Propaganda, and his contacts with heterogeneous figures inside or outside the War Cabinet gave pungency to a novel that resulted, *Lord Raingo* (1926). But when he wrote this he was a tired man, and the pathos of disillusionment transpires, almost involuntarily, in the latter pages. And yet, the year before he died, he delivered himself of another of his extravagances, *Imperial Palace* (1930), out of an unexhausted imagination fabricating marvels of invention and organization, almost like those with which H. G. Wells was equipping his worlds of the future, and substantiated it all with his usual realism. The resemblance is slight and only accidental; but it is of no small historical significance that *The Old Wives' Tale* and *Clayhanger* appeared contemporaneously with *Tono-Bungay* (1909), *Mr Polly* (1910), and *The New Machiavelli* (1911); Wells and Bennett were rivals, though the prizes and the rules of the competition were severally fixed at the will of each.

Novels of the Five Towns

In *A Man from the North*, a young fellow comes to London like Bennett, full of ambitions, and settles down eventually to the average lot. Local and autobiographical colour is at a minimum. But there is plenty of that in *Anna of the Five Towns*: Bennett's descriptions of the drab industrial background are so graphic that they tend to divide attention with the story. This already shows touches of his relish for paradox,

[1] The points at issue are discussed by Lafourcade (see especially pp. 2–3 and 234–236).

for instance, in Ephraim Tellwright, the rich miser, financier of Methodism, to whom "the circuit was a going concern," and who "reduced the cost per head of souls saved, and so widened the frontiers of the Kingdom of Heaven"; and in Anna, a poor workman's daughter, without education or the most elementary idea of the meaning of wealth, who receives an inheritance of £50,000 and remains as poor as ever. She is one of those strong, quiet, unassuming women, in whose very existence Gissing probably disbelieved, but whom Bennett draws over and over again, with unmistakable truth and in admirable variety. The man she loves disappears; he has committed suicide. Anna feels it her duty to marry another man.

She had sucked in with her mother's milk the profound truth that a woman's life is always a renunciation, greater or less. Hers by chance was greater. Facing the future calmly and genially, she took oath with herself to be a good wife to the man whom, with all his excellences, she had never loved. Her thoughts often dwelt lovingly on Willie Price, whom she deemed to be pursuing in Australia an honourable and successful career, quickened at the outset by her hundred pounds. This vision was her stay. But neither she nor anyone in the Five Towns or elsewhere ever heard of Willie Price again. And well might none hear! The abandoned pit-shaft does not deliver up its secret. And so—the Bank of England is the richer by a hundred pounds unclaimed, and the world the poorer by a meek soul stung to revolt only in its last hour.

The sole interest of *Leonora* (1903) and of *Sacred and Profane Love* (1905) is that they both look forward to *The Old Wives' Tale*, the one seeking and finding romance, or at least tragedy, in the plight of a middle-aged woman, unhappily mated and at odds with her daughters, the other a crude story of a Five Towns girl who runs off to the Continent and goes to the bad in the flashy, theatrical way of sensational fiction. *A Great Man* (1904) is not so cheap as that, but is only a rather lame effort at one of those hilarious extravaganzas which were to be among his particular if minor successes. Two sets of short stories followed, *Tales of the Five Towns* (1905) and *The Grim Smile of the Five Towns* (1907), mostly slight, but including the single one, "The Death of Simon Fuge," that can be set beside the title-piece in *The Matador of the Five Towns* (1912), as a miniature concentrating the look and sound and feel of a tract of the habitable globe which is dreary and repulsive in the extreme to those who have not the right vision. The point of the story is that no man is a prophet in his own country. "He may have been a great artist," says Mr Brindley, "or he may not. But for us he was simply a man who came of a family that had a bad reputation for talking too much and acting the goat!" Bennett finds the counterpart to his own impressionism in the painter whose talent is admitted with such crass indifference; Fuge "was exclusively preoccupied with the beauty and the romance of the authentic." He, also, can see the poetry in all the grime and gloom and glare, beauty and sublimity in the fierce contrasts of light and darkness and the infernal clamour of vast forces at work. Any and every aspect of the mundane drama enthralled Arnold Bennett, and challenged him to convey his sense of it. He revelled in his craftsmanship, as in his material, the stuff of existence. He found interest even in the prose and sawdust of human nature; and as an enterprising workman devoured with curiosity he would experiment with it, and find ever new matter on which to exercise his wits. He would see how it worked in other and subtler ways, make it react to novel conditions, play with it by inventing circumstances and situations. Hence the zest for such extravagances as *The Grand Babylon Hotel*, *Buried Alive*, *The Glimpse*, *The Card*, some of which yielded more than mere entertainment, whilst some were a fiasco. One in the present group belongs to this experimental category, *Whom God Hath Joined* (1906), and its ingenuity and curious emphasis on the logic of events give it almost the air of a problem-novel. It is the history of a pair of divorce cases in two closely related households, in the Five Towns. The impeccable realism, the sure insight into the characters of the women in particular, the erring wife, and the injured wife and daughter, give power and cogency to the ill-starred drama. "The foundation of good fiction is character-creating, and nothing else." [1] If the data

[1] *Things that have Interested Me*, iii. 192–193.

are sound, the action, story, plot, will work itself out incontrovertibly. There was bound to be some stage-management in a case where it was so necessary to make ends meet. But the probabilities are not too glaringly outraged; and it would be unfair to compare this with the parallel divorce cases in *The Forsyte Saga*, where the coincidence is purely accidental.[1]

"*The Old Wives' Tale*"

There is more than ever about the Five Towns in *The Old Wives' Tale*; but this is a novel that stretches out in both time and space. The perspective widens; the great manufacturing towns and London are on the horizon, and even Paris is the scene of protracted episodes before the march of events comes to a final rest in Bursley where it started. Like Galsworthy's *Forsyte Saga*, it is a novel of manners which has developed into a piece of social history, with glances at world events; it unfolds the passage of an epoch, the submergence of the Victorian era by the tide of modernity. The Five Towns imperceptibly but inexorably disappear in a vast industrial metropolis, hideous with the crudity and vulgarity of the present day. This, however, is only incidental. The basic theme is one of the great old commonplaces, the one celebrated so often in French poetry, the tragedy of advancing and remorseless time. "There is an extreme pathos in the mere fact," says the preface, "that every stout ageing woman was once a young girl with the unique charm of youth in her form and movements and in her mind. And the fact that the change from the young girl to the stout ageing woman is made up of an infinite number of infinitesimal changes, each unperceived by her, only intensifies the pathos."

"Ha! vieillesse felonne et fière,
Pourquoi m'as si tost abatue?"

cries Villon's Belle Heaulmière. Bennett was in a Paris restaurant when the thought struck him, and set him brooding over a scheme for such a novel. Maupassant had written one already. "*Une vie* relates the entire life history of a woman." But he resolved to "go one better" than Maupassant, and to

[1] *In Chancery*, Part II.

give "the life history of two women instead of one." He would have two heroines. "Constance was the original; Sophia was created out of bravado." Meanwhile, he let the project simmer at the back of his mind, and wrote five or six novels of smaller scope. In 1907 he sat down in a village near Fontainebleau and wrote the first part of *The Old Wives' Tale* in six weeks, went to London and wrote the farcical *Buried Alive*, and then came back determined to finish, which he did by July, 1908. It is a thoroughly English novel written entirely in France. He had a great but essentially a simple subject, and he treated it with laudable simplicity; there are no complications either of plot or of character. The two sisters, whose lives are to be recounted from childhood to death, are well-marked individuals, but to be classified as far from uncommon types. The staid, serious Constance is one of those to whom nothing ever happens, when once they have settled down into the groove of conventional habits; she is staggered one day to realize that she is forty: the wayward, mettlesome Sophia is her perfect opposite. Their careers will be as different as their characters. The placid Constance stays all her life in Bursley; hers is the common humdrum lot. The spirited Sophia falls in love, elopes, and would have been victimized by a worthless husband had she not been clear-headed and capable; and, having rid herself of that encumbrance, she makes her own fortune in Paris during the siege, coming back eventually to the Five Towns an old woman. This is all there is of story, in the broad outlines, though of varied incident, denoting the chances and changes of life, the casual humours, the inescapable tragedies, and those tiny events the significance and decisiveness of which time alone reveals,[1] there is no stint. Even those which are out of the common, such as Daniel Povey's murder of his dipsomaniac wife, the sensational affair of Rivain's guillotining, and Sophia's experiences during the bombardment of Paris, are as normal and

[1] "All this," she (Sophia) reflected, listening in the dark to the ceaseless rattle of the street, "because mother and Constance wanted to see the elephant, and I had to go into father's room! I should never have caught sight of him [Gerald Scales] from the drawing-room window!" Old Baines died while she was out of the room talking to Gerald. It was the first time he had been left unwatched for years.

true to the phases of life portrayed as the petty events in the domestic history of Constance and Povey. Bennett found all the romance he wanted in the average lot and the daily routine. He often waxed lyrical in expressing his delight in the inexhaustible interest of human nature and mere existence. Had he, as he once intended, pushed the contrast between the two sisters to a more symmetrical extreme, by putting Sophia through all the stages of seduction, abandonment, and prostitution, he would have committed a crime against his art, and reduced a potential masterpiece to the level of his irresponsible fantasies.[1] If at one stage he thought of forcing the story into such a framework, he corrected himself in time. His was not an abstract, theoretic mind, one that would contrive a story to illustrate a thesis or fit a preconceived design. He worked empirically, gazing at life and seeing intuitively below the surface. He could tell what Sophia would do at the critical junctures. In no single act does she contradict her nature. Such a realist as Bennett has continually to deal with the incalculable; which does not mean that any act is unmotived, but only that it may be a surprise to such as do not know all the factors, or cannot in imagination identify themselves with the living individual. Compared with Arnold Bennett's, Galsworthy's characters are logical propositions, which the reader accepts, along with their doings, as irrefutable, unless he dissents from the whole theory on which they are constructed. There is no scientific test that can be applied to Bennett's. But perhaps the assent of the sympathetic reader's consciousness is just as infallible, though not susceptible of demonstration. If Sophia had yielded to the glamour of Chirac and gone irretrievably to the bad, she would not have been Sophia. She put Bennett right when he was inclined to go wrong; for she was a real, live woman to

[1] Frank Harris was disappointed with Bennett's moderation (see Lafourcade, 111–112, where it is urged that Sophia, "rather like a Dostoevskian heroine, without reason or motives," is made to refuse Chirac and "pursue her lonely road in unwarranted chastity"). But the assumption that either Bennett or Dostoevsky dispenses with "reason or motives" seems the most "unwarranted." It would have been more to the point to take her as another example of the contradictory thoughts, sentiments, impulses—the psychological discontinuities—the handling of which Bennett learned from Stendhal.

him, the child of his imagination whose behaviour when she had come of age he watched with paternal absorption.

Life in Bursley

The natural complement to his main story, to the girlhood of his two heroines, the life of the stay-at-home in Bursley, and their last days together after Sophia's return, is Bennett's fullest panorama of life in the Five Towns. Nowhere else, in some fifteen novels and collections of stories devoted to the subject, did he depict it in such immense detail. Here it is that he comes nearest to Balzac and Zola. Whatever he happened to be writing upon, Bennett's knowledge always seems inexhaustible; it is as if he were an expert on everything he touched. In this case, he had the advantage of old familiarity: he had lived, he said, "in the actual draper's shop of the Baines's, and knew it as only a child could know it."[1] No doubt, half at least of the people who figure in the foreground or even the background had been more or less intimate acquaintances. He touches off so many of their portraits with the caustic irony that shows he has not forgotten his likes and dislikes, reserving, however, his heavier satire for collective foibles, like the crude salvationism with which these Pharisees disguise and pamper their materialistic cravings. There is a mockery as withering as Voltaire's in the set-piece showing the congregation in the Methodist chapel—the "multitudinous rows of people, in easy circumstances of body and soul," kneeling in high pews and covering their faces, whilst "there floated before them, in the intense and prolonged silence, the clear vision of Jehovah on a throne, a God of sixty or so with a moustache and a beard, and a non-committal expression which declined to say whether or not he would require any more bloodshed," with white-winged creatures wafting themselves around, and afar off the obscene monstrosity, with cloven hoofs and tail, who took a malignant pleasure in coaxing you by false pretences into the fire in which he existed. Bennett clearly saw the intimate connexion between the religion which they had evolved and the motives that ruled their lives.

Who would have supposed that Mr Povey, a recent convert

[1] Preface.

from Primitive Methodism in King Street to Wesleyan Methodism on Duck Bank, was dwelling upon window-tickets and the injustice of women, instead of upon his relations with Jehovah and the tailed one? Who would have supposed that the gentle-eyed Constance, pattern of daughters, was risking her eternal welfare by smiling at the tailed one, who, concealing his tail, had assumed the image of Mr Povey? Who would have supposed that Mrs Baines, instead of resolving that Jehovah and not the tailed one should have ultimate rule over her, was resolving that she and not Mr Povey should have ultimate rule over her house and shop? It was a pewful that belied its highly satisfactory appearance. (And possibly there were other pewfuls equally deceptive.)

But there is a finer humour, bringing to mind Mrs Gaskell, or at least Mrs Oliphant at her very best, in the scene in which Miss Chetwynd comes to tea, and Mrs Baines at once exerts her ruling powers by convincing her that the girls must leave school at the end of the term, and also makes her own grand renunciation in allowing the restless Sophia to be apprenticed as a teacher, instead of taking her natural place with Constance in the shop. The climax is at the moment when the "pinched virgin of forty," who even in her own small sphere had been eclipsed by her elder sister, lets out with well-prepared nonchalance the great news that her sister is engaged to the Reverend Archibald Jones. Mrs Baines was taken aback; but she did nothing indiscreet, she kept her presence of mind. "This is really *most* interesting!" said she.

It was. For Archibald Jones was one of the idols of the Wesleyan Methodist Connexion, a special preacher famous throughout England. At "Anniversaries" and "Trust sermons" Archibald Jones had probably no rival. His Christian name helped him; it was a luscious, resounding mouthful for admirers. He was not an itinerant minister, migrating every three years. His function was to direct the affairs of the "Book Room," the publishing department of the Connexion. He lived in London, and shot out into the provinces at week-ends, preaching on Sundays and giving a lecture, tinctured with bookishness, "in the chapel" on Monday evenings. In every town he visited there was competition for the privilege of entertaining him. He had zeal, indefatigable energy, and a breezy wit. He was a widower of fifty, and his wife had been dead for twenty years. It had seemed as if women were not for this bright star. And here Elizabeth Chetwynd, who had left the Five Towns a quarter of a century before at the age of twenty, had caught him! Austere, moustached, formidable, desiccated, she must have done it with her powerful intellect! It must be a union of intellects! He had been impressed by hers, and she by his, and then their intellects had kissed. Within a week fifty thousand women in forty counties had pictured to themselves this osculation of intellects, and shrugged their shoulders, and decided once more that men were incomprehensible. These great ones in London, falling in love like the rest! But no! Love was a ribald and voluptuous word to use in such a matter as this. It was generally felt that the Reverend Archibald Jones and Miss Chetwynd the elder would lift marriage to what would now be termed an astral plane.

There is as much detestation of provincialism here as contempt for such aberrations of the religious instinct. Bennett, it must be confessed, is more in his element in this sarcastic tirade than in the quiet domestic comedy leading up to it. More characteristic are the scenes of popular riot and revelry, such as Bursley Wakes, the visit of Wombwell's menagerie, the execution of the elephant who nearly killed a man, and the crowning excitement when the whole town turns out and pilgrims arrive from far and near to view the huge animal's corpse. It is a long steady recital punctuated by such episodes, and by domestic incidents, some farcical, such as the mischievous Sophia's theft of Mr Povey's tooth, some the regular household tribulations, illnesses especially, with the medical treatment, if it be only a dose of castor oil or entail a prescription from Dr Stirling for some ailment with a very long name—which Bennett duly gives together with all the symptoms. Now and then there are glimpses of stupefying actualities, as when Samuel Povey is hurriedly called in at night by his cousin Daniel, and through an open door on the staircase giving on a yard catches sight of "a building, vaguely lit, and naked figures strangely moving in it." "What's that?

Who's there?" he asked sharply. "That's the bakehouse," Daniel replied, as if surprised at such a question. "It's one of their long nights." Sam had never penetrated so far into his cousin's secrets; and never after did he "eat a mouthful of common bread without recalling that midnight apparition. He had lived for half a century, and thoughtlessly eaten bread as though loaves grew ready-made on trees." But there is no homily on the callousness of our social system: Bennett was not a Gissing, or a Shaw or Galsworthy. Ideas were not in his line; as Chevalley lamented, he had no general vision of life.[1] Yet he can link an event with what is going on in the world outside and making history. When Critchlow and the widow stand over the pitiable corpse of John Baines—

They knew not that they were gazing at a vanished era. John Baines had belonged to the past, to the age when men *really* did think of their souls, when orators by phrases could move crowds to fury or to pity, when no one had learnt to hurry, when Demos was only turning in his sleep, when the sole beauty of life resided in its inflexible and slow dignity, when hell really had no bottom, and a gilt-clasped Bible really was the secret of England's greatness. Mid-Victorian England lay on that mahogany bed. Ideals had passed away with John Baines. It is thus that ideals die; not in the conventional pageantry of honoured death, but sorrily, ignobly, while one's head is turned.

And Mr Povey and Constance, very self-conscious, went and saw the dead elephant.

It is a great Morality, as it was bound to be, instigated by such an initial thought. Villon is recalled to mind again in Sophia's reflections on the final predicament of Madame Foucault. But—

Moral reprehension, though present in her mind, was only faint. Certainly she felt the immense gulf between the honest woman and the wanton, but she did not feel it as she would

[1] In his summing up he remarks, "Dieu sait que rien ne peut dépasser la compréhension, la pénétration d'Arnold Bennett dans son domaine. On regrette seulement qu'elle ne s'ordonne pas, s'arrête aux constatations et ne fournisse aucune idée, ne révèle aucune vision de la vie" (*Le roman anglais de notre temps*, 169).

have expected to feel it. "What a fool you have been!" she thought; not, "What a sinner!"

Yet, behind a cynicism that appears to be identical with Sophia's, it is clear enough that Arnold Bennett is at heart a puritan. That, however, was not why he abandoned any intention he ever had of letting Sophia succumb to the enticements thronging round her when she was left alone in Paris after the collapse of her union with Gerald Scales. The confutation of any such theory is to be found in the chapter ironically headed "A Crisis for Gerald," in which, faced by a dilemma so desperate, her common sense awakens, and she decides that she is ready "to pay the price of pride and of a moment's imbecility with a lifetime of self-repression. It was high, but it was the price."

Gerald had begun and had finished her education. He had not ruined her, as a bad professor may ruin a fine voice, because her moral force immeasurably exceeded his; he had unwittingly produced a masterpiece, but it was a tragic masterpiece. Sophia was such a woman as, by a mere glance as she utters an opinion, will make a man say to himself, half in desire and half in alarm lest she reads him too, "By Jove! she must have been through a thing or two. She knows what people are."

The Paris episodes were essential for the full development of Sophia's personality; but, though profoundly interesting, they are not composed of the same realism as the Bursley chapters. The bulk of the characters might almost have been a concession to vulgar English preconceptions of what foreigners are.

"*Clayhanger*"

After a misguided attempt to adumbrate post-mortem experiences through the sensations of a man in an epileptic trance, which he seriously entitled *The Glimpse (an adventure of the Soul)* (1909), and a comic affair, *Helen with the High Hand* (1910), only half redeemed by a handful of characters from the Five Towns, Bennett published a novel, *Clayhanger* (1910), worthy to go on the same shelf as *The Old Wives' Tale.* This is another wellnigh epical narrative of life in the same familiar region, the personal history co-ordinated with that of the whole community, and in this case developing into a love-story, complicated on the one hand by circumstance, and on the other by strange and contradictory aberrations of feeling. The complications are so obscure that they necessitated two further novels, the second, not a sequel, but the story told again from the other point of view, and the third the ultimate disentanglement after marriage. The early life of Edwin Clayhanger, as related in the first, continually recalls to mind *The Way of all Flesh*, by which it must have been deeply influenced. It is an indignant though matter-of-fact account of a son's revolt from the tyranny of a father who stands for the old order, and also from the bigotry, hypocrisy, and fundamental materialism of the religion preached and accepted in this purblind provincial world. Though without the same literal reproduction of facts, the autobiographical element is as implicit as in Butler's story, and the satire often as merciless. Early in the book the father's history is given in brief. Darius Clayhanger was the offspring of poor workpeople in the Five Towns, at a time when children of seven went out into the world to earn their living. He started work in the winter of 1835. Darius was rescued with his father, mother, and sister from the "Bastille" by the Sunday school superintendent Mr Shushions, the first steam-printer in Bursley, who got him a job as printer's devil, in a works which eventually became his own. This pathetic, almost blood-curdling preliminary gives due weight to old Clayhanger as the prosperous master-printer and Edwin's father, and also strikes the historical note of the trilogy as a compendium of social evolution. There follows the history of Edwin's boyhood, youth, and young manhood; his ambition to be an architect, and surrender to his father's will that he shall be second-in-command at the printing-house; his stroke for freedom, when his father would keep him a mere helot; and, lastly, his passages of affection for the captivating Janet Orgreave, the meeting with Hilda Lessways, and all the perturbations that are related from her side in the following book. The main subject of the trilogy is going to be something quite different; but in this part the reader watches Edwin striving to overcome the handicaps of his upbringing, thinking for himself, learning what culture is from the refined Orgreaves, and seeing himself almost as a champion of civilization in the midst of barbarism. Arnold Bennett might have been inspired by his namesake Matthew Arnold's campaign against the Philistines, in *Culture and Anarchy* and other books, read, no doubt, by the Orgreaves. In his Voltairian tableau of pseudo-Christian savagery at the mass-celebration of the Sunday school centenary, he far outwent Matthew Arnold's persiflage and his own satire of Methodism in *The Old Wives' Tale*. Listening to the hymns chanting the legend of the blood, and seeing "the meek, stupid, and superstitious faces, all turned one way, all for the moment under the empire of one horrible idea, all convinced that the consequences of sin could be prevented by an act of belief, all gloating over inexhaustible tides of blood . . . it seemed to him that the drums were tom-toms and Baines's a bazaar." "Look at it!" he says to Hilda. "It only wants the Ganges at the bottom of the Square——" And they have their first quarrel.

Edwin and Hilda

Edwin's character has been tried in these preliminary experiences, the conflict with parental despotism and with inimical surroundings; he now has to face a new conflict, of antagonistic temperaments in himself and the woman he cannot help loving. Hilda Lessways is an "amazing, incalculable woman, wrapped within fold after fold of mystery," at least to Edwin; and very soon after making her acquaintance at the Orgreaves' he is at his wit's end to penetrate her "tantalizing psychology." Once, when she failed in an appointment to visit the works, he himself realized that "his feelings were complex and contradictory, flitting about and crossing each other in his mind with astounding rapidity. . . . He wondered why he should care whether she came or not; after all she was only a young woman who wanted to see a printing-works; at best she was not so agreeable as Janet, at worst she was appalling, and moreover he knew nothing about her." Attraction alternates with repulsion; yet he is in the grip of some strange magnetism: "what he had said" to her "suddenly acquired a mysterious and wise significance and became oracular. She alone had the power of inspiring him to be profound. He had noticed that before, years ago, and first at their first meeting." The "original antipathy" has turned into something unanalysable, but something that subjugates him. Still in a state of bewilderment, he finds himself engaged. Then, suddenly, he hears, as a bit of casual news, that Hilda, who has gone away to Brighton, is married to a certain George Cannon. How he survives the shock he hardly knows. But this is not the end. Years pass, and presently it comes out that a charming little boy staying with Auntie Hamps and the Orgreaves is George Edwin Cannon and Hilda's son. Why is he here and not with his mother? They are obviously concealing something, though he learns that she is running a boarding-house at Brighton, is separated from her husband, and in embarrassed circumstances. He goes down and sees her; by degrees he gets to the bottom of the mystery. George Cannon is doing time on Dartmoor, he is a bigamist; Hilda is not even a widow, the boy is illegitimate. In a moving scene, Hilda tells him,

"You'll never understand what I had to go through, and how I couldn't help myself"—she was tragically plaintive—"but I shall tell you. . . . You *must* understand! . . . My heart never kissed any other man but you!" she cried. "How often and often and often have I kissed you, and you never knew! . . . It was for a message that I sent George down here—a message to you! I named him after you. . . . Do you think that if dreams could make him your child—he wouldn't be yours?"[1]

"Hilda Lessways"

Hilda Lessways (1911) puts the case from the woman's side, and is a still more searching investigation into the secrecies of the feminine heart. Hilda collaborates with the novelist in trying to unriddle her own enigmas, but is sometimes forced to admit to herself that "There were obscure grottoes in her soul which she had not had the courage to explore candidly." This gives the whole history of Hilda's young womanhood in

[1] See Lafourcade (132–136, 143–146, and 246–248) for an able study of the contradictory thoughts and feelings that succeed each other, especially in his heroines, with amazing rapidity. Bennett recorded in his *Journal* that he had been getting ideas from Stendhal's *De l'Amour* before writing *Clayhanger*, and it is shown that his addiction to such psychological "discontinuities" must have been derived from that novelist.

the Five Towns, her secretaryship to George Cannon, and the train of accidents that lead to her helping and then succeeding George's sister in the ownership of the boarding-house at Brighton. She marries Cannon, only to discover after the honeymoon that he has an old wife living. Going back to Bursley, she meets Edwin Clayhanger at the Orgreaves', and they fall in love. Then Hilda realizes that she is about to become a mother, and the story breaks off on a note of tragic suspense. Hilda repeatedly reminds one of Sophia, in *The Old Wives' Tale*; she has perhaps a still stronger individuality, but at any rate the phases of illusion, enlightenment, and struggle, especially with her own feelings, are strikingly parallel. Cannon's glossy self-sufficiency fascinates the artless girl just as Gerald had the ingenuous Sophia. But she already has more insight; she feels misgivings. She thought, "This must be love. This is love!" "And yet her conscience inarticulately accused her of obliquity. But she did not care, and she would not reflect. She thought that she wilfully, perversely, refused to reflect; but in reality she was quite helpless." Soon after the marriage, however, she has the experience of disappointment. "She no longer saw her husband as a romantic and baffling figure; she had explored and charted his soul, and not all his excellences could atone for his earthliness." This is some time before the facts come to light, and she finds what a plight she is in. The situation later when she and Clayhanger are in love is analogous to that of Sophia and Chirac; and she is moved chiefly by the same deep-seated sense of personal dignity.

Rather than let him know, in any conceivable manner, that, all unwitting, she was bearing the child of another at the moment of her betrothal to himself, she preferred to be regarded as a jilt of the very worst kind. Strange that she should choose the role of deceiver instead of the role of victim! Strange that she would sooner be hated and scorned than pitied! Strange that she would not even give Edwin the opportunity of treating her as a widow! But so it was. For her, the one possible attitude towards Edwin was the attitude of silence.

These Twain (1916) takes up the story a few years later.

"These Twain"

Hilda and Edwin are married, and Cannon's boy is living with them in the Five Towns. Few are aware that the father is a convict. It is a study of married life, perhaps the most searching of its kind in English fiction—a great study in "the science of life." "The lofty and incomparable marvels of human nature" are deeply explored in this history of quite ordinary people. One feels that such a master as Arnold Bennett could furnish as absorbing a drama out of the life-stories of any of the countless people who throng about us. Every one is a creature full of mysteries and marvels; an inscrutable individual, known only by the surface even to his intimates, incalculable even to himself. Bennett brings out the romance, the beauty, the grandeur, the immense pathos latent in the commonest actuality. On the other hand, Edwin is painfully sensible of his personal futility—"his life seemed to be a life of half-measures, a continual falling short." He is worried by questions that Gissing or the discussion-novel would have treated very differently; here they go properly into a concrete and artistic form, as part of Edwin and Hilda's mental and moral history. These girls, for instance, at their greasy task in the works—"these girls so close to him, so dependent on him, so submissive, so subjugated, so soiled, so vulgar, whose wages would scarcely have kept his wife in boots and gloves, gave rise to strange and disturbing sensations in his heart." The question kept piercing the complacency of his industrial success: is it right? "Is what right?" his father would have snapped, and even big James the confidential foreman would have been nonplussed. James was "cautiously in favour" of trade unions; Edwin's father late in life had not been an uncompromising opponent. Edwin tried to think the problem solved by the current theories which would make him and his serfs "the almost blind agencies in a vast process of evolution." But there remained misgivings, which turned into sudden fears of responsibility, that came and went. These are but minor episodes in the greater, the marital conflict. Hilda and Edwin suffer agonies from the friction and opposition of their two wills, till he makes "the great discovery of all his career"—

It was banal; it was commonplace; it was what every one knew. . . . If Hilda had not been unjust in the assertion of her own individuality, there could be no merit in yielding to her. To yield to a just claim was not meritorious, though to withstand it would be wicked. He was objecting to injustice as a child objects to rain on a holiday. Injustice was a tremendous actuality! It had to be faced and accepted. (He himself was unjust. At any rate he intellectually conceived that he must be unjust, though honestly he could remember no instance of injustice on his part.) To reconcile oneself to injustice was the master achievement. He had read it; he had been aware of it; but he had never really felt it till that moment on the dark canal-bridge. He was awed, thrilled by the realization. He longed ardently to put it to the test. He yielded on the canal-bridge. And in yielding, it seemed to him that he was victorious.

He thought confidently and joyously: "I'm not going to be beaten by Hilda! And I'm not going to be beaten by marriage. Dashed if I am! A nice thing if I had to admit that I wasn't clever enough to be a husband!"

Bennett's sense of humour

Bennett remarked, in the preface to *The Old Wives' Tale*, that his writings, when not dull, were charged by the critics with "a regrettable tendency to facetiousness." He was always lively, but rather in the manner of a brilliant journalist. The satire, when aroused, was modulated to every tone of irony; now gentle and bantering, anon bitter and scathing. He was given to the mock-heroic, as in the sketch of Mr Povey evolving the "new and wonderful word" "exquisite" to go on a window ticket, or in Sophia or Hilda's unsophisticated ideas of Gerald Scales and George Cannon. But he did not keep his eyes always open for the minor absurdities and subtler drolleries; there are not too many encounters between such characters of price as Miss Chetwynd and Mrs Baines. His finest exploit of that rarer quality is in *These Twain*, in the chapter telling how Auntie Hamps takes measures on her death-bed for sacking the general servant Minnie, who has got into trouble.

"Edwin!"
"Yes, Auntie?"

"Has—that girl—gone yet?"

"Who?" he questioned, and added more softly, "Minnie, d'you mean?" His own voice sounded too powerful, too healthy and dominating, in comparison with her failing murmurs.

Auntie Hamps nodded. "Yes—Minnie."

"Not yet."

"She's going?"

"Yes."

"Because I can't trust—Maggie—to see to it."

"I'll see to it."

"Has she done—the silvers—d'you know?"

"She's doing them," answered Edwin, who thought it would be best to carry out the deception with artistic completeness.

"She needn't have her dinner before she goes."

"No?"

"No." Auntie Hamps's face and tone hardened. "Why should she?"

"All right."

"And if she asks—for her wages—tell her—I say there's nothing due—under the circumstances."

"All right, Auntie," Edwin agreed, desperate.

Maggie, followed by Clara, softly entered the room. Auntie Hamps glanced at them with a certain cautious suspicion, as though one or other of them was capable of thwarting her in the matter of Minnie. Then her eyes closed, and Edwin was aware of a slackening of her hold on his hand. The doctor, who called half an hour later, said that she might never speak again, and she never did. Her last conscious moments were moments of satisfaction.

Less serious work

A needless addendum to *These Twain* was a product of the war time. In *The Roll Call* (1919), Clayhanger's stepson, George Cannon, architect, who inherits his mother Hilda's capacity, makes himself famous at the age of twenty-one by winning the competition for a great town hall. He has love-affairs, with Marguerite, who gives him up rather than desert her widowed father, and with Lois, whom he marries. But romance is reserved for the bizarre affair with the lovely, sphinx-like American, Irene Wheeler. The story halts rather than ends, when George joins up, and has his first taste of service in a trying march in the rain on the Surrey downs. Bennett had published half a dozen others since the trilogy, two or three of them as light-hearted and light-headed as his previous frolic, *Buried Alive*, in which an eminent and eccentric painter changes identity with his dead valet, whence many absurd complications and misunderstandings. In *The Card* (1911), a bland adventurer in the Five Towns, by dint of cheek, good humour, and bold reliance on his luck, makes his way from a slum to affluence and the dignity of mayor. The character-drawing is shallow but racy, and the hits at aldermanic bumptiousness and other civic infirmities make lively farce. Arnold Bennett is here letting himself go, and being off his guard reveals his own sentiments, his complacent regard for wealth and comfort, his homage to success and the admiration of the vulgar as the pole of endeavour and the standard of life.[1] In *The Regent, a Five Towns story of adventure in London* (1913), the Card, partly by accident and partly by shrewdness and his remarkable inspiration of the moment, acquires the option on a plot near Piccadilly Circus and puts up the Regent Theatre. The building of it, with the legal preliminaries, and the running of it for a year, bring him into touch with a motley set who provide much entertainment. The Azure Club and the young Yeatsian intellectuals, the mountebank actor-manager, Sir John Pilgrim, the boosted and boosting suffragette, and the like, are hit off with a pretty mixture of appreciation and satire. Edward Henry Machin himself, a compound of guilelessness and horse sense, innocence and readiness for the occasion, affords the best entertainment of all. "The Matador of the Five Towns," first in a collection of some twenty miscellaneous tales, is a poignant sketch of a great full-back,

[1] In an oft-quoted passage (*The Common Reader*, first series, 186–187), Mrs Woolf complains of the fundamentally coarse texture of the minds of Bennett, Galsworthy, and Mr H. G. Wells. "Mr Bennett is perhaps the worst culprit of the three, inasmuch as he is by far the best workman." Mrs Woolf might have quoted some instances of Bennett's instinct for evaluating works of art in pecuniary terms from his account of a visit to Toledo (*Things that have Interested Me*, 3rd series, 62–65)—"Statuary worth millions of pesetas, paintings worth millions of pesetas"; "there must be a ton and a half of pure gold in that room blazing with electric light"; "their uniforms had cost a lot of money," etc., etc. "The riddle is that Spain is a country full of potential riches—which riches are not exploited."

the darling of the Five Towns. Then in *The Price of Love* (1914) there was a reversion to the manner of the Clayhanger series, the careful and sensitive draughtsmanship of average character, draughtsmanship that sees below the surface and reveals the individual. The foremost three are well drawn and ably contrasted, whilst Mrs Toms the charwoman is a type of modest endurance to be compared with Flaubert's drawing of such menial figures, and she is, further, a being of enchanting humour.

The war time

The effect on Bennett of the relaxation of morals during the war is visible in his show of frankly and fearlessly exposing the seamy side at its worst, *The Pretty Lady* (1918). Ostensibly, it is the candid full-length of a harlot, with a pair of neurotic society women as her foils. The puritan in Arnold Bennett was aghast at the prevailing licence, and not least at the wild vagaries of such as Lady Queenie and Concepcion Smith, wealthy, idle, disillusioned women, busying themselves in theatrical efforts at war work, and a cynical frivolity, which was all a mask for ennui and despair, even to themselves. There are signs that he was bewildered as well as repelled by their excesses. But, if this is an honest effort to reveal the truth, Bennett unconsciously relapsed into one of his compromises. The harlot is toned down and sentimentalized, notwithstanding her outburst at English smugness. "Always you are pretending something. Pretending that you have no sentiments. And you are soaked in sentimentality. But no! You will not show it! You will not applaud your soldiers in the streets. You will not salute your flag. You will not salute even a corpse. You have only one phrase: 'It is nothing.' If you win a battle, 'It is nothing.' If you lose one, 'It is nothing.' If you are killed in an air-raid, 'It is nothing.' And if you were killed outright and could yet speak, you would say, with your eternal sneer, 'It is nothing.' You other men, you make love with the air of turning on a tap. As for your women, God knows—!" The two society women are mere sketches, adumbrations, not unauthentic but incomplete. In spite of their reckless and almost incredible extravagances, they are not overdone but underdone. The question is whether Bennett was scared and baffled in his efforts to comprehend, and brought up against something impenetrable; or simply withheld the clue, choosing to leave all in that uncertainty which is admittedly life's characteristic. Christine, in comparison, is true so far as she is analysed, but commonplace. A scene in which Concepcion seems most inscrutable, when G. J. Hoape shrinks from the job of breaking the news that her husband is shot, only to find that she already knows it, is after all in full accord with Arnold Bennett's principle, to show life going on but not to analyse. He does analyse G. J. and Christine; hence the man is a mere anybody, though the method was good enough for a very elementary woman. London in 1916, the time of the air-raids, is presented in all its aspects with overwhelming actuality. As one of many scenes of terse, biting realism, take the inquest on Lady Queenie, killed by stray shrapnel during a raid, through climbing beyond the wire netting above the roof of the marquess's palatial town house, and the imperturbable coroner's frigid remarks:

The Coroner understood that the wire netting did not extend over the whole of the house. "It extends over all the main part of the house," his lordship had replied. "But not over the back of the house?" His lordship agreed. "The servants' quarters, probably?" His lordship nodded. The Coroner had said, "The wire netting does not extend over the servants' quarters" in a very even voice. A faint hiss in court had been extinguished by the sharp glare of the Coroner's eyes.

It is not often that Arnold Bennett is guilty of even so quiet a hit at class grievances. In the irresponsible improbabilities of *Mr Prohack* (1922), about the man who comes in for tons of money which he and his son spend, if there be any moral, it is the absurdity of this senseless expenditure and the fools it makes of its devotees.

"*Riceyman Steps*"

The art which transcribed the collective and individual life of swarming humanity in the Five Towns is directed, in *Riceyman Steps* (1923), to a small group of characters in dull back streets in Clerkenwell. This is a patient and minute, ironical yet compassionate, anatomy of a miser, one who sacrifices his life to his mania, though he would be the last person in the world to be aware of what ailed him. Mr Earlforward—business name Riceyman—is a bookseller in this dreary limbo, whose penuriousness brings him and his wife to their death-beds in a year of married life: they die of under-nourishment. He pinches and starves himself, stays in bed to save a clean shirt, washes in cold water not to put a penny in the gas-meter. And he is in ecstasy when he thinks he has found a woman who is his very counterpart. "A shrewd woman! A woman certainly not without ideas!" He takes her for a walk through East-End streets. He is in torment with his crippled leg, but he will not take a cab.

> Paradise, surcease from agony, for one shilling and perhaps a twopenny tip! But he would not look at it. He could not. He preferred the hell in which he was. The grand passion which had rendered all his career magnificent, and every hour of all his days interesting and beautiful, demanded and received an intense, devotional loyalty; it recompensed him for every ordeal, mortification, martyrdom. He proudly passed the taxi-cab with death in his very stomach. Nowhere was there a chance of rest! Not a seat! Not a rail! . . . He led Mrs Arb down towards the nearest point of Farringdon Road, though this was not the shortest way home. The tramcars stopped at the corner. Every one of them would deposit him at his own door. Paradise for one penny! No, twopence; because he would have to pay for Mrs Arb! He had thought to defeat his passion at this corner. He was mistaken. He could not. He had, after all his experience, misjudged the power of his passion. He was as helpless as the creatures who were beginning to gather at the iron-barred doors of the public-houses, soon to open for a couple of too short hours; and also he had the secret ecstasy which they had. He could scarcely talk now, and each tram that passed him in his slow and endless march gave him a spasm of mingled bitterness and triumph. His fear now was lest his grand passion should on this occasion be overcome by bodily weakness. He did not desire it to be overcome. He desired it to conquer even if it should kill him.

For "there were two Mr Earlforwards: one splendidly

uplifted, the other ready to faint from pain and fatigue." The life of the married pair follows on, with a realism that eludes not the most infinitesmal detail, to its sorry close. But the appealing figure, whose simple and modest but heroic devotion ranks her with the angels, is that of the charwoman Elsie, the war-widow who gives her little pension to her mother, for "She's a widow, same as me, and she can't fend for herself." Elsie is a fuller development of the same type of character as Maggie, the humble domestic heroine in *Clayhanger*, the drudge with more than a germ of greatness in her, unperceived by herself or others. Her infinite patience, and her naïve struggles with a prickly conscience, when she cannot keep her hands off a cold potato or a crust in the larder, reveal a deep and wistful tenderness in Arnold Bennett and an unwonted delicacy in his humour.

One morning, Mrs Earlforward has taken her to task for not turning off the gas-tap of the geyser, though privately she has found the excessive warmth very pleasant. Far from resenting it, Elsie feels she is on her mettle. "You didn't have any tea this morning," says Mrs Earlforward, "for she had noticed that nobody had been into the kitchen before herself."

"No, 'm. It's no use. If I'm to get through with my work Monday mornings I can't waste my time getting my tea. And that's all about it, 'm."

Elsie, her brow puckered, seemed to be actually accusing her mistress of trying to tempt her from the path of virtue. The contract between employers and employed in that house had long since passed, so far as the employed was concerned, far beyond the plane of the commercial. The employers gave £20 a year; the employed gave all her existence, faculties, energy, and gave them with passion, without reserve open or secret, without reason, sublimely.

"It's her affair," muttered Violet as she mounted to the kitchen to finish preparing breakfast. If she chooses to work two hours on a Monday morning on an empty stomach, I can't help it." And there followed a shamed little thought: "It saves the gas."

This pathetic creature, so beautiful in her lowliness and unrecognized greatness, reappears in *Elsie and the Child* (1924). Arnold Bennett is charged, not without reason, with materialist views of existence; but he is by no means unmindful of the spiritual aspects. The love and respect for human nature which characterized all his more serious work meant a belief in the innate spirit that distinguishes humanity from all other forms of life—in human nature, that which loves, that which has self-consciousness, self-respect, an instinctive morality. *Riceyman Steps* is a representative as well as a masterly work. Its two main themes, the miserliness of old Earlforward and the humble magnanimity of Elsie, are both spiritual themes, the one for critical scrutiny, the other for loving appreciation. Here at any rate Arnold Bennett can bear the comparison or the contrast with Galsworthy.

His last novels

After this, his unchallengeable realism was applied to matters of less consequence, to make good some bold invention or enforce a satire. It all but saves *Lord Raingo* (1926) from the results of mere opportunism. In this he turned to account his experiences in his official role, in close touch with the War Cabinet. Raingo, the self-made millionaire, with his gift for organizing publicity, manages to be made a peer and Minister of Records. The autobiographic relevance is patent; even the liaison that fits rather awkwardly into the comedy of politics is a rendering of facts. At the end, it gives a more pathetic turn to the analysis of the sick man's consciousness. But the best thing in the book is the cartoon of strangely assorted figures in the Cabinet—Andy Clyth, the Prime Minister, from Eccles, with his cherished provincialisms, placid self-admiration, and "damnable wizardy of demeanour and tone when he was after something"; the unruly Tom Hogarth, the only one who is not afraid of the chief and can have his own way with impunity; the bluff, canny, genial, h-dropping Labour minister; the austere, melancholy, ascetic Chancellor of the Exchequer; and the urbane, magnificent earl, calmly nursing the privileges of his order and maintaining an unruffled courtesy in this menagerie of uncouth popular heroes. The continual skirmishes, the half-dissembled efforts to do each other down and push the interests of their own departments, the elaborate bluff and stage-play for the benefit of a fickle and unintelligent public, are dramatized with admirable finesse.

Bennett "always had a passion for organization," he said, and talking about his ministerial experience he remarked, "Next to running a great hotel, this business seemed to me to be the most sensational that any human being could indulge in."[1] He ran his hotel only in imagination. *Imperial Palace* (1930) was the last and most brilliant of his speculative fictions. The whole intricate economy of a vast luxury hotel, from the financial deals for gaining control of it down to the working of the laundry and the engine-room and what goes on in the staff dining-room, is laid bare with an eager delight in complex detail and the fascinations of such a spectacle of opulence and splendour. The director's sentimental skirmishes with the daughter of the leading financier, and his prudent marriage with the young woman who has worked her way up right through the business, share interest with the Imperial Palace itself.

To sum up

Henry James was impressed by the density of Bennett's knowledge of the world that he undertook to depict, his "saturation" with his subject-matter, "the firmness and fullness of his embrace of it."[2] Bennett continually astonishes with the extent and minuteness of what he knows; his keenness of eye was such that he missed nothing. And as a workman enjoying his job and simply performing it honestly he never annoys by his knowingness, never puts on that air of pert omniscience characteristic of a certain school. Novel-writing to him was an industry, a trade, a business. It was how he gained his livelihood. He makes no further claims. Though if anyone was entitled to talk about art and craftsmanship it was Bennett, he is content to look on himself as engaged in a branch of manufacture like other people. Obviously, he was cut out for the particular job. So insatiable was his curiosity, so intense his fellow-feeling, he seemed to crave nothing else

[1] *Things that have Interested Me* (3rd series, 78–79).
[2] *Notes on Novelists*, "The New Novel" (257–260).

than complete intimacy with any and every human being whatsoever. And the insight which was his best original faculty took him more than half-way to such a complete intimacy. "You are an astounding woman, Con!" someone says in *The Pretty Lady*. "Concepcion Smith never made a mistake in assessing fundamental character," says the author, and the same may be affirmed of himself. He apprenticed himself to Flaubert, Maupassant, and Zola, and then learned still more from Balzac and Stendhal.[1] Butler and the French-taught George Moore were his English masters. He singled out Turgenev as the one great novelist who neither "ignored technique nor failed to understand it,"[2] another case of Gallic affinity, though he was himself unconsciously more influenced by Dostoevsky. His conspicuous failing was disregard for the graces of style. He wrote fluently and vigorously, and often achieved marvels of pictorial and nerve-shaking description. But he seemed to be insensible to the finer elegancies, and to despise that scrupulous attention to the consecrated order and dignity of the language which is the mark of the man of letters. This carelessness, however, was not a handicap when it came to writing dialogue. It is in his vivid and eminently natural conversations that Arnold Bennett's master-strokes of style are to be found.

Galsworthy

Galsworthy was the opposite of Bennett in this matter of style, as well as in his particular way of throwing himself into the moving current of time. *The Forsyte Saga* may or may not be a superior work to *The Old Wives' Tale*; but it contrasts as much by its fastidious, refined, yet sensitive and perfectly adequate style as by the differences between a story told in a long succession of more or less historic moments, studied by a highly intelligent spectator who arrests and examines each as it comes, and the uninterrupted movement of ordinary narrative, pushing on to a future which always lies somewhere ahead. Time goes on, but Galsworthy dwells on the separate stages; and the differences of style are due as much to this static rather than dynamic attitude as to the different make and texture of his mind. The lives of the two novelists

[1] Cp. Lafourcade (70, 98, 104).

[2] *The Author's Craft*.

covered almost exactly the same span; but there was a notable difference in the areas of the human world which they surveyed. From their different situations, they tended from the outset to look at different sections of society. And then, Bennett's well-stocked memory and his instinctive conception of man's life as continual activity made him begin further back, and come down gradually to the present. Galsworthy concentrates on his own day, the cross-section of time that will be succeeded to-morrow by another. He stands somewhere between Bennett and H. G. Wells; more of a novelist than Wells, yet still primarily a critic of society; but, compared with Bennett, a novelist simply by his deliberate choice of a vehicle for his criticism. He portrays characters typical of existing society, in a typical environment; he produces something like a natural history of the age. Bennett found the centre of gravity of his world in the class from which he came, the vast middle class which is said to be the backbone of the country; Galsworthy found it in his own, usually styled the upper middle class, which may be distinguished as the head-piece, since it is this section of the community, embracing the professions and the propertied gentry, along with the aristocracy from which they are not widely or permanently sundered, that up to this era was not inaccurately called the governing classes.

A middle-aged novelist

John Galsworthy (1867–1933) was the son of a solicitor, and went to Harrow and then to Oxford; he was called to the Bar (1890), but never practised. He spent some years in travelling all over the globe, on one of his voyages being lucky enough to have Joseph Conrad as travelling companion and making him a permanent friend. His early life and the periods spent in his own country gave him that intimate acquaintance with the manners and characters of the upper classes to be seen in his novels and the problem-plays which appeared in between these. Some early novels and stories published under the name of "John Sinjohn," the best of which were preserved in the miscellany *Caravan* (1925), may be passed over. The first of his novels to count, and that only as a preface to more mature work, was *The Island Pharisees*

(1904), published when he was near the age of forty. He had evidently been thinking and making up his mind, during the years when he was seemingly lying fallow; doing the analysis of people and problems which enabled him later on to exhibit a wide range of characters all of whom he knew to the last fibre of their being. It was not the programme of any of his novels, except perhaps *Fraternity*, to take a set of characters and then proceed to analyse their motives and behaviour. He had carried out that part of his task beforehand, and was now able to show the results. Every important character of Galsworthy's bears the trace of having been taken to pieces and then put together again; it is the peculiarity that stamps them as his, and makes them such significant and valuable counters in the game now to be played out. Analysis, then synthesis; he was critical observer first, then portraitist or dramatist, making those he had singled out as the representative figures perform in such scenes or complications as would illustrate the phenomena of the age, the regular subjects of sociological inquiry. The characters and their behaviour, down to the smallest involuntary gesture—the one is the unfolding and manifestation of the other—are the concrete terms in which he sets forth his view of life and society, at a particular epoch. Though a missfire, *The Island Pharisees* showed that Galsworthy felt the times were out of joint, and that he was going to expose the emptiness or the sheer hypocrisy of half our most cherished conventions. In *The Man of Property* (1906) and *The Country House* (1907) he quietly dissected two leading classes, the comfortable, idle, moneyed society of the City and the West End, and their provincial compeers, the landed gentry; with calm penetration and an irony that made short work of disguises, he laid bare the ruling motives that half-consciously shape their lives and souls, the lust of possession, in the one case, and of personal domination over the small world of a country parish, in the other. *The Country House* was little better than *The Island Pharisees*, except that it contained one of his beautiful portraits of an elderly lady, in Mrs Pendyce; it was a novel on the old-established lines, and readers were probably taken by surprise at the strokes of satire. But *The Man of Property* revealed the virtues of the new Galsworthy method. Applied to the miscellaneous affairs of a large ramifying family, it afforded a near approach to a panorama of society at a changing epoch. Galsworthy added sequel to sequel, which developed gradually into *The Forsyte Saga* (1922) and *A Modern Comedy* (1929), with various addenda, such as some of the stories in *Caravan.* At the same time, he was treating cognate problems in plays that were well received, beginning with *The Silver Box* (1906) and *Joy* (1907). Several of the novels that appeared long before he had done with the Forsytes were almost of the nature of monographs on special phases of the life of society or of the individual. The hypersensitive and perilous nature of social relations is elaborately illustrated in *Fraternity* (1909); *The Patrician* (1911) appraises the claims on a well-meaning man of an irregular love-affair and of public duty; *The Dark Flower* (1913) is passion, the uprising of an antisocial force which is a recurrent theme in the *Saga* also; *The Freelands* (1915) deals with the problems of four brothers, offspring of a family of the landed gentry, one of them having revolutionary proclivities. There is a striking unity in Galsworthy's work taken in the mass; virtually, it is all one series, a more comprehensive *Saga.* It is the same with his two dozen plays. *Strife* (1909) was followed by *Justice* (1910), *The Pigeon* and *The Eldest Son* (1912), *The Fugitive* (1913), *The Skin Game* (1920), *Loyalties* (1922), and *The Forest* (1924). Some would put them above his novels. At all events, they must be taken into account, not only in any complete estimate, but more particularly in regard to the very different handling of the dramatic element in the novels. His dialogue here is as natural and spontaneous as there; it defines and crystallizes the issues without deteriorating into mere debate or specious summarizing of a case from the stage. It is always in the given situation and its denouement that the problem is worked out. Everything he wrote is an accusation. The novels are at bottom as polemical as the plays, though more quietly and reservedly, arraignment and satire in this ampler medium not having to be so concentrated and pointed. He called attention to their "negative method." All alike expose one or another of the many forms of Philistinism. In the novels, when drama does occur, it is mostly at the points where the show is moving on a pace, though there is always enough dramatic tension latent to keep the characters alive and on the alert.[1] For it is on them that the author must rely to bring off solutions, to furnish some sort of answer to the questions involved.

The novel of human relations

Arnold Bennett, with little apparent effort, was able to call back to life whole sections of humanity, and make them look unique individuals. Galsworthy had not that facility, nor was it the one that would best have furthered his different purposes. He said to me, and no doubt to others, that his artistic patterns were Flaubert, Turgenev, and Maupassant. This might not be gathered at once from the novels themselves, which seem to be a very modern counterpart to the revolutionary fiction of another cardinal epoch, when the eighteenth was passing into the nineteenth century, the time of Bentham, Paine, and Cobbett, of Mrs Opie and Mrs Inchbald, Godwin, Cumberland, and Holcroft.[2] Some of those were programme-makers and propagandists, which Galsworthy was not. But he had the same deep and rankling sense of the wrongs and miseries of the world, and the same passionate impulse to expose them. He was as serious, and as indignant at the state of humanity, as ever Carlyle and Ruskin, though he kept his resentment under control, and preferred irony as a weapon to violent denunciation. And yet some of his plays, *Strife* and *Justice*, for instance, were so heavily weighted that the critics demurred. *The Skin Game*, on the other hand, whilst it avoided exaggeration, was so neat and exact an embodiment of a social problem that it did not sound quite authentic, the sheer conclusiveness of its realism prompted hesitation—a frequent result of doctrinaire fiction, in either play or novel. Even Hardy had not always escaped it, and Gissing's gloomy pictures excited general distrust. Galsworthy went to work on a wiser plan in his novels. He, too, was a champion of

[1] Guyot says of the *Saga* in particular, "Elle consiste en une succession de moments dramatiques d'une égale intensité" (p. 79).

[2] Butler, Bernard Shaw, H. G. Wells, and Galsworthy are the obvious modern analogue to Bentham, Godwin, and Holcroft.

the poor and disinherited; but he did not begin with a lurid recital of the miseries of the downtrodden and unfortunate. He painted, with a critical but tolerant art, a gallery of portraits from those classes who have got the very best out of life, *The Island Pharisees*, *The Man of Property*, *The Country House*, *The Patrician.* The very titles were an indictment. And he brings out conclusively that these fortunate classes are demoralized by too much prosperity, by idleness and lack of vision, and that a society organized for their special benefit has in itself the seeds of disintegration. Even the unimaginative Soames Forsyte has some glimpse of the real trend of events, when he broods over Queen Victoria's funeral and all the changes he has seen since her accession.

Wellnigh two generations had slipped by—of steamboats, railways, telegraphs, bicycles, electric light, telephones, and now these motor-cars—of such accumulated wealth, that eight per cent had become three, and Forsytes were numbered by the thousand! Morals had changed, manners had changed, men had become monkeys twice-removed, God had become Mammon—Mammon so respectable as to deceive himself. Sixty-four years that favoured property, and had made the upper middle-class; buttressed, chiselled, polished it, till it was almost indistinguishable in manners, morals, speech, appearance, habit, and soul from the nobility. An epoch which had gilded individual liberty, so that if a man had money, he was free in law and fact, and if he had not money he was free in law and not in fact. An era which had canonized hypocrisy, so that to seem to be respectable was to be. A great Age, whose transmuting influence nothing had escaped save the nature of man and the nature of the Universe.

Years later, after the war, his son-in-law Michael Mont is assailed by a slightly different vision, on the eve of Fleur's libel-action against a rival leader in a much more frivolous society.

Gazing at a square foot of study wall which had escaped a framed caricature, he reflected on the underlying savagery of life. He would be eating a lobster to-night that had been slowly boiled alive! This study had been cleaned out by a charwoman whose mother was dying of cancer, whose son had lost a leg in the war, and who looked so jolly tired that he felt quite bad whenever he thought of her. The Bergfields, Swains, and Boddicks of the world—the Camden Towns and Mile Ends—the devastated regions of France, the rock villages of Italy! Over it all what a thin crust of gentility! Members of Parliament and ladies of fashion, like himself and Fleur, simpering and sucking silver spoons, and now and then dropping spoons and simper, and going for each other like Kilkenny cats!

In these two books, *The Forsyte Saga* and *A Modern Comedy*, the history of four generations of Forsytes, the history of the upper middle classes from Victorian times to the eve of to-day, is written down, and brought into its right perspective as one crucial phase in the history of civilization, a phase of social development or social decadence. No one has ever found a better form of story to answer to and express the social theorem at the back of his mind. The *Saga* keeps fairly well within the limits of intellectual realism. But Galsworthy loves his creations too well, and has too sensitive an eye for the beauty which is a by-product of that vanishing epoch, not to depict it with the affection and sense of enjoyment or regret that is the soul of art.[1] Whilst John Morley, Samuel Butler, Bernard Shaw, H. G. Wells stand as austere judges or caustic satirists, he lingers at the funeral of Victorianism like an uninvited mourner, whose grief is more sincere than that of the family, because he expects no legacy.

Pharisaism, "Pendycitis," Forsytism

The objects of satire in *The Island Pharisees*, *The Country House*, and *The Man of Property* differed only as sub-varieties of a national trait. They were identifiable as being always found together, as inseparable as cause and effect. It was English complacency, in the first, a kind of "cocksureness," based on our treasured respectability, which, it is shown, rests on a series of rooted fallacies, which are somewhat clumsily con-

[1] He says himself in the preface, "But this long tale is no scientific study of a period; it is rather an intimate incarnation of the disturbance that Beauty effects in the minds of men." He was, of course, thinking of one of the two central figures of the story told in the two huge volumes. "The figure of Irene, never, as the reader may possibly have noticed, present, except through the senses of other characters, is a concretion of disturbing Beauty impingeing on a possessive world."

futed. One chapter here is entitled "The Country House," and deals with a domain where it has its safest stronghold.[1] Complacency in this case is the foible of a country squire, who represents established authority, which he is never tired of exercising, and in a minor degree of the rector, who in his particular sphere makes the most of what ancient usages have conferred on him. It is summed up ironically for the former in the Pendyce Creed:

> I believe in my father, and his father, and his father's father, the makers and keepers of my estate, and I believe in myself and my son and my son's son. And I believe that we have made the country, and shall keep the country what it is. And I believe in the Public Schools, especially the Public School that I was at. And I believe in my social equals and the country house, and in things as they are, for ever and ever. Amen.

From the squirearchy to the prosperous, well-established moneyed classes who are the other obvious example of English complacency. Young Jolyon, who regards himself as "the missing link" between the Forsytes and other species of the human race, defines their characteristics.

> "We are, of course, all of us, the slaves of property, and I admit that it's a question of degree, but what I call a 'Forsyte' is a man who is decidedly more than less a slave of property. He knows a good thing, he knows a safe thing, and his grip on property—it doesn't matter whether it be wives, houses, money, or reputation—is his hall-mark."
>
> "They are," repeated young Jolyon, "half England, and the better half, too, the safe half, the three per cent half, the half that counts. It's their wealth and security that makes everything possible; makes your art possible, makes literature, science, and even religion, possible. Without Forsytes, who believe in none of these things, but turn them all to use, where should we be? My dear sir, the Forsytes are the middlemen, the commercials, the pillars of society, the corner-stones of convention; everything that is admirable."

[1] M. Guyot has no grounds for his contention (p. 142) that Galsworthy devoted an especially long period of elaboration to this work. The story is indeed dated back to 1891; but Galsworthy did not begin work upon his novels till much later. *Villa Rubein* appeared in 1900; and then he was busy continuously on both fiction and plays.

Stability, security, possessions, are the appanage of the Forsytes and their like, and the ground for their complacency; not caste, in this instance, for they are a family of commoners, descended from yeoman stock. The founder of their present fortunes was the Jolyon Forsyte, known as "Superior Dosset," who became a master-builder and died at Highgate in 1850 worth thirty thousand. He was father of the senior Forsytes, five of whom are still alive and "may be said to have represented Victorian England, with its principles of trade and individualism at five per cent and your money back—if you know what that means." Old Jolyon was his eldest son, James his second, and out of James was begotten Soames Forsyte, solicitor, nicknamed by old Jolyon "The man of property," whom young Jolyon describes as "the very embodiment, the corporeal sum as it were, of the possessive instinct." Galsworthy takes Soames as the representative Englishman of the successful classes, as almost the master-key to the social history of his generation; though in his after-life, recounted in *A Modern Comedy*, Soames finds himself out of his element in the emancipated post-war age, which he can only stare at in bewilderment and anxiety for those dear to him. The *Saga* is the history of the huge family down to the death of Queen Victoria, with all their divergent interests reduced, as it were, to this common denominator—property, the possessive instinct, and the various attitudes it breeds. Those interests are as heterogeneous as the faces in the great crowd; but all the rest are overshadowed by one dramatic complication, a case of this ruling principle applied to personal relationships.

"The Man of Property"

Well endowed with what are usually rated as sterling qualities, Soames is unfortunately one of the unlovable. But even this hard business man is a victim of that universal and incalculable influence which Galsworthy celebrated in *The Dark Flower*, in the infatuation of George Pendyce for Mrs Bellew in *The Country House*, and repeatedly in the various Forsyte chronicles. "A wild plant that, when it blooms by chance within the hedge of our gardens, we call a flower; and when it blooms outside we call a weed; but, flower or weed, whose scent and colour are always wild! And further—the facts and figures of their own lives being against the perception of this truth—it was not generally recognized by Forsytes that, where this wild plant springs, men and women are but moths around the pale, flame-like blossom." Soames will never to his dying day subdue his passion for Irene. Irene married Soames because she could not help it; to put it concisely, her mother made her. But she is all subconscious repulsion; and, as young Jolyon says, "Aversion's deeper than love or hate, because it's a natural product of the nerves." Irene herself remarks, "I once told Uncle Jolyon that love was for ever. Well, it isn't. Only aversion lasts." And she is well aware that the man of property regards his wife as one of his belongings, like his ox or his ass. "He had married this woman, conquered her, made her his own, and it seemed to him contrary to the most fundamental of all laws, the law of possession, that he could do no more than own her body—if indeed he could do that, which he was beginning to doubt." For he thinks he perceives from subtle indications that his wife and Bosinney are in love—Bosinney, the frank, humorous, supercilious young architect, a man cursed with the artistic temperament and nicknamed by the Forsytes "the Buccaneer," who is building a country house for him at Robin Hill. Then, as Jolyon many years later tells Jon, his son and Irene's, in the moving summary of her history when the boy falls in love with Soames's child by a second wife, "Soames Forsyte, the father of Fleur, one night, at the height of her passion for this young man, forcibly reasserted his rights over her." She reveals it to Bosinney, who, distracted with anguish and horror, meets with his death somehow in the streets—it is never quite cleared up whether by accident or suicide. Irene leaves Soames, and for twelve years lives alone. Then he tries to induce her to make it up and live with him again. Jolyon is her trustee, and watches all this going on. He realizes that he loves Irene, and, the jealous Soames attacking them with a divorce suit, they marry, with the ironical sequel, two decades later, of the tragic dilemma of Jon and Fleur.

The Man of Property continues with hardly a break in what are now the second and third book of *The Forsyte Saga*, "In

"The Forsyte Saga"

Chancery" and "To Let," and it takes another thousand pages in *A Modern Comedy* to complete the story of Irene and Soames. The principal events to be recounted in this final volume are foreshadowed at the end of the *Saga*, when Jon's sister Holly observes of the marriage of Fleur and Michael Mont that this young man "had caught her on the rebound . . . in the reckless mood of one whose ship has just gone down." The love between Jon and Fleur had been a nightmare to Irene. It was broken off, and he had gone to North Carolina. But what if he came back? The brief foregoing summary states what in a different sort of novel would be the plot, and enough is left over for complications equally momentous in the near future. But this is not an ordinary novel; it is a general history of the Forsytes, and what they are experiencing, feeling, thinking, and doing, throughout a long period. The Irene-Soames affair bulks large, because it is one affecting the most prominent member of the family; it is watched and canvassed by all, with a sense on the part of some that it is Forsytism itself which is at stake. Matters will come to a head in similar fashion later on, in the affair of Fleur and Marjorie Ferrar, ending in the libel suit, and in the reawakening of passion when Jon comes back; then again the dramatic interest will be like that concentrated into the pages of the ordinary novel. The vast crowd of major and minor personages in the *Saga*, all carefully drawn and differentiated, and, without anything in the least like a formal review, introduced one after the other with all their idiosyncrasies, is curiously reminiscent of that ancient species of fiction known as charactery.[1] It is a very modern and refined form of charactery, and like the old one depicts both types and eccentrics. Galsworthy, as a critical spectator of current life and a student of its problems, was interested first and foremost in the typical representatives of a period and a class; but he also had a connoisseur's taste for eccentrics, and so makes much, in the *Comedy*, of June Forsyte's vagaries in middle age and of that very broad-minded old aristocrat and disappointed inventor, the Marquess of Shropshire. In his very pessimistic novel *Fraternity*, the only person

[1] See Vol. II., chap. xiv.

he seemed fond of was his octogenarian author of "Universal Brotherhood," who bathes in the Serpentine all the year round, cooks his food himself, always eschewing the higher mammals, does his own room, and all the rest of the time writes his book. Galsworthy's eccentrics are always estimable people, in fact, eccentrics of genius. There are more of them in *Caravan*. One salient feature of his method is that each person is seen through the eyes of the others.[1] He calls attention himself to this in the case of Irene. But it is the same with the rest. It is through the inquisitiveness of old James or Swithin or Timothy, or the clearer eyesight of young Jolyon, that Soames's stubborn personality is bit by bit revealed. Chapter after chapter retails a chance meeting of brothers and sisters or cousins, and a domestic chat full of piquant revelations. Galsworthy has analysed them all long ago, and now lets them expound the results. The great triumph of his method is the enchanting figure of Irene, who is always felt to be not far off in the background, as one of the dramatis personæ most deeply concerned, even when she is not present. Bosinney's is a doubtful case. We know his situation, we watch his emotions, but do we know him? He comes on the scene over and over again; he talks and is witty, and, which is more to the point, his love-affair with Irene and its tragic end is of the most affecting character. And yet Bosinney himself remains elusive, almost as much a stranger and outsider to the reader as he was to the Forsyte clan. Was the preliminary study of the man's inmost nature scamped in this one instance; or, as is more likely, did Galsworthy leave him thus far enigmatic on purpose? Young Jolyon is the keenest-sighted in his observations and the most penetrating in his judgments. When he tries to discuss the position with Soames, and, taken aback by the latter's obstinacy in wanting to force Irene to return, asks himself, "Is he real, this man?" he wonders whether or not

[1] "Si nous connaissons vraiment le dedans psychologique des personnages—et M. Galsworthy tient tellement à nous l'ouvrir que, plutôt que de raconter et décrire lui-même, il aime à nous montrer les événements, les paysages et jusqu'aux figures mêmes de son roman dans l'image qui s'en réfléchit en chaque âme—si nous savons la situation, les moindres mots vont suffire à nous suggérer tout de suite, et, comme il arrive dans la vie, ce qu'ils recèlent d'inexprimé" (Chevrillon, 184).

"Instead of helping her, I've made things worse." Then suddenly Soames exclaims, "It would be the best thing that could happen to her in many ways." And Jolyon has one of those gleams of far-seeing vision which make him Galsworthy's best interpreter.

At those words such a turmoil began taking place in Jolyon that he could barely sit still in the cab. It was as if he were boxed up with hundreds of thousands of his countrymen, boxed up with that something in the national character which had always been to him revolting, something he knew to be extremely natural and yet which seemed to him inexplicable—their intense belief in contracts and vested rights, their complacent sense of virtue in the exaction of those rights. . . . It was uncanny and intolerable! "But there's something more in it than that!" he thought with a sick feeling. "The dog, they say, returns to his vomit! The sight of her has awakened something. Beauty! The devil's in it!"

The very tone of that close voice checks even compassion in young Jolyon. "What was there in the fellow that made it so difficult to be sorry for him?" But it is Irene who petrifies Soames when he demands from her a reasonable answer: "You can't have a reasonable answer. Reason has nothing to do with it. You can only have the brutal truth: I would rather die."

The beauty of the indirect method is that it lays open the mentality of the speaker at the same time as it reveals the person discussed. Take Roger and Nicholas, at the very beginning, talking about that "good-lookin' woman, that wife of Soames"—

"She'd no money" is the latter's objection.
"What was her father?"
"Heron was his name, a Professor, so they tell me."
Roger shook his head.
"There's no money in that," he said.
"They say her mother's father was cement."
Roger's face brightened.
"But he went bankrupt," went on Nicholas.
"Ah!" exclaimed Roger, "Soames will have trouble with

her; you mark my words, he'll have trouble—she's got a foreign look."

As to Bosinney, all they can make out is that "he's one of these artistic chaps—got an idea of improving English architecture; there's no money in that!" Always money! All that old Jolyon can say of his little study with the stained glass is "Shouldn't wonder if it made a big price some day!" His latter years are spent in excogitating "how, by some sort of settlement, he could best avoid the payment of those death duties which would follow his decease," in devising "how to round off his property and make eternal the only part of him that was to remain alive." Muddle-headed Aunt Juley is sometimes by a fluke unwittingly still more caustic.

Soames overhears her prattling: "Only last Sunday dear Mr Scoles had been so witty in his sermon, so sarcastic: 'For what,' he had said, 'shall it profit a man if he gain his own soul, but lose all his property?' That, he had said, was the motto of the middle class; now, what *had* he meant by that?" "'In my Father's house are many mansions' was one of Aunt Juley's favourite sayings—it always comforted her, with its suggestion of house property, which had made the fortune of dear Roger."

Humour

From *The Island Pharisees* to *The Country House*, Galsworthy's humour is consistently ironical and satirical. Very rarely, if ever, is he light-hearted enough to indulge himself in the charms of pure comedy. One of the finest of his lesser pieces, "A Stoic," in *Caravan*, of the sturdy old Liverpool merchant who calmly perpetrates an arrant fraud upon his shipping company, to provide an income for his illegitimate family, and, keeping the flag flying to the last, commits suicide by eating a good dinner, may be savoured in that spirit. Old Heythorp, however, is only a Forsyte with a sense of humour, one who keeps himself fresh and young at the age of eighty by shrewdly enjoying the irony of things. And that admirable passage in *The Man of Property*, when old James, for one thing scenting scandal, having heard this strange rumour about Bosinney and Mrs Soames, and for another wanting to know about that new house on which Soames was spending such a lot of money, goes down to Robin Hill to see it for himself, is excellent comedy, but comedy of the same satirical sort. He runs into the young architect, on whose face is "a kind of humorous scorn: 'How do you do, Mr Forsyte? Come down to see for yourself?' It was exactly what James, as we know, *had* come for, and he was made correspondingly uneasy." They walk up to the elaborate terrace laid round two sides of the house, James leading the way.

"Now what did *this* cost?" he asked, when he saw the terrace extending round the corner.

"What should you think?" inquired Bosinney.

"How should I know?" replied James somewhat nonplussed; "two or three hundred, I dare say."

"The exact sum!"

James gave him a sharp look, but the architect appeared unconscious, and he put the answer down to mishearing.

On arriving at the garden entrance, he stopped to look at the view.

"That ought to come down," he said, pointing to the oak-tree.

"You think so? You think that with the tree there you don't get enough view for your money?"

Again James eyed him suspiciously—this young man had a peculiar way of putting things: "Well," he said, with a perplexed, nervous emphasis, "I don't see what you want with a tree."

"It shall come down to-morrow," said Bosinney.

James was alarmed. "Oh," he said, "don't go saying I said it was to come down! *I* know nothing about it!"

"No?"

James went on in a fluster: "Why, what should I know about it? It's nothing to do with me! You do it on your own responsibility."

"You'll allow me to mention your name?"

James grew more and more alarmed: "I don't know what you want mentioning my name for," he muttered; "you'd better leave the tree alone. It's not your tree!"

He took out a silk handkerchief and wiped his brow. They entered the house. Like Swithin, James was impressed by the inner court-yard.

"You must have spent a dooce of a lot of money here," he

said, after staring at the columns and gallery for some time. "Now, what did it cost to put up those columns?"

"I can't tell you off-hand," thoughtfully answered Bosinney, "but I know it was a deuce of a lot!"

"I should think so," said James. "I should——" He caught the architect's eye, and broke off. And now, whenever he came to anything of which he desired to know the cost, he stifled that curiosity.[1]

Art and workmanship

The love of order and beauty which, as much as pity and a passionate craving for justice, lay at the root of Galsworthy's social philosophy, was as powerful a ruling instinct in his work. He had to create an image of the world showing how far it fell short of his canons of order and beauty, and he strove to make that image fulfil his canons of art. Not for him the careless spontaneity of re-creation which was the reflex of Arnold Bennett's rapt enjoyment of life and of the infinite possibilities of human nature. There was always some idea

[1] D. H. Lawrence rightly assessed *The Forsyte Saga* as satire, and criticized it from that point of view. "*The Man of Property* has the elements of a very great novel, a very great satire. It sets out to reveal the social being in all his strength and inferiority. But the author has not the courage to carry it through. The greatness of the book rests in its new and sincere and amazingly profound satire. It is the ultimate satire on modern humanity, and done from the inside, with really consummate skill and sincere creative passion, something quite new. It seems to be a real effort to show up the social being in all his weirdness. And then it fizzles out" (*Phœnix*, "John Galsworthy," 542). By "social beings," whom Lawrence regards as "distinct" from human beings, he means people whose individuality has been subdued by the influences dominating in the sphere of society to which they belong. A man "may give away all he has to the poor and still reveal himself as a social being swayed finally and helplessly by the money-sway, and by the social moral, which is inhuman." He becomes as the slave in the old civilizations. "The free moral and the slave moral, the human moral and the social moral: these are the abiding antitheses." "The Forsytes are all parasites, and Mr Galsworthy set out, in a really magnificent attempt, to let us see it." They have no individual life of their own. It could not be put better; but what does Lawrence mean when he says the effort manifested in *The Man of Property* "fizzles out"? He is alluding to the love-affair of Irene and Bosinney and "the sentimentalizing of old Jolyon," by which he says "the thing is fatally blemished." But Lawrence does not fully appreciate that the converse and foil to the Irene-Soames theme is the theme of young Jolyon and Irene. (What he meant by "the sentimentalizing of old Jolyon" is not clear. Did he mean young Jolyon, who is the opposite pole to Soames and the shrewdest critic of Forsytism?) The union of Irene and Jolyon is, surely, not "giving way to the Forsytes"! As the essay goes on, Lawrence grows more and more hysterical, carried away by his sexual monomania—"the emotions are faked, faked, faked. It is one great fake." That refers to the third book, "To Let," which is all about "money, money, money." "Just money" and "a certain snobbish silliness" are two of the things that Galsworthy is satirizing. Lawrence can't have it both ways!

to be illustrated in a representation of things as they are, or some burning question to be solved and answered or shown to be insoluble. Hence it was compulsory that his men and women should be typical exemplars of some definite phase of social existence; and, the story being simply the characters shown undergoing and reacting to certain experiences, all that happened must be typical of the time and circumstances. He was as strictly responsible for the accuracy of his likeness as if he had been a regular historian. Of the huge medley of individuals in the *Saga*, the book in which he best realized his aims, some are poor and some richer in personality. But all, except the outsiders, are more or less planed down by the social machine; individuality has submitted to convention. This would have been the burden of his protest, if overt protest had been his intention. The family likeness of such a crowd, all of whom can be recognized apart, is not more remarkable than his success in making the Forsytes subtle variants of a national type plainly recognizable in every single one. Galsworthy himself held aloof, with the calm detachment of a philosophic and rather fastidious spectator. He was a critical observer, who had made his notes, and now produced the information. Here again he is the very opposite of Bennett, who could be hail-fellow-well-met with any clever scamp who happened to be successful or amusing. Of course, he aimed at dealing impartial justice, in his character-drawing and the conduct and emotional attitudes which were the decisive clue to what he meant. But from time to time likes and dislikes did come out. Arnold Bennett called him over the coals for displaying such "extraordinary passionate cruelty towards the oppressors as distinguished from the oppressed," [1] of which the most egregious example was his harsh treatment of Soames Forsyte in the *Saga*. He is much kinder in the *Comedy*, where Soames makes himself a slave to his daughter's whims, and she responds worse than perfunctorily. The old man's solitude in this ironical sequel is pitiable. There is a striking change of atmosphere in the *Comedy*: the younger generation are the prey of all sorts of

[1] *Books and Persons*, "John Galsworthy," 215.

ephemeral crazes, fashions, and fevers, to which Fleur and her contemporaries react for the time being with a frivolous abandon very unlike the sober conservatism of their elders.[1] But is not this, like Fleur's ingratitude and Soames's loneliness and estrangement from the world about him, the nemesis he, the man of property, laid up for himself, as was recounted in the *Saga*. Perchance, the family name was intended to hint at something. Soames, the great representative of Forsytism, and in his sphere so noted for foresight, was in the long run strangely lacking in that priceless faculty. Galsworthy evidently put a vast amount of his own personal experience and day-by-day observations into the *Saga* and its sequel; they almost form a diary of the later Victorian and the subsequent ages, and their immediacy is matched by their liveliness. He must have seen and been transfixed by those sunsets, have known those very houses and gardens, watched with intense concentration the big events that absorb or at least divert the attention of his characters—the South African war, Irish affairs, the Liberal revival of 1906, and later on the Great War, with its aftermath of social changes, especially the general emancipation from old-fashioned restraints. He does not overlook even such current topics of the hour as spiritualism, Couéism, "Foggartism," the censorship of books, the novels of the Forward Wing. All these matters indirectly concern the Forsytes. Some of the clan enlist for South Africa; June was expected to go as a Red Cross nurse. Jolyon sees in British policy the same domineering motives as are dehumanizing the upper section of society to which he belongs.

A precious war! Domination of peoples or of women! Attempts to master and possess those who did not want you! The negation of gentle decency! Possession, vested rights; and anyone "agin" 'em—outcast! "Thank Heaven!" he thought, "I *always* felt 'agin' 'em, anyway!" Yes! Even before his disastrous marriage he could remember fuming over the bludgeoning of Ireland, or the matrimonial suits of women

[1] *E.g.* Guyot, 107–111: "Fleur elle-même, contrainte de renoncer à Jon, était un personnage de tragédie. Et voici que la même Fleur, à deux ans de distance, n'est plus qu'une jeune femme aux idées étonnamment désordonnées, etc."

trying to be free of men they loathed. Parsons would have it that freedom of soul and body were quite different things! Pernicious doctrine, that! Body and soul could not thus be separated. Free will was the strength of any tie, and not its weakness. "I ought to have told Soames," he thought, "that I think him comic. Ah! but he's tragic, too!"

The *Saga* might have gone on for ever; and, by the time Galsworthy thought fit to close the chronicle, he had not only reconciled himself with his old antipathy, but made warm friends with Soames. Galsworthy had the sensibility, though not the creative imagination, of a poet[1]; it shows in the breadth and also in the intensity of his vision. His insight sought to reach the soul, and share the responsiveness of the whole personality to all experiences.[2] Innumerable incidents, like the drive through Richmond Park, when, "as the amorous perfume of chestnut flowers and fern drifted too near, one would say to the other, 'My dear! What a peculiar scent!'" or Soames's twilight walk across the park from Kensington Gardens, when "starved as he was, the whispered sounds in the stillness, the half-seen forms in the dark acted on him like some morbid stimulant," show this profundity. The glimpse of sleeping Holly, "like a miniature Madonna," is a bit of an interlude which is all poem, "The Indian Summer of a Forsyte." The natural setting brings out these unnoticed influences on our inmost being; and so does the social setting, a roomful of people, for instance:

> A feeling of its being too dangerous to take a step in any direction, or hazard any remark, had fallen on them all. Something of the sense of the impending, that comes over the spectator of a Greek tragedy, had entered that upholstered room, filled with those white-haired, frock-coated old men, and fashionably attired women, who were all of the same blood, between all of whom existed an unseized resemblance.

[1] "Il est philosophe et poète, mystiquement poète, ce qui ne l'empêche pas d'être le plus précis et le plus systematique des réalistes" (Chevrillon, 168).

[2] Katherine Mansfield's complaint was that he left no "mystery," no "unplumbed depth" to feed the imagination upon (*Novels and Novelists*, 305). But, as Chevrillon points out, he deliberately left something unrevealed—"en ayant soin de ne jamais les décrire complètement" (p. 176).

Often mere things take on a symbolic reference, as at the dinner when June is growing painfully aware of what is going on between her lover and Irene. Smilingly Irene said, "The azaleas are so wonderful this year!" At which Bosinney murmured, "Wonderful! The scent's extraordinary!" June said, "How *can* you like the scent? Sugar, please, Bilson." Long silence followed the charlotte. Irene, beckoning, said, "Take out the azalea, Bilson. Miss June can't bear the scent." "No, let it stay," said June. A silver tray was brought, with German plums. There was a lengthy pause; all were eating them.

Bosinney counted up the stones. "This year—next year—some time——"

Irene finished softly, "Never. There was such a glorious sunset. The sky's all ruby still—so beautiful!"

He answered, "Underneath the dark."

Their eyes had met, and June cried scornfully, "A London sunset!"

Galsworthy could draw a likely sketch of a poet, in Wilfrid Desert, and even produced a fair specimen of a stanza from his next volume.

His artistic patterns

But where are the influences of Flaubert, Turgenev, and Maupassant to be looked for, those professed by Galsworthy himself? [1] Certainly not in the general design and method of the *Saga* and the *Comedy*. Flaubert, and more probably Turgenev, may well have been his models and standards in those parts of the *Saga* in which the more personal and the wider theme are most intimately fused. Those eloquent silences, that masterly use of suggestion, may have been learned from or at least tutored by the Russian novelist, although in the general economy of the work the differences outweigh the resemblances. But there had been many changes and inner developments in the novel, even in the sociological novel, in the hundred years since Godwin and Holcroft, his remote predecessors. Jane Austen may have taught him very nearly as much as Turgenev. George Eliot had shown how to explore the hinterland of feeling and motive;

[1] See above, 322.

Meredith had even put the reader inside his characters, and let them see the inner and the outer drama through a consciousness with which they were brought into immediate and responsive apposition. Galsworthy's indirect method attains much the same intimacy and clarity.[1]

"Fraternity"

Of the novels appearing between the consecutive instalments of the Forsyte history, two have interest as psychological studies, though they lack the concrete vitality of the *Saga*. In both *Fraternity* (1909) and *The Dark Flower* (1913), an intellectual theorem is set forth in a story that purports to be true to life. The characters are generalizations of tendencies that any intelligent observer recognizes, some of them brilliant generalizations; but they remain abstractions. In *Fraternity*, Galsworthy takes a curious problem of human intercourse and tries to find a solution, but gives it up in despair. The book may accordingly be read as a satire on the fallacy of most humanitarian interference with the lives of others, or as a blank assertion of the insolubility of the case presented by Gissing and his like. Better, perhaps, to accept it as both. It is a dual problem that is posed, first the estrangement of the dilettante novelist and the misunderstood wife, and then the distressing plight of the "submerged tenth," who here in Kensington live just round the corner—the world of the Forsytes and Gissing's world next door to each other. Before Galsworthy began writing *The Man of Property*, there must have been a long and brooding contemplation of the facts of life; he must have performed a task, not so much of creative imagination, as of the intellectual insight that analyses human beings to the core, grasps subtle concatenations of motive, and studies how one instinct or appetency may eventually come to dominate a man's whole nature. By the time he came to

[1] Chevrillon (217–224) deals luminously with Galsworthy's probable indebtedness to some French and other novelists, especially to Meredith. Galsworthy, however, was not such an innovator as seems to be assumed (*e.g.* pp. 176–177) in the use of indirect discourse, the reproduction of what is spoken only in the mind, and of the postures and involuntary movements that make evident what is going on there. It was already a common device, with Arnold Bennett and others. Henry James would have frowned upon it, and might perchance have inquired how the fact came out that old Jolyon, rather upset by a talk with his son, "in paying the cab fare, for the first time in his life gave the driver a sovereign in mistake for a shilling."

write, he knew his characters thoroughly, and had only to make them known to the reader. He knew how they would react to the play of circumstance, to new impressions, to the influence of old restraints. His own delicate responsiveness to every vibration of feeling enabled him to perceive and show in what subtle ways motives are determined. The characters had been completely analysed, tested, and registered, so to speak, beforehand. Here, however, the experiment is conducted, as it were, while you wait; and, what is more unsatisfactory, if the characters have been taken to pieces already, you have to watch the whole process of reconstruction, and be disappointed that they do not come to life at the end of it. Chevrillon said that Galsworthy was able to make visible the psychology of each personage [1]; these people might indeed be described as a set of walking psychologies, visible even to themselves; they are "those who live too consciously," ever employed in a process of self-analysis. Sad victims of modern inhibitions, they have deprived themselves of the ability to live any sort of life of their own. Hilary and Bianca are a pair of cultured, superfine beings, who have tried so hard to establish autonomous personalities of their own that by now they do not know themselves or understand each other. Thus, in the little matter, to them by no means unimportant, of their æsthetic surroundings at home, conscious of "the grave Philistinism of the upper classes, she and Hilary had ever kept their duty to æstheticism green," and had preferred a beautiful simplicity to comfort. Hilary is told by the candid young "Sanitist" that he is suffering from "atrophy of the nerve of action," and "there's no cure for that!" Galsworthy admitted to Conrad that Hilary was "a monster, a degenerate." [2] Presumably, in this case he was still pursuing what he called his "negative method." [3] The fact is, both Hilary and Bianca are "shadows," in another sense than old Mr Stone applies the term to "the waste products of the social process," that is, the helpless poor. They are composed of

[1] "Dans cette scène de passion, la psychologie propre de chaque personnage ne cesse pas d'être visible" (Chevrillon, 192).

[2] Reynolds, 230.

[3] *Ibid.*, 239.

familiar trends of mind and currents of feeling; and are indeed superlative modern examples of the art and science of charactery applied to the elucidation of types as a criticism of the age. Hilary is a degenerate; he is also degeneracy and atrophy in the abstract. Bianca is elaborately analysed several times; here, for instance, she is seen reduced to a shadow-play of abstract antitheses:

> Of all the dark and tortuous places of this life the human heart is the most dark and tortuous; and of all human hearts none are less clear, more intricate, than the hearts of all that class of people among whom Bianca had her being. Pride was a simple quality when joined with a simple view of life, based on the plain philosophy of property; pride was no simple quality when the hundred paralysing doubts and aspirations of a social conscience also hedged it round. In thus going forth with the full intention of restoring the little model to her position in the household, her pride fought against her pride, and her woman's sense of ownership in the man whom she had married wrestled with the acquired sentiments of freedom, liberality, equality, good taste. With her spirit thus confused, and her mind so at variance with itself, she was really acting on the simple instinct of compassion.

The story

It is only the so-called "shadows" that prove to have any substance in them: the poor charwoman with her baby; her husband, whose head was injured in the war, and who loses it to the undesigned fascinations of the little model; the little model herself, whose name Ivy symbolizes her helpless, clinging nature; and the old newsvendor who watches the domestic drama and makes comments that often hit the mark, like a character out of Dickens. Hilary's efforts come to grief in both directions. His well-meaning impulse to befriend the little model has the result he should have expected: she throws herself at his feet. Partly from a sense of responsibility, he is on the point of yielding. But his class instincts are offended; he cannot stand the cheap scent when she presses her mouth to his. And that unwary impulse of his has disturbed a whole group of people. Her departure from the Hughs's had led to a violent outbreak on the crack-brained husband's part. He has gone to gaol, and the baby has died, the mother's milk being dried up. An act of pity in a moment of unwisdom has set a whole train of accidents going. At the end, Hilary has only widened the gulf between himself and his wife, by rousing her latent jealousy, though she is too proud to admit it. They part irrevocably. Even the pathos of the baby's funeral is given a sardonic twist by the presence of the old newsvendor:

> "He's gettin' Christian burial. Who gives this woman away? I do. Ashes to ashes. I never suspected him of livin'."
>
> "Yes, he's a-gone," he thought; "another little baby. Old men an' maidens, young men an' little children; it's a-goin' on all the time. Where 'e is now there'll be no marryin', no, nor givin' out in marriage; till death do us part."

Galsworthy told Conrad he himself regretted that he was "barred by temperament, habits of life, possessions, from the complete flow of sympathy."[1] His heart was divided between pity for the world, on the one hand, and, on the other, disgust with mere sentiment and hatred for the "Justice administered by an upper class with a patch over one eye and a squint in the other." It is the young Sanatist, with his insistence on a cold-blooded scientific reformation, who characterizes it so. The irony of old Mr Stone's benevolent mania, and the rhapsodies he intones from his vast treatise on Universal Brotherhood, are a still more sarcastic comment.[2]

"The Dark Flower"

The idea in *The Dark Flower* is the fateful incalculability of love, one illustrated often enough in the *Saga* and *Comedy*, to say nothing of *Fraternity* and divers short stories. It is an odd book for Galsworthy, a cross between a lyrical apotheosis of the celestial—or infernal—power and a didactic exhortation: a Magnificat as a text for a sermon. The hero, Mark Lennan, is only a minor character, for he has nothing in him save some inexplicable charm for women. In the three parts,

[1] Reynolds, 240.

[2] H. W. Nevinson thinks that "the weight of all the world's misery fell upon Galsworthy too suddenly and too late; not gradually and in early life as it falls upon most of us. The horror of it seems to have overwhelmed him, just as the horror of a slaughter-house might overwhelm a dainty carnivorous woman if she once caught sight of it" (Nevinson, 243).

Spring, Summer, Autumn, first the youth at Oxford captivates and desolates the heart of a professor's wife, nearly twice his age; then the mature man is in the very act of delivering another lady from a hated husband, when the attempt is cut short by tragedy; and finally, in middle age, he only just manages to resist the supplications of a girl as young and innocent as he himself was in the first episode, and remains soberly true to the wife of his bosom. So he bids farewell to "the dark-red flower," and settles down presumably to winter, the season which is left unchronicled. Only towards the end is the import revealed of these impassioned idylls. "Passion comes when it will, goes when it will; and we poor devils have no say in it." "Passion never plays the game. . . . Well did the old painters limn it as an arrow or the wind!" But this is no excuse for libertarianism. The creed of Freedom is, of all "the most enchaining." Free will is the restraining force. Incidentally, there is satire reminiscent of Samuel Butler on the English Grundys with their alpenstocks met with in a Tyrol climbing-resort: "Why don't they keep to their Culture, where no one knows what it is to ache and feel hunger, and hearts don't beat?" Galsworthy could be ironical on the supercilious English assumption of an ironical attitude to their presumed inferiors, here in particular those of other races.

"Caravan"

Galsworthy published five collections of stories and sketches, beginning with *Villa Rubein* (1900) and *A Man of Devon* (1901), both of which were ascribed to a fictitious John Sinjohn.[1] He brought them all together, with some excisions, in *Caravan* (1925), which includes more than fifty items. He was not a born story-teller. He had his definite vocation, which was to exhibit a society and the types of people that make it, rather than to relate incidents and adventures. His dramatic powers he reserved in the main for the theatre. Hence it is not surprising that a large proportion belong to the genus charactery, which does not mean, however, that there are no happenings. The very first, "Salvation of a Forsyte" (1900), records an incident in the life of Swithin, one of the least enterprising of a breed not cut out for adventure—the one flash of romance,

[1] John Galsworthy, son of John Galsworthy.

poetry, sentiment, in a safe and humdrum career. But the interest in the incidents is only as they cast the glare of action and decision on a character that is scared by it. So the conclusion is ironical:

Her footsteps died away in the passage, but Swithin sat gazing intently at a single bright drop of spilt wine quivering on the table's edge. In that moment she, in her helplessness and emotion, was all in all to him—his life nothing; all the real things—his conventions, convictions, training, and himself—all seemed remote, behind a mist of passion and strange chivalry. Carefully with a bit of bread he soaked up the bright drop; and suddenly he thought, "This is tremendous!" For a long time he stood there in the window, close to the dark pine-trees.

"A Stoic" is far from being the only delineation of ripe and serene old age. One of the mellowest and most memorable is "A Portrait" (1908), of a Victorian, "son of a time between two ages—the product of an era without real faith—an individualist to the core." He was a Conservative Liberal in politics till Dizzy's time, when he became a Liberal Conservative. His finest quality, though it kept him from making his mark in public affairs, was "the extraordinary balance of his temperament." "He abhorred fanaticism." "There was something classical, measured, and mellow in his march adown the years, as if he had been god-mothered by Harmony." A beauty like that of Mrs Gaskell's virginal old ladies pervades the next story, "The Grey Angel" (1917), of the octogenarian widow whose toil and self-denial for the wounded poilus bring her to her death-bed from sheer exhaustion. That pity and tenderness, a life spent, though she knew it not, in "the quest of perfection," are Galsworthy's own most cherished qualifications, the basis of his social philosophy. Any suffering or injustice, any fine unconscious rectitude or innocence of spirit, touches him to the quick. That is the appeal of "Quality" (1911), about the old shoemaker who never gave himself time to eat, never had a penny in the house; "all went in rent and leather." "How he lived so long I don't know. He regular let his fire out. He was a character. But he made good boots." Take again "The Prisoner" (1909), the young fellow sentenced for life in a German prison; reduced to imbecility, but putting all his longings into the picture which was the hundredth version done in eighteen years' captivity. Some of the stories take the ironical turning, but not so often as the novels. "The Juryman" (1916) tells of a man who longed to make his wife understand, but was repulsed by her mere amativeness. In "A Hedonist" (1920), the narrator says he "was sorry—very sorry, at that moment, for Rupert K. Vaness"; but really he and everybody else rejoice at the reverse to that gentleman's "basking philosophy." "Defeat" (1916) comes off badly in the inevitable comparison with Arnold Bennett's *Pretty Lady*. They are women of the same profession, and both foreigners; and pity, or at least sympathy, is sought for both. The best that can be said for the pair in Galsworthy's tale is that they are accurate constructions, true to type, the one answering to the regular formula for a sound-hearted young officer, wounded in the war and heroizing his comrades, and the other, the forlorn outcast, in the land of her country's enemies. There are other stories in which the performers are not quite self-propelled; Galsworthy is inside the figure, like the man who worked the pretended automaton. "The Apple Tree" (1916), dated seven years after *Fraternity*, is a vulgarized pendant to the affair of Hilary Dallison and the little model, the pretty rural setting of which cannot absolve it from D. H. Lawrence's charge that it is an unsavoury plunge into sheer narcissism.[1] Those versed in the slangy technique of the turf will get most enjoyment out of the last, "Had a Horse" (1923); though anyone may appreciate Galsworthy's psychology, with Dickensian trimmings, of the poor devil of a bookie who for a few weeks of bliss runs a horse of his own.[2]

[1] *Phœnix*, 546.
[2] He confessed that at one time *Ruff's Guide* was his favourite book.

CHAPTER VIII

D. H. LAWRENCE

Lawrence and the foregoing

WHATEVER his place among English novelists in general, D. H. Lawrence (1885–1930) is the most incontestable case in the age of Hardy and Conrad, Kipling and Chesterton, of genius born not made, the product neither of education nor tradition; as to the subjects of the preceding chapter, Arnold Bennett and Galsworthy, he ran counter to them from the very beginning and in almost every particular of his character and his work. He hated abstractions, and protested against the "rather bony, bloodless drama" of his day; it was time for a reaction against Shaw and Galsworthy and Barker—"the rule and measure mathematical folk." [1] And, though he saw as clearly as Galsworthy the evils arising from "the blind spirit of possession" and the hollowness of civilization in the machine age, and was disposed to welcome him as a satirist, he disliked Galsworthy's mode of attack and accused him of paltering with the evil.[2] Arnold Bennett he described as a "sort of pig in clover," who was "overpowered by his gold watch-chain" and let himself go with the tide: "Never let it be said I was a Bennett." [3] With a defiant contempt for the formal qualities of art, he wrote his novels and poems as so much "pure passionate experience.[4] Whilst Bennett followed his intuitions in the history of his characters and their fellow-beings, and Galsworthy the intellectual method distinguished therefrom in the last chapter, Lawrence abandoned himself utterly and decisively to the powerful current of instinctive life. He strove to identify his consciousness with the innermost urge; he put himself in immediate contact with the dark region of semi-

[1] *Letters*, 103.
[2] See above, p. 333, n.
[3] *Letters*, 716–717.
[4] *Fantasia of the Unconscious*, 11.

conscious feeling and of impulses that defy analysis and disconcert the understanding. His characters are not the humorous treasure trove of the Dickens school, or the refined imaginative creations of the humanist; he is blind to or professes to despise these riches of individuality. His men and women are simply human nature, with the elemental endowment of instincts and passional impulses in more than the normal measure, people chosen as exponents of his view of life because they live with something like the same intensity as himself. In his novels he let them live to the full, and thus secured the virtue of immediacy to a degree probably unique in fiction. Unfortunately, he was a genius without a sense of humour; and much of his work exposed him to ridicule, which he courted rather than shunned, out of pure hatred and contempt for the conventional and puritanical and delight in provoking them. He will long remain a problem to those who would define him and determine his precise relation to the epoch.

Origin and early life

David Herbert Lawrence was born at Eastwood, a village in the colliery district on the borders of Nottinghamshire and Derbyshire, and was the fourth child of a miner. The circumstances of his boyhood and schooling, the family life, and the emotional trials he went through on coming to the age of puberty, are related with only a few departures from fact in his third novel, *Sons and Lovers* (1913), in which Paul Morel stands for Lawrence, Bert as he was known in the family circle. All his novels are more or less autobiographical, even if they deal with only a "thought-adventure," like *Kangaroo*. But this is the nearest to the literal truth, and is of cardinal importance as a key to his intricate and ofttimes paradoxical nature. His father was a good-natured, careless, tippling workman, good-looking with his curly beard, who had been at the pit since the age of seven. What the life of him and his mates and their families was actually like may be seen from the poignant realism of a little sketch, "The Miner at Home," [1] even better than from the novels, in which the interest lies elsewhere. The scene between the bullying, masterful coal-miner, who

[1] *Phœnix*, 775–779.

is cowardly enough at heart, and the starving and contriving wife, to whom he jauntily announces that the men are coming out on strike, has a force and pathos, and even a restrained humour, not too common in his stories. The mother was a superior woman, of some education, who had long repented of her bargain, but won her children's admiration by the way she kept the home together, in spite of her husband's weekly bouts, after which there were often violent scenes. Lawrence hated his father then; his mother said she knew why: "It happened before he was born. One night he put me out of the house. . . . He's bound to hate his father."[1] But in later life he did more justice to a vein of real tenderness under that rough exterior. His love for his mother was of abnormal intensity; in a fit of involuntary exaggeration he said he loved her like a lover, and he always believed there was a bond between them of pre-natal origin which could never be broken and which made it almost impossible for him to find a real mate in any other woman. It was this devotion to his mother that came into collision with his regard for the girl named Miriam in the novel. They had been comrades from boyhood and girlhood, reading the same books and exchanging ideas, visiting neighbours, and wandering about together in this patch of country between Sherwood and the Peak, where there were still many unspoiled nooks. Paul, or Bert, knew them by heart, and could tell the name and properties of every flower and weed. Nothing escaped his notice, from those early days till the time when he was inditing his very last books. But his mother affected to look down on "Miriam" as belonging to the common people; she was jealous, and did her best to detach her son, when people began to say that the pair ought to be engaged. The truth has been revealed with perfect candour and delicacy by the original of Miriam[2]; and it is evident that Lawrence was suffering from an inner division. He told her that he loved her spiritually, but that a wife must have sensual attractions which she did not possess. But that was very far from the whole truth. Lawrence was anything but a normal man. In him, the strength of genius was strangely

[1] *D. H. Lawrence*, by E. T., 138.

[2] *Ibid.*, *passim.*

mingled with some obscure weakness. In every book he wrote there are continual allusions to some inscrutable terror that haunted him. When Paul, in *Sons and Lovers*, looks out on town and country as he sits in the tramcar, he feels as if he has no place in the human world.

Whatever spot he stood on, there he stood alone. From his breast, from his mouth, sprang the endless space, and it was there behind him, everywhere. The people hurrying along the streets offered no obstruction to the void in which he found himself. . . . He got off the car. In the country all was dead still. Little stars shone high up; little stars spread far away in the flood-waters, a firmament below. Everywhere the vastness and terror of the immense night which is roused and stirred for a brief while by the day, but which returns, and will remain at last eternal, holding everything in its silence and its living gloom. There was no Time, only Space. Who could say his mother had lived and did not live? She had been in one place, and was in another; that was all. And his soul could not leave her, wherever she was. . . . "Mother!" he whimpered—"mother!" She was the only thing that held him up, himself, amid all this. And she was gone, intermingled herself. He wanted her to touch him, have him alongside with her.

The subconscious fears that held him down in Italy or in Mexico were of the same nature and origin.[1] From the darkest recesses of his blood came a terrible echo at the name of Mount Eryx, something quite unaccountable. "The name of Athens hardly moves me. At Eryx—my darkness quivers." Kate Leslie, in *The Plumed Serpent*, who is only Lawrence adventuring in Mexico, is always sensible of a state of "curious reptile apprehension" which comes over dark people, and a panic fear which she herself cannot resist, "a sense of devilment and horror thick in the night air." Her husband had explained whence it arises; and it is significant that it comes from sources older than ourselves: "that evil was the lapsing back to old life-modes that have been surpassed in us," in the civilized, who are however liable to be revisited at the incitation

[1] One of the most memorable of these harrowing visitations is the subject of that chapter in *Kangaroo* entitled "The Nightmare."

of the barbaric drums and rhythms—"consciously reverting to the savage." Lawrence needed protection, someone to lean upon; the only mate for him was one who could give him the sense of security he had had at home—he wanted to be mothered. The uniqueness, the sensitiveness that endeared him to "Miriam," were bound up with this fatal vulnerability. She was painfully aware of his tragic predicament. There were moments when she saw Lawrence "dizzily poised on the edge of an abyss," and was powerless to help him. "There were moments, too," she writes, "in our desperate struggle, when we seemed to touch another sphere of existence, and it flashed upon me that never here in this life, but somewhere beyond the human bourne, lay the unity we were striving for."[1] They never married. When Lawrence went to Croydon as teacher in a school, they corresponded at intervals, and he made "Miriam" his confidant in various love-affairs of the lightest description. She hoped he would return to her; but she was deeply hurt by the unfair version of their attachment given in *Sons and Lovers*, in which "Lawrence handed his mother the laurels of victory," and the shock "gave the death-blow to our friendship." By now, Lawrence had met Frieda Weekley, wife of a professor at the University of Nottingham, a woman older than himself and the mother of three children; and he felt that he had found in her the strength and tenderness he needed. They went away together to Germany, her native country, and as soon as she was free they married (1913).[2]

First writings and the War

Lawrence says it was at Miriam's farm that he got his first incentive to write.[3] He used to send her his poems and other work as it was finished, including the initial version of *Sons and Lovers*. They read Fenimore Cooper, Stevenson, George Eliot, Thackeray, the poets, and then Maupassant and Flaubert, and talked them over earnestly. When they were seeming most estranged, he begged her to read *Sentimental Tommy* and

[1] E. T., 147.

[2] Mark and Mary Rampion, in *Point Counter Point* (1928), by Aldous Huxley, are drawn from Lawrence and Frieda. Rampion, the man of genius, the man of unerring insight, is the only male character who meets with any approval in this caustic review of the age.

[3] *Letters*, 674.

its sequel, and say if his was not a parallel case. It was she that sent some of his poems to Ford Madox Hueffer, who printed them in *The English Review* (1908). She knew his faults, no one better, and also what allowances had to be made for them; she has painted the vividest and most spontaneous portrait of Lawrence in his young manhood. "One could not help being affected by his vitality and charm. Mother made a remark that set me speculating. She said, 'I should like to be next to Bert in heaven.'"[1] She read his first novels, *The White Peacock* and *The Trespasser*, before they were published; and Lawrence actually sent her the proofs of *Sons and Lovers* after his union with Frieda. That appeared in 1913, after a volume of *Love Poems*. His play, *The Widowing of Mrs Holroyd* (1914), was likewise based on his own household experiences. Holroyd is a miner who drinks and runs loose with women, and neglects his hard-working wife, an heroic woman who brings up her children well in spite of poverty. A respectable man loves her, and she is inclined to respond, when Holroyd is killed by a fall of rock, and she has a revulsion of feeling, dismissing Blackmore and accusing herself of having driven her man to his death. Lawrence's revolt, the revolt of the man of nature, from the artificial self-consciousness and mere automatism of "societal" man, from the same standardized and imitative life of society to-day, in fact, and the underlying uncleanness and disease due to "this insatiable struggle and desire to possess, to possess always and in spite of everything,"[2] as had been stripped of its shams by Galsworthy, in the *Saga* and the *Comedy* and also in *Fraternity*, dates back to long before the War, but it was exacerbated by the War, which Lawrence regarded as the direct result of this general baseness and degeneracy.[3] "The War finished me: it was the spear through the side of all sorrows and hopes," he wrote to Lady Cynthia Asquith.[4] He was driven further back into his unbalanced self; and, tortured by his isolation and separateness,

[1] E. T., 31.

[2] *Letters*, 244–245.

[3] "It is by fulfilling the *lowest* truth that money is honour and glory—that we have come to war and pretty nearly to bankruptcy" (*Ibid.*, 358).

[4] *Ibid.*, 217.

he fell more and more into what detractors called his "mindless trances" and his sudden wild fits of rage. Whether his novel *The Rainbow* ought to have been suppressed, or his exhibition of paintings closed by the police, are irrelevant questions. Lawrence was singled out by British philistinism and officialdom as an easy mark; the fact that he was physically unfit was made the excuse for wanton outrages at the tribunals, and the German origin of his wife laid them both open to absurd suspicions and to their being evicted from their humble refuge in Cornwall by the military authorities. Lawrence was a crusader for love, which "universalizes the individual." "Love is the great creative process, war is the opposite," and he was in direct opposition to the principle of war.[1] It almost killed him, he said, to think, as an artist, of the British public in its present state. "I hate democracy so much. . . . But then I think that 'aristocracy' is just as pernicious, only it is much more dead. They are both evil."[2] For the time being, he could only forget, and turn his eyes towards another world, as yet uncreated. His letters are full of the perfectly valid reasons why he left England. "You mustn't think that I haven't cared about England," he wrote again to Lady Cynthia. "I have cared deeply and bitterly. But something is broken. There *is not* any England. One must look now for another world. This is only a tomb."[3] So the Lawrences went wandering from Italy to Sicily and Malta, right on to Australia, and then to California and Mexico, in search of a habitable country. They must often have enjoyed themselves; and yet they met with disillusionment of some kind everywhere, and Lawrence's travel-books as well as the novels written by the way are full of querulousness, besides his regular outbursts of subconscious dread stirred up by some experience which to others seemed innocuous. He long nursed a project for a new life and some new form of community, and intermittently sought to enlist coadjutors. His scheme was too vague and visionary to appeal to any but a few waverers who quickly fell away; but he clung to the idea that after the War mankind would repudiate the past and unanimously insist upon

[1] *Ibid.*, 265. [2] *Ibid.*, 344. [3] *Ibid.*, 397.

a new way of life. To live, all must unite, and bring all knowledge into a coherent whole, "cast all personalities into the melting-pot, and give a new humanity its birth." "One must destroy the old Moloch of greediness and love of property and love of power. But think what a splendid world we shall have, when each man shall seek joy and understanding rather than getting and having." [1] Lawrence beheld himself as the prophet of a new order, a sort of Blake, Shelley, or Nietzsche, almost as a superman. But he was a genius who certainly could not take care of himself. He was another "ineffectual angel," who was often mistaken for a demon. A heretic he was,[2] but in no wise a charlatan. He took himself only too seriously, realizing only in part the internal weakness that paralysed so much of what was great in him. His fundamental mistake was to scoff at the reasoning faculty, because it was weak in himself, in comparison with other ways of knowing. He built up a philosophy of life, or, rather, a theosophy, on bases that he never tested or was able to test; and he could never give a rational account of it, though he repeatedly tried and thought he had succeeded. It was the old doctrine, traceable in Shaftesbury, Rousseau, Blake, and indeed much further back, to "follow instinct"—a sound doctrine if combined with the proviso that the dictates of our nature should be examined, verified, and corrected. But Lawrence never saw the necessity for such a careful inspection, and went on blindly to the end, making remarkable discoveries in this obscure mental tract, but never clearly knowing, that is by the intellect, what he was discovering, or gauging its validity by the reason. His letters, more even than the rest of his writings, abound in swift perceptions and instantaneous yet sure generalizations. Wisdom does not come, however, of such incoherent flashes of insight. He had the makings of a great personality, but was unable to fuse them together in a balanced unity. He himself was acutely aware of this inability; yet he obstinately strove to erect a complete manhood and theory of life on those

[1] *Letters*, 231–232.

[2] "Lawrence is for my purposes an almost perfect example of the heretic" (T. S. Eliot, *After Strange Gods*, 36–37).

impulses of his which had from time to time the ascendancy. Now and then, in a lucid interval, he saw himself as he was, and confessed to the bee in his bonnet, one of them at any rate.[1] If he had only had a more vigilant sense of humour! There was something that would be grotesque if it had not been tragic in this incessant self-tormentor; but more utterly grotesque were the fulsome adulation of his disciples and their mutual recriminations. Lawrence had a gift for throwing others off their balance as well as himself.

First novels

Lawrence rejected the humanitarian philosophies, and arrived at subversive conclusions of his own. Trusting his pre-natal instincts, he found in them plenary authority for repudiating thought and accepting the dark admonitions of the unconscious as infallible.[2] He expounded his doctrines in his novels, with more and more confidence as he went on. They were novels, right enough, that is, works of creative art, for he was possessed by his creative imagination as much as by his fundamental convictions. He tried more than once to state and explain these in the ordinary intellectual way, for his reasoning seemed conclusive to himself and he felt sure it would convince others; but the imaginative was the only method that he had at easy command.[3] Hence his novels, whilst definitely works of art, were always didactic, or, rather, apostolic, for he regarded the dictates of the unconscious as sacred: "Primarily," he said, "I am a passionately religious man, and my novels must be written from the depth of my

[1] Writing to Lady Cynthia Asquith about his new novel, *The Lost Girl*, he said: "That bee in my bonnet which you mention, and which I presume means sex, buzzes not overloud" (*Letters*, 504). A good account of the antics of his adorers, and also of the persecution Lawrence and Frieda suffered during the War, will be found in the study by Hugh Kingsmill, a common-sense review, if a little unsympathetic—at any rate, a wholesome counterblast to the "high-faluters." Kingsmill is mentioned in Middleton Murry's *Between Two Worlds* (p. 175) as "a breezy, disarming fellow" with whom the writer evidently has no affinity.

[2] "Logic might be unanswerable because it was so absolutely wrong" (*Lady Chatterley's Lover*, v).

[3] "Man thought and still thinks in images. But now our images have hardly any emotional value. We always want a 'conclusion,' an end, we always want to come, in our mental processes, to a decision, a finality, a full stop. This gives us a sense of satisfaction. . . . Whereas of course there is no goal. Consciousness is an end in itself. We torture ourselves getting somewhere, and when we get there it is nowhere, for there is nowhere to go" (*Apocalypse*, 90–91).

religious experience."[1] Art, to him, was art for *his* sake.[2] He felt an irresistible urge to write, and found writing good for himself. "One sheds one's sicknesses in books—repeats and presents again one's emotions to be master of them."[3] He also wrote, "I do think that art has to reveal the palpitating moment or the state of man as it is."[4] He told Middleton Murry that he considered art a social activity, and instanced Shakespeare in *Hamlet* and *Lear*, as one working "towards a more perfect social conception—of fraternity as opposed to paternity, and now of complete fraternity on this earth."[5] From the outset, his novels were an exploration and an exposition of the self in its relations to others and to the universe, and it was inevitable that they should be based upon his own inmost experience. His first, *The White Peacock* (1911), superficially like a Hardy novel, was about a set of young people, it might be the Lawrences and their intimates, growing up together in the semi-rural region where he lived. The main story is of a disappointed lover who marries unhappily and takes to drink. But the most pregnant character is Annable the gamekeeper, an anticipation of Mellors in *Lady Chatterley's Lover*. Both are reflexes of Lawrence. This is a man of "one idea—that all civilization was the painted fungus of rottenness. He hated any sign of culture. . . . He was a thorough materialist. . . . 'Be a good animal, true to your natural instinct,' was his motto." E. T., who disliked Annable, objecting to his cynical brutality, remonstrated with Lawrence, who replied, "He *has* to be there. Don't you see why? He makes a sort of balance. Otherwise it's too much of one thing, too much *me*." That is, he was a makeweight to young Cyril, who in his relationship to Emily corresponds to Paul, Miriam's peccant lover, in the later novel. To account for Lawrence's

[1] *Letters*, 190. He said in *Reflections on the Death of a Porcupine* (1925)—on "The Novel"—"Most great novelists have a didactic purpose up their sleeve. . . . You can tell me Flaubert had a 'philosophy' not a 'purpose.' But what's a novelist's philosophy but a purpose on a higher level? And since every novelist who amounts to anything has a philosophy—even Balzac—any novel of importance has a purpose" (p. 104). "But the novel must be 'quick' and its characters 'quick'" (p. 110).

[2] "I always say, my motto is, 'Art for *my* sake'" (*Ibid.*, ix).

[3] *Ibid.*, 757.

[4] *Ibid.*

[5] *Reminiscences of D. H. Lawrence*, 65.

obsession with keepers, E. T. recalls an incident in which he was caught trespassing, and was deeply hurt by the insolence of a gamekeeper.[1] It is Annable who likens the peacock, fouling the statue of the angel on which it perches, with the soul of a lady—"a woman to the end, I tell you, all vanity and screech and defilement." E. T. read with a critical eye the next novel also, *The Trespasser* (1912), a slighter thing which is more directly autobiographical, being Lawrence's poetized account of his flirtation with a girl who went with him to the Isle of Wight. He begged E. T. not to mind, telling her the story of the shirt of Nessus. He felt a need for Helen—Helena in the novel—"but I must *always* return to you . . . only you must always leave me free." [2]

"Sons and Lovers"

As already indicated, *Sons and Lovers* (1913) is autobiography in a much more serious sense; Lawrence himself admitted it, although he had altered important facts, making the Miriam of the novel, for instance, yield to Paul Morel's solicitations. It appeared after Lawrence had found the woman he craved in Frieda. Though there were "flashes in his blood," Paul could not get across to Miriam. She was "the threshing-floor on which he threshed out all his beliefs," but he learns presently that he loves her only with his soul; another woman comes on the scene, who exerts a more sensuous attraction. The new love is another man's wife, who continues for some time to hold part of him whilst another part craves for Miriam. Free at last of the siren, he is again offered the saint, or rather the woman who seemed to perceive the saint beneath his husk. "Oh, why did he not take her? Her very soul belonged to him. Why would he not take what was his? . . . He felt, in leaving her, he was defrauding her of life. But he knew that in staying, stifling the inner desperate man, he was denying

[1] E. T., 117–118.

[2] E. T., 181–182. Kingsmill finds in Siegmund's sense of a failure as Helena's lover one of the earliest clues to Lawrence's alleged sexual inferiority, to which many have attributed his everlasting preoccupation with the sexual act. He is supposed to have got sex on the brain through this form of "inferiority complex." "The phallic cult which fills so much of his writing originated in his diffidence with women" (Kingsmill, 45). To Middleton Murry, on the other hand, "Sex is for Lawrence a *pis-aller*, a means of escape"—"from the anguish of his own inward division, and from the sense of isolation that is inseparable from it" (*Son of Woman*, 53–54).

his own life. And he did not hope to give life to her by denying his own." So on a note of interrogation, like all Lawrence's fiction up to now, this finest of his early novels comes to an end. It has been hailed by authorities on the subject as the first genuine example of psycho-analytical fiction in English. There had been plenty of novels of psychological analysis ever since George Eliot and Meredith had set writers plunging farther and farther into the deeps, and revealing the play of unconscious impulses. The line of development led directly to the work of James Joyce, Virginia Woolf, and Dorothy Richardson, who have been intent on what they call "the stream of consciousness." But "the novel of psychological analysis has at bottom nothing to do with the psycho-analytical novel," declares uncompromisingly one of the leading authorities on that special science.[1] The teaching of Havelock Ellis, Samuel Butler, and others, who applied a frank and more or less scientific treatment to sex problems, heredity, and similar questions, paved the way for the general interest shown in psycho-analysis later on, especially during the years 1917–1925, when it became an everyday topic, and novelists, and still more critics, made great play with the technical terms, sometimes with only a cloudy notion of what they meant. Even Arnold Bennett sometimes showed he had an inkling of the new theories, as when in *The Pretty Lady* he makes G.J., "in the desolation, the dismay, the disillusion, the nausea which ravaged him," "unwillingly conscious of fragments of thoughts that flickered like transient flames far below in the deep mines of his being," not to say when he sketched those "astounding" women Concepcion and Lady Queenie; and Galsworthy, much earlier than that, in *The Man of Property*, sometimes appeared to be poetizing a bit of Freudian analysis. When Soames exclaims to Irene, "The truth! there's no such thing with women. It's nerves—nerves," he hears her whisper, "Yes, nerves don't lie. Haven't you discovered that?" When the Forsyte brothers are gazing on the dead body of Bosinney,

1 "Der Roman mit psychologischer Analyse hat mit dem psychoanalytischen Roman prinzipiell nichts zu tun" (*Der Einfluss der Psychoanalyse auf die englische Literatur*, von Reinald Hoops (1934), p. 30.

whose subconscious nature was so utterly foreign to theirs, "in each one of them the trend of his nature, the odd essential spring, that moved him in fashions minutely, unalterably different from those of every other human being, forced him to a different attitude of thought." But the psycho-analysts would have given a very different turn to some of the Forsyte problems, and to the deep antagonism between the clan and those outsiders, Irene and Bosinney. Lawrence's first two novels were in the older tradition, like the first of May Sinclair's, who wrote under the influence of Walt Whitman and Butler, of Havelock Ellis and Edward Carpenter, and of the teaching of Herbert Spencer, Haeckel, Maudsley, and Ribot, on heredity. In later novels, however, she openly applies the theories of Freud, Jung, and Adler to explain her psychological cases, in *The Three Sisters* (1914), for instance, which appeared the year after *Sons and Lovers*.[1] The central situation in Lawrence's novel is an example satisfactory to the psycho-analysts of what they term the Œdipus complex. In its original form, to which Lawrence intended to give the title "Paul Morel," but which was returned by the publishers with searching criticisms by Edward Garnett, the conflict between love for the mother and a very different affection for the girl is unfolded without reference to any psychological theory. At that time, Lawrence had not read Freud. But he now went to Germany with Frieda, who perused the rejected manuscript, and appears to have introduced him to the new theories, which they discussed together.[2] The final version, with the new title, *Sons and*

[1] Hoops, 41–45.

[2] He says in a letter dated 5th October 1913: "I never did read Freud, but I have heard about him since I was in Germany" (*Letters*, 142). This view is set forth by Hoops (64–67), who points out that, although the Œdipus complex in Paul is the central motive, it is not the only one that affiliates Lawrence with the psycho-analysts. There is also the conflict between man and woman, the "duel of sex," and there is the human tendency to consign personal defects and anything disagreeable to the region of unconsciousness. Hoops illustrates all this from passages in the novel. Miriam suffers from the inferiority complex; and is even supposed to be infected with the incest motive, in her ecstatic love for her little brother Hubert (Hoops, 67–69). Middleton Murry contends, on the other hand, that Lawrence "had independently arrived at the main conclusions of the psycho-analysts, and the English followers of Freud came to see him," etc. (*Reminiscences of D. H. Lawrence*, 39). Lawrence, it will be seen, made the inner meaning of his fiction perfectly clear in his two little books on psycho-analysis later on. But his doctrine never

Lovers, bears the impress of this initiation, and is thus a document in the history of Lawrence's mental development and in that of the English novel.[1] Traces could also be pointed out in the dozen tales collected under the title *The Prussian Officer, and other stories* (1914). Militarism is stigmatized in the first, which shows how an uprush of elemental impulse, physical rather than mental, may launch a man into crime. The clash between the two internal forces is also the theme of "Daughters of the Vicar"; one sister fights down physical repulsion and marries a poor reed of a man who saves her from her father's poverty, the other defies class prejudice and marries a sturdy collier. As bitter tragedy, though of the bloodless order, "Shadow in the Rose Garden" is a little masterpiece: a wife tells her husband of a pre-marital affair with an army officer, who is now a lunatic. There is another of his gamekeepers in "The Shades of Spring," the successful lover who discomfits the dilettante Syson. It is of crucial significance that Hilda tells the latter, the man "doesn't matter so much. . . . It is one's self that matters . . . whether one is being one's own self and serving one's own God."

Lawrence on sex

As sexual relations were continually his subject, and his very next novel, *The Rainbow* (1915), was condemned in a police court as an obscene book, something must be said here on Lawrence's attitude to sexual questions. To him, not only was sex the way woman fulfils her being and man one of his chief creative functions, for which reason he always extolled marriage, but the sexual experience was also a door to new realms of consciousness, an initiation into divine mysteries, the mystery of the other world that is close beside us. He says in this novel, of Lydia and Tom Brangwen's coming together again after a period of estrangement, "It was the entry into another circle of existence, it was the baptism to another life, it was the complete confirmation. Their feet trod strange ground of knowledge, their footsteps were lit up with dis-

coincided exactly with orthodox Freudism, and became more and more peculiar to himself. Herr Hoops finds his *Lebensanschauungen* most completely and most artistically exhibited in *The Plumed Serpent* (1926).

[1] "Es ergibt sich somit, dass *Sons and Lovers* der erste psychoanalytisch beeinflusste Roman in der englischen Literatur ist" (Hoops, 73).

covery." [1] "And always the light of the transfiguration burned on in their hearts. He went his way, as before, she went her way, to the rest of the world there seemed no change." But God had taken up His abode with them. "Now He was declared to Brangwen and to Lydia Brangwen, as they stood together." Lawrence insisted on the sacred nature of sex, on the religious element in its consummation. He was by no means the voluptuary that he is sometimes depicted: "No one was less a sensualist," says one of his harshest critics,[2] he always lived on the spiritual level. He had not the remotest intention, in writing *The Rainbow*, of shocking the puritanical or truckling to the prurient. He and "Miriam" had read Hardy's novels together, and discussed *Tess of the D'Urbervilles*; and, so far, he had not claimed more freedom than was exercised there in the handling of such situations. Hence he was dumbfounded, nonplussed. It seemed to him monstrous that "a serious and profound piece of work" like *The Rainbow* should be suppressed.[3] It sounds a paradox to many to call Lawrence a puritan, but it is the truth. In the *Fantasia of the Unconscious*, he carefully distinguishes between the lower and the higher planes of being and consciousness, the sensual and the spiritual [4]; and both here and in his novels it is on the spiritual significance of sex that he lays his emphasis. He condemns those like Oscar Wilde and Maupassant who, in the Epicurean spirit, "embrace feeling" and make themselves martyrs to it. "When man loses his deep sense of purposive, creative activity, he feels lost, and is lost. When he makes the sexual consummation the supreme consummation, even in his *secret* soul, he falls into the beginnings of despair." "With sex as the one accepted prime motive, the world drifts into despair and anarchy." [5]

[1] In his introduction to Lawrence's *Letters*, Aldous Huxley compares him with Kierkegaard, quoting from the latter, "And God the Father, the Inscrutable, the Unknowable, we know in the flesh, in Woman. She is the door for our in-going and our out-coming. In her we go back to the Father; but like the witnesses of the transfiguration, blind and unconscious; otherwise it is a revelation, not of divine otherness, but of very human evil" (*Letters*, xii).

[2] *After Strange Gods*, by T. S. Eliot, 60. Contrast this with the malice of Wyndham Lewis's characterization of *Sons and Lovers*: "The book is an eloquent, wallowing mass of Mother-love and Sex-idolatry" (*Paleface*, 180). "Women in Love is again the same thick, sentimental stew" (*Ibid.*).

[3] *Letters*, 387.

[4] Chap. iv.

[5] Chap. ix.

"The psycho-analysts, driving us back to the sexual consummation always, do us infinite damage." His books are full of his hatred of animality; *Sea and Sardinia*, for instance, continually waxes violent with his outbursts of revolt. *The Rainbow* was condemned, and Lawrence was subjected to a contemptible persecution, really because he had married a German and inveighed against war as a "method of barbarism."[1] When he wrote *Lady Chatterley's Lover*, the suppression of which may well be defended, he had gone through a lifetime of abuse and interdiction; and it is easy to understand how he was driven at last to let himself go. That book, as he wrote it, may be regarded as an indiscretion into which he was goaded by his scorn for the prurient who posed to the world and themselves as the moralists.[2] And yet its frankness and downrightness were a token of Lawrence's honesty. Having been charged with all sorts of personal depravity and with wilfully trying to demoralize his readers, charges that simply bewildered him, he turned on his enemies and showed them what their rash statements really amounted to. All he had done hitherto was to set down what he meant without beating about the bush, but with none of the alluring accompaniments of the average sentimental novel. He flung back in their faces their own dirty words, the unequivocal expressions they had been asking for and pretended to have blushed at. It was his translation of the gospel into their own vernacular.[3]

[1] "They can say all they like about 'obscenity,' but you and I know in our bones that the real reason for the attack was that he denounced War. And you [Frieda] were German, so of course Lawrence was plotting to bring the Prussian Guards into Cornwall in submarines" (Richard Aldington: introduction to *Apocalypse*, 1932). See also Maurois (p. 309), "Qui ne comprend pas que l'essence même de Lawrence, c'est un respect religieux pour la vie sexuelle, ne comprend rien à Lawrence."

[2] To the prurient all things are prurient. One critic posing as a psychologist and alienist collected his reviews in a book, and in the chapter on Lawrence catalogued all the passages describing what he called "amorous love" that had "irritated" him, thus providing a handy guide for lubricious readers.

[3] Lawrence did not say that he wrote like this to out-Herod Herod; possibly, he did not analyse his motives so far. He told Rolf Gardiner that it was "a phallic novel: a delicate and tender phallic novel," and "strictly a novel of the phallic consciousness as against the mental consciousness of to-day." "I've got to sell it too: for I've got to live" (*Letters*, 713). "S'il n'a pas voulu précisément 'épater les bourgeois,' dans son for intérieur il défiait les pouvoirs qui l'avaient insulté jadis, en condamnant, pour de moindres offenses son *Rainbow*: 'Vous n'aimez pas cela? Vous allez voir pis!'" (De Reul, 146).

"*The Rainbow*"

The same half-industrialized region furnishes the scenes of *The Rainbow* (1915), in which the chequered histories of three pairs of love-makers, of three generations, only approximate to the perfect unity of two in one, the dark and the light, symbolized by the rainbow. In this and the belated sequel, *Women in Love* (1921), there is a certain variety in the character-drawing; or, to put it more accurately, character is shown in some diversity of situation, nurture, and development. For it is human character rather than characters that interests Lawrence; he disapproves of the established fashion of novel-writing, "which causes one to conceive a character in a certain moral scheme and make him consistent. The certain moral scheme is what I object to. In Turgenev, and in Tolstoi, and in Dostoievsky, the moral scheme into which all the characters fit . . . is, whatever the extraordinariness of the characters themselves, dull, old, dead." [1] He would go deeper, to the elements of human being, to the essence of the ego, which may pass through, "as it were, allotropic states," which may require a deeper sense than we are used to exercise to recognize as states "of the same radically unchanged element." In these two novels, Lawrence's impressions of people do stamp with a certain measure of individuality a certain number of the characters, and a certain sarcastic insight is as effective as the sense of humour of the classic novelists in accentuating individual traits and giving dramatic force to the clash of temperaments. But here, far more than in the classic novelists, it is the impulses and weaknesses of human nature in general that are shown active in these various selves, with their intimate feelings and reactions, not very different from those of other human beings. This it is that makes them apt exponents of a fundamental antagonism, no less apt if inclined to give way, in the strife between man and woman—a strife in which there is no such thing as submission, only subjection on one part or the other. The Brangwens are farmers long established in the strip of arable land remaining on the county border near Ilkeston. The one in possession, somewhere about 1840, marries Lydia Lensky,

[1] See his letter to Edward Garnett and Aldous Huxley's remarks thereon (*Letters*, Introduction, xxi–xxii).

a Polish widow, whose wider experience of the classes, due to her foreign origin and sharper experience of the different ranges of people in the world, makes her a piquant contrast to the rough yeoman. He is thrilled by her foreignness; and the conjunction has humorous aspects, which however are irrelevant in Lawrence's reading of the case. Tom is a primitive, a man of instinct, who had been a dolt at school, and does not aspire to be much else. Yet he has a strong inner life, and is vehemently conscious of all the unknown things going on around him. A meeting with a stranger, apparently a foreigner, makes him wonder, "What was there outside his knowledge, how much? . . . what did everything mean? Where was life, in that which he knew or all outside him?" Five years later, he finds himself married to the exile's widow. They settle down in the equilibrium of physical intimacy, and he and she seem to have found fulfilment. But each of us is separate and distinct; each of the pair is conscious of latent antagonisms: "Such intimacy of embrace, and such utter foreignness of contact!" For a long while, Tom is bewildered, desperate, "plunged in a revolt that knew no bounds." Then they come together again, after two years of married life, and it is more wonderful than at the beginning. He did not understand her foreign nature; but what did it matter? What was her dead husband to him "but an unfulfilled possibility to which he, Brangwen, was the reality and the fulfilment"? "God was her father and her mother. He had passed through the married pair without making Himself fully known to them." The love and married life of his foster-child Anna Lensky and his cousin Will Brangwen are the same thing, subtly differenced by the more complicated nature of Anna and the religious mysticism and æsthetic interests of Will, which she cannot share. They are thrown together at the farm, and mere physical contact is enough to convince them that they must be married. The world is transfigured for both of them. To Will, as he passes under the bridge on the dull canal to the collieries, "the evening glowed in its last deep colours, the sky was dark blue, the stars glittered from afar, very remote and approaching above the darkening cluster of the farm, above the paths of crystal along the edge of the heavens." When they met, "he dared not lift his face to look at her." There follows an exquisite idyll, their mutual, impulsive avowal, as they are gathering the sheaves together under the harvest moon. But the young believer, the artist, the Ruskinian, takes Anna to Lincoln cathedral. He sees divine infinity in the soaring arches [1]; she notices only the mocking faces of the imps. But when she has outraged his poetic soul and pooh-poohed his Adam and Eve, constraining him to burn his cherished bit of sculpture, she relents and is chastened in spirit, so that "a new, fragile flame of love came out of the ashes." It flashes on him that sceptical, practical, instinctive Anna was "like a running stream." He is in love with her again. A beautiful interlude in their married life is Anna's dancing before the mirror in her pregnancy—a scene that was one of the chief counts against the book in the famous prosecution which resulted in its being suppressed. Both these pairs achieve, if not a consummation, at least some measure of equilibrium, if only a compromise. Lovers want complete absorption, but the other self resists. It is usually the woman that resists; they must have their inner life. But Anna and Will, after their clashes, agree to live and let live. "She had conquered, really. . . . She and the baby and himself, they were one." "The passionate sense of fulfilment, of the future germinated in her, made her vivid and powerful." And "little by little, as she learned to love him better, she would put herself aside, and when she felt one of his fits upon him, would ignore him, successfully leave him in his world, whilst she remained in her own." Less fortunate is the third love-ordeal, of Anna and Will's child Ursula and the young officer Anton Skrebensky, son of an exiled Pole. The fault is Ursula's, though she is morally Anton's superior, for she is uncompromising; she thinks that the one thing that matters is—"It matters whether people have courage or not." She flings herself at his head, and then realizes that she was not truly in love.

[1] But he cannot escape Lawrence's metaphors from the process of procreation. "His soul leapt up into the gloom, into possession, it reeled, it swooned with a great escape, it quivered in the womb, in the rush and the gloom of fecundity, like seed of procreation in ecstasy."

"She knew that Skrebensky had never become finally real. In the weeks of passionate ecstasy he had been with her in her desire; she had created him for the time being. But in the end he had failed and broken down." So, after the wild spasms and the rapture of surrender, they separate, and he marries a commonplace girl, leaving Ursula to vision hope in the rainbow. It is Ibsen's doctrine—or that of Nietzsche—of the self: Anna apprehends at last by instinct what it is her soul is in quest of—her self. But most are "separate people with separate destinies. Why should they seek to lay violent hands of claim on the other?"

A sequel to "The Rainbow"

The proscription of *The Rainbow* was a serious mishap to Lawrence, and with the depression of spirit caused by the War and his persecution by the military authorities accounts for a long period of comparative silence. Publishers were chary of accepting anything from the author of a prohibited book, and he would not compromise with the enemy; on the contrary, he was ready at any moment for a violent counter-attack. For a long while he and Frieda were living from hand to mouth, in Italy and then across the Atlantic, looking for the earthly paradise they never found, whilst he wrote spasmodically. He actually finished his sequel, *Women in Love*, in 1916, but could not get it published till 1921, a year after *The Lost Girl.* The alternative title, "Day of Wrath,"[1] which he suggested to the publisher, Secker, would have been appropriate to the circumstances under which the book was produced, with a quotation from the *Dies Iræ* for the motto. But it would no doubt have been interpreted too sweepingly as referring to the disasters that fall in the end on such as Gerald, the "born lover," as Lawrence in the person of Birkin calls him, though he is at bottom the typical egoist and exploiter of men as well as women. Gerald is one of the ruthless captains of industry and pillars of a standardized society that Lawrence's soul abhorred. When he enters the paternal firm, he seems to be possessed by a furious and destructive demon; he gets rid of the grey old clerks, removing them as so much lumber, to make room for efficient successors. Business

[1] *Letters*, 507.

man, soldier, explorer, sportsman, he acquits himself in all these roles with the same efficiency. But to Lawrence he stands, not for life, but for death, and his violent end in a winter accident in the Alps is evidently symbolical. There are a quaternion of lovers, Gudrun and Gerald, Ursula and Birkin, two of the Brangwen sisters, that is, in new relations. Gudrun is alleged to be an unkind portrait of Katherine Mansfield.[1] Lawrence projected himself this time into Birkin; and, if he did not mean Ursula to be a direct likeness of Frieda, he certainly tried to express the deep and tolerant affection between them. But to begin with, he, or at any rate Birkin, has to get rid of another person who is said to be drawn from the flesh, Lady Hermione, wealthy patroness of the arts and fulsome manifestation of intellectual snobbery, believed to be an ill-natured fling at Lady Ottoline Morrell, to whom many of Lawrence's most thoughtful letters were addressed in the early years of the War. He eliminates Birkin's "spiritual bride," as Ursula calls her, in a way that would hardly have occurred to a man with much sense of humour. One day, she is so sore at the muteness of Birkin, who has been bored by her political guests and the glib enunciation of views very different from those of himself or of Lawrence, that she picks up a heavy paper-weight and nearly stuns him by dropping it on his head, as he sits reading Thucydides. After this, there could not be much further amity between them. But even Ursula finds it hard to see eye to eye with Birkin, who is certainly fond of laying down the law, on the recondite nature of love, for instance. Ursula admits to Gudrun that he is "too much of a preacher. He is really a priest." He tells her that there is "a final me, which is stark and impersonal and beyond responsibility. So there is a final you." He wants to meet her, "not in the emotional, loving plane, but there beyond, where there is no speech and no terms of agreement." She was a woman who wanted to be "made much of, to be adored." Gudrun is satisfied to have given herself one feverish night to Gerald; she would never marry him. Birkin

[1] If a portrait of Katherine, she is "a singularly fantastic one," writes Middleton Murry (*Reminiscences of Lawrence*, 95).

congratulates himself on being fit to unite with such a woman as Ursula. To him their marriage was "his resurrection and his life." And yet there were "infinite distances of silence between them": they are happy, but Ursula feels that their bliss is not yet complete. She has to be satisfied with being loved. Birkin tells her that he can live all his life with her; but he adds, "to make it complete, really happy, I wanted eternal union with a man too—another kind of love." It is not altogether easy to understand why Lawrence liked this best of all his books.[1] At all events, it is a good theoretic example of his method, or rather of the penetrating instinct that at once seizes the inner consciousness of everyone. The characters are presented, as it were, from the inside, but without any laborious analysis. They are minds and feelings to begin with, instead of the visible personalities that have to be laid bare by such a process. Inner mind seems to respond directly to inner mind, outer circumstances having then to fall into due subordination. It is not quite so difficult to comprehend why he told Garnett, in one of many letters elatedly heralding this particular novel, that it might be found good by "the Meredithy public."[2] But, if he meant any close comparison with the poetic comedy of the great panegyrist of "brain-stuff," he was certainly still more wrong. He might as well have compared the *Fantasia of the Unconscious* with the *Essay on Comedy*.

"*The Lost Girl*"

Lawrence wrote *The Lost Girl* (1920) in Italy. He wanted to rehabilitate himself at Mudie's, and thought it was unexceptionable from their point of view, though he made no bones about altering one page to which the libraries objected.[3] A full-blooded Lawrentian novel was hardly to be expected under the general circumstances. In fact, whether he did or did not thus take virtue out of it, the book turned out after all the labour and worry only a cross between genuine Lawrence and the regular novel of manners. This is probably the only novel in which he tried to write like Dickens, as he did in the characterization of Miss Frost, his heroine Alvina's maternal,

[1] He confesses this in a latter to Douglas Goldring (*Letters*, 514).

[2] *Ibid.*, 105.

[3] "Quite passable, from Mudie's point of view" (*Letters*, 504). He calmly puts it, with regard to one disturbing passage, "So it had to be altered" (*Ibid.*, 510).

bespectacled governess, of Miss Pinnegar, her father's devoted secretary, and that benevolent old man of business himself. It opens in the same mining district as had now become familiar from the other novels. Alvina perturbs her father by wanting to carve out for herself an independent career. But she goes to Italy and promptly falls in love with the peasant Cicio, an example physically of the Italian who is "attractive, supple, and beautiful," such as had been depicted in *Twilight in Italy* (1916), but only a vivacious animal who had formerly got his living as an artist's model. But she quits him, and returns to England, and in an interlude less Lawrentian than Tolstoyan works as maternity nurse in a hospital, refuses the offer of the visiting physician, and goes out to Italy again to confront the risks of marriage with Cicio.

"*Aaron's Rod*"

Lawrence says in *Kangaroo*, "Now a novel is supposed to be a mere record of emotion-adventures, flounderings in feelings. We insist that a novel is, or should be, also a thought-adventure, if it is to be anything at all complete." He took up again his authentic mission in *Aaron's Rod* (1922), a book that shows by the grace of the narrative and the beauty of the descriptive passages the tranquillizing results of his sojourn in Italy. It sets out the problems that obsessed him, if not their final solutions, in the life of a common man. He had tried to formulate and solve them in the orthodox logical way in two small volumes, *Psychoanalysis and the Unconscious* and the more elaborate *Fantasia of the Unconscious*, both to be published the same year. They had emerged from his random musings, and had been stated with all the clarity at his command, in one of the most charming chronicles of his meditative wanderings, *Twilight in Italy* (1916). But the parabolic or symbolical method was to prove fairly apposite to doctrines that were mystical in basis. The urgent problem at the moment was to find some issue from the chaos of disintegrating principles and incoherent ideas and ideals after the War, when everything seemed to be in a state of revolution and there was no terminus in sight. Both Aaron Sisson the miner and his friend and mentor Lilly are in their several ways exponents of Lawrence's craving for self-fulfilment and his maturing forecast of a direction and a goal. Tired of giving in to his wife, sexually in chief, Aaron leaves her and the little ones, and, earning enough to keep going with his flute, crosses the Alps into Italy, where he joins forces with Lilly, and they talk and talk, and Aaron does at last establish "self-responsibility, aloneness." Lilly instructs him in the theory of the new life, in which or to which women must submit with full and hearty acceptance. "Give thyself, but do not give thyself away." Better "the deep, fathomless submission to the heroic soul in a greater man." Here there is a hint of Lawrence's later trend towards the totalitarian creed, or at least the gospel of the leader, the superman. Some of Lawrence's expositors have interpreted it that Lilly was urging tenderer bonds of affection between man and man. When Aaron crossed into Italy, it was as if he had passed a barrier in time as well as in space. Lawrence displays his wonderful descriptive magic in evoking mountains and glaciers, lakes and glints of distant seas, towns hardly less beautiful than nature, all without the least effort at the grandiose. Then Aaron is a troubled spectator of the street-fighting during the revolution. It is the same thing on the larger scale as the blindness and helplessness of the individual man in his struggle to discover his function in life and fulfil it. Things have moved on since Lawrence quietly considered his problems in *Twilight in Italy*, and congratulated the Italian on having held aloof from Northern industrialism and found "the absolute, the god-like" in the senses, the consummation of man "in the Self and in Selflessness."

By great retrogression back to the source of darkness in me, the Self, deep in the senses, I arrive at the Original, Creative Infinite. By projection forth from myself, by the elimination of my absolute sensual self, I arrive at the Ultimate Infinite, Oneness in the Spirit. They are two Infinites, twofold approach to God. And man must know both.

He had repudiated "synthetic love" between men and women: "there is only passion, and passion is fundamental hatred, the act of love is a fight." He seemed to make those discoveries of his, in *Twilight in Italy*, in a state bordering upon semiconsciousness—in a twilight, indeed. But, though he says in *Fantasia of the Unconscious*, "I don't like mysticism,"[1] he is perhaps less cryptic to minds that boggle at abstractions in such a parable as this, characteristic of his style in *Aaron's Rod*:

"You are your own Tree of Life, roots and limbs and trunk. Somewhere within the wholeness of the tree lies the very self, the quick; its own innate Holy Ghost. And this Holy Ghost puts forth new buds, and pushes past all limits, and shakes off a whole body of dying leaves. And the old limits hate being empassed, and the old leaves hate to fall. But they must, if the tree-soul say so."

"Fantasia of the Unconscious"

As Lawrence declared that the theories set forth in his *Fantasia of the Unconscious* (1922) were deduced from his novels and poems, this little book may be taken as a vade-mecum to the personal philosophy underlying these. Written in 1920, as a recast of or a supplement to the shorter *Psychoanalysis and the Unconscious*, it has been pronounced by Middleton Murry his greatest book, and by such a severe critic as T. S. Eliot "a criticism of the modern world to be read and re-read." Yet it is a work that may well discomfit the reader who looks in it for clear and straightforward reasoning. Lawrence was well aware of his failings on the intellectual and logical side, though he was apt at any moment to hazard an argument in general terms and regard it as clinching.[2] He repudiated modern science as vehemently as he inveighed against our "technical civilization": "Our science is a science of the dead world. Even biology never considers life, but only mechanistic functioning and apparatus of life." Modestly admitting that he is not even a scholar, though he has found hints in scholarly books, from the Yoga and Plato down to Freud and Frobenius, only hints, however, he says he proceeds by intuition, and is well content to describe his effort as "pseudo-philosophy" or "pollyanalytics," which some may regard as "a wordy mass of revolting nonsense." His main object is to rebut Freud, who attributes a sexual motive to all human activities. And he

[1] Introduction.

[2] Thus a seasonable and well-meaning article, "Pornography and Obscenity" (*Phœnix*, 170–187), is woefully muddled and self-contradictory, though it is often cited by admiring critics as a piece of holy writ.

lays it down at once that "the essentially religious or creative motive is the first motive of all human activity." The sexual motive comes second. And there is a great conflict between the interests of the two, at all times. We are ignorant of the origin of life and the goal of death. It is a good thing that the First Cause is to us unknowable. But he admits almost with shame that he believes in the souls of the dead, and even that they somehow re-enter the souls of the living, however much he dislikes mysticism.[1] There ensues a long discursus on the plexuses and ganglions, which purports to show that these bodily organs, usually ranked as inferior, are centres of knowing and being as important as the brain, or more so. The object is to prove that "the vast bulk of consciousness is non-cerebral."[2] He is willing to concede that there are two planes of being and consciousness, the sensual and the spiritual. Thought is instrumental only, "just a means to action and living," life and action taking their rise "actually at the great centres of dynamic consciousness." The aim of education should not be mental consciousness: "We want *effectual* human beings, not conscious ones." He would shut up all schools at once, and let humanity lie fallow, "for two generations at least." What requires education, leading out, is our "pre-mental, non-mental" consciousness, the dynamic consciousness. "Sex is a vital polarity"; wherefore it is advisable to keep boys and girls apart as much as possible, and initiate them later with the utmost care into a right understanding of so dangerous a matter. Sex must be "subordinated to the great dominating male passion of *collective* purpose. When it is accepted as the one prime motive, the world drifts into despair and anarchy." Lawrence attacks some views that Freud never advanced; but at any rate he rejects the Freudian theory of dreams and their sexual interpretation, deriding in particular the idea that incestuous desires lie at the root of neuroses and

[1] Hence his lyrical digression on the Sun as "materially composed of all the effluence of the dead"—"to the Sun fly the vibrations of the molecules in the great sympathy-mode of death, and in the Sun they are renewed," etc., etc. "The Sun's quick is polarized in dynamic relation with the quick of life in all living things" (*Fantasia*, xiii, "Cosmological").

[2] *Psychoanalysis and the Unconscious*, iii, "The Birth of Consciousness."

insanities. He will have nothing to do with the doctrine of repressed desires and their sublimation when brought into the light of full consciousness. Love must be subordinated to the great purposive passion, "and no great purposive passion" or motive, ideal, or social principle, "can endure for any length of time unless based on the sexual fulfilment of the vast majority of individuals concerned." On the other hand, "assert sex as the predominant fulfilment, and you get the collapse of living purpose in man. You get anarchy." We talk continually about self-preservation as our great object in life, implying, as he put it in his study of Thomas Hardy, "that this struggle for the means of life is the essence and whole of life." "As if it would be anything so futile, so ingestive!" [1] The object of life is the achievement of oneself. If we secure not that, "then the remainder that we do possess will be taken away from us." "Life and action take rise actually at the great centres of dynamic consciousness"; this is not, like mental consciousness, static. He told Lady Ottoline Morrell that it is better to lapse back into the unconscious self—"Only then you will act straight from the dark source of life, outwards, which is creative life." [2] And he told Katherine Mansfield, "We must grow from our deepest underground roots, out of the *unconscious*, not from the conscious concepts which we falsely call ourselves." [3] Aldous Huxley quotes him as saying, "My great religion is a belief in the blood, the flesh, as being wiser than the intellect." [4] To think and feel in unison with this primal consciousness is to have creative imagination, though Lawrence seems sedulously to shun that familiar word. He is very explicit on the various levels of consciousness, in *The Boy in the Bush*, especially on that higher level on which the soul in its entirety is "conscious, super-conscious, far beyond mentality." "Man's divinity and his ultimate power is in this super-consciousness of the whole soul . . . not in

[1] *Phœnix*, 404. [2] *Letters*, 286. [3] *Ibid.*, 290.

[4] Introduction to the *Letters*, xiv. See also the editor's penetrating comparison with Wordsworth's awareness of "unknown modes of being" (xi), and the admirable account of Lawrence's sense of the "divine otherness" lying beyond the borders of man's conscious mind (xii). In the sexual experience, "the immediate, non-mental knowledge of divine otherness is brought, so to speak, to a focus—a focus of darkness." Hence his preoccupation with the subject of sex.

skill or intelligence alone, but in the soul's extreme power of knowing and then willing."

Two Australian novels

Lawrence and Frieda were in Australia in 1922, before going to Taos in New Mexico, whither his admirer, the rich American, Mabel Dodge, who was living with the Indian Luhan, had long been trying to persuade him to come. The result of his sojourn and his talks and meditations was the novel *Kangaroo* (1923), and also another, *The Boy in the Bush* (1924), originally written by Miss M. L. Skinner, which, recognizing that it had "good stuff" in it, he took and completely transformed. *Kangaroo* is his closest approximation to the contemporary discussion-novel, consisting largely of long-winded talks and reveries on life and the present state of the civilized world; a "thought-adventure" he called it. Lawrence is to be recognized in the Englishman R. L. Somers, who comes to Australia with his wife, and is all but captured by the revolutionary Australianism of the self-appointed liberator Kangaroo. Already in the *Fantasia* he had urged that social salvation could come only from "a higher, responsible, conscious class," the masses being swayed by such knowledge as is "symbolical, mythical, dynamic." Mankind is craving for leadership. "But men must be prepared to obey, body and soul, once they have chosen the leader." Watching a flight of birds swirling up with one accord from the water, Somers asks himself whether some sort of telepathy is not the clue to all herd instinct. The mass is "driven, goaded mad," by the pricking of some god-urge that it cannot interpret. Both Capital and Labour see the situation as clear as daylight. But it is this "god-urge" that drives them mad, "the bot-fly of the Holy Ghost, unlistened to, that is the real cause of everything." A dark, mysterious God hovers behind the human conflict, and the victory is with those who can seize and identify themselves with this dark master of human destiny. But Somers shrinks from the thought of this dark God even when he has declared his adhesion. "He shrank from the effort." He is too like his creator, no man of action, though it has been argued by some that his failure to throw in his lot with Kangaroo, who presently dies, was a characteristic result of a divided mind in Lawrence himself, who was certainly not cut out to be either a leader of men or a submissive follower. The Lawrences stayed most of the time in an Arcadian spot in New South Wales; their ephemeral discords and occasional quarrels are presumably reflected in the inability of the Somers couple to understand each other completely. At all events, Lawrence was in love with the land that "as yet has made no great mistake, humanly"; and the Australian scene has never been painted more magically or the mentality of the people more admirably summed up. And yet *The Boy in the Bush* (1924), which he only rewrote, is a more Lawrentian book than *Kangaroo*, which is all his own; as if, with the story already given, he only had to put himself into it, himself or the dark God which he salutes as the Holy Ghost. Meredith saw in man's nature a trinity—blood, brain, and spirit. Lawrence disregards the two latter elements, and sees man as nature, instinct, a secret soul, by discovering and obeying which he who is strong enough to free himself from the meaningless shackles of society as it is may grow into a free agent. This is what Jack Grant succeeds in doing. Miss Skinner apparently contributed the rich and intimate knowledge of unkempt life in Western Australia, and probably gave accuracy to the singularly coarse and brutal dialect; Lawrence would never have objected. Jack is sent out by his people after he has come a cropper at school. He is the right stuff for the rough existence in front of him, and for the self-development which is the main thesis. He finds himself in a family of distant connexions, among whom there are some he takes to, some that he instinctively hates. Easu, for instance, against whom he is thrown in instinctive antagonism, personifies the evil forces which it is his congenital impulse to combat. Jack fights Easu, now getting the better of him and now the worse; in the end it becomes a life-and-death struggle and Jack kills him, in self-defence against a murderous attack. Easu seduces the girl whom Jack loves in his peculiar way; Jack marries her and fathers the child. But this is no mere love-story. One of the few persons in Australia who see the inwardness of things is the old grandmother, who tells him, tenderly enough, "Ye're a bundle of conventions, like y'r granfather. . . . Folks are tough in Australia, tough as whit-leather. Y'll be tempted to sin, but y' won't be tempted to condemn. . . . Trust yourself, Jack Grant. Earn a good opinion of yourself, and never mind other folks. You've only got to live once. You know when your spirit glows—trust that. That's you! That's the spirit of God in you." But the spirit of God is without, as well as within. "It seemed to Jack this sound in the bush"—of the mocking-bird—"was like God. Like the call of the heroic soul seeking its body . . . sounding through the immense dead spaces of the dim, open bush, strange and heroic and inhuman." He makes good right enough. He feels himself entering a new grey-blue paradise, in the bush, a paradise "where man has to begin all over again," if it was a human way of life at all that he wanted. But Jack's must be a lonely kind of individualism; he is half-consciously aiming to be a sort of superman. "A certain real amiability in him, and a natural kindly disposition towards his fellow-men, combated inside him with a repudiation of the whole trend of modern human life, the emotional, spiritual, ethical, and intellectual trend. . . . Casually, he could get on with anybody. Intimately, he could get on with nobody. . . . Therefore it was his friends who suffered most from him." It is not with human beings at all, but with those creatures that are nearer the original source of life, that he has real fellowship, with the bright bay stallion, for instance, with which he harmonized so that they made a sort of centaur. The primitive man wants to live primitive, like Abraham in the wilderness, with his wives and children around him. He wanted "a little world" of his own, in the north-west.

"A little world of my own. . . . And my children growing up like a new race on the face of the earth, with a new creed of courage and sensual pride, and the black wonder of the halls of death ahead, and the call to be lords of death, on earth. . . . A little world of my own! As if I could make it with the people that are on earth to-day! No, no, I can do nothing but stand alone! And then, when I die, I shall not drop like carrion on the earth's earth, I shall be a lord of death, and sway the destinies of the life to come." Nietzsche's individualism has developed into a mysticism which is Lawrence's own. Jack is not one of the tame dogs who are put into the earth as carrion, but one of the wild, untamed souls that walk on "over the border into the porch of death, to be lords of death and masters of the next living." He is realizing the spiritual body which men like Easu know and hate, Easu who typifies "the natural body fiendishly subjugating the spiritual body."

"Man is like this. He has various levels of consciousness. When he is broken, killed at one level of consciousness, his very death leaves him on a higher level. And this is the soul in its entirety, being conscious, super-conscious, far beyond mentality. It hardly needs eyes or ears. It is clairvoyant and clairaudient. And man's divinity, and his ultimate power, is in this super-consciousness of the whole soul. Not in brute force, not in skill or intelligence alone, but in the soul's extreme power of knowing and then willing. On this alone hangs the destiny of all mankind."

Shorter stories

The Lawrences sailed from Australia in August and reached Taos in September, 1922, after a brief stay in San Francisco. Lawrence had two sets of stories ready for publication, most if not all rewritten after they had appeared in various magazines. Three of medium length were included in *The Ladybird, The Fox, The Captain's Doll* (1923); and ten short ones in *England, my England* (1924); *St Mawr, together with The Princess* (1925), he wrote at Taos, like all or most of those in *The Woman who Rode Away, and other stories* (1928). It was often very wholesome for Lawrence to be kept compulsorily within the limits of a magazine story, to be denied too much freedom to pour himself out in afterthought and wider speculation. He gained in incisiveness and perfect relevance and consistency, without any serious self-suppression. Both *The Ladybird* and the two stories annexed demonstrate compellingly his insight into dark tracts of consciousness. The Bohemian count, though he may be only a transfiguration of Lawrence himself, touched as it were by the great god Pan, and the thrilled society woman who yields to the mysterious call, the infernal witchery, of a deeper world than that of her old conventional self and her solid English husband, are not easy to forget; they have a glamour, they cast a spell. The other two stories are of the incalculable elemental impulses aroused by sensual contacts. The soldier-boy in "The Fox" kills a woman by a calculated accident, out of some unconscious hate or homicidal urge. The older woman responds to some occult lure in the boy, who is otherwise her natural antipathy. But the only character here having very distinct lineaments is March, his girl; in whom, however, the chief interest attaches to her inscrutable shynesses and repulsions and her paralysis of nerves in the presence of the fox or the foxy man. In "The Captain's Doll," the comedy of women's submission to the sheer masterfulness of the other sex is rendered picturesque by the quaint position of the countess and the baroness reduced to earning their living by making rag dolls. The irony is summed up in the doll made by Countess Hannele in the likeness of her Scottish suitor, who in marriage requires a patient Griselda, a woman to honour and obey him, love being a negligible consideration. Several of the ten tales in *England, my England*, are glimpses into the deeper being of the really live man, who has that "sheer immediacy of blood-contact with the substantial world" which Lawrence holds to be essential for happiness. Thus "The Blind Man" who lost his sight in the War finds a richer intimacy with those whose nature is not superficial, and a happiness he never had before. The raciest are tales of those homely people in the Midlands among whom he grew up, and there are glints of humour in the divers modes in which sex makes its appeal, as in "You Touched Me," "Samson and Delilah," or "Fannie and Annie." "Tickets, Please," gives the comedy of manners and the off-and-on sweethearting of the stalwart girls who ride to the works on an antediluvian tram-line; and "Monkey Nuts," a tale of land-girls and Tommies, has a characteristic sketch of the woman who throws the handkerchief—which in this case is not picked up by the chosen boy.

Lawrence kept harping now on the same favourite string, the strength and rightness to be derived from the pre-mental,

"St Mawr" and "The Princess"

the dark founts of a life that is really creative.[1] In St Mawr a wife perceives a strength that is grotesquely lacking in her husband. St Mawr is a horse, a very real horse, and also a symbol. To the two women whose feelings and inmost yearnings are the whole matter of the story, he stands for the wild, untamed life of natural things that is in irreconcilable opposition to the domesticated existence of men to-day, men who are not really alive. To talk about the mere animal in man is absurd. "You say they are too animal," says the ennuyée American, married to the English baronet who paints and would like to be something more than a dilettante. "It's the animal in them has gone perverse, or cringing, or humble, or domesticated, like dogs. I don't know one single man who is a proud living animal. But then, men always do leave off really thinking when the last bit of wild animal dies in them." They persuade the husband against his will to buy St Mawr, and the mettled beast nearly kills him—he had killed two men already. St Mawr has that which Butler called unconscious memory, and something else.

In his dark eye, that looked, with its cloudy brown pupil, a cloud within a dark fire, like a world beyond our world, there was a dark vitality glowing, and within the fire, another sort of wisdom. She felt sure of it, even when he put his ears back, and bared his teeth, and his great eyes came bolting out of his naked horse's head, and she saw demons upon demons in the chaos of his horrid eyes. Why did he seem to her like some living background, into which she wanted to retreat? When he reared his head and neighed from his deep chest, like deep wind-bells resounding, she seemed to hear the echoes of another darker, more spacious, more dangerous, more splendid world than ours. . . . And she wanted to go.

In the process called civilization, men have eliminated such inchoate cravings; hence they have eliminated life. Their

[1] He had told Katherine Mansfield long ago that "we must grow from our deepest underground roots, out of the *unconscious*, not from the conscious concepts which we falsely call ourselves" (*Letters*, 290). This was in 1915, and he added, "Murry irritates me and falsifies me, and I must tell him so"; whence it is no wonder that Middleton Murry derides both *St Mawr* and *The Princess* (*Son of Woman*, 337–338).

fundamental nature has become a ghost; they shrink from it in terror, and are easily satisfied with their half-existence, the precursor of death. "And the horse, is he to go on carrying man forward into this—this gutter? No! Man wisely invents motor-cars and other machines, automobile and locomotive. The horse is superannuated, for man. But, alas! man is even more superannuated, for the horse." Even death has become a matter of routine, now that we have lost our proud individuality, our sense of incessant conflict with the mystery and terror.

Mrs Witt mistrusted death too. She felt she might pass out as a bed of asters passes out in autumn, to mere nothingness. And something in her longed to die, at least, *positively*: to be folded then at last into throbbing wings of mystery, like a hawk that goes to sleep. Not like a thing made into a parcel and put into the last rubbish-heap.

Lawrence's humour is always sarcastic, never genial: he was not a lover of his species, at least as he saw it around him. That scorching humour shows excellently in the scene where Mrs Witt, with her formidable plainness of speech, puts to flight the Dean and his horrified wife. Nor is Mrs Witt's daughter behindhand, with her poor impression of our finished society men, "with their bare faces or their little quotation-mark moustaches" who *are* so tremendously male. Take the fox hunting set. "Like little male motor-cars. Give him a little gas, and start him on the low gear, and away he goes: all his male gear rattling, like a cheap motor-car." After a horse like St Mawr, men are flat and uninteresting, and society repulsive. Mother and daughter end their tour on a ranch in the Arizona mountains, and the pages evoking the scenery are unsurpassed by any descriptive writing in English. The companion story, "The Princess," is also worth reading for its landscape-painting alone—of New Mexico and the Rio Grande canyon, with "far, far off, the blue mountains like a fence of angels on the horizon." The exquisite, fairy-like descendant of legendary Scottish kings, poor but so proud, irritates the Calibans of this sensual world and the "real Mediterranean . . .

to whom the phallic mystery was still the only mystery." But, if you peel everything away from people, "in the middle of everybody there is a green demon that you can't peel away . . . there is a green, upright demon in every man and woman; and this demon is a man's real self, and a woman's real self. It doesn't really care about anybody, it belongs to the demons and the primitive fairies, who never care." And it is this unconscious self that unconsciously consents when she goes off alone with the guide Romero to a remote hut in the Rockies, and in the cold midnight he asks, "You want me to make you warm?" and she says "Yes." Next day, she repulses him, and he holds her captive, confiscating her garments and brutally violating the helpless girl, till she is rescued by the men of the Forest Service, who shoot Romero dead.

"The Plumed Serpent"

But the chief record of his stay in Mexico, the novel that he evolved out of his experiences there as he had evolved *Kangaroo* out of those in Australia, although Lawrence does not figure in it himself even by proxy, and the adventures are those of a woman visiting the country and becoming involved in its political movements, is *The Plumed Serpent* (1926). It is not surpassed even by *The Bible in Spain* or *Eōthen* as a graphic revelation of the spirit of a country and a race. Kate Leslie, who has lost her husband, finds herself thrown up against two leading Mexicans, a political chief of Spanish descent and an Indian general, who are trying to reconstruct society and the State on the basis of a revival of the ancient religion; and after long hesitation throws in her lot with them and stays in Mexico as the general's wife. But that is only a bald summary. It is an exploration of the dark soul of a people, and the history of an attempt to establish a Fascist regime in a country where "the white man, let him bluster as he may, is hollow with misgiving about his own supremacy." In the *Fantasia*, Lawrence had urged that "for the mass of people, knowledge *must* be symbolical, mythical, dynamic. This means that you must have a higher, responsible class; and then in varying degrees the lower classes, varying in their degree of consciousness"[1]; and that "man must be prepared

[1] P. 68.

to obey, body and soul, once they have chosen the leader. And let them choose the leader for life's sake only."[1] It was a similar attempt at the totalitarian idea that he had described in *Kangaroo*.[2] Like him, Kate loathes "the rabble"; she has a "ghastly fear of the rabble; and during the War, nations were nearly all rabble."[3] Kate also experiences that nameless dread which so often visited Lawrence. There was something "for ever gruesome and macabre" in this country of famous revolutions, which "began with *Viva!* but ended always with *Muera!* Death to this, death to the other, it was all death! death! death! as insistent as the Aztec sacrifices." "Why had she come to this high plateau of death?" "She thought again of going back to Europe. But what was the good?" There, "it was all politics or jazzing or slushy mysticism or sordid spiritualism." "She felt she could cry aloud for the unknown gods to put the magic back into her life, and to save her from the dry-rot of the world's sterility." "Give me the mystery and let the world live again for me!" Kate cried in her soul. "And deliver me from man's automatism."

She had thought that each individual had a complete self, a complete soul, an accomplished I. And now she realized as plainly as if she had turned into a new being, that this was not so. Men and women had incomplete selves, made up of bits assembled together and somewhat haphazard. Man was not created ready-made. Men to-day were half-made, and women were half-made. Creatures that existed and functioned with certain regularity, but which ran off into a hopeless jumble of inconsequence.

These were, of course, the thoughts that went through Lawrence's mind during his sojourn in Mexico. It might be objected—and it is a valid criticism—that he came with a mind ready prepared, and hence that his verdict must be discounted. But this is simply saying that he was an experienced traveller, equipped with the knowledge and having

[1] P. 79.

[2] See above, p. 372.

[3] "Kate had known the agony of cold social fear, as if democracy were a huge, huge cold centipede, which, if you resisted it, would dig every claw into you. And the flesh would mortify round every claw" (chap. viii, "Night in the House").

the address for diagnosing the deeper elements of race, perceiving what is like and what different in the aboriginal instincts and in the results of alien culture. His sensitivity to those impulses of human nature which are bound up with the physical part of us gave him a peculiar comprehension of a people like the Mexicans, who are intellectually and spiritually backward. He was convinced that a full and vigorous life for such backward races must be based on religion, and that the religion must be one that they can assimilate. There is one mystery, he contends, but many manifestations of the divine. "The mystery is one mystery," says Ramon Carrasco, the Fascist leader, "but men must see it differently"; and he tells his wife Carlota, "If the real Christ has not been able to save Mexico—and He hasn't—then I am sure, the white Anti-Christ of Charity, and socialism, and politics, and reform, will only succeed in finally destroying her." So he and Cipriano set about restoring the ancient religion, and incarnate themselves as two of the national gods.

"If I want Mexicans to learn the name of Quetzalcoatl, it is because I want them to speak with the tongues of their own blood. I wish the Teutonic world would once more think in terms of Thor and Wotan, and the tree Igdrasil. And I wish the Druidic world would see, honestly, that in the mistletoe is their mystery, and that they themselves are the Tuatha De Danaan, alive, but submerged. And a new Hermes should come back to the Mediterranean, and a new Ashtaroth to Tunis; and Mithras again to Persia, and Brahma unbroken to India, and the oldest of dragons to China. Then I, First Man of Quetzalcoatl, with you, First Man of Huitzilopochtli, and perhaps your wife, First Woman of Itzpapalotl, could we not meet, with sure souls, the other great aristocrats of the world, the First Man of Wotan and the First Woman of Freya, First Lord of Hermes and the Lady of Astarte, the Best-Born of Brahma, and the Son of the Greatest Dragon? I tell you, Cipriano, then the earth might rejoice, when the First Lords of the West met the First Lords of South and East, in the Valley of the Soul."

In this strange novel, compound of poetry and realism,

Lawrence indulges to the full his trust in the pre-rational instincts and his cosmic imagination. He lets Carlota have her say, and also the bishop, both conscientious objectors to a Nazism that drapes itself in a mythology salvaged from prehistoric and barbaric depths. She declares, "It is just the male vanity. . . . Don't you think, Señora, that the beginning and the end of a man is his vanity? Don't you think it was just against this danger that Christ came, to teach men a proper humility? But that is why they hate Christ so much." The bishop, speaking also for the archbishop, recoils from Ramon's plea for a Church that will accept all the Saviours, a "Catholic Church of All the Sons of Men," for "The Saviours are more than one, and let us pray they will still be increased. But God is one God, and the Saviours are the Sons of the One God." Ramon does not wish to quarrel with Rome, or have bloodshed and enmity. "Should there not be peace between the men who strive down their different ways to the God-Mystery?" "Once more desecrate the Altars! Bring in strange idols. Burn the images of our Lord and our Lady, and ask for peace?" falters the poor bishop, who helplessly longs to be left alone. No doubt, he knew that Ramon was essentially a fighter, as Lawrence confesses, in a letter written under the hanging stars in New Mexico at this time, that he himself was—"to wish me peace is bad luck—except the fighter's peace." Lawrence was saying at that very moment, "one just *knows* that all our Pale-face and Hebraic monotheistic insistence is a dead letter—the soul won't answer any more." [1] Kate reluctantly, having married Cipriano, consents to be a goddess, and take her place beside the new Quetzalcoatl and Huitzilopochtli. She feels a little uneasy when she is pressed against the small but strong and assertive body of Cipriano, "with its black currents and storms of desire"; and Lawrence cannot get rid of "the bee in his bonnet," and must stage another of his dramas of attraction and repulsion, with more about the phallic mystery, which has now become mere rigmarole. What with this and the protracted ceremonies and hymns and incantations, and much repetition of the same kind of scene in other conjunctures, the

[1] *Letters*, 604.

book is spun out to at least double its proper length.[1] It is an epitome rather of Lawrence, and his peculiar vision of the boding soul of mankind, than of Mexico. It is fiction striving to actualize such a vision, and doing it by making solid realities transparent to gleams of a vague but ineffable beyond. The very landscapes seem opalescent. So it is with the whole history of this strange adventure. Through it another world is glimpsed, or, rather, the celestial or infernal foundations of this one. As a feat of fantastic creation, a spectacle of exotic, barbaric life, it challenges comparison with *Salammbô*; it is a similar evocation of the splendid and the gruesome. But the relevant comparison is with *Kangaroo*, in which the same sort of inquisitive and speculative visit to a strange country is reported in a recital equally imaginative and suggestive of his personal views of present, past, and future.[2]

"The Woman who Rode Away"

The title-piece of his next collection, *The Woman who Rode Away, and other stories* (1928), was another part of his harvest from Mexico. It is a compact and a more compulsive variant of *The Plumed Serpent*, and one of those masterly tales of his the inner meaning of which is as clear as that of any treatise or tractate. No one was better than Lawrence at a story, when the drift of it coincided tellingly with his cherished convictions.[3] A young Californian, wife of the owner of a silver-mine in Mexico, lured by the spirit of adventure, by curiosity, and by some obscure itch to know the Indians who live afar off in the mountains, sets out on a solitary ride up the great valley. When she is deep in the passes, three Indians accost her, and she accepts them as guides. But presently she finds herself a prisoner in their village. For ages the Indians have been waiting for a white woman to sacrifice to their gods, so that they might regain the supremacy which had been usurped by

[1] Dorothy M. Hoare (*Some Studies in the Modern Novel*, 112) is not convinced of Lawrence's "final impressiveness." He "tries very hard to make us believe that his solution is the final one, but one cannot help suspecting that he is at the same time trying to persuade himself. Ramon, who represents his views best, is really conscious of defeat," *et seq.*

[2] Lawrence's dream of establishing the nucleus of a new life in Mexico came to nothing. Interesting and far from unsympathetic personal reminiscences of this and his rich but incoherent self will be found in *A Poet and Two Painters*, by Knud Merrill (1938).

[3] See comparison of novel and story (Vol. IX, 58–60).

the whites. She is laid on a great flat stone, and slain with due ceremony by the priest. It is an imaginative story which can be read with imaginative assent and no questions asked. But some of the others have a more familiar and realistic setting, and it may be justly objected that Lawrence makes hay of the probabilities when he constrains a set of ladies and gentlemen in ordinary society to expound his mystical ideas and act upon them with unhesitating confidence. In "Glad Ghosts," a little party in a Derbyshire house consciously take it upon themselves to demonstrate his theory of "the unborn body of life hidden within the body of this half-death which we call life." There are two confirmed spiritualists, one of whom is haunted by his dead wife; and Lawrence weaves with gusto and dramatic effect the haunted atmosphere which was now the air that he preferred to breathe. The story is told, it must be acknowledged, with superlative skill, through suggestion and innuendo. It goes off into poetry, but not into any spurious blend of prose and romance. The ghosts are those dead wives who never knew the bodily tenderness that their nature had a right to demand. "She forgot to be flesh and blood while she was alive, and now she can't forgive herself, or the Colonel," says the story-teller's host, of the Colonel's wife. Whatever interpretation is to be placed upon the dream which is the climax, it is more than hinted that the host's wife came in the darkness to the man who tells the tale, and the haunted man's wife to their host. Such trifling improprieties never daunted Lawrence, any more than improbabilities. In "Jimmy and the Desperate Woman" it has to be accepted that the broad-minded editor, with his theoretic views of life, would offer to marry a collier's wife in the West Riding simply because she had sent a strong poem for his magazine and he wanted a wife of "character." But there are sparks of humour in several of these pieces, and some satire may be suspected on the "high-brow" Jimmy. "The Last Laugh"—of Pan at Hampstead—is a flight of imagination from the most commonplace of platforms. On the other hand, "Two Blue Birds," "Smile," and "In Love" are delicate little studies of the interplay of temperament that seem at first entirely outside

Lawrence's orbit. But, as in "Sun," a simple tale of sun-bathing, drawing at the fount of nature, his occult vision is always there at work, strictly fastened upon the essentials. This has a dexterous sting in the tail, for the benefit of the puritanical.

"The Man who Died"

"The Man who Died" (1931), or to give it its first title, "The Escaped Cock," which appeared after Lawrence's death, must be mentioned here, as having some distant relationship with the supernaturalism of *The Plumed Serpent* and some links of thought with "Glad Ghosts." The colonel there exclaims how wonderful it is to be flesh and blood, to be alive, in comparison with being dead "and merely spirit." "Think how ghastly for Jesus, when he was risen and wasn't touchable! How very awful, to have to say *Noli me tangere*." Jesus comes out of the tomb still alive, for he has only been in a swoon, and he is changed altogether in mind. He is worn out and disillusioned; the day of his interference is over, the teacher and the saviour are dead in him. He has arisen into the life of the body: which, too, "has its little life, and beyond that, the greater life." He falls in with a young priestess of Isis, who anoints his wounds and chafes his hands and feet; and in the fragrant and sanctified dusk of the shrine they embrace. Their issue is to be Osiris reborn. There is an accomplished artistry and much incidental beauty in this story, which is executed in a manner learned probably from Flaubert and Pater, but nearer still to the manner of Anatole France, though the sardonic but unaggressive under-meaning is without the mordant wit of this last. It has been repeatedly pointed out that in the initial event Lawrence asserts the same thing as Butler had about the Resurrection.

"Lady Chatterley's Lover"

It must be borne in mind that throughout the greater part of his literary life Lawrence felt he was fighting against time. His physical condition was such that he never had what the assurance companies term a fair expectation of life; and his latter years were an agonizing race, in which he never lost courage, but was more and more aware of all that he had missed which makes for the fullness of man's existence. His novels, dogmatic and assertive as they are on the objects of human effort, were investigations and inquiries rather than confident statements; and the quest was continued in the very last of them, in which one who poses as a detached spectator asks, "Isn't the whole problem of life the slow building up of an integral personality, through the years? living an integrated life?" Lawrence was still struggling to find the meaning of life, and to find himself and his proper function in the world of men. This novel, *Lady Chatterley's Lover* (1929), appeared the year before he died. It was the complete "phallic novel" which he had long contemplated—"a novel of the phallic consciousness as against the mental consciousness of to-day."[1] He believed in the novel as a means of directing "the flow of our sympathetic consciousness"; properly handled, it "can reveal the most secret places of life; for it is in the *passional* secret places of life above all, that the tide of sensitive awareness needs to ebb and flow, cleansing and refreshing."[2] This, like *The Rainbow*, was suppressed by the authorities; as already observed,[3] Lawrence went to extreme lengths in it in spurning those whom he regarded as hypocritical objectors to plain speaking. The book in fact is full of gibes at the hideousness and humbug of so much of our modern world, testifying to "the utter death of the human intuitive faculty"—the squalor of his own old neighbourhood, the streets and shops where "all went ugly, ugly, ugly, followed by the plaster-and-gilt horrors of the cinema, with its wet picture announcements, 'A Woman's Love,' and the new big Primitive chapel, primitive enough in its stark brick and big panes of greenish and raspberry glass in the windows." He satirizes even what he considers some of the fallacies of the educational system, and is in such a mood of discontent that he goes out of his way to be unsympathetic about his namesake C. E. Lawrence — obviously meant when he speaks of "the famous C. E. Florence"—and his "unsatisfactory mysticism." The "ruling class" which he had so often reproached is here represented by his baronet Sir Clifford Chatterley, who may talk sense about "an integrated

[1] *Letters*, 713. [2] *Lady Chatterley's Lover*, chap. ix.
[3] See above, p. 360 and note.

life," but is after all only "a buffoon," panting after "the bitch-goddess, Success," and on the whole inferior even to the mere sensualist Michaelis—"Michaelis was a heroic rat, and Clifford was very much of a poodle showing off." The book must have been put together somewhat hastily; and these satirical passages, which were necessary to make the whole meaning clear, look too much like digressions. The central affair is the history of a woman in this purposeless modern world who, being married to the baronet, a man wounded in the War and now impotent, finds the sexual fulfilment to which she is entitled in her husband's gamekeeper. In this rough and coarse but shrewd individual she discovers that blood-affinity which Lawrence puts foremost among the requirements for a genuine union; and she finds happiness. He initiates her in the candid and brutal language of the smoking-room and the bar-parlour, and their experiences together are monotonously described at full length in these terms, naked and unashamed. The ultimate result is a dreary and painful book. And yet Lawrence meant it as a great eulogy of that physical tenderness which he contends is spiritual in essence, his axiom being accepted that the body is the soul. It is also another of his appeals for a general admission that man and woman have equal delight in the sensual side of love. From such assertions of the moral value of the novel as those already quoted, it is evident that Lawrence wrote this one with the best intentions. He was honestly and firmly convinced that it was a puritan work; it is certainly a violent hit at the merely puritanical. "I put this forth," he says in the preface, "as an honest, healthy book, necessary for us to-day." Only people without minds will be shocked, and "they don't matter." There is no need to contend again, after what has been said of his work in general, that he invariably addressed himself to this chosen theme, the one that be believed himself called upon to deal with frankly, with what he held to be the best motives.[1] A short posthumous novel, *The Virgin and the Gipsy* (1930), is a less probable story of a Derbyshire rector's

[1] "Lawrence est, au fond, puritain" (André Maurois: *Magiciens et Logiciens*, 309). See also Paul de Reul, 150.

daughter who finds herself in much the same predicament as Lady Chatterley.

His art of the novel

Lawrence would have been the last person to view himself as an artist; he was too much in earnest, though if he had stopped to ask if the great painters and other artists that he admired were not in earnest he would have been hard put to it for an answer. His novels actually compose a natural history of the sexual life, concerning themselves as they do with what he held to be the most momentous group of incidents in the whole course of man's initiation and absorption in the general life of the universe and the consummation of the self. It has been seen how differently he regarded his characters from the way of most novelists; character to him was not a cluster of permanent tendencies, habits, idiosyncrasies, acquired qualities, and what not. The individual is a centre of consciousness, held by a will. But the will is a kinetic force the working of which is obscure, and should be left in obscurity. "Do not keep your will in your conscious self," he tells an intimate correspondent; "let your will lapse back into your unconscious self."[1] It is in that obscure region of unconsciousness that he carried out most of his explorations, a psychological world that the older novelists had hardly even discovered. And it was through the reactions of the body that he thought he was in close touch with this region. His own personal complex was mainly responsible for his finding the secret of life mainly in the body; whence to him "the body *is* the soul," the true self; a man's body may be, to another as well as to him, "the central body of all life."[2] One result of this preoccupation with what is usually regarded as merely the outward envelope is that Lawrence often seems to be aggressively physical, and even gross on principle, as indeed he often was out of sheer impatience with his censors, out of a spirit of defiance. It was inevitable that words should often fail him in trying to expose all that was going on in the dark regions beyond the daylight of consciousness. His vision may be rapt and penetrating, and reveal as by flashes of lightning. It may be charged with the contagious quality of personal ecstasy, and

[1] *Letters*, 286. [2] *Rainbow*, chap. iv.

his prose may beat lyrically in unison. But when he keeps on in the same old strain, ringing the changes on his favourite metaphors, the loins, the womb, the midriff, the afflatus seems to be akin to monomania. It is such passages that reveal most deplorably his lack of a normal sense of humour. He was one of those who can employ Biblical rhythms without ever coming to grief; how sedulously he read the Bible in his youth is patent in his familiarity with the old stories; but it is also evident in the easy flow and the incisiveness of his own narrative style. It gave dignity to his prose, also, when that was required; his very last book, *Apocalypse* (1934), illustrates this conspicuously. But Lawrence was woefully careless in matters of style. He had little sense of the niceties of verbal expression, could be loose in grammar, and slovenly or worse over his punctuation. It often seems as if he wrote well only by accident. And so it was, only the accident was inspiration of some sort. The sheer momentum of the story or the feeling imparts itself to the prose. And when Lawrence was thrilled by great scenery, in the Alps or in California, or his epicurean regard for beauty of any order was truly aroused, his whole being seemed to concentrate itself for the moment, and pour itself out in spontaneous syllables that instantly called up the same live and burning image in the soul of his reader. In all he did there was this unevenness qualifying the brilliance, corresponding to a certain unevenness in the working of his mind—or soul.[1]

A pioneer of neo-realism

Lawrence will inevitably be singled out by future historians as exemplifying in work after work the gradual and halting transition from old to new. During his last years and since his death, novelists have been engaged in getting rid of the old-established forms and machinery and installing new plant for a totally different system of psychological investigation and of technical procedure in showing forth the results. To them,

[1] The chronology of Lawrence's works is in a state of confusion, largely owing to the fact that some were published first in America—sometimes under different titles. I notice that Paul de Reul and Manly and Rickert both give 1922 as the date for *England, my England*, whereas my copy, Secker's edition dated 1924, purports on the face of it to be the first. I do not pretend to have cleared up these doubtful points.

he was only a pioneer, struggling in blind discontent and impatience with worn-out and obsolete methods, and striking out new ones of his own which were often only a makeshift. The complete exponents of the various forms of neo-realism do not come within the purview of this account of the English novel. This is a history that does not end with a definite epoch; it simply breaks off with the death of Lawrence in 1930. Not only would it have been hazardous for a circumspect person to try to deal adequately with writers still living; the present age is not an historian's business. There are obvious gaps in the foregoing chapters; it was hard yet cheering to have to omit Wells and Shaw from the story of fiction since the advent of Butler, not to mention others who appear in footnotes. There might, it is true, have been a chapter to summarize conclusions, like the final one in Saintsbury's history of the French novel, or to attempt to forecast the outcome of recent developments. But it would have been straining chronology to discuss such topics as surrealism, extra-realism, the stream of consciousness, expressionism, dadaism, etc., in a work devoted to the writers who have passed away. It might have been not only venturesome and indiscreet but even misleading to lay all the emphasis that would satisfy the innovators on the revolutionary ideas and methods now dominant. Fashions have established themselves for longer or shorter periods, in the moral and social and the æsthetic attitudes of novelists; and these, together with the technical discoveries and improvements that won acceptance, have been noted at the relevant points in this long survey. But it has doubtless been remarked that doctrines and theories have never left anything like the deep impress of the great personalities who have appeared from time to time and changed the direction of fiction. Such is the individualism of the English genius—in Conrad's case it was a foreigner, but the exception only emphasizes the rule—it has always been apt to twist and divert traditions and tendencies, however general and however well-established. It is the born novelist whose example and renovations have had decisive effects. The ruling character, direction, and purport have been the result of personal influence, of those whose imagination was most responsive to the circumstances and spirit of their age, as well as expressive of their own social and spiritual values. Even the new views so forcibly enunciated by Samuel Butler were not so influential as the impact of his trenchant personality. The history of English fiction is best summarized in a list of the great names —Defoe, Swift, Fielding, Sterne, Jane Austen, Scott, Dickens, Thackeray, the Brontës, Meredith, Hardy, Henry James, Conrad, Butler, Wells, Kipling. And you may group the French and even the Russians much more easily than you can these. They may indeed not stand for definite æsthetic principles, but they do stand for something which will probably go on having effects upon the novel of the future.

SELECT READING AND REFERENCE LIST

GENERAL

BATHO, EDITH, and DOBREE, BONAMY. *The Victorians and after, 1830–1914* (*Introduction to English Literature*, iv). 1938.

CAZAMIAN, MADELEINE L. *Le Roman et les idées en Angleterre.* 2 vols. 1923–1935.

CHESTERTON, GILBERT K. *Heretics.* 1905.

Kipling, Wells, Moore, Celts and Celtophiles, slum novelists, etc.

CHEVALLEY, ABEL. *Le Roman anglais de notre temps.* 1921.

CRUSE, AMY. *The Victorians and their Books.* 1935.

DOBREE, BONAMY. *The Lamp and the Lute: studies in six modern authors.* 1929.

Ibsen, Hardy, Kipling, E. M. Forster, D. H. Lawrence, T. S. Eliot.

DREW, ELIZABETH A. *The Modern Novel: some aspects of contemporary fiction.* 1926.

Galsworthy, Wells, Bennett, Conrad, etc.

ELIOT, T. S. *After Strange Gods: a primer of modern heresy.* 1934.

GARNETT, EDWARD. *Friday Nights: literary criticisms and appreciations.* 1922.

Hudson, Conrad, D. H. Lawrence, Jefferies, etc.

GOULD, GERALD. *The English Novel of To-day.* 1924.

HENDERSON, PHILIP. *The Novel of To-day.* 1936.

HOARE, DOROTHY M. *Some Studies in the Modern Novel.* 1938.

James, D. H. Lawrence, Hardy, Conrad, Moore, Katherine Mansfield, etc.

Maurois, André. *Magiciens et Logiciens.* 1935.

Kipling, Wells, Shaw, Chesterton, Conrad, Strachey, Mansfield, Lawrence, Huxley. Translated as *Poets and Prophets* (1939).

Muir, Edwin. *Transition: essays on contemporary literature.* 1926.

D. H. Lawrence, etc.

Overton, Grant. *The Philosophy of Fiction.* 1928.

Read, Herbert. *Reason and Romanticism: essays in literary criticism.* 1926.

Rickword, Edgell (ed.). *Scrutinies.* Vol. ii. 1931.

The later period of D. H. Lawrence, by Peter Quennell. Note on Form in the Novel, by Brian Penton.

Roz, Firmin. *Le Roman anglais contemporain.* 1912.

Meredith, Hardy, Mrs Humphry Ward, Kipling, Wells.

Swinnerton, Frank. *The Georgian Scene: a panorama.* 1935.

Verschoyle, Derek (ed.). *The English Novelists: a survey of twenty contemporary novelists.* 1936.

Meredith, Butler, James, Hardy and Conrad, D. H. Lawrence and Aldous Huxley.

Whitehead, A. W. *Science and the Modern World.* 1926.

Wilson, Edmund. *The Triple Thinkers.* 1938.

Woolf, Virginia. *The Common Reader.* 2 series. 1925–1932.

CHAPTERS I–II.—CONRAD, WITH HIS NEXT OF KIN

Conrad, Joseph. *Notes on Life and Letters.* 1921.

Crankshaw, Edward. *Joseph Conrad: some aspects of the art of the novel.* 1936.

Curle, Richard. *Joseph Conrad: a study.* 1914.

Elton, Oliver. *C. E. Montague: a memoir.* 1929.

Fernandez, Ramon. *Messages.* 1926.

L'Art de Conrad.

Ford, Ford Madox. *Joseph Conrad: a personal remembrance.* 1924.

Freeman, John. *The Moderns: essays in literary criticism.* 1916.

Shaw, Conrad, Wells, etc.

Herman Melville (*English Men of Letters*). 1926.

Interesting for the points of comparison with Conrad (see the index).

Jean-Aubry, G. *Joseph Conrad: life and letters.* 2 vols. 1927.

The reader will find this a better repository of information than it looks from the index. This was made by someone who did not know the rudiments, and put several dozen stories and novels under the catchword "The"!

Las Vergnas, Raymond. *Joseph Conrad* (*Grands écrivains*). 1938.

This, which arrived *après coup*, is one of the most thorough and perceptive studies of Conrad's psychological method in any language. A carelessness in matters of detail, *e.g.*, *à propos* of *The Secret Agent*, which is located in "Green Park" he says, "l'observatoire saute en effet," when the point is that *il ne sautait pas*, should not excite mistrust of the critical soundness.

Megroz, R. L. *Joseph Conrad's Mind and Method.* 1931.

Morf, Gustav. *The Polish Heritage of Joseph Conrad.* 1930.

Tschiffely, A. F. *Don Roberto: life and works of R. B. Cunninghame Graham.* 1937.

Walpole, Hugh. *Joseph Conrad* (*Writers of the Day*). n.d.

CHAPTERS III VI.—KIPLING, SCOTS AND IRISH, WOMEN NOVELISTS, SATIRISTS, ETC.

Boyd, Ernest A. *Ireland's Literary Renaissance.* 1916.

Chevrillon, André. *Trois études de littérature anglaise.* 1921.

La Poésie de Kipling, Galsworthy, Shakespeare et l'âme anglaise.

Rudyard Kipling. 1936.

This includes the study of Kipling's poetry as its first part.

DARLINGTON, W. A. *J. M. Barrie.* 1938.

LAS VERGNAS, RAYMOND. *Portraits anglais: Chesterton, Belloc, Maurice Baring.* 1936.

MACAULAY, THURSTON. *Donn Byrne, bard of Armagh.* 1929.

MANTZ, R. E., and MURRY, J. MIDDLETON. *The Life of Katherine Mansfield.* 1933.

RATTRAY, R. F. *Samuel Butler: a chronicle and an introduction.* 1935.

RICHARDS, JOHN MORGAN. *Life of Mrs Craigie told in her Correspondence.* 1911.

CHAPTER VII.—BENNETT AND GALSWORTHY

GUYOT, EDOUARD. *John Galsworthy.* I. *Le romancier.* 1933.

KAYE-SMITH, SHEILA. *John Galsworthy* (*Writers of the Day*). 1916.

LAFOURCADE, GEORGES. *Arnold Bennett: a study.* 1939.

MARROT, H. V. *The Life and Letters of John Galsworthy.* 1935.

REYNOLDS, M. E. *Memories of John Galsworthy.* 1936.
By his Sister.

SIMONS, J. B. *Arnold Bennett and his Novels.* 1936.

CHAPTER VIII.—D. H. LAWRENCE

CARSWELL, CATHERINE. *The Savage Pilgrimage.* 1933.

GEORGE, W. L. *A Novelist on Novels.* 1918.
D. H. Lawrence, etc.

HOOPS, REINALD. *Der Einfluss der Psychoanalyse auf die englische Literatur.* 1934.

KINGSMILL, HUGH. *D. H. Lawrence.* 1938.

MERRILL, KNUD. *A Poet and Two Painters: a memoir of D. H. Lawrence.* 1938.

MURRY, JOHN MIDDLETON. *Son of Woman.* 1931.

Reminiscences of D. H. Lawrence. 1933.

Between Two Worlds: an autobiography. 1935.

REUL, PAUL DE. *L'Œuvre de D. H. Lawrence.* 1938.

T., E. [MIRIAM]. *D. H. Lawrence: a personal record.* 1935.

INDEX

INDEX

A

ALDINGTON, RICHARD, 360, note
Allen, Grant, 214, 249
Andersen, Hans, 158
Anderson, Sir Robert, drawn in *The Secret Agent*, 51
"Anstey, F.," 249
Arnim, Gräfin von, 227, note
Arnold, Mathew, 248, 305
Asquith, Lady Cynthia, 350, 351, 353, note
Aubry, G. J., 17, note
Austen, Jane, 199, 337
"Ayscough, John," 254

B

BACON, FRANCIS, 89
Bage, Robert, 252
Banim, Michael and John, 188
Balzac, Honoré de, 125, note, 291, 299, 354, note
Barlow, Jane, 189, 193–194
Barker, Granville, 345
Barrie, Sir James, 157, 158, 160, 161–182, 186, 251, 349
— *The Admirable Crichton*, 176
— *Auld Licht Idylls*, 165, 166
— *Better Dead*, 162, 164
— *Dear Brutus*, 177, 179
— *The Little Minister*, 167
— *The Little White Bird*, 181
— *Margaret Ogilvy*, 161, 162, 163, 165, 182, and note
— *Mary Rose*, 177–178, 179, 182
— *My Lady Nicotine*, 165
— *The Old Lady shows her Medals*, 175

Barrie, Sir James, other plays, 177
— *Peter Pan*, 163, 179–181, 182
— *Quality Street*, 175
— *Sentimental Journey*, 164, 167–170, 179
— *Tommy and Grizel*, 163, 167–170, 182
— *What Every Woman Knows*, 163, 164, 176–177
— *When a Man's Single*, 162, 163, 164
— *A Window in Thrums*, 165, 166
Barry, William, 249
Baudelaire, P. C., 238
Beerbohm, Max, 249, and note
Bellamy, Edward, 253
Belloc, Hilaire, 271, 287
Bennett, Arnold, 100, note, 152, 247, 250, 287, 288–318, 333, 334, and note, 338, note, 345
— *Anna of the Five Towns*, 292, 293–294
— *The Author's Craft*, 293, 318, note
— *Books and Persons*, 293
— *Buried Alive*, 293, 295, 297, 310
— *The Card*, 293, 295, 310
— *Clayhanger*, 289, 292, 293, 303, 306, note, 312, 315
— *Elsie and the Child*, 316
— *The Glimpse*, 295, 303
— *The Grand Babylon Hotel*, 295
— *A Great Man*, 294
— *The Grim Smile of the Five Towns*, 294
— *Helen with the High Hand*, 303
— *Hilda Lessways*, 304, 305, 306–307
— *Imperial Palace*, 293, 317
— *Leonora*, 294
— *Lord Raingo*, 293, 316
— *A Man from the North*, 292, 293
— *The Matador of the Five Towns*, 295, 311
— *Milestones*, 292
— *Mr Prohack*, 313
— *The Old Wives' Tale*, 289, 292, 293, 294, 295–303, 305, 307, 309, 318
— *The Pretty Lady*, 312–313, 318, 344, 356

Bennett, Arnold, *The Price of Love*, 312
— *The Regent*, 293, 310
— *Riceyman Steps*, 292, 313–316
— *The Roll Call*, 310
— *Sacred and Profane Love*, 294
— *Tales of the Five Towns*, 294
— *These Twain*, 307–310
— *Things that have Interested Me*, 293, 295, note
— *Whom God Hath Joined*, 295
Benson, A. C., 254
Benson, E. F., 253
Benson, R. H., 253
Bentham, Jeremy, 322
Beresford, J. D., 247, 254
Bergson, Henri, 291, note
Besant, Sir Walter, 252
Blake, William, 222, 224, 352
Blake-Forster, C. H., 191
Bland, Hubert, 143, note, 156, note
Bland, Mrs Hubert, 215
Bodkin, M. M., 195–196
Borrow, George, 87, 97
— *The Bible in Spain*, 379
Boyd, E. A., 188, 189, note, 190, note
Brontë, Charlotte, 75
Brontë, Charlotte and Emily, 222
Brontë, Emily, 75, 225
Brooke, Emma Frances, 214
Broughton, Rhoda, 210, 211–213, 248
Brown, G. B., 168
— *The House with the Green Shutters*, 187
Brown, Stephen, 190, note
Browning, Robert, 149, 158
Bullock, Shan F., 188, 192, 194–195
Bunyan, John, 159
Burnand, Sir Francis, 248
Burns, Robert, 122
Butler, Samuel, 239, 244–270, 304, 318, 357, 385

Butler, Samuel, *Alps and Sanctuaries*, 256
— *Erewhon*, 244, 246, 247, 250, 251, 252, 255, 258, 259–263, 268, 270
— *Erewhon Revisited*, 259, and note, 263–267, 268, 269, 270
— *Ex Voto*, 256
— *The Fair Haven*, 255
— *God the Known and God the Unknown*, 259, note
— *Note-Books*, 265, 276
— *The Way of all Flesh*, 244, 245, 246, 247, 250, 254–255, 257, 267–270, 304
Byrne, B. O. Donn, 196–198

C

Caine, Hall, 221
Calverley, C. S., 248
Cannan, Gilbert, 247
Carleton, William, 188
Carlyle, Thomas, 322
Carpenter, Edward, 357
Carr, H. Wildon, 291, note
"Carroll, Lewis," 181, 248
Chartists, 115
Chateaubriand, F. R. de, 89
Chekhov, A. P., 238, 239, 241, 242
Chesterton, G. K., 154 and note, 155, 217, 218, 221, 251, 271–287, 345
— *The Ball and the Cross*, 279
— *The Club of Queer Trades*, 275
— *The Flying Inn*, 284
— *Heretics*, 273
— *The Incredulity of Father Brown*, 280–282
— *The Innocence of Father Brown*, 280–282, 283
— *Magic*, 275, note, 282–283
— *The Man who was Thursday*, 277–279
— *Manalive*, 284–286
— *The Napoleon of Notting Hill*, 274
— *Orthodoxy*, 273, 274, 275

Chesterton, G. K., *The Secret of Father Brown*, 280–282
— *Tremendous Trifles*, 275–276
— *The Wild Knight*, 272
— *The Wisdom of Father Brown*, 280–282
Chevalley, Abel, 302
Chevrillon, André, 110, note, 115, note, 118, note, 136, note, 148, note, 152, note, 329, note, 336, note, 338, note, 339, and note
Cholmondeley, Mary, 214
Clifford, Sir Hugh, 11, and note, 19, note, 34, note
Clifford, Mrs W. K., 214
"Colette," 239
Colum, Padraic, 188
Conrad, Joseph, 11–104, 105, 124–125, 142, 144, 153, 250, 259, note, 270, 319, 339, 341, 345, 350
— *Almayer's Folly*, 18–22, 45, 70, note, 73, 78
— *The Arrow of Gold*, 68–69
— "The Black Mate," 38
— "The Brute," 35–36
— *Chance*, 42, 58–66, 72, 73, 74, 76, 83–84
— "The Duel," 18, 34–35
— "The End of the Tether," 29, 31–32, 83
— "Falk," 66
— "Freya of the Western Isles," 36–38, 76
— "Gaspar Ruiz," 36
— *Heart of Darkness*, 17, 26, 29, 30–32, 54, 72
— "The Informer," 18, 35
— "Karain," 33, 83
— "The Lagoon," 33
— *Lord Jim*, 22–29, 33, 39–41, 42, 45, 70, note, 72, 74, 76, 85, 104
— *The Mirror of the Sea*, 14, 26, 47, 68, 83
— *The Nigger of the "Narcissus,"* 26–29, 42, 66, 73, 76, 82, 83
— *Nostromo*, 18, 33, 42, 45–51, 66, 72, 76, 79, 83
— *The Outcast of the Islands*, 20–22, 31, 78
— "An Outpost of Progress," 34
— "The Partner," 38
— "The Pearl of the Ocean," 38

Conrad, Joseph, "Prince Roman," 38
— *The Rescue*, 37, 69–70
— *Romance*, 45
— *The Rover*, 42, 47, 71, 79
— *The Secret Agent*, 51–55, 58, 65, 74, 76
— "The Secret Sharer," 38, 79
— *A Set of Six*, 34–36
— *The Shadow-Line*, 66–68
— "A Smile of Fortune," 38
— *Suspense*, 47, 71–72
— "The Tale," 38–39
— *Tales of Hearsay*, 38–39
— *Tales of Unrest*, 26, 33–36
— Tragedy in Conrad, 42–44
— *'Twixt Land and Sea*, 36
— "Typhoon," 26, 29, 42, 45, 72, 76, 82
— *Under Western Eyes*, 22, 55–58, 65, 72, 76
— *Victory*, 18, 42, 73, 79, 85
— "The Warrior's Soul," 38
— *Within the Tides*, 38
— "Youth," 26, 29–30, 42, 72, 83
Cooper, J. Fenimore, 12, 349
Corelli, Marie, 221
Cowper, William, 88
Craigie, Mrs. *See* "Hobbes, John Oliver"
Crane, Stephen, 11, 23, note
Crashaw, Richard, 158
Creighton, Cuthbert, 270
Crockett, S. R., 157, 161, 183–184
Cruse, Amy, 174, note

D

Darlington, W. A., 162, note, 169, note
Darwin, Charles, 244–245, 251, and note, 256, 257
Daudet, Alphonse, 12
Defoe, Daniel, 92, 98
De la Mare, Walter, 271, note
De Quincey, Thomas, 162

Dickens, Charles, 32, 75, 87, 109, 200, and note, 248, 250, 276, note, 344, 346, 366
Disraeli, Benjamin, 219, and note, 220
Dobree, Bonamy, 153, note, 156, note
Dodge, Mabel, 372
Don Juan legend, 245
Dostoevsky, Theodor, 13, 239, note, 291, 298, note, 318, 361
Dostoevsky and Conrad, 55, 57
"Douglas, George." *See* Brown, G. B.
Downey, Edmund, 195, 249
Dowson, Ernest, 238
Doyle, A. Conan, 51
Dudeney, Mrs, 215
Dumas, Alexandre, 183
Du Maurier, George, 253
Dunsany, Lord, 188
Dunsterville, L. C., 140

E

"E., A." *See* Russell, G. W.
Eddington, Sir A. S., 259, note
Eglinton, John, 188
Eliot, George, 43, 170, 199, 200, 210, 213, 222–223, 224, 246, 291, 337, 349, 356
Eliot, T. S., 352, note, 359, note, 369
Ellis, S. M., 263, note
Elton, Oliver, 103, note

F

Farrar, F. W., 140
Fascism. *See* Nazism
Ferguson, Sir Samuel, 189
Fernandez, Ramon, 26, note, 34, note, 72, 74, note
Ferrier, Susan, 157
Fielding, Henry, 23, 175
Flaubert, Gustave, 12, and note, 245, 318, 322, 337, 349, 354, note
— *Salammbô*, 383

Ford, Ford Madox, 45, 51, 350
Fowler, Ellen Thorneycroft, 215
France, Anatole, 12, 36
Freud, Sigmund, 247, 259, note, 357, and note, 369, 370
Frobenius, Johannes, 369

G

Galsworthy, John, 150, 247, 287, 288, 289, 298, 302, 311, note, 318–344, 345
— "The Apple Tree," 344
— *Caravan*, 319, 321, 328, 329, 331, 342–344
— *The Country House*, 320, 323, 324, 326, 331
— *The Dark Flower*, 321, 326, 338, 341–342
— "Defeat," 344
— *The Eldest Son*, 321
— *The Forest*, 321
— *The Forsyte Saga*, 289, 290, 296, 318, 321, 324, 326–336, 337, 338
— *Fraternity*, 320, 321, 328, 338–341, 344, 350
— *The Freelands*, 321
— *The Fugitive*, 321
— "The Grey Angel," 343
— "Had a Horse," 344
— "A Hedonist," 344
— *The Island Pharisees*, 319, 320, 323, 324, 331
— *Joy*, 321
— "The Juryman," 344
— *Justice*, 321, 322
— *Loyalties*, 321
— *A Man of Devon*, 342
— *The Man of Property*, 320, 321, 323, 324, 327, 331, 333, note, 338, 356–357
— *A Modern Comedy*, 321, 324, 326, 328, 334, 337, 350
— *The Patrician*, 321, 323
— *The Pigeon*, 321
— "A Portrait," 343
— "The Prisoner," 344

Galsworthy, John, "Quality," 343
— "The Salvation of a Forsyte," 342–343
— *The Silver Box*, 321
— *The Skin Game*, 321, 322
— "A Stoic," 343
— *Strife*, 321, 322
— *Villa Rubein*, 325, note, 342
Galt, John, 157, 159, 166
Gardiner, Rolf, 360, note
Garnett, Edward, 13, 19, 24, 39, note, 66, 87, note, 88, note, 96, 253, 357, 361, note, 366
Garnett, Richard, 249
Gaskell, Mrs, 175, 199, 200, 215, 300, 343
Gibbons, Stella, 226, note
Gilbert and Sullivan, 249
Gissing, George, 236, 291, 302, 308, 322, 338
Godwin, William, 322, 337
Goldring, Douglas, 366
Goldsmith, Oliver, 166
Goncourt, Jules and Edmond de, 245
Gorky, Maxim, 238, 239
Gould, S. Baring-, 221
Grady, Standish James, 190–191
Graham, R. B. Cunninghame, 11, 38, 86, and note, 94–97, 99, 154, 250
"Grand, Sarah," 214
Grant, James, 160
Graves, A. P., 189
Gregory, Lady, 188, 189, 190, 196
Griffin, Gerald, 188
Guyot, Edouard, 325, note, 335, note
Gyp, 109, note

H

Haeckel, E. H., 357
Hardy, Thomas, 11, 26, and note, 28, 35, 43, 153, 221, 222, 224, 225, 250, 273, 291, 322, 345, 359, 371

Harker, Lizzie Allen, 215
Harraden, Beatrice, 215
Harris, Frank, 298, note
Harte, Bret, 109, and note, 250
Hartog, Marcus, 257, note
Hegel, G. W. F., 275
Henderson, Philip, 156, note
Hepburn, T. N. *See* "Setoun, Gabriel"
Herbert, George, 88
Hichens, R. S., 249
Hoare, Dorothy M., 383, note
"Hobbes, John Oliver," 216–221
Hockley, W. B., 97
Hogg, James, 158, 178
Holcroft, Thomas, 322, 337
Homer, 244
Hoops, Reinald, 356, note, 357, note, 358, note
Hope, Thomas, 97
Housman, Laurence, 287
Howells, W. D., 253
Hudson, W. H., 11, 85, 86–94, 95, 100, 253, 256, note
— "El Ombú," 36
Hueffer, Ford Madox, 350
Hull, Eleanor, 189, 196
Huxley, Aldous, 74, note, 146, note, 273, 287, 349, note, 359, note, 361, note, 371
Hyde, Douglas, 189

I

Ibsen, Henrik, 238, 273, 279, 364
Irish novelists, 187–198

J

Jacks, L. P., 287
Jacobs, W. W., 249
James, Henry, 26, note, 33, note, 72, 73, 75, 81, and note, 160, note, 210, note, 219, 250, 317, 338, note

Jefferies, R., 253
Jeffery, Francis, 159
Jenkins, J. E., 248
Jerome, Jerome K., 249
Johnston, Harry, 186
Joyce, James, 187, 188, 189, 356
Jung, Carl, 247, 357

K

"Kailyard School," 157–187
Kaye-Smith, Sheila, 288, note
Keats, Gwendoline. *See* "Zack"
Keddie, Henrietta. *See* "Tytler, Sarah"
Kellett, E. E., 148, note
Kickham, C. J., 191–192
Kierkegaard, S. A., 359
Kinglake, A. W., *Eōthen*, 379
Kingsmill, Hugh, 353, note, 355, note
Kipling, John Lockwood, 105
Kipling, Rudyard, 11, 15, 85, 86, 89, 104, 105–156, 181, 215, 238, 250, 345
— *Actions and Reactions*, 150
— *Barrack-room Ballads*, 106, 121, 142, note
— "The Brushwood Boy," 135, 147, 150
— *Captains Courageous*, 107, 122, 140
— "The City of Dreadful Night," 132
— *The Day's Work*, 106, 129, 140, 144–146, 150
— *Debits and Credits*, 107, 149, 151
— *Departmental Ditties*, 106, 121
— *A Diversity of Creatures*, 131, 151
— *The Five Nations*, 106, 121, 147
— *From Sea to Sea*, 106
— "Georgie Porgie," 113–114
— *In Black and White*, 106, 121, 132
— *The Jungle Books*, 107, 112, 136–139, 155
— *Just-so Stories*, 107, 135, note
— *Kim*, 105, 107, 110, 122, 140–143, 147, 149, note, 155

Kipling, Rudyard, *Life's Handicap*, 106, 112, 113–114, 115, 116, 125, 126, 132, 136, 146
— *The Light that Failed*, 106, 115, 122
— *Limits and Renewals*, 107, 151
— "M'Andrews' Hymn," 144, 145–146
— "The Man who Was," 128
— "The Man who would be King," 119, 133
— *Many Inventions*, 106, 108, note, 112, 116, 125, 126, 127, 130, 134, 136, 137, 147
— *The Naulahka*, 106, 122
— *The Phantom 'Rickshaw*, 106, 118
— *Plain Tales from the Hills*, 106, 110–112, 115, 116, 124, 126, 134
— *Puck of Pook's Hill*, 107, 143–144
— "Recessional," 148, 155
— *Rewards and Fairies*, 107, 143–144
— *The Seven Seas*, 106, 121
— *Soldiers Three*, 106, 108, 116, 117
— *Stalky & Co.*, 105, 107, 140
— *The Story of the Gadsbys*, 106, 114, 117, 142
— "The Strange Ride of Morrowbie Jukes," 119, 133
— "The Taking of Lungtungpen," 117
— "The Tents of Kedar," 114
— "They," 107, 134, 135, note, 147
— *Traffics and Discoveries*, 131, 146, 147
— *Under the Deodars*, 106, 118
— "The Village that voted the Earth was Flat," 130
— *Wee Willie Winkie*, 106, 120
Knoblock, Edward, 292
Knox, W. L., 279, note
Koran, 97, 148, note

L

Lafourcade, Georges, 293, note, 306, note, 318, note
Lang, Andrew, 109, note
Las Vergnas, R., 80, note
Lawless, Emily, 189, 192–193, 194

Lawrence, C. E., 386
Lawrence, D. H., 227, 247, 287, 291, 333, note, 344, 345–389
— *Aaron's Rod*, 367–368
— *Apocalypse*, 353, note, 360, note, 389
— "The Blind Man," 376
— *The Boy in the Bush*, 371, 372, 373
— "The Captain's Doll," 375, 376
— "Daughters of the Vicar," 358
— *England, my England*, 375, 376
— "Fannie and Annie," 376
— *Fantasia of the Unconscious*, 345, 359, 366, 367, 369–371, 379
— "The Fox," 375, 376
— "Glad Ghosts," 384, 385
— "In Love," 384
— "Jimmy and the Desperate Woman," 384
— *Kangaroo*, 346, 348, note, 367, 372–375, 379, 380, 383
— *Lady Chatterley's Lover*, 353, note, 354, 360, 385–387, 388
— *The Ladybird*, 375
— "The Last Laugh," 384
— *Letters*, 350, note, 351, note, 352, note, 354, note, 359, note, 360, note, 361, note, 364, note, 366, note, 371, note, 382, note, 386, note
— *The Lost Girl*, 364, 366–367
— *Love Poems*, 350
— "The Man who Died" ("The Escaped Cock"), 385
— "The Miner at Home," 346
— "Monkey Nuts," 376
— "Night in the House," 380, note
— *The Phœnix*, 346, note, 369, note, 371, note
— *The Plumed Serpent*, 348, 358, note, 379–383, 385
— "Pornography and Obscenity," 369
— "The Princess," 377, and note, 378–379
— *The Prussian Officer*, 358
— *Psychoanalysis and the Unconscious*, 367, 369, 370, note
— *The Rainbow*, 351, 358–364, 386, 388, note
— *Reflections on the Death of a Porcupine*, 354
— *St Mawr*, 375, 377–378

Lawrence, D. H., "Samson and Delilah," 376
— *Sea and Sardinia*, 360
— "The Shades of Spring," 358
— "Shadow in the Rose Garden," 358
— "Smile," 384
— *Sons and Lovers*, 346, 348, 349, 350, 355, 357, 359, note
— "Sun," 385
— "Tickets, Please," 376
— *The Trespasser*, 350, 355
— *Twilight in Italy*, 367, 368
— "Two Blue Birds," 384
— *The Virgin and the Gipsy*, 388–389
— *The White Peacock*, 350, 354
— *The Widowing of Mrs Holroyd*, 350
— *The Woman who Rode away*, 375, 383–384
— *Women in Love*, 361, 364
— "You Touched Me," 376
Lawrence, G. A., 128, 212
Le Fanu, J. S., 188
Le Gallienne, Richard, 108, note
Lesage, A. R., 89
Lever, Charles, 188, 194
Lewis, Wyndham, 359, note
Linton, Mrs Lynn, 214
Locke, John, theory of duration, 23
Loti, Pierre, 12, 28, 89, 170
Lover, Samuel, 188
"Lyall, Edna," 214
Lytton, Lord, 244, 252

M

Macaulay, Rose, 273
MacCarthy, Desmond, 258, note
MacDonald, George, 157–159
M'Ilroy, Archibald, 195
Mackenzie, Henry, 157, 161
"Maclaren, Ian," 157, 160, 161, 183, 184–186

"Macleod, Fiona," 158, 186, 187
MacManus, Seumas, 195
Macnaughtan, Sarah, 186
Maeterlinck, Maurice, 238
"Malet, Lucas," 214
Mallock, W. H., 248
Malory, Sir Thomas, 196
Mangan, J. C., 189
Mansfield, Katherine, 226–243, 247, 336, note, 365, and note, 371, 377, note
— "The Doll's House," 236–237, 241
— *The Doves' Nest*, 229
— *The Garden Party*, 228, 233–236, 241
— *Journal*, 229, note, 236, 240, note
— "Prelude," 229–232
— *Something Childish*, 229, 231–238
Mantz, R. E., and J. Middleton Murry, 228, note
Marryat, Captain Frederick, 12
Martin, Violet. *See* "Ross, Martin"
Martyn, Edward, 188
Mathers, Helen, 213
Maudsley, Henry, 357
Maugham, W. Somerset, 247
Maupassant, Guy de, 12, 32, 53, 81, note, 118, note, 238, 239, 245, 296, 318, 322, 337, 349, 359
Maurois, André, 124, 360, note, 387, note
Mégroz, R. L., 13, note, 17, note
Melville, Herman, 13, 15, 28, note
Mencken, H. L., 13, 80, note
Meredith, George, 101, 129, 158, 170, 171, 174, and note, 199, 219, 222, 238, 250, 263, note, 267, note, 270, 291, 338, and note, 356, 373
— *Essay on Comedy*, 366
Merrill, Knud, *A Poet and Two Painters*, 383, note
Meyer, Kuno, 189
Moir, D. M., 157
Molesworth, Mrs, 160
Montague, C. E., 11, 85, 86, 99–104, 154, 250

Moore, George, 153, 187–188, 197, 198, 273, 318
Morf, Gustav, on Conrad, 50, 78, 80, note, 128
Morier, J. J., 97
Morrell, Lady Ottoline, 365, 371
Morris, William, 253, 276
Munro, Neil, 160
Murry, J. Middleton, 227, 228, note, 353, note, 354, 355, note, 357, note, 365, note, 369, 377, note, 388, note

N

Nazism, 372, 380, 381, 382
Nevinson, H. W., 142, note, 341, note
Nietzsche, F. W., 273, 352, 364, 375
Nisbet, Edith. *See* Bland, Mrs Hubert
Noble, Edward, 11, 104

O

O'Byrne, M. L., 101
O'Grady, Standish Hayes, 189
Oliphant, Laurence, 248
Oliphant, Mrs, 159, 199–210, 211, 300
— *A Beleaguered City*, 210
— Carlingford novels, 199, 201–209
— *The Cuckoo in the Nest*, 202
— *The Land of Darkness*, 210
— *A Little Pilgrim in the Unseen*, 210
— *Miss Marjoribanks*, 200–201, 205–209, 210
— *Old Mr Tredgold*, 209
— *The Perpetual Curate*, 202, 204–205, 210
— *Phœbe Junior*, 205
— *The Rector*, 202, 204
— *Salem Chapel*, 203–204, 205
— *The Warden*, 202
Ollivant, Alfred, 187, note
Onions, Oliver, 247
O'Riordan, Conal, 188

P

Pain, Barry, 249
Palgrave, W. G., 98
Phillpotts, Eden, 221, 292
Pickthall, Marmaduke, 11, 97–99
Plato, 369
Platt, J. Arthur, 257, note
Poe, E. A., 109, note
Problem novel, 213, *et seq.*
Pugh, Edwin, 221

R

Rabelais, 277, 284
Rattray, R. F., 259, note
Read, Herbert, 58, note
Reade, Charles, 160
Reul, Paul de, 360, note, 387, note
Reynolds, M. E., 339, note
Ribot, T. A., 357
Richards, I. A., 24, note
Richardson, Dorothy, 356
Richardson, Samuel, 285
Ritchie, Lady. *See* Thackeray, Anne Isabella
"Ross, Martin," 194
Rousseau, J.-J., 352
Roz, Firmin, 109, note, 118, note, 125, note, 138, note
Ruskin, John, 322
Russell, G. W., 271, note, 188
"Rutherford, Mark," 203, note

S

Saint-Pierre, B. de, 89
Saurat, Denis, 149, note
Scott, Dixon, 101, note, 140, and note, 169, note, 178, note, 183, 186, 188
Scott, Sir Walter, 157, 159

Scottish novelists, 157–187
"Setoun, Gabriel," 186
Shaftesbury, 3rd Earl of, 352
Shakespeare, William, 102, 125, note, 154, 238, 266, 354
— comparison of Conrad, 37, 39, 41, 42–43, 79, 87, note
Sharp, William. *See* "Macleod, Fiona"
Shaw, G. Bernard, 238, 244, 245, 246, note, 255, note, 257, note, 261, note, 262, note, 269, note, 270–271, 272, 273, 274, 279, 288, 291, 302, 322, note, 345
Sheehan, P. A., 195
Shelley, P. B., 352
Sigerson, George, 189
Sinclair, May, 247, 357
Skelton, Sir John, 160
Skinner, Miss M. L., 372
Smollett, T. G., 27, 157
Somerville, E. Œ., 194
Spencer, Herbert, 357
Steel, Flora Annie, 215–216
Stendhal, 298, note, 306, note, 318
Stephens, James, 187, 188, 189
Sterne, Laurence, 23–24, 168, 169, 174
Stevenson, R. L., 11, 46, 64, 82, 160, 183, 186, 276, 349
Stokes, Whitley, 189
Street, G. S., 249
Swettenhan, Sir Frank, 34, note
Swift, Jonathan, 245, 248, 251, 252, 262, 270
Swinnerton, Frank, 247, and note
Symons, Arthur, 238
Synge, J. M., 188, 190

T

"T., E.," 347, note, 349, note, 350, note, 354, 355, and notes
Thackeray, Anne Isabella, 210–211
Thackeray, W. M., 170, 250, 349
Thomas the Rhymer, 178
Tolstoy, L. N., 88, note, 195, 242, 361

Tomlinson, H. M., 11
Totalitarianism. *See* Nazism
Traherne, Thomas, 88
Trollope, Anthony, 199, 211, and note, 212
Tupper, Martin, 221
Turgenev, Ivan, 13, 238, 318, 322, 337, 361
Twain, Mark, 109, note, 250
Tynan, Katherine, 189, 194
"Tytler, Sarah," 160

V

Vaughan, Henry, 158
Verlaine, Paul, 238
Villon, François, 296, 302
Voltaire, Arouet de, 299, 305

W

Walpole, Sir Hugh, 247
Ward, Mrs Humphry, 214, 222, 248
Webb, Mary, 221–226, 239
Wells, H. G., 15, note, 238, 247, 253, 271, note, 273, 288, 291, 293, 311, note, 319
"West, Rebecca," 247
Whistler, J. M., 273
Whitehead, A. N., 259, note
Whiteing, Richard, 253
Whitman, Walt, 357
Wilde, Oscar, 82, 238, 249, 273
Williams, Orlo, 267, note
Women novelists, 199–243
Woolf, Virginia, 247, 311, note, 356, 359
Wordsworth, William, 88, 226, 371, note

Y

Yeats, W. B., 188
— *Cathleen ni Houlihan*, 190

Yeats, W. B., *The Celtic Twilight*, 190
— *Deirdre*, 190
— *On Baile's Strand*, 190
— *The Secret Rose*, 190
— *The Shadowy Waters*, 190
Yoga, 369
Yonge, Charlotte, 211

Z

Zola, Émile, 31, 211, 245, 279, 291, 299